EDUCATIONAL and PSYCHOLOGICAL MEASUREMENT

EDUCATIONAL and PSYCHOLOGICAL MEASUREMENT

George K. Cunningham
University of Louisville

MACMILLAN PUBLISHING COMPANY
NEW YORK

Collier Macmillan Publishers
London

Printed in the United States of America

Macmillan Publishing Company
866 Third Avenue, New York, New York 10022

Collier Macmillan Canada, Inc.

Library of Congress Cataloging in Publication Data

Cunningham, George K.
Educational and psychological measurement.

Bibliography: p.
Includes index.
1. Educational tests and measurements. I. Title.
LB3051.C86 1986 371.2'6 85-7125
ISBN 0-02-326330-X

Printing: 5 6 7 8 Year: 1 2 3 4

ISBN 0-02-326330-X

To Nancy and Sarah

PREFACE

This textbook is intended for use in measurement and evaluation courses that fall between those offered to prospective classroom teachers, for whom test-construction techniques are emphasized, and those offered to graduate students, for whom the focus is psychometric theory. Courses for which this textbook would be appropriate are offered to upper-division undergraduate and graduate students. Enrolled in such courses would be students who are majoring in elementary or secondary education, educational psychology, special education, educational administration, counseling, or any one of several other education majors. In addition, it can be used in measurement courses taught in psychology departments because it includes all of the topics included in such courses, along with content more closely related to education.

The book covers those topics that one would expect to find: derived scores, reliability, validity, test construction, standardized tests, mental ability testing, and personality assessment. Material also is covered that is not usually found in textbooks intended for this audience. For instance, an entire chapter is devoted to computer applications in measurement. Although references to computers and examples of their application to measurement can be found throughout this book, the chapter on computer applications is intended to provide the measurement student with more specific information about the ways computers are used in the field of measurement and evaluation. Information is included on how to get started with a computer, methods of entering data, and data analysis options. Specific information about such topics as item analysis, test banking, tailor-made tests, and computerized standardized test scoring and interpretations can also be found.

Another important advance in the measurement and evaluation field is the application of latent-trait theory to practical measurement problems. Presently the most important application of these techniques is in improving sophisticated standardized tests. In addition to the possibility of increasingly precise and useful methods of interpreting scores, these techniques can be used to develop test banks and create tailor-made tests. One major stumbling block in the application of this theory is its mathematical complexity and consequent inaccessibility to those with a limited background in math. In Chapter 8 there is a readable but detailed explanation of latent-trait theory that even students without a strong mathematical background can grasp. Although there is not sufficient detail for students to begin applying latent-trait theory, there is an adequate amount of coverage to permit them to understand the increasing number of references and examples of its use that they are likely to encounter.

Another important area of study associated with educational measurement is criterion-referenced testing. It is a very attractive approach to assessment and has seen widespread adoption by school systems across the country. In general it has been accepted in an uncritical fashion and in many cases it has been oversold. Too many of its practitioners have a poor understanding of the correct methods for its implementation. As a result, the types of criterion-referenced tests that are widely accepted in the public school sector are often quite different from those described by experts on criterion-referenced testing. Even though the experts are moving in the direction of more sophisticated descriptions of learning objectives, such as domain referencing, most existing criterion-referenced tests are better described as objective-referenced tests, which are considered to be an inferior approach to evaluation. If criterion-referenced tests are to be used on an increasingly widespread basis, then educators are going to need to become much more knowledgeable about how to use them. Chapter 10, "Criterion-Referenced Testing," provides a description of what is currently known about this approach, the methods of implementation, and the problems associated with its use.

Minimum competency testing is a topic that has received a great deal of attention over the last several years. It is a measurement-oriented response to perceived educational failures. Its historical development, legal implications, strengths, weaknesses, successes, and failures are outlined in Chapter 11. The reader will find the most current information on this controversial topic in this book.

The preparation of material on ability testing presents one of the most difficult tasks for the author of a measurement textbook. Unlike most other aspects of measurement, where the students arrive in class knowing little about the subject, most students already possess a modicum of information on this topic. Although some of it may be accurate, much of it may consist of strongly held prejudices. The textbook writer and the instructor not only are faced with the task of teaching the basic concepts, to permit the student to gain an understanding of ability testing, but they also must disabuse students of their existing misconceptions and deal with their deeply held prejudices. Exacerbating this problem is the emotional aura surrounding the topic. Ability testing is not a subject about which it is easy to remain neutral. Our society harbors radically divergent views on the subject, ranging from those who would put an end to all such assessment to those who view ability tests as a justification for the stratification of our society along racial or ethnic lines. Many of these extreme views are in conflict with the known facts about such testing.

Because most of the disagreement surrounding this topic stems from definitional confusion, the definitions are clarified. The intention is to treat controversial aspects of ability testing in an evenhanded, clear, and easily understood fashion. Each side of the issues is presented, and the reader is placed in a position where he or she can draw conclusions based on facts.

Textbooks for measurement and evaluation courses are filled with methods and techniques for performing statistical operations and obtaining scores and coefficients. The reader is usually not given much information concerning why one method of technique is selected over another. The tone instead tends either to be nonjudgmental, or one of several methods is recommended without explanation. Often there is no single clearly acceptable technique, and different experts may have their own ideas about which should be used. In this book, rationales are provided to assist the reader in deciding which method or technique should be used.

The field of measurement and evaluation is filled with issues and controversies. These range from minor technical questions about selecting appropriate statistical techniques to some of the most fundamental philosophical questions in Western science, such as the relative importance of the influence of heredity and environment on intelligence. Textbooks sometimes try to avoid these issues by presenting both sides of an argument without taking a position. The reader will find this textbook to be different in that respect. Although both sides of controversies are presented, this book takes a position on the major issues and provides a rationale for the student to help him or her understand what is really going on. Furthermore, the controversies are presented in their historical and social context. This avoidance of equivocation and emphasis on context gives the student a better opportunity to understand why things are done the way they are in measurement to enhance interest and understanding.

I would like to express my appreciation to Norm Gronlund, Daniel Mueller, and Jerome Kapes for their invaluable comments and suggestions on the earlier drafts of the book. I would also like to thank my editors at Macmillan: Lloyd Chilton, for his support and assistance in bringing this project to fruition and Wendy Polhemus, for her help in the production of the book. Finally, I wish to thank Becki McGinty for the outstanding job she did in supervising the typing of the ennumerable draft versions of the manuscript.

G. K. C.

CONTENTS

1 Introduction to Measurement 1

2 Statistics 18

3

Derived Scores

62

4

Computer Applications to Measurement

79

5

Reliability

99

6
Validity
120

7
Classroom Testing
134

8
Improving Achievement Tests
152

9
Assigning Grades
171

10
Criterion-Referenced Testing
187

11
Minimum Competency Testing
205

12 Achievement Testing 218

13 Mental Ability Testing 242

14
Individual Intelligence Tests
263

15
Group Mental Ability Tests
285

16
Personality Assessment
310

17
Selecting Tests, Reporting Results, and the Future of Measurement
346

EDUCATIONAL and PSYCHOLOGICAL MEASUREMENT

1

Introduction to Measurement

OVERVIEW

The purpose of this first chapter is to introduce the reader to the basic assumptions upon which this textbook is predicated. A brief history of the development of the measurement field is provided; it is divided into those developments that occurred as a result of the need to solve practical problems and those that have a more theoretical basis. Opposition to testing and its causes, along with the reasons why testing is needed, are included. Finally, a rational basis for measurement, which depends on the importance of constructs, is presented.

OBJECTIVES

From this chapter you will learn about the history of testing and some of its theoretical underpinnings. Specifically, you will learn the following:

- The relationship between measurement and science.
- The purpose of measurement.
- The historical developments that led to the establishment of measurement as a field of study.
- The reason that there is so much opposition to testing.
- Why tests are needed.
- Some of the theoretical bases for testing.

Measurement and Science

In the nineteenth century, psychology was more a branch of philosophy than it was a science. Behavior was explained by means of descriptions in the form of a narrative, utilizing the techniques of the novelist or journalist. At the same time science was in a state of ascendancy, and there was the general belief that the problems of the world could be solved through empirical processes. Eventually this same attitude began to permeate psychology, and among some psychologists there arose the desire to model the field more closely after the hard sciences.

One characteristic that differentiates science from nonscience is the precision of measurement. Physicists in particular have taken the position that before one can argue for the existence of something it is necessary to first possess an operational definition that specifies how it is to be measured. For example, space is measured by a ruler whereas time is measured by a clock. If something has no operational definition, its existence can be questioned. Physicists seem to have an advantage because they deal with a world that is easily measured, but they are faced with subatomic particles that are exceedingly difficult to quantify. These particles can be affected or even transformed by the process of their assessment in the same way that measuring humans often affects their behavior (Wolf, 1981).

Until the end of the nineteenth and beginning of the twentieth centuries, most of what psychologists did was unmeasureable. Before psychology could be accepted as a science, there was a need to develop techniques for operationally defining its constructs.

The introduction of objective measurement techniques allowed psychology to move from being mere armchair philosophy to a position where it could claim respectability along with the more traditional areas of scientific study. According to Edward Wilson (1978), one of the founders of sociobiology, the various sciences are arranged in a hierarchy according to the level of organization they study, their objectivity, and the degree of precision with which they describe their environment. Under such circumstances it is only natural that the social sciences have endeavored to become more like "hard" science and thus more respectable. To reach this goal it is necessary to find even more precise means of quantifying behavior because this enhances their precision and objectivity.

The Purpose of Measurement

The purpose of measurement in the social sciences is to provide a numerical index for quantifying traits to permit the study of human behavior based on mathematical models. Such an approach provides for the objective discussion of an attribute because we are able to talk in terms of actual amounts rather than vague approximations. The assumptions that undergird this approach will be the topic of discussion throughout this book. It will be emphasized from the beginning that the process of assigning numerical values to traits and then manipulating these numbers through mathematical models can be no more legitimate than the soundness of the assumptions on which it is based.

Historical Development

The historical development of the field of measurement in education is closely related to similar developments in the field of psychology. This can be understood along two dimensions. First there is the practical dimension where the methods and techniques used are directly tied to their ability to fulfill an immediate need. This is illustrated by civil service and educational testing. The second dimension is theoretical and is based on a scientific interest in individual differences. It is exemplified by the field of ability testing. Of course ability testing also can be viewed in terms of its practical aspects.

The Practical Dimension

Civil Service in China According to P. H. Dubois (1970), a measurement historian, the first systematic program of testing was initiated in China as far back as 2200 B.C. At that time China had no hereditary ruling class, and initial appointments as well as continuance in employment were based on examinations. The tests covered the examinee's knowledge of civil law, military affairs, agriculture, revenue, and geography. Civil servants were tested every three years, and prospective appointees went through a grueling process of three exams to determine whether they were qualified for office. This procedure was discontinued in favor of a university system as a result of the need for a scientific rather than a classical preparation for office.

British Civil Service The Chinese method of selecting government employees was used as a basis for the establishment of the Indian civil service. The first British civil service commission was set up in 1850.

Civil Service in the United States Following its successful use in England the Chinese method for selecting government employees was eventually adopted in the United States. The first civil service was established in 1883. Tests were developed for many occupations, including postal clerk, draftsman, botanist, and physician. As a means of validating the tests, attempts were made to show that there was a statistical relationship between scores on the test and later performance on the job.

Academic Testing Formal testing in schools did not commence until the introduction of paper in the 12th century. It was passed on by the Arabs during the Crusades, who had acquired the technique from the Chinese. Assessment by means of written tests was first used by Jesuits at St. Ignatio (Dubois, 1970).

The development of academic tests was pioneered in Britain, particularly at the University of London. Under its initial charter, testing and awarding degrees was recognized as a legitimate basis for decision making, from awarding degrees and permission to practice a profession to admission to civil service. It was on this foundation of civil and academic testing that psychological testing was founded.

The Theoretical Dimension

The birth of psychology as a science is believed to have taken place in the laboratory of Wilhelm Wundt in Leipzig, Germany. His approach to gaining an understanding of human consciousness proceeded by means of reducing the process of thought to its most fundamental parts. His focus was on establishing what was typical rather than elucidating individual differences, and he placed great emphasis on measurement. The measurements that were made during this procedure were mainly psychophysical—that is, sensory acuity and reaction time.

Although Wundt's work was methodologically useful, it did not make a great contribution to the theoretical understanding of human abilities. Its biggest contribution was in a negative sense because the two main branches of learning theory (cognitive and behavioral) began as reactions against the Wundt school of psychology.

Individual Differences Before the science of measuring human abilities could be developed, a theory of individual differences was needed. The belief that humans differ in terms of ability and that these differences are relevant to success in life is an idea peculiar to Western societies. It is a view of the world that has gained acceptance only in recent times. Prior to the second half of the nineteenth century, man was not expected to aspire beyond the role dictated by his heritage. Differences between humans were understood in terms of religious beliefs and predestination. The individual who soared above his peers was usually thought to be the beneficiary of divine providence, whereas the soul that fell below was doing penance for his or her sins.

Genetics and Heredity Although a vague belief in the influences of heredity already existed, little was known about its mechanics until Gregor Mendel (1822–1884) reported the results of his study of garden peas. His findings and conclusions later became known as Mendel's laws. It was not until the beginning of the twentieth century that his work became generally accepted. The understanding of the influence of inheritance, or "blood," as it was described at the time, was crude. This is best illustrated in the literature of the times. For instance, Charles Dickens loved to tell stories about the child of well-bred parents who, through accident, disaster, or the untimely death of his mother and/or father, is separated from his family and is raised in a poor and deprived environment. His personality and behaviors always match his genteel background rather than his rough surroundings. Even his speech was likely to be that of his natural parents. Sometimes the converse story is told where, through some accident, the child of a deprived or even criminal background is raised in a genteel setting. At some point a terrible crime is committed by this individual of seemingly well-bred background. When the cause of the senseless behavior is sought, it is traced to the criminal blood coursing through the hapless individual's veins, which inevitably results in his inability to refrain from violence.

Charles Darwin An important factor in the increased acceptance of the importance of individual differences was the publication by Charles Darwin of *The Origin of* *the Species* in 1859. Darwin had studied to be a physician at Edinburgh but decided that he disliked the sight of blood. He then went on to earn his degree at Cambridge and seemed headed for a career as a clergyman when he was offered the position of naturalist on the *H.M.S. Beagle*, a survey ship headed for the coast of South America. It was on this voyage that he amassed the large amount of data on unusual life forms that later formed the basis for his theory of evolution.

The explanation of evolution that existed prior to the acceptance of Darwin's theory of interspecies differences was based on the Argument from Design, which, simply stated, asserts that creatures differ because God designed them that way. The adaptation of different species to their environment was viewed as support for the belief in the omniscience of a higher being (Plomin, et al., 1980).

Upon returning to England Darwin began to doubt the validity of the Argument from Design and began to develop his own explanation, which became his theory of evolution. Darwin knew that what he was proposing was controversial, and he was a very careful man. He wanted to make sure that he was really prepared before he announced his theory. His friends and associates urged him to hurry before someone published a version of this theory before him. Then it happened. A young biologist named Alfred Wallace sent Darwin a manuscript that, although based on less solid evidence than Darwin possessed, presented a theory that was similar. Darwin did not know what to do, but his first instinct seems to have been to step aside. At this point, his colleagues, along with those of Wallace, agreed to arrange for simultaneous presentations (Plomin, 1980). It is of course Darwin's name that is associated with evolution, not Wallace's, and this is believed to be because Wallace's later work focused on the occult, which led other scientists to discount him as a fellow (Jaynes, 1976).

The publication of Darwin's work was immensely controversial at the time and remains so to this day. The growing sophistication concerning the mechanics of genetics has led to a number of changes in Darwin's original theory, but his fundamental thesis is still generally accepted. According to his theory of evolution, species differ and their differences are genetically based and passed on to offspring. If the environment contains conditions that favor one sort of difference then there is a greater likelihood of that trait being passed on. Over a number of years a species will evolve in the direction of those traits that lead to the greatest possibility of survival. Although Darwin used the term *survival of the fittest*, it is probably more precise to talk about reproduction by the fittest (Plomin et al., 1980). It was later that the realization that acquired characteristics could not be inherited became generally accepted. Thus the acquisition of the long neck by the giraffe did not come about because of use, but rather it was the result of the selectively greater survival capacities of individual giraffes with long necks in a time of food scarcity. In each generation those giraffes with longer necks were more likely to survive, along with offspring who shared the common gene pool characterized by the predisposition toward longer necks.

Sir Francis Galton The development of psychological testing, although presaged by the research conducted in Germany by Wundt, really got its start with Sir Francis Galton, a cousin of Charles Darwin. Galton was strongly influenced by Darwin and gained from him an appreciation of the importance of individual differences; unlike his cousin, however, he focused on the importance of differences for humans.

At the age of twenty-two, Galton inherited a sizeable fortune and led the life of a country gentleman. He became interested in a wide range of activities from geography to photography and is credited with important explorations and discoveries in Africa at the same time that Stanley, Livingston, and Sir Richard Burton were seeking the source of the Nile River. Perhaps because of the influence of his illustrious cousin, he eventually settled on the subject of heredity and individual differences as his field of study.

A major interest of Galton involved the study of highly superior individuals, labeled geniuses. He studied them using biographical material and concluded that although environment played a part, it was heredity that was of greatest importance. He came to this conclusion by studying the family trees of geniuses. Of course his only means of identifying those geniuses was by their reputation and success in life. Not surprisingly, he found that the occurrence of other equally distinguished individuals in a family was a function of how closely they were related to the individual of great prominence. Although he acknowledged its possible importance, he tried to discount the environmental effects of close association with a highly gifted individual and the increased opportunities this brings to the rest of the immediate family.

Of far greater importance, from a measurement standpoint, was his interest and insights into the subject of individual differences. Just as Darwin had emphasized that individual differences in animals constitutes the key element in natural selection, Galton was fascinated by differences in human abilities. He often used as an example the vast differences in performance elicited from students on the lengthy math exams given at Cambridge University (Galton, 1892). Although Galton did not discount the influences of environment, he thought that heredity placed limits on the capacity of the individual. He believed that even with no training it was possible for an individual to perform at a level that surpassed what could be achieved by those with a more meager endowment, despite extensive training. He cites the pure cockney bank clerk with no training as a runner who, in a track meet, defeated well-trained runners from the Scottish hills (Galton, 1892).

At this time the existing measurement techniques were unsophisticated, and the assessments of higher-level mental functioning that would be considered routine today were unknown. Galton, therefore, saw little alternative to emphasizing the sort of anthropomorphic, psychophysical, and sensory measurements used by Wundt. He measured such things as height, arm span, strength of squeeze, strength of pull, breath capacity, vision, memory for form, and discrimination of color. He justified this approach by asserting that what we know we have learned through our senses.

In cooperation with the International Health Exhibition, which took place in London in 1884, Galton arranged to take a series of measurements on visitors to the fair. After the exhibition closed, he moved his laboratory to the Science Museum in South Kensington and continued to collect data. By the time he finished, he had collected data on 9,337 individuals (Dubois, 1970). During the remainder of his career, Galton focused his energy on analyzing this mass of data, a task much more difficult than it would be today because it was done without the aid of computers. He made some initial attempts to establish norms and standard scores, having developed a rudimentary understanding of the normal distribution from M. Quetelet (Galton, 1892). He also laid the foundation for the development of the correlation coefficient, which constitutes an extremely important advancement in understanding how different measurements on the same person are related. Credit for the discovery of the correlation coefficient must be shared by Galton with Karl Pearson, and there are those who would also give credit to Axel Oehrn (Guilford, 1967). Galton's most important contribution was probably his emphasis on individual differences and his insistence that those differences had consequences for behavior. This idea is the cornerstone of the field of psychological measurement.

The Galton tradition of testing was brought to the United States by James McKeen Cattell, who had studied with Wundt at the University of Leipzig and later worked as an assistant in Galton's laboratory. There he naturally came under the influence not only of Galton but of Darwin as well. He left Britain with an appreciation for individual differences. Unfortunately, he chose to emphasize the more sensory type of skills, as suggested by Galton, rather than the higher-level mental processes that Alfred Binet was beginning to study in France. His rationale for studying the Galton-type items was his belief that Binet's more complex processes could be reduced to simple sensory operations.

At the turn of the century, Cattel brought his interest in psychological testing to the University of Pennsylvania and later to Columbia University where he established a psychological laboratory and began testing the sensory abilities of incoming freshmen. Clark Wissler applied the correlation techniques of Galton and Pearson and related the testing results to grades (Guilford, 1967). Not surprisingly, he obtained correlations that were too low to give comfort to those who continued their advocacy of Galton-type items, although he did find that there were substantial correlations among grades for different courses.

Alfred Binet Many of the methods now used in psychological testing can be traced back to Binet's work. As a child psychologist working in Paris at the turn of the century, Binet became interested in the assessment of human abilities. Rejecting the psychophysical measurement of Galton and Wundt in favor of higher-level mental processing, he developed the first intelligence test that measured high level mental functioning, the 1905 scale, together with Theodore Simon. Later he developed two additional scales called the 1908 and 1911 scales.

Binet reported individual intellectual level in terms of mental ages and did not use, nor would he have endorsed, the use of IQ scores. His important contributions were as follows: (1) a focus on the assessment of higher-level mental functioning, (2) the inclusion of the assessment of varied aspects of cognitive functioning summarized into a single score, and (3) the employment of criterion groups, which greatly enhanced the validity of the instrument.

Louis Terman There were a number of translations of the Binet-Simon tests into English, but for the most part they were literal translations that had technical limitations. It was Louis Terman who provided the definitive translation. Calling on his previous experience, he added his own items to those of Binet and in 1916 published the Stanford-Binet. This test provided the first well-standardized, carefully developed test of intelligence and was much more refined than the other translations. Terman reported test results with IQ scores in addition to mental age scores. The introduction of the IQ was both an advance and a source of future problems. Although it provided technical advantages over the mental age, there was a tendency to attribute a degree of importance and significance to the measure that has led to misunderstandings and misuse.

The test was revised in 1937 and two forms were developed to provide an alternate when a child needed to be retested. In 1960 the test was again revised by including the best items from the two forms. Even though it is still accepted as an important individual intelligence test, its use declined after the introduction of the Wechsler tests. The Wechsler tests provide a series of subscale scores that enable the psychologist to make much more detailed interpretations. The Stanford-Binet is now used mainly as an alternative form for the Wechsler tests or to assess low-functioning young mental retardates. Individual intelligence tests and the similiarities and differences between the Stanford-Binet and Wechsler tests are discussed in more detail in Chapter 14.

The Army Alpha and Beta At the beginning of World War I, the American Psychological Association (APA), under the presidency of Robert Yerkes, was anxious to be of assistance in the war effort. The armed services were faced with the difficult task of inducting hundreds of thousands of soldiers, deciding what they should do in the military, and training them in a short amount of time. It was decided that psychologists would develop tests that could be used to classify the inductees according to the role that their abilities suggested. At this point, group tests of abilities did not exist, and it was clear that it would be impractical to administer an individual test like the Stanford-Binet. Terman was a member of the committee charged with developing the screening instrument. Fortunately he had a graduate student, Arthur Otis, who was already working on ways to translate the Stanford-Binet into a test that could be administered to groups. Using his methods two tests were developed: the Army Alpha for inductees who could read and the Army Beta for those who could not. Nearly two million soldiers were tested and an eight-hundred-page report was written. Although some debate exists concerning the actual usefulness of those tests, they had an enormous impact on ability testing because they led to the development of commercially published tests: intelligence as well as achievement and personality tests.

Opposition to Testing

Psychological testing has been embroiled in controversy since its inception. It is an aspect of the overall educational process in the United States that seems to uncover a raw strain of competitiveness within our society because it promises rewards to some and an unhappy life for others and magnifies the social inequalities that already exist. To the extent that differences in ability exist, testing makes them more obvious.

Theoretical Bases for Defending and Criticizing Testing

The role of testing in our society can best be understood in terms of two conflicting philosophical positions: meritocracy and egalitarianism.

Meritocracy The philosophy of those advocating a meritocracy is centered on the belief that a society benefits when its members are rewarded according to a system based on an individual's actual accomplishments and ability. Such a view incorporates an emphasis on the principle that human differences determine who is successful and who is not and is consistent with the view that tests and other assessment instruments are useful. Even though our society is generally believed to reflect such values and is probably moving even more so in that direction, the movement has not been universally accepted as beneficial. Opposition to the establishment of a meritocracy has often taken the form of criticism of the use of ability tests.

Egalitarianism Espousing egalitaranism usually involves opposition both to testing and to establishing a meritocracy. It places emphasis instead on a belief in equal treatment for all, with the corrollary view that there is something wrong with any practice, in or out of education, that emphasizes individual differences. In addition there is the belief that jobs and education are rights that should be available to everyone.

Causes of the Opposition to Testing

First of all, discussions of the value of testing often reflect underlying differences in philosophy between those who advocate the use of tests supporting a meritocracy and those who oppose it and advocate egalitarianism. Opposition to testing is also cyclical. In the 1950s, testing seemed to be above criticism. In the 1960s and 1970s it was found that the widespread use of standardized tests had the effect of resegregating newly desegregated schools. As a result, there were demands that the use of standardized tests be curtailed. The National Education Association (NEA) went on record in opposition to standardized testing, the Association of Black Psychologists (ABP) urged a moratorium on intelligence testing (Cleary, 1975), in New York group intelligence tests were banned, and in California the use of individual intelligence tests to place minority students in special education classes was prohibited. Furthermore, in New York, publishers of aptitude tests used for admission to colleges and graduate schools must now make the content of their tests—the actual items—available to those taking such tests. Along with this is an underlying antipathy toward tests which should not be surprising given the differences that exist in our society, the contrasts between students in terms of academic performance, and the natural tendency to blame the bearer of bad tidings for the bad news itself. When an individual, class, or school system does poorly on a test, it is only natural that some of the anguish associated with the disappointment in performance should be focused on the test itself. It is therefore not unusual for students to blame their poor performance on the inadequacies of the test they failed. When the effect of this generally negative view of testing is coupled with the fact that there is a tendency for divergent performances to be elicited when different cultural or socioeconomic groups are compared, it should be expected that there would be calls for the abolishment of all standardized testing.

The Need for Tests

Despite the fact that both constructing and taking tests are rather unpleasant activities and that the argument for their elimination is at times persuasive, tests are a necessary part of any educational system. Educational testing, specifically classroom testing, forms the basis for the assignment of grades. Although it is possible to develop grading systems that do not require testing, those that have been tried have not worked well and have also engendered considerable opposition.

Motivation Tests provide motivation for students, rewarding those who are prepared and providing negative consequences for those who are not. Because the frequency of an individual's behaviors is increased by reinforcement, it can reasonably be said that tests cause students to study more. If you are a student taking two classes, and in one there is a comprehensive program of evaluation, while in the other there are no tests, you will probably find yourself devoting most of your time to the class in which you are evaluated.

Diagnostic Uses Tests also provide useful diagnostic information to the instructor about students' strengths and weaknesses and they can provide a useful basis for the modification of the instructional program. They also tell the instructor about the effectiveness of his or her instruction. Furthermore, the use of good evaluation procedures forces the instructor to define objectives. Whether or not they accept the value of formally stated instructional objectives, all teachers have goals, even when they are not explicitly stated. The process of constructing tests clarifies those objectives because, despite what an instructor might say, students view as important the things about which they are tested.

Certification Schools have responsibility in the area of certification both on a formal and an informal basis. When a student completes a class, the instructor who awards a passing grade is warranting that the student has learned the knowledge covered in the course. In public schools there is a growing movement toward accountability, with parents appearing in court to sue schools when they feel that their children have not received the education to which they are entitled. State legislatures have also entered this arena by passing laws mandating that students must have mastered certain basics before being awarded a diploma. This movement has already encompassed a majority of states, and many others are considering the adoption of such laws. Minimum competency testing will be considered in detail in Chapter 11.

Special Education During the 1960s, when the federal government was spending large amounts of money on special education, there was a tightening of the rules surrounding admission requirements. Schools were required to include individual intelligence tests as one aspect of the procedures for assignment to special education classes. This was an improvement over previous screening procedures, which were sometimes based on nothing more than a teacher's recommendation. In the 1970s, there was a growing concern about the disproportionate number of minority children in such classes. This resulted in criticism and the outright banning of the use of individual intelligence tests for the purpose of special education placement in some localities.

Intelligence tests are only one component of the assessment of students referred for possible placement in special classes. Although some criticism is certainly justified, it is doubtful that their elimination would result in better assessment.

Admission to Colleges, Universities, and Graduate Schools Ability testing for the purpose of admitting students to programs with restricted enrollments has led to increased social mobility and a minor revolution in higher education. In the past, admission to highly selective universities and graduate schools was based largely on family background and social class because these were the only data available. With the general acceptance of standardized admissions tests, students began to be admitted on the basis of measured ability. Mental tests allow bright students from the lower classes to rise on the socioeconomic ladder and those from upper classes who lack sufficient ability to drop a few rungs.

Much of the present day criticism of college aptitude tests has focused on their unfairness to students from culturally different and/or lower socioeconomic backgrounds. This is ironic because these are the individuals that these tests were intended to benefit.

A Theoretical Approach to Measurement

To paraphrase Wilson (1975), the physical world is not constructed in such a way that it facilitates comprehension by the human brain; conversely, the human brain is not constructed in such a way as to make easier the understanding of the physical world. Despite this, the scientific world proceeds with its purpose of describing the universe. It does this by imposing its models and schemes onto the chaos it encounters. Its most powerful tools are mathematical. When the observed world can be made to conform to the artificial requirements of mathematical models, explanatory power is greatly enhanced because prediction is made possible.

The field of measurement has a special role to fill in this process. It is the goal of measurement to take the irregular behaviors of humans and quantify them. It is the central dogma of measurement that words used to describe the traits and characteristics of humans can be expressed as numbers. This is not an easy process. The single words on which the numbers are based may be far from adequate descriptors of behavior, and the use of numerical indices tends to further abstract the words from their original meaning.

Measurement As a Physical Characteristic

Early measurement done with humans focused on physical characteristics. When Galton was measuring visitors to his booth at the International Exposition of 1884 and later to the Kensington Museum, he had for his focus anthropometric traits: hand, arm, and body lengths, as well as reaction time and sensory acuity. This emphasis on physical measurement led to an acceptance of the view that all measurement could be thought of in the same way as the physical characteristics of the individual. Even when the emphasis in measurement shifted to higher-level mental processing, this view of measurement continued.

The belief was also consistent with older superstitions about the basis of personality traits. Medical theory in the Middle Ages took the view that our health and behavior were determined by the balance of humors in the body. Hippocrates mentions four: sanguine (cheerful and active), choleric (angry and violent), melancholic (sad), and phlegmatic (passive and unassertive). Although this manner of describing behavior is rejected in a medical sense, the spirit of the approach is retained in the way measurements of human behavior are explained. We talk of giving a child motivation as though we could give him a cup of one of Hippocrates' humors when what we really want to do is change the child's behavior. Even though such attributes as height and weight are concrete and directly measureable, most of the focus of psychological measurement is on descriptions of behaviors rather than physical attributes. When we say that a person is anxious, we should not be thinking in terms of possession of a given amount of a substance labeled anxiety; instead we should understand that we are characterizing his or her behaviors as best being described and labeled as anxious.

Measurement Error

Theoretical approaches to measurement generally focus on measurement error. It is the possibility, or even the inevitability, of measurement error that causes psychologists and other social scientists to have this theoretical interest. The chemist measuring a reagent can safely assume that his or her scale is accurate. It is unlikely that he or she would show much interest in a theory of measurement.

True Scores and Measurement

The term *true score* has several meanings within a measurement context. It is first of all associated with such formal psychometric theories as classic true score theory. It also has other more general meanings in measurement. It is sometimes used to designate a hypothetical, perfectly accurate score, free of any measurement error, which can be contrasted with an individual's actual score and which is referred to as the obtained score. True scores can be described as platonic truth and/or in terms of operational definitions.

Platonic Truth Even though all existing measurements are imperfect, it is at least conceivable that perfectly accurate measurements exist somewhere. This is sometimes thought of as a Platonic truth because Plato believed that pure forms could exist somewhere, if only in another world visible to other worldly beings.

This point of view stems from the understanding of measurement that arose at the end of the nineteenth century when the field was in its infancy and mainly utilized psychophysical assessments. It is under these circumstances that the idea of a Platonic true score makes the most sense. For instance, at one time it was believed that intelligence was directly related to skull size. In measuring the circumference of skulls it is certainly reasonable to think that inaccuracies in measurement can be related to the true circumference of the skull.

Suppose you are conducting research that involves determining the weight of the participants in your experiment. Because of budgetary limitations you are forced to use an old bathroom scale—the kind that, when you find yourself unsatisfied with your weight, you reweight yourself on, knowing that you are likely to obtain a different weight, perhaps more to your liking, the second time you try. The inaccuracies of such a scale are most easily understood in terms of a comparison between the weight obtained on your shoddy bathroom scale and the true weight as determined by a physician's highly accurate scale. The degree to which the two weights differ can be determined precisely. According to classic true score theory, the reliability of the obtained score is a function of the relationship between it and the true score as obtained using the physician's more precise scale. Of course there is error even in the physician's scale, just as there can always be the possibility of an even more precise scale.

Operational Definitions The existence of a true score seems reasonable in the case of physical measurements. However, with the more abstract material associated with psychological assessment the existence of true scores is problematic. For instance, an individual's true level of intelligence, creativity, or anxiety is difficult to conceptualize. For this reason, the true score is now usually described operationally. In modern usage it often is defined as the mean of a large number of parallel forms of the test. Two tests are parallel if they are made up of items randomly selected from the same pool of items. The true score can also be defined as the score that could be obtained if all of the possible items for a test were administered. This total collection of items is called the domain of observables.

Constructs in Measurement

The field of measurement has for its focus human attributes or characteristics. Numbers are associated with characteristics as a means of quantifying the degree of the latter's presence or absence. This is sometimes misinterpreted to mean that those things we are measuring are actual physical entities, or can be thought of as though they were.

The attributes being assessed by psychological and educational tests are constructs rather than physical entities. A *construct* is a generic terms for a class of behaviors. For instance, the word *creativity* does not exist independently but refers instead to behaviors that, when present in sufficient quantity, cause us to say that a person is creative. Examples of constructs are schizophrenia, paranoia, reading ability, anxiety and rigidity. The field of measurement is concerned with the extent, existence, quantity, and consistency of the domain of observables defining a construct. Another way of viewing constructs is as a created entity, as compared to something that already exists. Trees exist whether we have a name for them or not, but the existence of intelligence is dependent on our provision of a label and a means for its assessment.

Much of our communication is based on the use of constructs. When we use the word *depressed*, we are referring to a set of behaviors that are intended to reflect depression. It is our anticipation that a colleague hearing that term conjures the same set of behaviors in his or her mind.

When we communicate it is with the expectation that our intended meaning can be put into words and arranged in the appropriate order according to accepted syntactical rules in such a way as to enable the meaning to be transferred to the person with whom we are communicating. In measurement we use a single word or a number representing that word to describe someone's behaviors. There is a considerable risk of confused meaning when we do this.

The associations that one person has with a certain word may be quite different from someone else's. If you are told that an individual is tall, you might not have any trouble identifying the person to whom the reference is being made, but if the individual is described as creative, you may not know about whom the reference is being made.

Constructs are quantified by the use of finer delineations of individual words rather than more complicated word structures. This approach is different from psycholinguistic approaches which emphasize syntactical structures as a means of facilitating the communication of meaning. Human language conveys meaning at a number of different levels from the sounds (phonemes), fundamental meanings (morphemes), and words to phrases and sentences. The meaning in what we say is carried not only in our words, but in their juxtaposition with other words and the order of the sentence. The words themselves represent only a part of our language capabilities. The numeral representing a single word is quite limited in the information it can convey when compared to the richness of languages.

The assignment of a single number to a construct assumes the existence of a trait with a unitary meaning. Unfortunately, the single score obtained through a specific measurement technique usually represents many factors, rather than just one. The single score obtained on a reading achievement test represents the sampling of a wide range of behaviors. The person using the score is likely to be unaware of all that is being assessed. Many of the terms we use to describe human behavior have a multiplicity of meanings, and yet by a single number we imply only one meaning.

The description of traits using numbers serves a useful and necessary purpose, but it should be done with the knowledge that this procedure, while creating the impression of great precision and scientific objectivity, involves quantifications that are at best inexact.

Constructs are more difficult to use than object names because they are more abstract. This fact is often ignored, and there is a tendency to treat the construct as though it had objective reality. The process of viewing an abstract term as concrete is called reification. Another problem with constructs is the tendency to use them to explain behaviors, which is called nominalism. An example of this would be an explanation of a child's inability to read by the statement that he or she had a reading disability. This is a logically flawed statement because our best evidence of the diagnosis of a reading disability is the fact that the child cannot read. Diagnosing a reading disability on the basis of a child's inability to read and then stating that the child cannot read because of a reading disability is not particularly useful. Another example would be the diagnosis that a child's withdrawn behavior was caused by emotional disturbance. This is "circular" logic because the diagnosis of emotional disturbance was based at least partially on the withdrawn behavior in the first place.

The biggest problem with the use of constructs is the considerable disagreement that can emerge concerning which behaviors belong to the domain of a given construct. Attempts to develop tests to assess creativity, for instance, have not met with success because there is a lack of agreement concerning the behaviors that belong in the domain of observables for this construct. Although there is more agreement about a construct like reading comprehension, such tests developed by different publishers often vary markedly in their content. As has been emphasized, the purpose of educational and psychological measurement is the quantification of constructs in the form of specific test behaviors. This works and makes sense to the extent that the attribute can be described by a set of behaviors that has general acceptance.

The legitimacy of the interpretation of constructs is sometimes compromised by the item-selection process. Tests tend to be composed by the test maker and seldom consist of items randomly selected from the domain of observables (Nunnally, 1967). This can have an adverse impact on the legitimacy of inferences made about a score (test validity).

Another problem is that the limitations of the objective test process sometimes force us to select items that do not actually measure the construct of interest. This is the weakness of operational definitions. When we use the phrase "reading comprehension ability," we are usually referring to an individual's capacity to read, retain, and understand what has been read. Because we cannot assess this directly in an objective fashion, we are forced to construct items that come as closely to this goal as possible. As a result the construct actually being measured may not be what is usually thought of as reading comprehension at all.

Values

Some attributes are not so much constructs as they are values. Whether an individual is judged to possess a given trait becomes more a function of the perception of the observer than an objective characterization of the individual being observed. When we talk about a child's reading ability, this is clearly a trait of the child and the subjectivity of the observer plays a minimal role. In other more value-laden settings, the predisposition of the person observing the behavior can become even more important than the nature of what is being observed. In studies of the reaction of parents following the imposition of plans to facilitate busing, it was found that those parents who removed their children from public schools denied that their decisions were the result of opposition to desegregation (Cunningham and Husk, 1979). In fact, they often expressed favorable attitudes toward desegregation. Without even mentioning opposition to desegregation, they would discuss quality of education and the inconvenience of the busing itself. In analyzing these responses the social scientist is thrust into the position of making a value judgment. The parents can be described as making legitimate responses based on a concern for the welfare of their children, or their behavior can be labeled as racist. In this case racism is a value-laden construct that is quite difficult to define.

The Structure of This Textbook

The emphasis in this textbook is on three areas. The first is the mechanics of measurement, which includes such topics as descriptive statistics, standard scores, reliability, and validity. The second is a description of the different types of tests used in education and psychology, including educational tests, ability tests, and personality tests. The third is the appropriate uses for tests. This book has been written with two assumptions: tests are powerful tools with the capacity to do good when their results are applied correctly, and they have the potential for great harm when used inappropriately.

SUMMARY

1. Psychology started out more as a branch of philosophy than a science.
2. It was the introduction of more precise methods of measurement that allowed psychology to become more scientific.
3. Measurement in the social sciences provides the techniques for quantifying human behaviors so that they can be studied empirically.
4. The historical development of measurement proceeded along two dimensions, one practical and the other theoretical.
5. Standardized testing probably began in China in the form of civil service tests that were later adopted first by Britain and then by the United States.
6. The theoretical development of the field of measurement had its start with studies of individual differences.
7. Galton pioneered the development of the instruments for measuring individual differences, whereas Binet, along with Simon, is credited with the development of early tests for assessing higher-level thought processing.
8. The first standardized mental ability tests intended for administration to large groups were the Army Alpha and Beta.
9. Testing, measurement, and assessment are topics that have their strong advocates and equally adamant detractors.
10. Questions about theory as it relates to measurement typically focus on whether the measurements of humans can use as a model the physical measurements used in the hard sciences.
11. Another important focus in measurement theory is the meaning and quantification of errors in measurements.
12. Measurement is largely involved with the quantification of constructs.

SUGGESTED READINGS

DUBOIS, P. H. (1970). *A history of psychological testing*. Boston: Allyn and Bacon. [This is generally considered the most important book about the history of tests and evaluation. You will encounter many references to this source in any discussion of the historical developments in the field of measurement.]

GOULD, S. J. *The mismeasure of man*. (1981). New York: Norton. [This is a popular and very readable account of some of the early developments in the history of psychological, and particularly intelligence, tests. It provides a historical perspective for an extremely critical view of these assessment techniques.]

GUILFORD, J. P. (1967). *The nature of human intelligence*. New York: McGraw-Hill. [The first chapter of this book provides an excellent historical account of the development of the field of intelligence testing.]

NUNNALLY, J. C. (1978). *Psychometric theory*. New York: McGraw-Hill. [Chapter 3 in this book provides a helpful explanation of the use of constructs.]

2

Statistics

OVERVIEW

Measurement involves identifying human attributes, placing them on a continuum, and attaching numbers that represent the amount of the attribute possessed. On a test this is done by summing across a large number of behaviors in the form of items and coming up with a single score that is intended to represent a measure of typical performance. A raw score on a test is therefore the sum of a large number of observations. The purpose of this chapter is to describe the methods that have been developed for summarizing and manipulating these values. The emphasis is on the basic operations that an individual needs to know in order to use measurement techniques effectively.

Descriptive statistics are emphasized because these are the types of computations that are most often used with measurement. Central tendency, variability, and correlations are the focus of most of the chapter, but probability and multivariate statistics are also introduced.

OBJECTIVES

From this chapter you will learn the computational methods associated with statistics. Specifically you will learn the following:

- The rationale for attaching numbers to traits.
- The meaning and uses of assumptions.
- The theoretical basis for scales.
- The appropriate computations that can be used with each scale.
- The difference between descriptive and inferential statistics.
- The uses and misuses of frequency distributions.
- The computation and uses for the three measures of central tendency.
- The reasons why the mean is the most often used measure of central tendency.
- The computation and uses for the three main measures of variability.

- The reasons for the domination of standard deviation and variance as measures of variability.
- The theoretical basis and derivation of the normal curve.
- The computational methods for the Pearson Product-Moment correlation.
- The methods of interpreting correlations.
- Factors that affect the magnitude of a correlation coefficient.
- Additional correlational methods.

Introduction

A major purpose of educational and psychological measurement is to bridge the gap between psychology as a philosophy and psychology as a science by providing the numbers that allow the construction of theoretical models for describing human behavior. Statistics provide the means for constructing these mathematical models that help us to understand our environment.

If you wanted to know the average age of all of the students in a college, you could assemble the students in a field, place them in rank order by age and then select the one in the middle as the average. It would, of course, be easier to take the numbers representing ages and manipulate them, particularly if you could store the information in a computer. By manipulating numbers it is easy to find the individual whose age is located in the middle, to find the age that occurs most frequently, or to add up all of the ages and divide by the total number of students to obtain the mean. It is far easier to push numbers around and manipulate them than it is to do the same with people. Of course, before we initiate this process we must be sure that we are going to get the same results from manipulating the numbers as we would if we manipulated the people.

Math Phobia and Statistical Anxiety

The reader is cautioned not to allow him- or herself to be intimidated by the use of the word *statistics*. The term has a very broad range of meaning and can include anything from the most arcane theoretical math approaches to simple arithmetic computations. The treatment of statistics in this chapter assumes only a minimal level of mathematical sophistication. We will seldom go beyond that which might be expected of a seventh- or eighth-grade student. Although some of the material covered in this chapter may be difficult, its difficulty will not be the result of its mathematical complexity.

Attaching Numbers to Traits

In measurement we attach numbers to the characteristics and traits that we use to describe others. Instead of talking about a child being either a good or poor reader, we provide reading test scores that convey this information with a much higher degree of specificity and in a manner that lends itself to mathematical computations. We lose something when we do this because we are taking the richness and complexity of the words in our language and simplifying them into unidimensional metrics.

The theoretical problems associated with this approach were introduced in Chapter 1, and they will be further elaborated in Chapter 5. The purpose of the present chapter is to explain how the numbers are to be treated once obtained.

The mere fact that we can attach a number to a person does not mean that we are justified in performing mathematical operations on the numbers. For instance, knowing the average value of the numbers on the back of football jersies tells us nothing useful about the teams or the players. Such a procedure would be of little use because the numbers were not intended for any purpose other than identification.

Assumptions

We use models to explain causal relationships among variables. A model is constructed from a series of statements that we believe to be true. We have no way of establishing the truth of those statements. They may be untestable, the cost of finding out about them may be prohibitively high, or they may represent a point of fact that is obvious or trivial. The unverified aspects of a model are handled by means of assumptions. An assumption is an assertion that we neither prove nor disprove but that must be true in order for any conclusions about our model to be valid. In the event that our assumptions are not true, the conclusions drawn from any analysis based on these assumptions is invalid.

When you examine the results of a reading achievement test for an individual child you make a number of assumptions. You assume that the test was administered in a standardized fashion, that the child was given neither too much nor too little time, and that there were no disruptions that interfered with his or her performance. Furthermore, it is assumed that there was not some mechanical breakdown in the scoring process that resulted in invalid results. It is also assumed that the score reported is the correct one for the child and is not a transposition of some other child's score. There would be no easy way of testing all of these assumptions, but if one or several of them are not true then the results of the test may be invalid. If a child who has always been an excellent student—who has obtained good grades and high scores on similar tests—gets a very low score on a reading achievement test, we would be likely to question some of the assumptions surrounding the test results.

Scaling

The appropriateness of the mathematical treatment of numbers is a function of characteristics that we call scaling properties. The scaling properties of test scores and other data used in the social sciences are of interest because they determine the type of statistical analysis that can be employed. Concern about scaling has declined over recent years, but during the 1950s it was one of the hottest topics in the field of statistics. Interest in the subject was increased by the consequences that were likely the result from a rigid adherence to scaling dogma. Such a position was likely to lead to the view that much of the statictical analysis being performed in the social sciences was inappropriate because the data were not of the proper scale.

Types of Scales

Data can be classified into one of the four scales: nominal, ordinal, interval, or ratio.

Nominal Scales The most basic type of measurement involves placing objects or persons into categories. For example, we can divide a group of people into males and females and label them *M* or *F*, *A* or *B*, or any other title that we might find appropriate or convenient. Often numbers are used, such as a 1 for males and a 2 for females. Other examples of nominal data are religion, ethnic background, and marital status. The main assumption on which the nominal scale is based is the requirement of *equivalence*. This means that subjects in the same category cannot be different with respect to the classification attribute, and subjects in different categories cannot be the same with respect to that attribute.

When we use numerals as labels they just indicate differences, not ranking or hierarchy. For instance, in a school district there might be four high schools. Each student is in one high school, and a student cannot simultaneously be in two different schools. We could label them 1, 2, 3, and 4, but this would not mean that school 4 was better than the other three or had more of any attribute than the others. It is possible that there is order to the four schools according to some attribute. Perhaps the average reading level is lowest in school 1, and higher in each successive school, with school 4 having the highest reading level. As long as we are just focusing on the differences between the schools, we have nominal data. When we focus on the hierarchal characteristics, we are assuming that the numerals used to designate the high school in which a student is enrolled is of a higher scale.

Suppose a group of judges observes the behavior of a group of children on the playground. The judges then provide a set of scores assessing each child's behavior on a number of different dimensions. The judges are particularly interested in studying the misbehavior of children in this setting and decide to classify misbehavior into one of three categories: (1) overly aggressive behavior; (2) dangerous behavior, such as jumping off the top of the jungle bars; and (3) whining and crying behavior. In order to simplify the recording of the children's behavior it is convenient to code the behavior. A 1 could be assigned to the first category, a 2 to the second, and a 3 to the third. It should be obvious that these assigned numerals are not isomorphic with numbers, and it would make no sense to treat them mathematically. What we have is clearly nominal data.

Ordinal Scales When it is possible to assume that the categories can be ranked, they take on the properties of the next higher level, which is the ordinal scale. For instance, our judges, observing behavior on the playground, might focus on aggressive behaviors and categorize children into three groups according to the frequency of their aggressive behavior. We have now established a relationship between three categories, and the magnitude of the numbers takes on meaning because they indicate order. We could give the children who are most often agressive a score of 3, those who are least often agressive a score of 1, and those in between a score of 2. We could use the numbers 5, 7, and 132, but these would likely cause confusion.

The numerals used represent an efficient way of indicating rank order, but they do not bear any direct relationship to the actual amount of the attribute. When we have an ordinal scale, if two subjects are placed in separate categories, then one or the other must have a higher ranking. They cannot be equal. If $A \neq B$, then either $A > B$ or $A < B$. This characteristic is called connectedness. If $A > B$, then B cannot be greater than A. This quality is called asymmetry. Furthermore, if A has more of a quality than B and B has more of a quality then C, then A must have more of the quality than C, and this is called transitivity.

Not all ordinal data are the same, and it makes sense to think of two kinds: first of all, there are ordinal data that consist of ranking categories. It is just a step up from nominal data and should not be treated in any way other than as though it was of an ordinal scale. This sort of ordinal data will be referred to as type 1 ordinal data. The scale obtained when individuals are categorized according to their occupation is of a nominal scale, but when occupations are ranked according to their status it becomes an example of a type 1 ordinal scale. They can be contrasted with achievement test scores that are not, strictly speaking, interval data because the intervals between scores are not perfectly uniform. On the other hand, saying that they are nothing more than ordinal data is not accurate. They are almost, but not quite, interval data and are therefore called type 2 ordinal data. The intervals between occupations, ranked according to their status, may show no regularity. Consequently, only statistics deemed appropriate for ordinal data should be employed. Test scores that are type 2 ordinal data can be and are treated as though they were interval data.

Interval Scales With interval data the numerals attached to objects or persons refer to the amount of the attribute, rather than merely indicate the relative positions in a series. We are not only able to say that A has more of a trait than B, but also how much more of the trait A has. A yardstick is of an interval scale, therefore 3 inches plus 4 inches is the same as 5 inches plus 2 inches. This characteristic is called additivity; without it we cannot justifiably add, subtract, multiply, and/or divide. For individuals ranked in terms of tennis ability, it would be wrong to say that the difference between the first and the second and the ninth and tenth rated players is the same. Furthermore, it would not be fair to make up a doubles team consisting of the first- and sixth-rated player and think that they would be equal to one consisting of the third- and fourth-rated player, even though their rating in both cases sums to seven. Only if their ability was measured on an interval scale could this be done. The importance of the assumption that one has interval data resides in the mathematical properties it confers. Mathematical computations on actual scales can only be conducted with either interval or ratio data and not with nominal or ordinal data. Test scores and the results of most psychological instruments are assumed to have meaningful intervals, which permits mathematical computations. As we shall see, this is an assertion that it is often difficult to defend.

With interval scales we do not know about the relative magnitude of scores because we have not established an absolute zero. In most psychological measurement we typically use the mean as a point of reference, and a person's score is interpreted in terms of variability around the mean. We do not really know what it means to say that a person has an IQ of zero or what a zero would mean on an instrument measuring self-concept. For this reason we cannot legitimately state that one person's score is twice as high as someone else's.

Ratio Scales Ratio scales differ from interval scales by having a zero point that is not arbitrary, but that instead represents the complete absence of the relevant trait. This characteristic permits statements about the relative amount of the trait possessed by an individual. It is permissible to say that one child is twice as tall as another child because height is measured on a ratio scale; but it is not permissible to say that one child has twice the reading ability of another child because reading ability is only measured on an interval scale. Ratio scales are seldom used in psychological measurement and one must search diligently to find examples of their use in the social sciences. Height, weight, and time are examples, as is Kelvin temperature (Fahrenheit and Celsius are only of an interval scale).

Assigning the Appropriate Scale to Data

The four scales are cumulative. That is, data that are ordinal are at the same time nominal, and data that are interval are also both nominal and ordinal. Ratio data, therefore, have all of the properties of nominal, ordinal, and interval scales, along with those characteristics that make them unique. Each step up the scaling ladder assumes the characteristics of the subordinate levels. The different scales are described in Table 2.1.

Assumptions The relevance of assumptions must be kept in mind when the scaling properties of sets of data are considered. We make conclusions about the scaling characteristics of data that we have no easy way of verifying. We are therefore dealing with assumptions. In the event that our assumptions are wrong, the validity of our results is likely to be adversely affected.

Continuous and Discrete Data Another way of illustrating a distinction among these scales is in terms of *continuous* and *discrete* data. With discrete data there

TABLE 2.1 Description of Scales

Scales	Assumptions		Descriptions	Examples
Nominal	Equivalence		Individuals are placed into categories.	Occupation Sex Race
Ordinal	Equivalence Connectedness Asymmetry Transition	Type 1	Individals are placed into categories and these are ranked.	Basketball rankings Class rank
		Type 2	Individuals are placed on a continuum characterized by a scale on which the units may not be completely uniform.	Grade point average Scores from classroom tests
Interval	Equivalence Connectedness Asymmetry Transitivity Additivity		Individuals are placed on a continuum characterized by a scale on which the units have uniform intervals.	IQ scores Standardized test scores Fahrenheit and Celsius temperatures
Ratio	Equivalence Connectedness Asymmetry Transitivity Additivity An absolute zero		The same characteristics inhere as for interval data, except that ratio scale data have an absolute zero, which permits interpretations that include relative comparisons.	Height Weight Kelvin temperature

are no decimal values. A subject is assigned a 1, a 2, or a 3, with no values in between. Nominal data and most ordinal data are discrete. Interval and ratio data are generally considered continuous and can have values that are intermediate between integers, in the form of decimals. You must be aware, however, that it is possible to have data reported in decimal values, which does not meet the criteria necessary for an interval scale.

Controversies in Scaling

The scale of a set of data is not a fixed property of the data but is what we designate it to be. In a more formal sense, it is determined by the assumptions we make—and of course some assumptions are more reasonably associated with a given measure than others. By definition assumptions are never tested, and if we have made assumptions that are not justified, then the resulting analysis of data based on these assumptions will be flawed and the degree of the inaccuracy will be unknown. Consider several judges observing a gymnastic performance and assigning numbers to the performers at the conclusion of their routines. How would you know the scale of the assigned numbers? There is no way to respond without knowing which assumptions have been made. It is possible that the judges are only classifying the performances into categories designated by a number, with no attempt made to differentiate among the performances in any other way. They could, for instance, be assigning a 1 for floor exercises, a 2 for the balance beam, a 3 for the rings, and so forth. In this case what we have is clearly a nominal scale. If the judges rank ordered the performers according to their performance, then we would have data of an ordinal scale. If scores are awarded based on the perceived quality of the performance and those qualities are on a continuous scale—and, furthermore, are to be averaged—then an interval scale must be assumed.

During the 1950s a school of thought concerning scaling emerged that can best be described as fundamentalist. Two major exponents of this view were Virginia Senders (1958) and Sidney Siegel (1956), whose textbooks strongly supported this position. They argued that a set of scores is either nominal, ordinal, interval, or ratio, and that these scales are ordered in ordinal fashion according to the level of assumptions required of each, with each scale of course subsuming the assumptions of all of the lower scales. According to this view, if a data set does not meet the assumptions of one scale, it must be of a lower scale. The scales are therefore viewed as discrete rather than continuous entities. There is also the implication that the scale of data must be capable of being established through ostensible characteristics. Using these criteria, most measures used in psychology and education, if examined very closely, would fail to meet the requirements of the interval scale. For example, grade-point averages, IQ scores, and test scores in general cannot easily be proven to be interval. If one accepts this fundamentalist view, then arithmetic computations should not be performed on most of the data collected by social scientists.

In order to fill the need for statistical techniques to be used when traditional approaches were deemed inappropriate, a new branch of statistics was developed called nonparametric statistics, to differentiate it from the more often used parametric statistics. Although these methods are promoted as analogs to the more generally used statistical methods, they are less powerful and require a reorientation of our thinking in statistics and the learning of an entirely new set of techniques. The dogmatic view that any data that could not be proved to be interval must be ordinal is hard to maintain in the face of careful scrutiny. Type 1 ordinal data should be treated statistically as such, but it is shortsighted to treat type 2 ordinal data in the same way. Using computer technology it is possible to simulate the effect of violating scaling assumptions; the results of such studies have shown that most of our statistical operations are robust to the violation of scaling assumptions. For this reason you should not be too concerned if you have type 2 ordinal data rather than interval data.

When computing correlations you are supposed to use the Product-Moment Correlation coefficient with interval data and the Spearman Rank Order correlation coefficient with ordinal data. If you use the Product-Moment correlation for data that are ordinal, but that do not deviate too far from being interval, the results will be quite similar to that obtained using the Spearman formula.

As a practical matter almost all data collected by social scientists are treated as though they are interval, whether they are or not. This sometimes is done as a result of an awareness of the robustness of the statistics to violations of scaling assumptions and sometimes out of ignorance.

There are instances where a concern for scaling is relevant. For example, performing mathematical operations on grade equivalents or percentiles can result in a considerable distortion in the results of data analysis. Scaling, as it relates to derived scores, will be covered in the next chapter.

Types of Statistics

One type of statistics, nonparametric, has already been mentioned, but there are many other ways that statistical approaches can be categorized. The two most often-used categories are *descriptive* and *inferential* statistics. This book, and in particular this chapter, focuses on descriptive statistics.

Descriptive Statistics

After grading the tests taken by a class of thirty-four students, the teacher is faced with thirty-four numerals representing the performance of the class. Studies of the brain have shown that, although it is possible to look at an aggregate of seven different scores and to understand and process them, the human mind is generally not capable of making sense out of larger sets of numbers. It is believed that this is the point where the brain switches from left- to right-brain processing. A teacher, or anyone dealing with aggregates of numbers, needs techniques for organizing data and turning them into information. The teacher with the thirty-four students needs to summarize the data in such a way that they can become meaningful. The processes involve the risk of losing information, because when you focus on summary data about a group as a whole, you have given up specific information about individuals in the group. The purpose of descriptive statistics is to take raw scores and treat them mathematically in such a way that they can be interpreted meaningfully.

Inferential Statistics

Although descriptive statistics form the basis for the interpretation of measurement results and the foundation for inferential statistics, inferential statistics constitutes the chief methodology for conducting research. With inferential statistics we are seeking to understand large groups labeled populations by looking at the characteristics of randomly selected subgroups called samples. The results of the computations involving samples are called statistics, whereas those obtained from the populations are called parameters. Samples are used to understand populations not because they provide better information, but for convenience and to increase the generalizability of results. If you want to describe the reading level of all third-grade students in a school system, it would of course be possible to administer a reading test to them. This approach would be expensive and time consuming, but the information obtained would be very precise. However, if it were possible to obtain results that would be almost as accurate utilizing a smaller subgroup, or sample, then it would make sense to do so. It is possible to test all of the third-graders in a school district, but if one is interested in making generalizations about all third-graders in the United States, it is obviously not realistic to think that you could test each child in the population. The techniques of inferential statistics, which are based on the use of random samples, provide a methodology and a rationale for making generalizations about populations from samples, as well as techniques for determining the accuracy of the results of such an approach.

Using Statistical Methods in Measurement

Frequency Distributions and Graphs

Suppose you are enrolled in a class in which there are fifty students. You have just taken the first test, which consisted of seventy-five multiple-choice questions. You are of course anxious to know how you did, so when you see your instructor you ask about your performance. After looking in his grade book, he tells you that you received a score of sixty. This may not tell you very much. It could be a terrible score, because the test may have been very easy, and you could have had the lowest grade in the class. On the other hand, the test could have been very hard, and you may have the best score of anyone in the class.

Frequency Distributions What is needed is a way of communicating to you how the entire class did, so that you know how you did in relation to everybody else. The simplest approach would be to construct a frequency distribution, which would indicate how many students received each score. Table 2.2 provides an example of this.

Such a chart is an improvement over having fifty scores spread out in a disorganized fashion, but to the extent that the scores are spread over a wide range, such an approach does not result in the summarization of much data. A better approach is to put the data into a grouped frequency distribution such as is seen in Table 2.3. It is relatively easy to understand and easy to construct.

Notice how, when we shift from the frequency distribution to the grouped frequency distribution, we have a trade-off between specificity about individual scores and a more coherent summarization. The field of statistics is full of such trade-offs, and the statistician must decide the format in which data are to be reported in the context of both the amount of information to be conveyed and the ways the data can be best used.

Graphs The frequency distribution can be made graphic by extending a column from the midpoint of each interval in such a way as to indicate the relative amount of each attribute being measured. This is called a histogram, or bar graph. Its use is illustrated in Figure 2.1.

Another method of presenting data graphically is the frequency polygon. It is constructed in a similar fashion to the histogram, except that instead of using a

TABLE 2.2 Frequency Distribution of Test Scores

Test Score	Number of Cases	Test Score	Number of Cases
75	0	56	4
74	0	55	3
73	1	54	3
72	1	53	4
71	2	52	1
70	1	51	2
69	0	50	1
68	0	49	1
67	2	48	1
66	1	47	0
65	2	46	2
64	0	45	0
63	0	44	2
62	1	43	1
61	3	42	0
60	2	41	1
59	1	40	1
58	2	39	0
57	4	38	0

TABLE 2.3 Grouped Frequency Distribution of Test Scores

Score Interval	Frequencies
30–39	0
40–49	10
50–59	25
60–69	10
70–79	5
80–89	0

horizontal line to indicate the frequency, a point is located at the center of the interval and at the proper height to indicate the frequency. These points are joined by straight lines that are connected to the midpoint of the zero frequency at both ends of the distribution. The frequency polygon is illustrated in Figure 2.2.

Instead of a straight line, a curved line can be fitted to the points. This is illustrated in Figure 2.3.

There are many other ways of graphically displaying data, and in the future these techniques can be expected to be used on an even more widespread basis because of the graphic capabilities of small computers. The increasing availability of software capable of doing this makes the construction of elaborate graphs easy and the reporting of data appealing.

Although graphs serve the purpose of presenting data in an easily understood and attractive fashion, they are uneconomical in terms of space and do not lead to further analysis. They also can be constructed either intentionally or unintentionally in a misleading manner. Because they emphasize relationships it is important

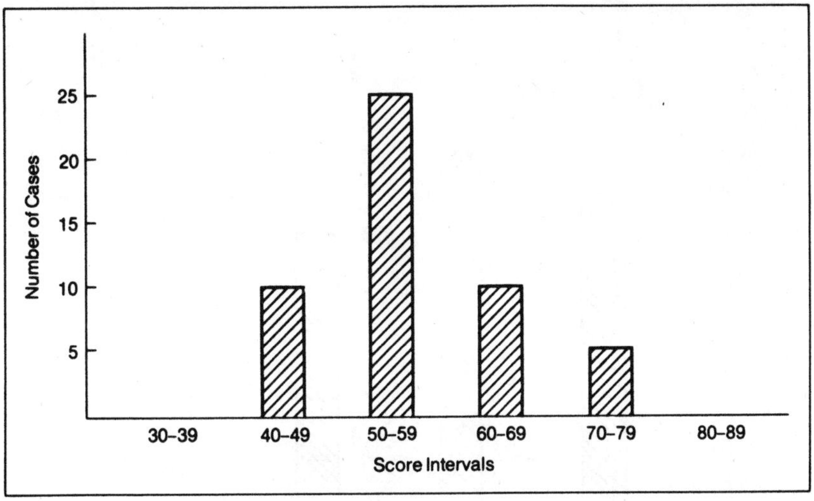

Figure 2.1
Histogram of test scores.

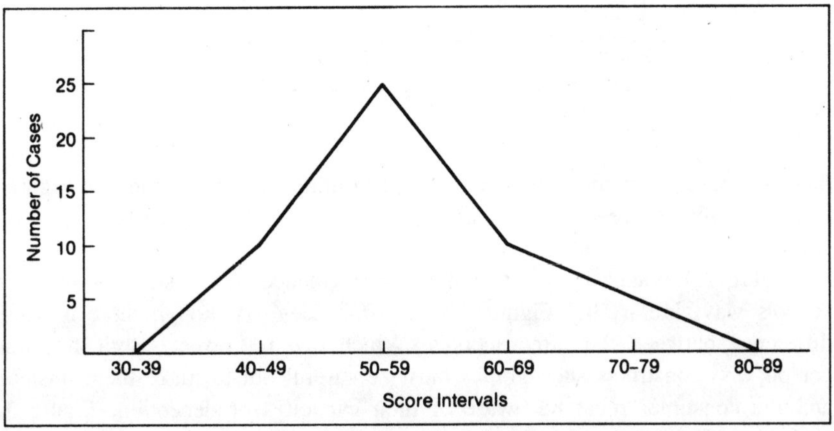

Figure 2.2
Frequency polygon of test scores.

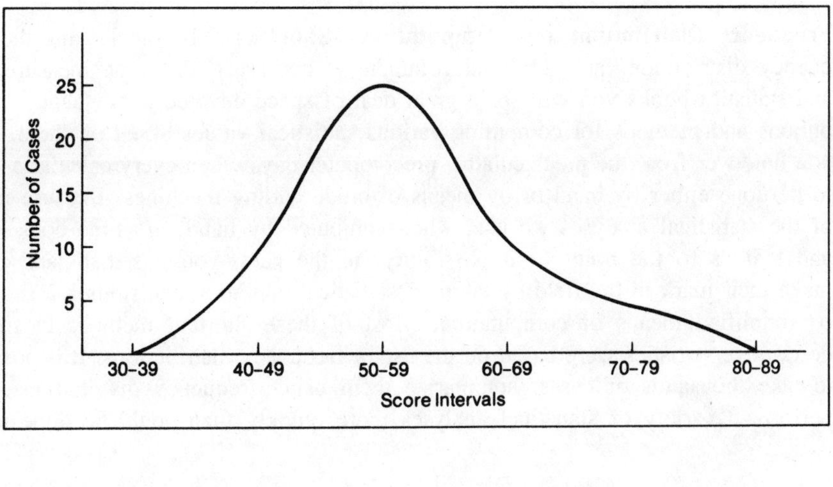

Figure 2.3
Smooth curve of test scores.

Figure 2.4
Graph of reading test scores with zero point.

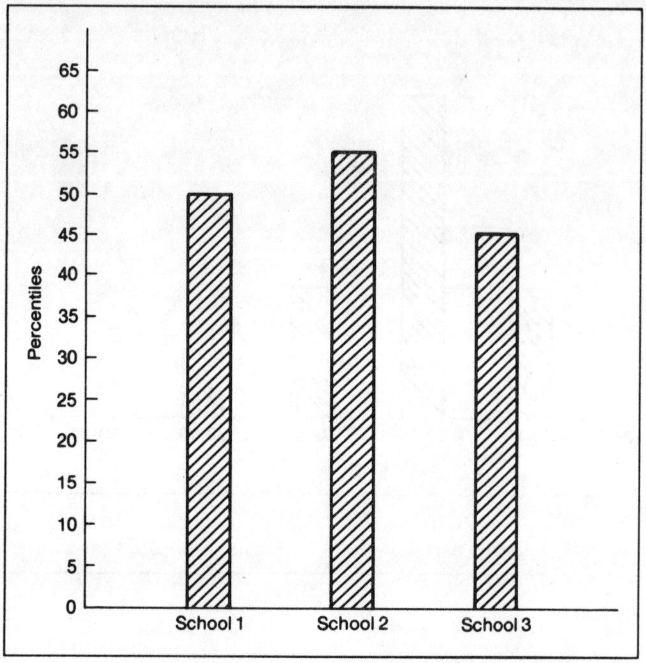

that the abosulute zero of the data be kept in mind. The histograms in Figures 2.4 and 2.5 report the result of a reading achievement test for three schools, but they convey information that is quite different.

Figure 2.4 makes it appear that the performance of the students in the three schools was similar, but Figure 2.5 makes it seem as though there is a sizable difference between the three schools. Which one is correct? Both are, but the person who constructs such graphs must be careful not to make them misleading, and the consumer must be aware of their capacity for deception. Figure 2.4 is probably a better representation of the data because it takes the absolute zero into consideration.

Frequency Distribution and Computational Shortcuts Before leaving the frequency distribution, an additional comment is necessary. In some measurement and statistics books you will see a great deal of space devoted to frequency distributions and methods for computing various statistical values based on them. This is a holdover from the precalculator, precomputer days when every calculation had to be done either by hand or by means of crude adding machines. Because many of the statistical analyses we use, when computed by hand, are time consuming and tedious to the point of impossibility, in the past, young statisticians could make their mark in the field by taking a statistical operation and finding a shortcut or simplified means of computation. Most of these shortcut methods in simple descriptive statistics were based on the use of frequency distributions. It is possible to take thousands of cases, summarize them using frequency distributions, and perform a variety of statistical analyses more quickly than could be done using

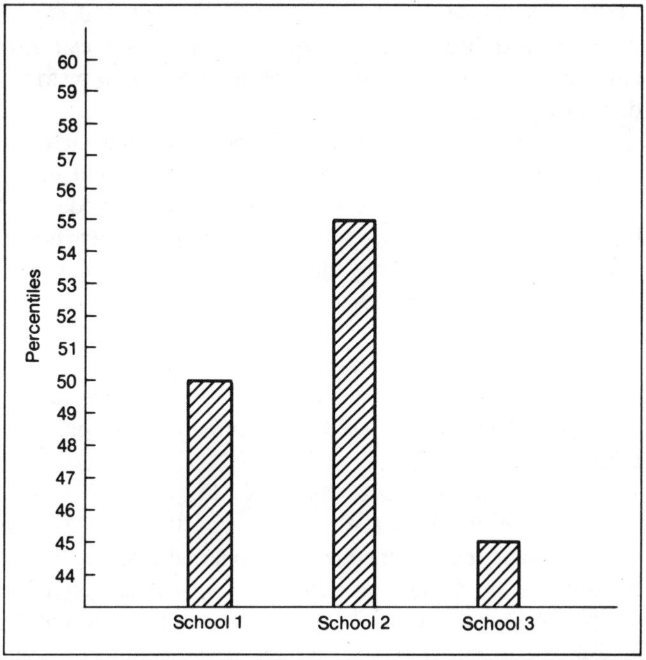

Figure 2.5
Graph of reading test scores without zero point.

raw data. There is a long tradition of statistical analysis based on the use of frequency distribution. These habits die hard, and some statistics and measurement books devote a great deal of time to old-fashioned methods of statistical computations.

It is now possible to purchase an inexpensive and simple-to-operate calculator that can handle raw data easily. In addition, the availability of easy-to-use statistical packages makes computations easy to perform on large-scale computers that are available at most universities and colleges and in many school districts. Although the use of personal computers for statistical computations is still in an undeveloped state, with the increasing sophistication of both hardware and software they are likely to become an important tool for data analysis. These three levels of electronic data processing and analysis render the use of frequency distributions for anything other than simple descriptive statistics unjustified.

Central Tendency

The most efficient way of describing a set of data is by means of a single value. What we are looking for is a number that is most typical of all of the scores. When we do this we must give up the idea of describing the group completely, because we are inevitably going to lose information about the individual. Of course that is one of the trade-offs we must accept when using descriptive statistics. The three major ways of computing the typical score are mode, median, and mean.

Mode The mode is the easiest type of central tendency to compute. It is simply the score that occurs most frequently. The mode can also be used with data of any scale, from nominal to ratio, because it is least restrictive in terms of the scale of data it requires.

If all of the scores occur with the same frequency, we say that there is no mode. If two scores occur with equal frequency and they are adjacent, we select a score at the midpoint between the two as the mode. If there are two relatively high scores, each located at a different point, we describe the distribution as bimodal. If there are more than two, we say it is multimodal. We can also refer to major and minor modes.

Median The median is the point that divides a set of ordered scores in half in such a way that there are as many scores above that point as there are below it. The median can be used with either ordinal or interval data but not with nominal data.

Consider the following scores: 10, 15, 15, 20, 35, 42, 45. The median is 20 because there are three scores above and three scores below. Note that the first step in computing the median is to place the scores in ascending order and that the two 15s are counted as separate scores. If all sets of scores contained an odd number of scores and the scores in the middle were not the same, computing the median would be relatively easy. Now consider these scores: 10, 15, 15, 15, 35, 36, 42. What is the median? Your first guess might be 15, but not if you remember the definition: the median is the point at which there are as many scores above as there are below. There is only one score below 15, which is 10, but there are three scores above it: 35, 36, 42. Therefore, by definition, the median cannot be 15. If the data are interval, there is a straightforward mathematical solution to the problem; if it is ordinal, no such mathematical solution can be applied. All we can do is plead for more precise measurement to eliminate the problem of identical scores.

With ordinal data it is perhaps better to think of the median as being the person, object, or score that divides the ordered set of data in half, with as many scores above as there are below. If you have an even number of scores, you have a problem because you cannot cut a person in half. Suppose a school has a six-member tennis team whose players are ranked by playing ability. You would have a hard time finding the median player. All you know is that it is the person located between the third and fourth player, but that is not much help. In this case there really is no median. With interval data if there is an even number of scores, the median is the point between the two middle scores. If there are tied ranks around the middle score, the median is the midpoint as long as the distribution is symmetrical; if there is a different number of scores above from the number below this point, however, computing the median utilizes a more complex process. This process involves interpolation and requires the assumption that the data are continuous, meaning that the scores can have any decimal value. When data are continuous, no two scores should be the same. When this happens we assume that our measurement was not sufficiently sensitive, and that subjects with the same scores would have differed had our techniques of measurement been more precise. Suppose that three students at the center of the distribution obtain the same score on a test. If the three students obtained test scores of 72, we should assume that a more precise measure of the attribute would spread the scores between the real limits of 72, or 71.5 and 72.5. At this point we do not know, nor do we need to know, which of the students had the most of the trait and which had the least. To compute the median under these circumstances, it is necessary to determine the point between the real limits that should be identified as the median. To do this, we use the following formula:

$$\text{Median} = \text{Lower limit} + \frac{\dfrac{\text{Total cases}}{2} - \text{Cases below}}{N} \qquad [2.1]$$

where

Lower limit = the tied score − .5

Total cases = the number of cases in the data set

Cases below = the number of cases below the tied scores

N = the number of tied scores in the middle of the distribution

Consider the example presented earlier that included the following scores:

10, 15, 15, 15, 35, 36, 42

Using formula 2.1 we obtain:

$$\text{Median} = 14.5 + \frac{\dfrac{7}{2} - 1}{3} = 14.5 + .83 = 15.33$$

Mean The mean is the arithmetic average computed by dividing the sum of the scores by the number of scores. It is the most frequently used measure of central tendency and requires data that are at least of an interval scale.

The mean is the building block for all statistical analyses; each of the increasingly more complex computations we will examine is based on the mean. The mean has a number of important characteristics that make it useful in such computations.

It is based on every score. Unlike the mode and the median, the mean takes every score into account. If even one score is changed, the magnitude of the mean will change. This is not true for the other measures of central tendency.

It is the best estimate of the population average. Suppose you want to know the average age of all 18,000 students enrolled at a university. You could compute the mean of the entire 18,000, but that would of course be awkward. Alternatively, you could randomly select a sample of, let's say, 100 students. This means that each of the 18,000 students in the population would have an equal chance of being among the 100 students in the sample. Computing the average age of the 100 would allow you to infer the average age of the population of all students. The best estimate of the population average would be the mean. The reason it is the best estimate is that it is the most stable. If you obtain successive samples of 100 subjects and compute the mean, median, and mode on each sample, the means would tend to be more similar than the medians and modes for each sample.

The deviations around the mean always sum to zero. The deviation is the value obtained when the mean is subtracted from a score. If you sum the deviations, the resulting value will always be zero.

In Table 2.4 we are presented with five values (5, 5, 4, 1, 0). The mean of these values is three (15/5 = 3). As has been shown, when the mean (3) is subtracted from every score the sum of these deviations is 0. If you were to select any other number, the sum of the deviations would not be 0. For instance, consider 2 and 4, one digit below and one digit above the mean. The sum of the deviations around the values is plus and minus 5, respectively.

The squared deviations are always smallest around the mean. The sum of the deviations squared for the data in Table 2.4 is 22 when the deviations are computed using the mean, but when either 2 or 4 is used, the sum of the deviations squared is 27. This illustrates the general principle that when the deviations are squared and summed using any value other than the mean, the obtained value is larger than when the mean is used.

Summary of the mean's traits. The mean has four important traits: (1) it is affected by every score in the data set on which it is calculated, (2) it is the best estimate of the population average, (3) deviations around the mean always sum to zero, and (4) the sum of the squared deviations is always smallest when computed using the mean.

These characteristics of the mean, although of minor interest by themselves, are extremely important for understanding further statistical computations such as variability.

Choosing Between the Mean and Median The mean is easier to compute than the median because it does not require awkward interpolations and there is no need

TABLE 2.4 Characteristics of the Mean

X		$\overline{X}$	x	x^2
5	−	3	2	4
5	−	3	2	4
4	−	3	1	1
1	−	3	−2	4
0	−	3	−3	9
$\Sigma X = 15$			$\Sigma x = 0$	$\Sigma x^2 = 22$

$\overline{X}$ = the mean
X = a score
N = number of cases
x = a deviation
Σ = sum of
Σx = sum of deviations
Σx^2 = sum of squared deviations

to place the data into rank order. With a few scores, putting data in rank order is not much of a problem, but this process can be quite time consuming in the case of large data sets. Because of the necessity to rank order data first, you cannot directly compute the median on a calculator, although it can be done on a computer. The mean is easily computed using any hand-held calculator because the data can be entered in any order.

You might be wondering at this point why we would use the median at all. There are a number of situations where the median is useful. First of all, if the data are ordinal you cannot use the mean, so you must use the median or mode. Second, the two computations treat extreme scores differently. The magnitude of the median is not dependent on the size of any scores except the middle scores. For example, the median of the following scores: 35, 46, 51, 67, 70, 75, and 81 is, of course, 67. If we change the 81 to 810, the median remains 67. This makes the median different from the mean because the mean is affected by all scores, including extreme "outlying" scores. Although this characteristic of the median can be a disadvantage—because it results in the loss of information—there may be situations where we prefer not to have disparate extreme scores distort the data.

Suppose you own a small but successful business with four workers: two receive \$10,000 a year; one \$11,000; another \$15,000; and you pay yourself the handsome salary of \$49,000 a year. After hearing complaints from your workers concerning their salaries, you tell them that they have no reason for complaining because you pay an average salary, using the mean of \$19,000. The median is of course \$11,000 and the mode is \$10,000. Outlying, extreme scores cause a great deal of difficulty in statistical analyses, and the use of the median is one approach to dealing with the problem.

In a study of learning disabilities that had the purpose of determining a definition for this condition (Kaiser, 1974), a questionnaire was sent to experts in the field asking them to estimate the probability that a child had a learning disability given the presence of a specific symptom. For instance, they were asked the probability of a child having a learning disability when it was known that the child was hyperactive. One expert might say 60 percent, another 70 percent, a third 65 percent, and still another 55 percent. A fifth expert, with a somewhat different orientation, might say 10 percent. The mean is 52 percent, whereas the median is 60 percent. In this case the median seems to be far more justifiably called the typical score. In further analysis of the data, when an average score was needed, the median was used instead of the mean.

Variability

Let us return to the earlier hypothetical situation where you have asked your instructor about your performance on a recent test. You were told that you got 60 out of 75 questions correct, which is not very helpful. That could be a good or bad score, depending on how everyone else did. Now that you know about central tendency, you can ask your instructor what the mean for the class is. Suppose the mean is 56. Remembering that your score was 60, you now know more than you did before. You know that you did better than the average student, but you do not know how much better you did. If all of the scores are grouped around the mean, you may have one of the best scores in the class. On the other hand, if the scores are spread out, your score of 60 might be only slightly above the mean. What is needed is a method for quantifying how well a measure of central tendency describes a set of scores.

Any time you compute a single value that is to represent a group of values, a loss of information is implied. For example, consider two groups of students in a math class. Each group has five students. Group 1 has the following scores on a math test: 53, 47, 49, 51, and 50; the scores for Group 2 are 35, 50, 65, 45, and 55. The mean for both groups is 50. This provides an accurate reflection of all of the scores in Group 1 because they cluster around 50. The mean of 50 for Group 2 is not very typical and does not convey much information about the scores in the group because they deviate so much from the mean. Measures of variability are ways of quantifying how much information is lost. This characteristic makes measures of variability, like measures of central tendency, very important to the field of measurement. This is important in the field of measurement because we have a great interest in how much scores differ from what we expect and how much error is involved in our assessments.

The four methods of measuring variability are as follows: range, semi-interquartile range, variance, and standard deviation. Unlike central tendency, where it was possible to describe typical situations in which the mode or median might be the statistic of choice, the range and the semi-interquartile range are seldom used.

Range The range is simply the difference between the highest and lowest scores. To compute the range the lowest score is subtracted from the highest score. Sometimes a 1 is added to make the range inclusive of all of the scores. The range is not a very useful index of variability because the magnitude of the value is determined by only two scores, the largest and the smallest. On a classroom test for instance, the majority of the class may have scores in the 80s and 90s, but if one student has a score that is well below this, the range will be greatly inflated.

Semi-Interquartile Range The semi-interquartile range is computed by subtracting the first quartile from the third quartile and dividing by two. The first quartile is the point that separates the bottom one fourth of the scores from the upper three fourths of the scores. The third quartile is the point where three fourths of the scores are below and one fourth of the scores are above. The actual computation of the quartile requires a process of interpolations similar to that used in the computation of the median. The semi-interquartile range is used so infrequently that it is not neccessary to understand it further. It is enough to know that it is a measure of variability.

Standard Deviation and Variance The most important methods for determining variability are the variance and the standard deviation. These computations, along with the mean and correlation, are the most frequently used statistics throughout the field of measurement. The standard deviation and variance are computed in essentially the same way. The standard deviation is the square root of the variance, which of course means that the variance is the square of the standard deviation.

The standard deviation is a better descriptive statistic than the variance. The variance is usually used for data analysis that goes beyond description and is often used as a basis for more sophisticated data analysis.

The computation of the standard deviation is based on what has already been learned about the characteristics of the mean. The manner in which a set of scores deviates around the mean is at the heart of the computation of the standard deviation. Clearly, knowing how much each score differs from the mean is a clue to how much variability there is in a data set, and that is the basis of the formulas used to compute the standard deviation. As was the case with central tendency, we are seeking a single value to indicate variability.

Definitional Formula There is no single formula for computing the standard deviation, but rather there is a family of formulas, all algebraically equivalent. The definitional formula is useful in understanding how the process works, whereas the various computational formulas provide for ease of computation. The definitional formula follows:

$$\sigma = \sqrt{\frac{\Sigma x^2}{N}} \qquad \textbf{[2.2]}$$

where

σ = the standard deviation

Σx^2 = sum of the deviations squared

N = the number of cases

The use of the definitional formula is illustrated in Table 2.5.

Why do we square the deviation and then find the square root? You, as well as many others, are probably curious about the reason for such a complex approach. Why find the square of the deviations and then turn around and find the square root of the total of squared deviations? It is not possible, of course, to find the average of the deviations because they always sum to zero. The next best option would be to eliminate the minus signs and find the average of the unsigned deviation obtaining a statistic called the average deviation (AD). Squaring values to eliminate the negative sign is a more accepted practice among statisticians than just eliminating the signs.

There is another reason for the unpopularity of the AD. If it is used a decision must be made concerning whether to compute deviations around the mean or the median. The median might be used because the sum of the unsigned deviations is smallest around that statistic. Go back and look at Table 2.4 and notice how the sum of the unsigned deviations around the mean is 10. Now figure out what it is when the median is used. As you can see it is 9. With any set of data, when the mean and the median are not the same, the sum of the unsigned deviations using the median will be less than if computed using the mean. Because the mean is a more stable measure and takes all scores into account, it is clearly a better value

TABLE 2.5 Computation of the Standard Deviation Using the Definitional Formula

Score (X)		Mean ($\bar{X}$)	Deviations (x)	Squared Deviation (x^2)
7	−	4	3	9
4	−	4	0	0
2	−	4	−2	4
1	−	4	−3	9
7	−	4	3	9
4	−	4	0	0
4	−	4	0	0
3	−	4	−1	1
$\Sigma X = 32$[a]			$\Sigma x = 0$	$\Sigma x^2 = 32$[a]

$$\sigma = \sqrt{\frac{32}{8}}$$

$$\sigma = \sqrt{4}$$

$$\sigma = 2$$

[a] These values are the same only for these particular scores. With other scores these values will not be the same.

to use. When it is used the more involved process of computing the standard deviation seems warranted, and it is the statistic that is almost always employed, despite the more complex procedures that it entails.

Computational Formulas The definitional formula (2.2) is useful for computing the standard deviation when there are only a few values and/or the data has been selected in such a way that the mean is an integer rather than a decimal value. Its main advantage is that its use in computing the standard deviation gives the person doing the computation a better idea of what the standard deviation is. It is impractical for larger data sets because it cannot easily be computed using a calculator. There are a number of formulas, each algebraically equivalent to the definitional formula, that permit an easier computation of the standard deviation.

The formula that follows was developed for use with early versions of adding machines and electronic calculators that had only two memories; its use simplifies the computation of the standard deviation. Of course it is too abstracted from the meaning of the standard deviation to provide any insight into its computation.

The computational formula follows:

$$\sigma = \sqrt{\frac{\Sigma X^2 - \frac{(\Sigma X)^2}{N}}{N}} \qquad [2.3]$$

where

ΣX^2 = the total of all scores squared (the scores are squared first and then totaled)

$(\Sigma X)^2$ = the square of the total of all scores (the scores are totaled and then squared)

N = the number of cases

If you use formula 2.3 with the data presented in Figure 2.9, you will obtain the same value obtained using the definitional formula.

Two points about the computational formula should be emphasized:

1. It eliminates the use of deviations and uses only the actual values in the data set and their squares.
2. When you square each value and find the sum of their squares, you obtain a value smaller than if you add up the values and square the total.

The computational formula "works" at a mathematical level because it is algebraically equivalent to the definitional formula. It also works at an intuitive level. Consider the values in Table 2.6. The three values in each of the three sets of data sum to 12, the square of which is 144. In the computational formula this is written $(\Sigma X)^2$. It is the value ΣX^2 that varies in these three instances. When all of the values in a data set are the same, ΣX^2 is smallest; in example 1 it is 48. Because 144 $[(\Sigma X)^2]$ divided by N (which is 3) is also 48, the numerator in the formula becomes 0 and the standard deviation becomes 0. If all of the values in a set of data are the same, it makes sense that the standard deviation would be 0.

TABLE 2.6 Computation of the Standard Deviation for Three Sets of Data Using the Computational Formula

Example 1		Example 2		Example 3	
Scores (X)	X^2	Scores (X)	X^2	Scores (X)	X^2
4	16	8	64	10	100
4	16	3	9	1	1
4	16	1	1	1	1
$\Sigma X = 12$	$\Sigma X^2 = 48$	$\Sigma X = 12$	$\Sigma X^2 = 74$	$\Sigma X = 12$	$\Sigma X^2 = 102$
$(\Sigma X)^2 = 144$		$(\Sigma X)^2 = 144$		$(\Sigma X)^2 = 144$	
$\sigma = \sqrt{\dfrac{48 - \dfrac{144}{3}}{3}}$		$\sigma = \sqrt{\dfrac{74 - \dfrac{144}{3}}{3}}$		$\sigma = \sqrt{\dfrac{102 - \dfrac{144}{3}}{3}}$	
$\sigma = \sqrt{\dfrac{48 - 48}{3}}$		$\sigma = \sqrt{\dfrac{74 - 48}{3}}$		$\sigma = \sqrt{\dfrac{102 - 48}{3}}$	
$\sigma = 0$		$\sigma = 2.94$		$\sigma = 4.24$	

The more different the values in a data set, the greater the value of X^2 as compared to $(\Sigma X)^2$, and consequently the larger the standard deviation. This can be seen in Table 2.6, examples 2 and 3.

Estimating populations from samples. It is not unusual to see either the computational or definitional formulas written with $n - 1$ as the denominator instead of just N, which we have used up to this point. This is because the meaning and interpretation of the statistic changes depending on how they are being employed. Up until now we have viewed the standard deviation and variance as measures of variablity that stood alone as descriptors of the set of data with which we were interested. However, in the field of statistics, we are often concerned with the realtionship between samples and populations and in using statistics to estimate the parameters of the population.

The mean of a sample is an unbiased estimator of the mean of the population. In other words, the estimate of the mean of a population, based on the mean of a sample drawn randomly from the population, is just as likely to overestimate as underestimate this value. This is why the mean provides a good estimate of the central tendency of the population. The standard deviation and variance, when computed using the formulas presented up to this point, are biased estimators. They consistently underestimate the population parameter. This underestimation is greatest for small samples and less noticeable for larger samples. For this reason when one wishes to make inferences about the variability of the population, it is necessary to change the formula for computing the variance and standard deviation in such a way that it no longer results in an underestimation of these values. This is done by changing the denominator from N to $n - 1$.

The use of this value results in a sizable increase in the value of the standard deviation and variance for small samples and a smaller increase for larger samples. The symbols for the standard deviation and variance changes from σ and σ^2 to s and s^2 when $n - 1$ is used in the denominator. These changes in symbols are not made merely to confuse students, but to cue the consumer of such statistics as to the nature of the computations that were performed. Unfortunately, everyone in the field of measurement and statistics does not adhere to these conventions. What is presented is the most accepted use of the symbols.

You might wonder why $n - 1$ is used. Why not $n - 2$ or $n - 1/2$? The conclusion that the correct value was $n - 1$ was based on a rather cpmplex mathematical proof, which you will be spared. This correction procedure makes the sample variance an unbiased estimator of the population variance; however, the sample standard deviation is not a completely unbiased estimator of the population standard deviation. Even with the corrected formula, the standard deviation of a sample will underestimate this parameter of the population to some degree. The bias is still greatest for small samples. The degree of bias is also related to the shape of the distribution. The greater the deviation from normality, the more bias.

The fact that there are two ways of computing the standard deviation, each with a different denominator, can cause confusion when you are using a calculator that is preprogrammed for computing the standard deviation. Generally you enter each value using a specific key designated Σx. Then, with the push of another button, you are presented with the standard deviation. There is a catch though:

you must check the manual that came with your calculator to see exactly which formula was used. Some of the more sophisticated calculators provide a choice of formulas, but most calculators use the formula that includes $n - 1$ in the denominator. You can check to see which is used by entering a set of data for which the standard deviation is known. For instance, try entering 4, 2, 4, 2 and then compute the standard deviation. If the result is 1, you know that N was used in the denominator; however, a value of 1.15 would indicate that $n - 1$ was used. If your calculator uses the formula with $n - 1$ in the denominator, the obtained value can easily be converted to the value that would have been obtained using formula 2.3. This is accomplished by multiplying the obtained value by one less than the number of cases ($n - 1$), dividing by n, and then pushing the square root button.

Using the standard deviation. In the same manner that interval data are needed before mathematical computation is permissible, we must also be sure that any two scores that are to be combined have similarly sized standard deviations. We cannot, for instance, add the results of two tests with different standard deviations and expect the results to be meaningful.

If you are seeking a single score to characterize a student's reading ability and you want to consider both the number of books read and the score on a reading achievement test, it is clearly not permissible merely to add the number of books to the reading score. If you did that, the score on the reading test would be weighted much more heavily than the number of books. This is because the standard deviation from the reading test is much greater than the standard deviation of the number of books read. No rational person would knowingly do this, but there is seldom any hesitation about adding the raw scores from two tests, even though their standard deviations are quite different. The only way to ensure that two tests can be compatibly combined is to make certain that they have similar standard deviations. This can be most easily accomplished by transforming the scores into derived scores. The specific methods for accomplishing this will be covered in the next chapter. Another important aspect of the standard deviation is its relationship to the normal curve. This relationship forms the basis not only for standard scores, but also for inferential statistics.

The Normal Curve

A particularly important aspect of statistics and measurement is the normal curve, or distribution. It represents an aspect of measurement that is emphasized far more often than it is understood. You will probably recognize its classic bell-shaped form, as illustrated in Figure 2.6.

The normal curve, or distribution, can be understood in three contexts: (1) as a natural phenomenon, (2) through probability, and (3) by means of its mathematical formula.

Natural Phenomenon If you take a sufficiently large number of measurements of a naturally occurring phenomenon and create a histogram, you are likely to

Figure 2.6
The normal curve.

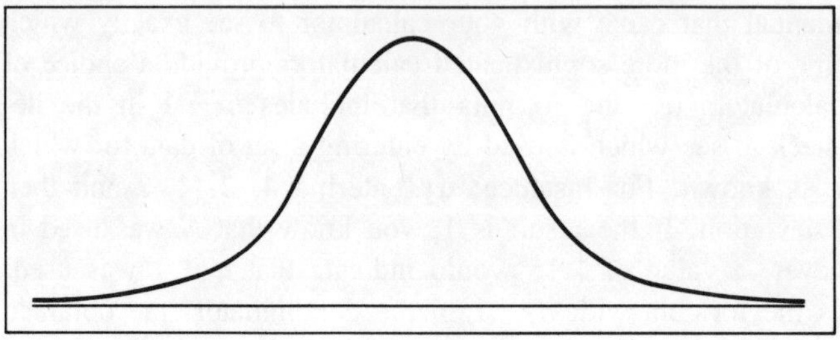

obtain a shape that is tall in the center and short at the extremes. Similarly, if you examine the results of students' performance on a test, you will find that most students are about average and that there are relatively few scores at either extreme. Of course, there are naturally occurring phenomena that do not yield a normal distribution, and test scores obtained using instruments that are either too easy or too hard will have scores piled up at the extremes. It is reasonable to think of the normal curve as a naturally occurring phenomenon, and this becomes more evident as the size of the sample increases. Unless you have a very large number of subjects, or are very lucky, you will not obtain a graph that looks exactly like the one illustrated in Figure 2.6, but it may be similar.

Measurements of height taken on very large samples by the armed services appear to be normal, as is true of large samples of intelligence test scores, such as those shown in Table 2.7. This table shows a comparison between actual IQ scores obtained by Weschsler in his norming sample for the Weschsler Intelligence Scale for Children–Revised (WISC-R), along with the theoretical normal distribution. As can be seen, the two are nearly identical.

It is reasonable to assume that it is possible to find among naturally occurring phenomenon distributions that are either normally distributed or nearly so.

Probability Take a coin and flip it ten times. Count the number of times it comes up heads, and then repeat the process many times. If you construct a histogram of the number of times a head comes up in each ten flips, the results will look like the classic bell-shaped, or normal, curve. Although a small number of trials may not provide a very good approximation, the more trials you use, the closer you will approach the classic shape. However, if the first several trials deviate from the expected shape, do not expect the next trials to compensate. Each new trial is independent from what has happened before. The reason large samples, or a large number of trials, lead to closer approximations to the normal curve is that values that do not fit the model—which can be expected to happen occasionally—will have a minor effect when compared to many other trials. It is of course possible, in a finite number of trials, for any shape to emerge. It is possible, although certainly unlikely, to have every flip of a coin come up heads over one hundred trials.

The same type of results that we obtain by flipping coins can also be obtained by tossing dice, spinning a roulette wheel, dealing cards, or utilizing the results of any other game of chance or process in which chance operates. It should not come as a surprise that naturally occurring events, such as the height of a large

TABLE 2.7 A Comparison of the Distribution of WISC-R Scores with the Normal Distribution

		Percent Included	
IQ	Classification	Theoretical Normal Curve	Actual Sample[a]
130 and above	Very superior	2.2	2.3
120–129	Superior	6.7	7.4
110–119	High average (bright)[b]	16.1	16.5
90–109	Average	50.0	49.4
80–89	Low average (dull)[b]	16.1	16.2
70–79	Borderline	6.7	6.0
69 and below	Mentally deficient[b]	2.2	2.2

[a] The percents shown are for Full Scale IQ, and are based on the total standardization sample (N = 2,200). The percents obtained for Verbal IQ and Performance IQ are essentially the same.

[b] The terms *High average (bright), Low average (dull), and Mentally deficient* correspond to the terms *Bright normal, Dull normal, and Mental defective,* respectively, used in the *WPPSI, WAIS,* and 1949 *WISC* manuals.

SOURCE: David Wechsler, *Wechsler Intelligence Scale for Children–Revised.* New York: The Psychological Corporation, Table 8, p. 26, 1974. Reproduced by permission from the Wechsler Intelligence Scale for Children–Revised.

number of army enlistees, trace a normal curve similar to that obtained by tossing dice or flipping coins. In very large samples the genetic and environmental factors that determine height involve chance combinations that can reasonably be considered random. Some factors may raise a person's height above the mean and others may push it below, but with a large sample the various factors tend to cancel each other out.

Bernoulli. The relationship between chance occurrences and the normal curve is not coincidental. The normal curve was created in such a way that it matches that which is obtained through chance occurrences. The study of the normal curve stemmed from attempts to understand probability and was partially a response to the needs of gamblers anxious to improve their chances at gaming tables by being able to compute the probabilities of certain events happening. One of the earliest mathematical treatments of probability is found in *Ars Conjectandi* written by James Bernoulli in the seventeenth century. Bernoulli developed a method for determining the probability of an event occurring a specified number of times over a given number of trials when the probability of the event occurring in one trial was known.

$$\text{Probability of } n_1 = \left[\frac{n!}{n_1!(n - n_1)!}\right]\left[(p)^{n_1}(q)^{n - n_1}\right] \quad \textbf{[2.4]}$$

where

Probability of n_1 = the probability of obtaining n_1 "successes" in n trials where "successes" refers to the condition that you are trying to predict. If, for instance, you are trying to predict the number of heads, then "successes" would be the number of heads

n = the number of trials
n_1 = the number of successes you are trying to predict
p = the probability of success
q = the inverse of the probability of success or $1 - p$
$!$ = a factorial

As formidable as this formula might appear, there is only one aspect that should be new to the reader, and that is the *factorial*. A factorial is a number multiplied by one less than itself, 2 less than itself, then 3 less, until 1 is reached. For instance, the factorial for 4 is $4 \times 3 \times 2 \times 1$. The symbol for the factorial is !. The factorial for 4 is written 4! and is read four factorial.

The logic that Bernoulli propounded is applicable to all sorts of chance occurrences, but they can be most easily illustrated by the flipping of coins, where, if the coin is fair, there is a fifty-fifty chance of obtaining either a head or a tail. The type of problem that this formula might solve is the probability that one would obtain three heads after flipping a coin ten times. Applying formula 2.4 we get the following:

$$\text{Probability of } n_1 = \left[\frac{10!}{(3!)(7!)}\right]\left[(.5)^3\,(.5)^7\right].$$

By breaking the formula down into its two components we get

$$\frac{10!}{(3!)(7!)} = \frac{(10)(9)(8)(7)(6)(5)(4)(3)(2)(1)}{\left[(3)(2)(1)\right]\left[(7)(6)(5)(4)(3)(2)(1)\right]}.$$

After canceling we then have

$$= \frac{(10)(9)(8)}{(3)(2)(1)} = 120 \quad \text{and because}$$

$$(.5)^3(.5)^7 = (.5)^{10} = .000976,$$

the probability of $n_1 = (120)(.000976) = .117$.

The computation of the factorial of small numbers is simple, but even slightly larger numbers can require tedious computations. The factorial of 10 is 3,628,800. Try to compute the factorial of 20. Without a calculator or computer that treats the numbers exponentially, the computation is virtually impossible. Because none of these aids were available to the early gamblers, what they needed was a method of computation that bypassed the need for factorials.

Probability and the bell-shaped curve. In the search for the solution to this problem, an interesting phenomenon was discovered. The histogram of probabilities computed in the manner already described traces a bell-shaped curve. It is the same curve that is seen in many naturally occurring phenomenon. Figure 2.7

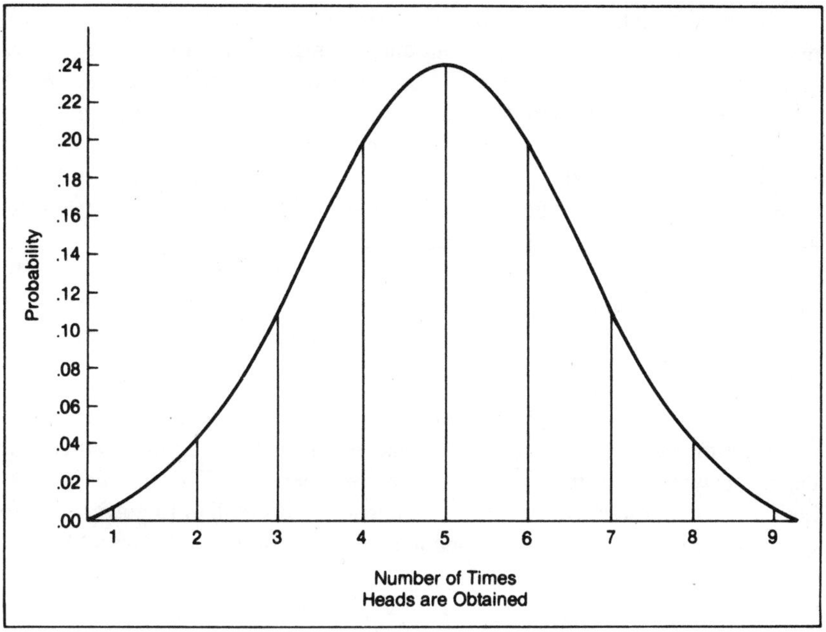

Figure 2.7 Graph of the probabilities of obtaining heads in ten flips of a coin.

illustrates the graph of the probabilities of obtaining specified numbers of head after ten flips.

The fact that the graph of probabilities traces a characteristic bell-shaped curve led mathematicians to the conclusion that what was needed was a mathematical function that defined the curve. The function then could be used for solving probability problems.

As a Mathematical Formula To meet the needs of gamblers and to satisfy the curiosity of other mathematicians, De Moivre (1667–1754) devised a mathematical formula that approximated the naturally occurring normal curve and greatly simplified the problems of computing probabilities. The formula is too complex to reproduce here, but sophisticated calculators as well as computers with the appropriate software can provide these data with the push of a button (or several buttons).

Variations in the Normal Distribution There is not one normal distribution but a family of distributions. Some of these may not look like the classic normal distribution, but may still be derived from the normal curve formula. The classic bell-shaped curve is a standard normal curve with a mean of zero and a standard deviation of one. Two important variations from the classic bell shape are defined as *kurtosis* and *skewness*.

Kurtosis involves the degree to which a curve tends toward being more pointed (leptokurtic) or flatter (platykurtic) than the classic bell shape, which is described as mesokurtic. The larger the standard deviation, as compared to the mean, the more platykurtic the distribution, and the smaller the standard deviation the more leptokurtic. The kurtosis of a distribution can vary, and the distribution may still meet the requirements for normality.

Regardless of the relative size of the mean and standard deviation, the normal distribution is always symmetrical around the mean. Lack of symmetry is referred to as skewness. If you construct a histogram of the results of a test and the test is too easy, the scores will pile up at the high end. In this case we say that the curve is skewed negatively (the direction of the skewness is determined by the location of the tail of the curve). If the test is too hard, the scores pile up at the bottom end of the distribution and we label the curve as positively skewed. Kurtosis and skewness are illustrated in Figure 2.8.

There are many ways that a distribution can differ from the classic bell shape of the normal distribution. It could be rectangular—that is, every score could occur with equal frequency. Instead of one peak at the center of the distribution, it could have two and be bimodal or have many peaks and be multimodal.

Computing skewness and kurtosis. In the cases of both kurtosis and skewness there are mathematical computations that permit us to determine, numerically, the degree to which a distribution has these characteristics. The skewness of a distribution is equal to the average of the *z*-scores raised to the third power. The formula for a *z*-score (which will be discussed in more detail in the next chapter) follows:

$$z = \frac{X - \overline{X}}{\sigma} \qquad [2.5]$$

where

X = the score
$\overline{X}$ = the mean
σ = the standard deviation

When a distribution is symmetrical, the skewness is zero. If the value is negative, we say that the distribution is negatively skewed. If it is positive, we say that it is positively skewed. The larger the skewness value, the less symmetrical the distribution.

Kurtosis is the average of the *z*-score raised to the fourth power. A mesokurtic distribution has a kurtosis of three. When the kurtosis statistic is greater than three it is leptokurtic, and the further from three it deviates, the more leptokurtic it becomes. Kurtosis values that are smaller than three are labeled platykurtic.

It is unlikely that you would compute either kurtosis or skewness by hand, but many descriptive statistics computer programs, in providing the statistics for a set of scores, routinely include skewness and kurtosis.

Important Characteristics The normal curve has three important characteristics. The first is that the point of deflection, or the place where the curve switches from being concave to convex, occurs one standard deviation on either side of the mean. The second is that the normal curve never actually touches the *X*-axis. No matter how far along the axis one goes away from the mean, the possibility of a score still exists. The third is that with the normal curve there is a fixed proportion of cases between any two points along the *X*-axis in terms of *z*-scores.

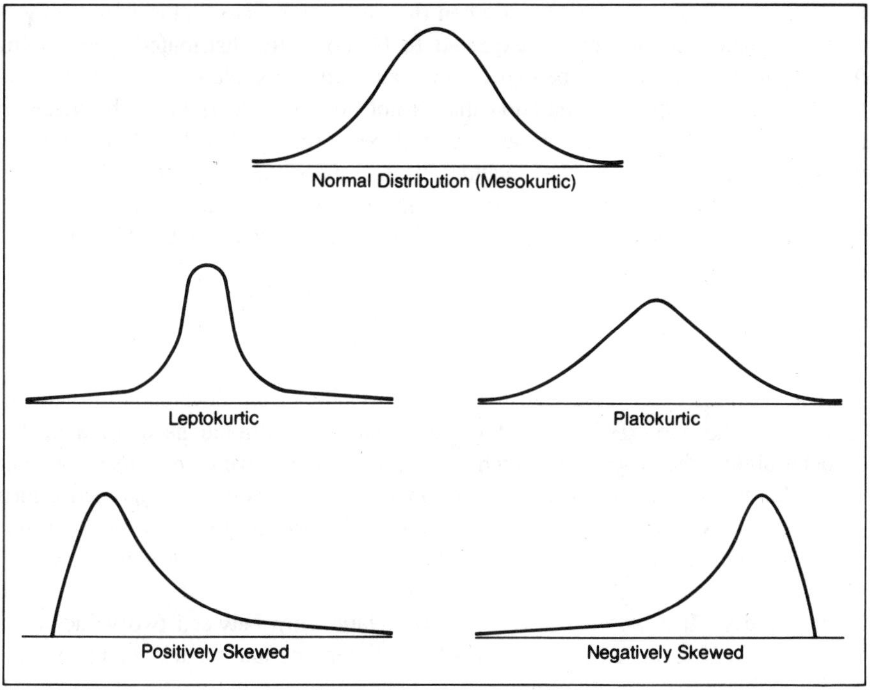

Figure 2.8
Examples of deviation from normality.

The third characteristic is of particular importance because it makes it possible—as long as a normal distribution can be assumed—to convert raw scores to percentages. The first step is to convert the raw scores into *z*-scores by subtracting the mean from the score and dividing by the standard deviation.

By utilizing the information from Table A.1 in the Appendix, this value can be converted to a percentage. For instance, 68 percent of cases lie between -1 and $+1$ standard deviations around the mean; and 95 percent of cases are between -2 and $+2$ standard deviations. Given any two values, expressed in terms of standard deviations, it is possible to compute the proportion of cases. This can be done as long as it is reasonable to assume that the data are normally distributed. The area under the curve is considered "one," or unity, and values reported in the tables represent the proportion of cases between the mean and the *z*-score.

The Assumption of Normality Although it is often legitimate to assume that naturally occurring phenomena approximate the normal curve, this is not always true. The existence of distributions that are close to normal is dependent on the operation of random factors. There are many factors that prevent a distribution from approaching normality. The most important factor in measurement is the skewness that results from the truncation accompanying tests that are too easy or too hard, causing scores to pile up at either end of the distribution. Another cause of skewing is the response sets that are often encountered with personality tests.

The fact that many sets of scores do not appear to be normally distributed is not cause for alarm, despite the fact that so much of statistics and measurement is based on this assumption. Even when the underlying distribution is not normal, errors in measurement can be expected to be normally distributed. This is true because the factors that can be expected to cause error operate in a random fashion. In a like manner with a population that is not normally distributed, the means of a sufficiently large number of samples will be normally distributed. In addition, many statistical operations that include an assumption of normality seem to work very well when that assumption is not met. Even when violations of normality affect the conclusions, statisticians are left with no alternatives but to use them.

Correlation

The types of descriptive statistics already covered were developed prior to this century. In the early 1900s test developers had an additional need for a method of determining the degree to which two sets of scores were in agreement. This was a major concern of Galton's, as he investigated various anthropometric measurements on which his research was based. He wanted to know whether they were independent or related to each other and/or other factors in some way.

Scatter Plots It is possible to display the relationship between two values using a scatter plot. If you examine the scores for both reading and math of eight students, shown in Table 2.8, the relationship is evident, but when the scatter plot is drawn, the relationship becomes more obvious. The scatter plot of the data in Table 2.8 is shown in Figure 2.9. The closer the points in a plot approximate a straight line, the more closely the two variables are related. If the plotted points slope upward from left to right, as in Figure 2.9, then the relationship is labeled positive. In this case low math scores are associated with low reading scores, whereas high scores in math are associated with high scores in reading.

When the plot slopes downward from left to right, it is said to be negative because the higher values in one variable are associated with the smaller values in the other. When it is not possible to discern a slope or any linearity, we say that there is no relationship.

Pearson Product-Moment Correlations Scatter plots, like frequency distributions and histograms, are useful for their visual characteristics, but they are a statistical

TABLE 2.8
A Comparison of Eight Fourth-Grade Reading and Math Scores

Student	Math Score	Reading Score
A	70	80
B	40	30
C	20	30
D	10	10
E	70	100
F	40	80
G	40	30
H	30	40

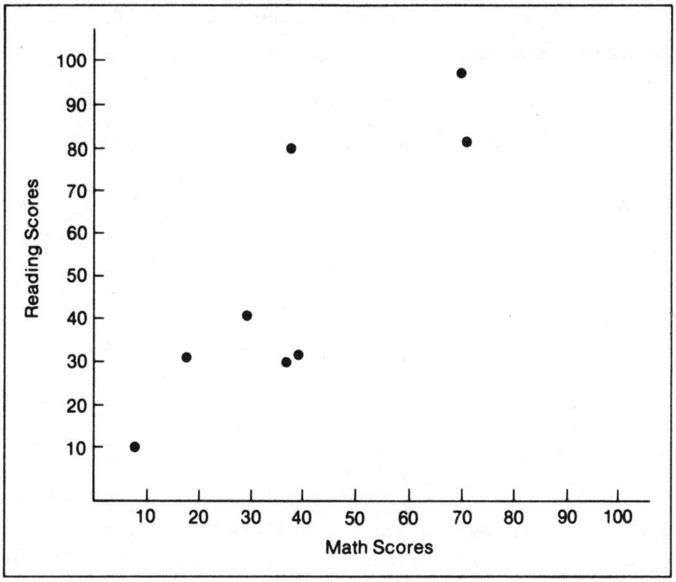

Figure 2.9 Scatter plot of fourth-grade reading and math scores.

dead end because no further analysis is possible. In addition, their interpretation is subjective, and it is not always easy to examine two scatter plots and determine which shows the greater relationship. This was the problem that faced Sir Francis Galton when he was trying to analyze the mass of anthropometric data he had collected. He therefore developed the framework for the correlation statistics that were later revised and named after Karl Pearson (Dubois, 1970). What he wanted was a single value that would indicate the degree of relationship between two variables. It was to be so constructed that it was never greater than one or smaller than minus one. Positive values were to indicate a positive relationship, while negative values were to indicate a negative relationship, or correlation. The closer the correlation coefficient approached one or minus one, the greater the relationship and the closer to zero the lesser relationship. The final correlational techniques developed by Pearson had all of these characteristics.

When you encounter the term *correlation*, it will generally refer to the Pearson Product-Moment correlation developed by Karl Pearson. You may also see or hear it referred to as the Product-Moment correlation, the PM correlation, the Pearsonian correlation, or just correlation. The value itself is called the coefficient.

The definitional formula. As was the case with the standard deviation, there are both definitional and computational formulas for the correlation coefficient. The computational formula for computing the correlation is quite intimidating to the nonmathematically inclined, although it is more lengthy than complex. Computing the correlation coefficient using the definitional formula involves two components. The first step requires the conversion of each value to a *z*-score, which is done internally within the computational formula. To obtain the correlation, it is necessary to cross multiply the *z*-score and divide the sum of the cross-products by the number of cases. The definitional formula for the Product-Moment correlation coefficient follows:

$$r = \frac{\Sigma z_x z_y}{N} \quad \textbf{[2.6]}$$

where

r = the correlation coefficient
z_x = the z-score for the first variable
z_y = the z-score for the second variable
N = the number of subjects

An example of a positive correlation. The computation of the correlation coefficient for math and reading test scores is illustrated in Table 2.9. As can be seen, a value of .85 is obtained. This is, as you might anticipate from the scatter plot, a fairly high correlation. Notice how positive z-values are multiplied by positive z-values and negative z-values by negative z-values, which in both cases results in a positive cross-product. Under these circumstances the sum of the cross-products is relatively large, and the result is a correlation coefficient of .85. The sum of the cross-products (the numerator) can never be larger than the denominator because that would mean that the correlation coefficient was larger than

TABLE 2.9 Computation of the Pearson Product-Moment Correlation Between Math and Reading Test Scores Using the Definitional Formula

Student	*Math (X)* Raw Score	*Math (X)* *z-Score*	*Reading (Y)* Raw Score	*Reading (Y)* *z-Score*	*Cross-Products*
A	70	1.5	80	1.00	1.50
B	40	0	30	−.67	0
C	20	−1.0	30	−.67	.67
D	10	−1.5	10	−1.33	1.99
E	70	1.5	100	1.67	2.50
F	40	0	80	1.00	0
G	40	0	30	−.67	0
H	30	−.5	40	−.33	.16
	$\bar{X}$ = 40		$\bar{X}$ = 50		$\Sigma z_x z_y$ = 6.81
	σ = 20		σ = 30		

$$r = \frac{\Sigma z_x z_y}{N}$$

$$r = \frac{6.81}{8}$$

$$r = .85$$

1. Remember, except for purposes of illustration in an example such as this, an N of 8 is far too small to obtain meaningful results.

An example of near-zero correlation. In Table 2.10 the computation of the correlation between a math test score and a test of physical education proficiency (PEPT) is computed. As can be seen, the two variables are unrelated. In some cases (for example, student E) a high score in math is associated with a high PEPT score; in others a low score in math is associated with a low score on the PEPT (for example, student C). In both situations the resulting cross-product is positive because positive values multiplied by positive values and negative values multiplied by negative values both yield positive products. In other cases high scores in math are paired with low scores on the PEPT (for example, student A), or low scores in math are paired with high scores on the PEPT (for example, student D). In both of these situations the resulting cross-products are negative because when a positive and a negative value are multiplied, the product is negative. When all of the cross-products are added, the sum is a small value because the negative values cancel the positive values. In the case of the data in Table 2.9, the sum of the cross-products is .34. When this is divided by the number of students ($N = 8$) the resulting correlation coefficient is only .042.

An example of a negative correlation. When two sets of data are negatively correlated, positive z-values are paired with negative values and vice versa, which yields a numerator that is negative and relatively large when compared to the denominator. This results in a negative correlation coefficient. This is illustrated in Table 2.11, where reading test scores are correlated with the average number

TABLE 2.10 Correlation Between Math Test Scores and Physical Education Proficiency Test (PEPT)

Student	*Math Scores* Raw Score	*Math Scores* *z*-Score	*PEPT* Raw Score	*PEPT* *z*-Score	*Cross-Products*
A	70	1.5	30	−.67	−1.00
B	40	0	40	−.33	0
C	20	−1.0	10	−1.33	1.33
D	10	−1.5	100	1.67	−2.50
E	70	1.5	80	1.00	1.50
F	40	0	80	1.00	0
G	40	0	30	−.67	0
H	30	−.5	30	−.67	.33
	$\bar{X} = 40$		$\bar{X} = 50$		$\Sigma z_x z_y = .34$
	$\sigma = 20$		$\sigma = 30$		

$$r = \frac{\Sigma z_x z_y}{N}$$

$$r = \frac{.34}{8}$$

$$r = .042$$

TABLE 2.11 Correlation Between Reading Test Scores and the Average Number of Hours Spent Watching Television per Day

Student	*Reading Score*		*Hours TV per Day*		*Cross-Products*
	Raw Score	***z*-Score**	**Hours**	***z*-Score**	
A	80	1.00	3	−.5	−.50
B	30	−.67	4	0	0
C	30	−.67	4	0	0
D	10	−1.33	7	1.5	−1.99
E	100	1.67	1	−1.5	−2.50
F	80	1.00	2	−1.0	−1.00
G	30	−.67	7	1.5	−1.00
H	40	−.33	4	0	0
	$\overline{X}$ = 50		$\overline{X}$ = 4		$\Sigma z_x z_y = -6.99$
	σ = 30		σ = 2		

$$r = \frac{\Sigma z_x z_y}{N}$$

$$r = \frac{-6.99}{8}$$

$$r = -.874$$

of hours of television watched per day. Notice how the best readers are the ones who watch the least television and vice versa.

Why the correlation can never exceed ±1. In order to understand why the correlation can never exceed 1, positively or negatively, consider how a variable could be related to another variable in such a way as to yield the highest possible correlation. This would occur when the *z*-score for both variables was the same, as is illustrated in Table 2.12.

The sum of the cross-products is the same as the sum of squared deviations because the mathematical procedure for obtaining the sum of squared deviations and for obtaining the sum of the cross-products is identical. Because the standard deviation of a set of *z*-scores is always 1, the sum of the squared deviations divided by *N* must always be equal to 1. Because the correlation coefficient is equal to the sum of the cross-products divided by *N*, computing the correlation under the preceding circumstances involves the same process as computing the standard deviation of the *z*-scores. For this reason the maximum value for a correlation is 1. The computational formula for the Pearson Product-Moment correlation coefficient follows:

$$r = \frac{N\Sigma XY - \Sigma X \Sigma Y}{\sqrt{N\Sigma X^2 - (\Sigma X)^2}\ \sqrt{N\Sigma Y^2 - (\Sigma Y)^2}} \qquad [2.7]$$

TABLE 2.12 Correlation Between Reading Test Scores and Teacher Ratings of Reading Ability

Student	*Reading Score*		*Teacher Rating*		*Cross-Product*
	Raw Score	***z*-Score**	**Rating**	***z*-Score**	
A	80	1.00	8	1.00	1.00
B	30	−.67	3	−.67	.45
C	30	−.67	3	−.67	.45
D	10	−1.33	1	−1.33	1.77
E	100	1.67	10	1.67	2.79
F	80	1.00	8	1.00	1.00
G	30	−.67	3	−.67	.45
H	40	−.33	4	−.33	.11
	$\bar{X} =$ 50		$\bar{X} =$ 5		$\Sigma z_x z_y =$ 8.02[a]
	$\sigma =$ 30		$\sigma =$ 3		

$$r = \frac{\Sigma z_x z_y}{N}$$

$$r = \frac{8.02}{8}$$

$$r = 1.00$$

[a] This value is not exactly 8.0 because of rounding error.

Computational formula. This formula combines the two operations already described. In actual practice, other than for instructional purposes, correlations are seldom computed without the aid of a computer. Even a calculator sophisticated enough to compute correlations directly is not of much help because the amount of data and number of buttons to push result in a high likelihood of error. When an error is made, the entire process of entering data must be started again. Even when no error is made there is a tendency to think that there was, and it is difficult to suppress the urge to repeat the computations as a check. If the results of the two computations are not in agreement, a third computation must be performed in hopes that it will match one of the previous two. This problem is exacerbated by the fact that we seldom compute a single correlation but are usually interested in a series of correlations or intercorrelations, which makes any computational method that does not use a computer impractical. An explanation of how computers can be used to compute correlations is provided in Chapter 4.

Interpreting Correlations The first question that emerges in the interpretation of correlations concerns how large a coefficient should be before we begin attaching importance to it. There is no easy answer to this question, but as a start we can say it depends on the variables being related. For instance a .60 correlation would be high if you were showing the relationship between scores on a personality test and behavioral observation; it would be incredibly high if you were relating a job aptitude test to performance on the job; but it would not be very impressive if it were the correlation between an academic aptitude and a reading comprehension test.

Index of determination. There is another method of judging the magnitude of correlations that involves relating them to the amount of information conveyed or how much one score helps predict another. This is the index of determination, which is obtained by squaring the correlation coefficient. The index of determination indicates the proportion of variance in the first variable explained by the second variable and vice versa.

Because correlations are always one or less, squaring leaves a product smaller than the original. The main use of the index seems to be to make us humble about our correlations because the value obtained is always less than the original. The interpretation of correlations is not really made easier by this mathematical transformation, and it is as difficult to explain as the correlation itself.

Significance of correlations. It is also possible to determine the significance of a correlation. The term *significance* as it is used here takes on a special meaning within the realm of inferential statistics. It does not refer to "importance" but to the probability that a relationship that is found in the sample actually exists in the population.

We know that it would be a very unusual occurrence to obtain a correlation of exactly zero. Even if two variables are unrelated, a very small coefficient—either positive or negative—will usually be obtained when the correlation coefficient is computed. What we are interested in determining is how large this correlation needs to be before it can no longer be considered a chance occurrence. This is mainly a function of sample size. The specific level of significance of a correlation coefficient can be determined using Table A.2 in the Appendix. Small samples require larger coefficients to be considered significant. For example, with a sample size of 100, you could expect a correlation within a sample to be as large as .19 (in a population where the correlation was zero) only 5 percent of the time by chance. With a sample size of 10, the correlation would have to be .63 to meet that standard. This means that with large samples, very small, inconsequential correlations can be labeled as significant. Technically this means that any correlation coefficient other than zero can be called significant at some level of probability. For these reasons you should be dubious about the usefulness of a correlation coefficient when this characteristic is based only on its being significant. Just because there is a nonzero correlation coefficient between two variables does not mean that the relationship is meaningful.

Causality In measurement, statistics, research, and in science in general, causality is of great importance. Unfortunately it is exceedingly difficult to establish causality. One factor that makes dealing with causality troublesome is that our intuitive grasp of causality is often wrong. It is all too easy to fall into the trap of surmising that two events that occur together must have a causal relationship. The decision concerning which is causal and which is caused is often determined capriciously. It is also easy to assume that when two variables are correlated one of the variables must have caused the other. This decision concerning which did the causing too often is made based on the prejudices of the researcher. Examples abound.

Confusing cause and effect. It has been established in numerous studies that there is a relationship between the score on a measure of self-concept and a student's performance in class. The conclusion usually made is that a child's self-concept somehow determines his or her performance in class. This is used as a justification for classroom activity aimed at increasing academic performance by means of enhancing self-concept. Raising the self-concept of children may be a legitimate part of a child's education, and activities that enhance self-concept may have a positive effect on school performance, but the existence of a nonzero correlation does not prove that this causal relationship exists. The fact that students who are successful in school are likely to develop good self-concepts as an outgrowth of their successes cannot be ignored.

The same phenomenon occurs when researchers conclude that a high correlation between parental expectations about their child's performance in school and their child's actual performance justifies programs intended to improve a child's performance by increasing parental expectations. In this case the researcher is making an assumption about the direction of causality that has little basis other than wishful thinking. It is far more likely that parents' expectations are affected by their child's past performance than the other way around.

Third factors. These two examples illustrate errors in identifying the direction of cause. Another common error occurs when a third factor affects both variables. In this case the two variables may have no connection other than their relationship with the third factor. For example, it is possible to obtain a reasonably high correlation between the number of books in high school libraries and the percentage of graduates who attend college. This does not mean that a school system is likely to increase the rate of college attendance by buying more books for their libraries. Clearly the most important factor is the socioeconomic level of the community. Schools in more well-to-do areas not only can afford more books for their school libraries but are more likely to have a large proportion of students attending college. In addition, the overall educational level of wealthier communities is higher, and college-educated parents are more likely to see to it that their children attend college.

Factors Affecting the Size of Correlation

Nonlinearity. The Pearsonian correlation is sensitive only to linear relationships, although these are not the only way that two scores can be related. One type of a nonlinear relationship is the curvilinear relationship. An often-cited example involves the relationship between anxiety and test performance. As seen in Figure 2.10, performance is poor when anxiety is low. As anxiety increases, so does performance; however, when anxiety becomes too high, performance begins to decline. The resulting plot of such a relationship is a curve. Despite the fact that there is clearly a relationship between test performance and anxiety, the obtained correlation coefficient will be small.

Reliability. The reliability of the variables being correlated also places a limit on the size of the correlation. Although we might believe that there is a high relationship between a job aptitude test and on-the-job performance, if we base our assessment of job performance on ratings that are unreliable, we are unlikely to obtain a correlation coefficient that is very large.

Sample size. The size of the sample affects the stability of the correlation. Correlations tend to be unstable with small samples. This is because the structure

Figure 2.10
The relationship between anxiety and test performance.

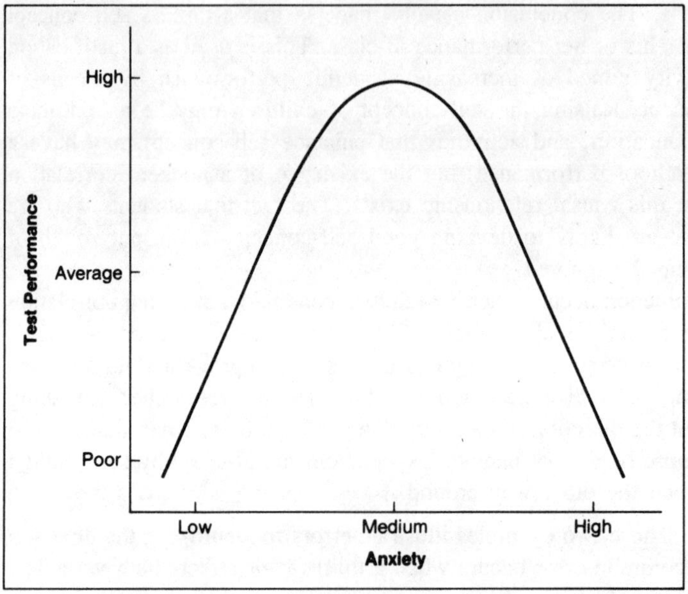

of the formula causes deviant scores to be heavily weighted. If you are computing the correlation between eight sets of scores, such as shown in Table 2.13, where seven pairs of scores are clearly related but the eighth is very different, you obtain a correlation of .27. If you correlate just the first seven values, the coefficient is .67. With larger sample sizes the effect of the deviant score is muted. Because chance factors can easily affect a single score, small samples give us little confidence in the resulting correlations.

Restricted range. A subtle but important cause of suppressed correlations is a phenomenon called restricted range. This occurs when the range of scores is small. In the correlation of test scores, this is often a result of the selection process. For example, one method of establishing the validity of an aptitude test like the Graduate Record Exam (GRE) is to correlate test scores with grade-point average (GPA) in graduate schools. A high correlation argues for the validity of the test. Of course, if only students with high scores are accepted, there will be a narrow range of GRE scores. In addition, the grades assigned in graduate school are usually high, because only an A or a B is considered passing. As a result, both the GRE and grades may have restricted ranges. The dotted section of Figure 2.11 shows what the distribution might look like if the range was not restricted. The shaded section shows the result of range restriction. Under the latter condition the obtained correlation could be expected to be small. This same problem occurs, to a lesser degree, with the Scholastic Aptitude Test (SAT) At the present time the median validity coefficient over many studies is .41. But, there is a tendency, as enrollments decline, for schools to pay less attention to these scores because of declining enrollment. As a result there may be less restriction in range in the future and the result may be higher validity coefficients (Bracey, 1980).

TABLE 2.13 Computation of the Correlation Between Reading Test Scores and Verbal Intelligence Test Scores

Student	*Reading Scores* Raw Score	*z*-Score	*Verbal IQ* Raw Scores	*z*-Score	*Cross-Products*
A	70	1.5	80	1.00	1.50
B	70	1.5	80	1.00	1.50
C	40	0	40	−.33	0
D	40	0	30	−.67	0
E	40	0	30	−.67	0
F	30	−.5	30	−.67	.33
G	20	−1.0	10	−1.33	1.33
H	10	−1.5	100	1.67	−2.50
	$\bar{X} =$ 40		$\bar{X} =$ 50		$\Sigma z_x z_y =$ 2.16
	$\sigma =$ 20		$\sigma =$ 30		

$$r = \frac{2.16}{8}$$

$$r = .27$$

Additional Correlation Terms Without the aid of a computer, and even with a calculator, the computation of the Pearsonian correlation coefficients is very tedious. For this reason there have been several short-cut methods developed for use when one of the variables to be correlated, or both, is dichotomous. An example of dichotomous data is sex (male or female). The use of such variables may seem like a violation of the requirement that variables correlated using the Product-Moment formula be interval. However, it is possible to treat this sort of nominal

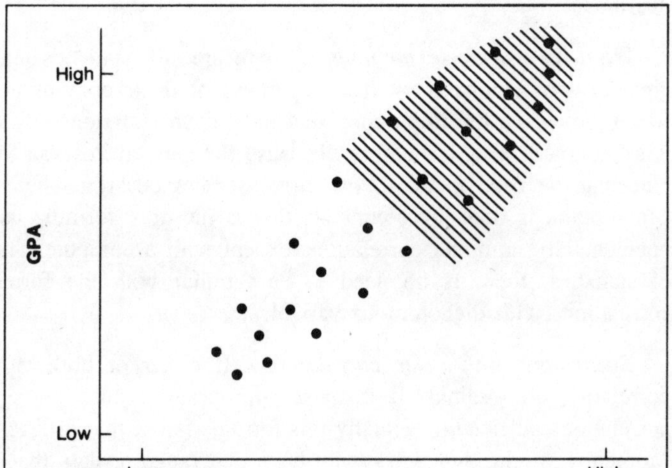

Figure 2.11
Effects of restricted range.

data as though it were at an interval scale with no harmful effects. This works only with data that are divided into two categories.

Point-biserial correlation. The point-biserial correlation coefficient is used when one variable is continuous and the other is dichotomous: for instance, for correlating sex with the score on a reading comprehension test. The point-biserial is algebraically equivalent to the longer Pearsonian formula, which means that you get exactly the same result regardless of which you use; but if you are doing the computation by hand, it is easier and quicker to use the point-biserial.

Biserial correlation. The biserial is used in the same situations as the point-biserial, but it is even easier to compute. It is an estimate rather than an algebraic equivalent, and for this reason will not yield exactly the same results as the Product-Moment correlation. It also requires an additional assumption not required when the point-biserial is used. The dichotomous variable must have started out as a normally distributed interval-scaled variable before it was dichotomized. Therefore, you could not correlate reading comprehension and sex using the biserial correlation because sex does not meet the assumption of underlying normality. However, you could compute the correlation between these two variables using the point-biserial correlation because it does not require this assumption.

Reading comprehension and intelligence could be correlated using the biserial correlation by first obtaining the IQ scores; dividing the group of students in half at their median, labeling one half *1* and the other half *2*; and then performing the biserial correlation. This is legitimate because intelligence meets the assumption of underlying normality.

Methods used when both variables are dichotomous. The phi coefficient is used when both variables are dichotomous. Like the point-biserial it is algebraically equivalent to the Pearsonian correlation. The tetrachoric correlation also is used when both variables are dichotomized; however, it, like the biserial, is only an estimate that requires the assumption that both dichotomical variables be normally distributed.

When to use these methods. There are still statistics textbooks that place a great deal of emphasis on the proper use of these computational methods. They sometimes leave the impression that in a given situation only one of the formulas is appropriate. This is incorrect because the general Pearson Product-Moment formula can be used in all of the circumstances described here. In fact, when the computation is done by computer, that is the only formula used. Because we do not generally compute correlations except with a computer, in the modern world of statistics, there is no need to be familiar with the formulas for computing correlations with dichotomous variables.

Spearman rank-order correlation. If either or both variables that you are correlating are ordinal, it is more appropriate to use the Spearman rank-order correlation coefficient. Actually this formula is not that different from the Product-Moment formula, and unless you have tied ranks or data that deviate a great deal from being interval, the coefficients obtained using either formula will be very similar.

Multiple correlation. A very powerful correlational tool that was made practical only with the availability of computers is multiple correlation. This permits the computation of the correlation coefficient of one variable (the dependent variable) with any number of other variables (independent variables). The independent variables can be continuous or categorical. Although these computations are virtually impossible to compute by hand, they are easily calculated using a computer. By adding and deleting variables, it is possible to determine how much variance each independent variable explains.

Regression analysis. By using a series of computations closely related to those employed with correlations, it is possible to establish weightings that can be used to predict one variable when another related variable is known. This also can be done with a multiple-correlations model, where a dependent variable is predicted by a series of independent variables. A good example of this is the algorithms used by colleges and universities to determine admission policies. The dependent variable is grade-point average. The two most important independent variables are high school GPA and SAT or ACT scores. In addition, other factors of interest can be included, such as number of extracurricular activities, quality of the high school, educational background of the parents, and so forth. The multiple-regression analysis can then provide a basis for admission policies by establishing how much to weight each independent variable.

Factor Analysis When we create an assessment instrument consisting of items from which we derive a single score, we must assume that we are measuring a single trait. If we are wrong in our assumption and it turns out that we are measuring several distinct and independent traits, our score will not be very meaningful.

For instance, teaching at the college level is often evaluated using a rating scale made of items that assess some aspect of teaching. Once the students have completed the instrument, the responses are tallied and the results reported. They can be reported either in terms of individual items, or the items can be summed to produce a single composite score. The issue of whether the composite score is legitimate is addressed by a determination of whether the quality of teaching can best be thought of as a single trait. If it is possible to say that some teachers are good and some are poor, without qualifying this statement by the specification of the ways in which they are poor and the ways in which they are good, each item is measuring the same trait and the composite score is meaningful.

When such rating systems are evaluated, however, it is found that two distinct traits are being measured. The first trait involves the overall competence of the instructor and includes such characteristics as knowledge of the field, preparation, quality of exams, skill in presentation, and so forth. The second trait involves affective characteristics, such as willingness to respond to questions and helping students after class, along with other general positive personal characteristics of the instructor. A single composite score made up of these two traits can be misleading because the highly competent instructor who is poor in affective skills looks the same as the much less competent instructor who is strong in the affective area. They both appear to be about average, but this is clearly an inaccurate picture of their teaching ability. The composite score is also affected by the number of items included for each trait. The more items measuring a given trait, the greater the weighting that trait will receive.

In Chapter 5, "Reliability," methods for quantifying the degree to which a set of items measures the same trait will be discussed. It is also of interest to determine whether, among a set of items, there is a single trait or several traits and which items belong with a single trait. The procedure for doing this is called factor analysis.

The computation technique. Factor analysis is a statistical technique for taking the items appearing on a test or a collection of tests and determining mathematically which should be grouped together. The grouping is then called a factor. The determination of whether a factor exists is based on two considerations: (1) the degree to which the items that make up the factor are related to each other, and (2) how independent the factor is from other factors. Because different methods for conducting factor analysis weigh these considerations differently, they tend to come up with different factors.

In addition to selecting factors, it is necessary to decide how many factors there should be. A point must be established where a factor is so weak that it no longer deserves to be called a factor. For example, consider the following list of objects: apple, hamburger, carburetor, orange, windshield, banana, potato, transmission. What are the most logical groupings? Certainly carburetor, windshield, and transmission should be grouped as parts of a car. But should apple, orange, and banana be grouped separately as fruits or lumped with hamburger and potato as foods, or should potato be grouped with them as vegetables? The decision concerning how they should be grouped is arbitrary and based on the relative importance placed on the two criteria for determining a factor.

There are two major approaches to factor analysis. The orthogonal rotation approach emphasizes differences between factors. Using this approach one is likely to identify few factors. Using oblique rotations the internal consistency of a factor is emphasized and more factors tend to emerge. If we analyze data characterized by a strong factor structure, we are likely to get the same results, regardless of our approach. Unfortunately that is not always the case, and when we are faced with data with a weak factor structure, the type of analysis may determine the results.

SUMMARY

1. The quantification of human attributes permits the construction of mathematical models that can greatly enhance the explanatory power of those trying to describe human behavior.
2. Statistics provide the techniques for the manipulation of the numbers obtained from the quantification of human attributes.
3. The number used for the quantification of human behaviors can be categorized as belonging to one of the four scales: nominal, ordinal, interval, and ratio.
4. We are generally safe in treating most scores obtained in measurement as though they were of an interval scale, even though—strictly speaking—some of them may be only of an ordinal scale.
5. In measurement we are mainly interested in descriptive statistics.
6. The most fundamental method of describing data is by means of frequency distributions and graphs.

7. There are three methods for describing central tendency: mean, median, and mode.

8. The mean is considered the most useful of the three methods for describing central tendency because it is affected by all scores. In a distribution it is the most stable, and it is most useful in conducting further computations.

9. There are also three methods of describing the variability of a set of scores (range, semi-interquartile range, and standard deviation/variance), but the standard deviation is the one that is most often used in connection with measurement.

10. The standard deviation is not only useful for its descriptive capabilities, but because of its relationship to the normal distribution.

11. The relationships between variables are quantified by means of correlation coefficients and scatter plots.

12. Correlations range between -1 and $+1$ with the degree of the relationship indicated by how much the value deviates from zero.

13. Negative values indicate negative relationships, positive values positive relationships, and values approaching zero no relationship.

14. The most important thing to remember about the interpretation of correlations is that the mere existence of a nonzero correlation does not indicate a causal relationship.

15. Nonlinearity, reliability, sample size, and the existence of a restricted range can all affect the size of a correlation coefficient.

16. Point biserial, biserial, phi, and tetrachoric correlation coefficients are examples of computational methods used with dichotomous data which simplify hand calculations.

17. The availability of computers has rendered these easier-to-compute methods obsolete.

18. Multiple correlation techniques permit the correlation of a dependent variable with any number of independent variables.

19. The use of regression techniques permits the prediction of a dependent variable with either one or several independent variables.

20. Factor analysis provides a method for determining the number and relative strengths of factors in a group of items.

SUGGESTED READINGS

FREEDMAN, D., PISANI, R., & PURVES, R. (1978). *Statistics*. New York: Norton. [This book provides an up-to-date view of descriptive statistics that incorporates computer applications as well as the use of hand calculators.]

HAYES, W. L. (1981). *Statistics for the social sciences* (3rd. ed.). New York: Holt. [This is perhaps the lengthiest and most complete basic statistics book that you will encounter. It includes both descriptive and inferential statistics.]

PEDHAZUR, E. J. (1982). *Multiple regression in behavioral research*. New York: Holt. [This is the most readable, yet one of the most complete, books on multivariate analysis.]

SIEGEL, S. (1956). *Non-parametric statistics*.. New York: McGraw-Hill. [This is the classic book on nonparametric statistics.]

3

Derived Scores

OVERVIEW

It is difficult for test users to interpret raw scores directly because such scores do not have much absolute meaning. It is only when they are compared to something that they become meaningful. The task of interpreting raw scores is even more difficult with standardized tests than with informal tests, because when a test constructed by individuals other than those interpreting it, the meaning of raw scores is difficult to establish. For this reason, raw scores need to be transformed into derived scores to be interpreted. The purpose of this chapter is to provide information concerning which types of transformations, or derived scores, are most appropriate under differing circumstances. A full range of derived scores is presented from grade equivalents to scaled scores derived from latent trait models. This is an important chapter because derived scores represent the interface between psychometrists, test developers, and test consumers.

OBJECTIVES

From this chapter you will learn the methods of computing and using derived scores. Specifically, you will learn the following:

- The advantages and disadvantages of age and grade equivalents.
- Methods of computing percentiles.
- The computation and use of *z*-scores.
- The computation and uses for *T*-scores.
- The computation and uses for the other standard scores.

Introduction

Bob's mother has a conference with her son's teacher and is told that, on a standardized test of reading comprehension with 50 questions, her son obtained a score of 36. This information is unlikely to be of much use to Bob's mother because she has no way of knowing whether this is a high or low score, how it compares with the scores of other students in the class, or how much learning a score of 36 represents.

Bob's mother could be informed about her sons's progress either in terms of absolute or relative performance. Information about absolute performance would involve the provision of details about exactly what tasks her son had mastered and which he had not. This is best done using the type of domain-referenced methods described in Chapter 10.

Relative performance refers to how a student compares with other students. There are a number of different ways of making these comparisons, called derived scores. These include grade and age equivalents, percentile ranks, and standard scores.

Any of these derived scores could be computed for a classroom test, with the other students in the class used as the comparison group. In actual practice, the comparison group is usually large and selected so as to be representative of a larger, usually national, population. This permits the determination of how an individual compares to students in the same grade nationwide. Test publishers provide norm tables that allow teachers to determine the equivalent derived score for each raw score. These tables can be used to determine the simpler derived scores, but for those based on the more complex item response theory, computer analyses are necessary.

It is not always easy to decide which derived score to use because each has its advantages and disadvantages. One solution to the problem of deciding which to use is to utilize several different derived scores. Test publishers generally have test-scoring facilities and test-scoring programs that they lease for scoring, which will provide any or all derived scores that might be needed. The following section includes a description and explanation of the different methods of computing derived scores.

Grade and Age Equivalents

Grade Equivalents

The purpose of grade equivalents is to tell us how a student is progressing in school in terms of grade level. Tables are constructed in such a way that for each raw score there is a grade equivalent score. Each grade equivalent is intended to represent the average performance of students at that level. The score consists of the grade, a decimal, and a number representing months. The grades can range from *K* for Kindergarten to 12. Grades above 12 are sometimes used, but they are not particularly meaningful. The months range between 1 and 10, representing the ten months of the year, under the assumption that a child's performance will not increase during the two months of summer. For example, the average score for a child halfway through the fifth grade would be 5.5.

The Advantages of Grade Equivalents The main advantage of grade equivalents is the apparent ease with which they can be interpreted. Anyone can look at a grade equivalent and get an idea of how a student is doing in school. The use of these scores avoids the need for any understanding of statistics or measurement. Actually, this advantage is illusory because grade equivalents provide more misinformation than information, and many measurement specialists believe that their use should be discontinued.

The Disadvantages of Grade Equivalents The biggest problem with grade equivalents is that the information they provide about a student's level of functioning is often misleading or incorrect. This is a result of the methods that are used to construct the tables used for determining grade equivalents. When a third-grader obtains a grade equivalent of 6.3, the parent and teacher quite reasonably assume that the child obtained the same score as the average child in the third month of the sixth year in school. In all likelihood no children of that level ever took the particular test that the third-grader took. In order for grade-equivalent norm tables to reflect how children at one grade level actually compare to children at other grade levels, it would be necessary either to give all students the same test or, if there were different tests for different grade levels, to require that children across all grades take every test.

Once that information was obtained it would be possible to interpret an individual's score by establishing the grade level to which the score is similar. The reading test performance of a fifth-grade child could then be described as being at the eighth-grade level, and we would know that the child had performed similarly to an eighth-grader. If no eighth-grade child actually took the fifth-grade level test, such comparisons really cannot be made with any degree of accuracy.

Of course it would not be practical to administer the same test to every child, nor could each level of a test be administered to every grade because of the enormous amount of testing that would be required. Besides, such a practice would be inhumane. It would require test publishers to administer high school reading tests to first-graders, most of whom would not be able to answer any questions, and a first-grade test to high school students, which would similarly not make sense. Instead of administering every test to each grade, each grade-level test is adminstered only a few grades above and below. The scores outside this range are then obtained through extrapolations and those in between by interpolations. A fifth-grader who obtains an 8.0 grade equivalent on a math achievement test is therefore not compared to the actual performance of eighth-graders but to the hypothetical performance that would have been expected had eighth-graders taken the test.

In Figure 3.1 the interpolation of scores for a math test administered to fifth-graders is illustrated. The test was actually administered only to third-, fourth- and fifth-grade students. By projecting a straight line through the average scores of these three grades it is possible to estimate the average grade that would have been obtained if students in other grades had taken the test. Therefore, a child who obtained a raw score of 90 would have a grade equivalent of 7.0 because his or her performance is similar to the score that would be expected from a student in seventh grade. Points in between are determined by means of interpolation.

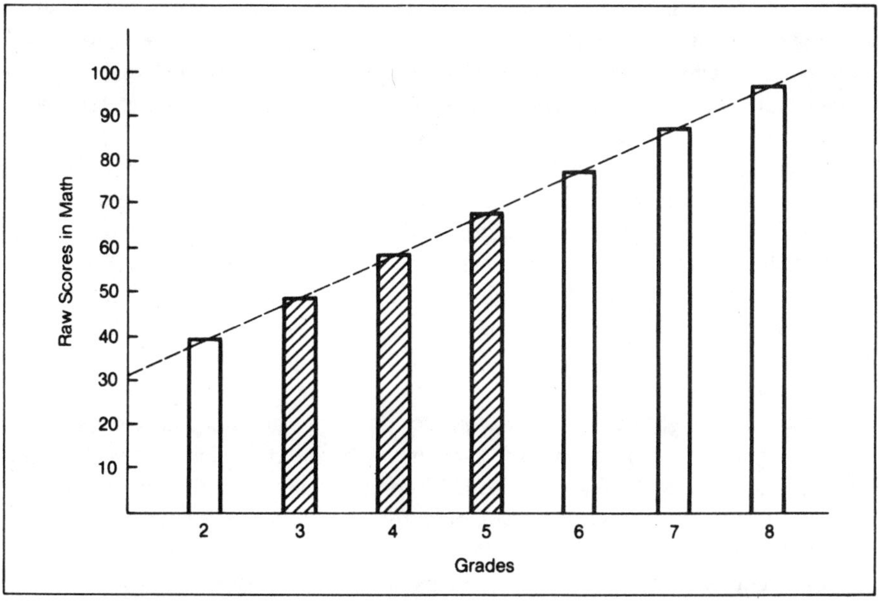

Figure 3.1 Actual and extrapolated performance on a math test administered to fifth-graders.

There is not a single accepted method of determining the average. Sometimes the mean and sometimes the median is used. The process of extrapolation used to estimate the average scores of students in the grades on one particular level of the test is also quite imprecise. Slight measurement errors will be magnified through the process of extrapolation, providing a diminished confidence in the meaning of a grade level the farther it is from the child's actual grade.

As is the case with age norms, the construction of grade norms is based on the assumption that growth in the trait measured takes place in a linear fashion. This means that performance increases gradually and at a stable rate over an extended period of time. This seems to work best with broad rather than narrow topics. Specific aspects of mathematics, such as the multiplication tables, could not be evaluated with grade equivalents because a student gains complete mastery in a relatively short period of time. Even broad areas like biology, which are normally taught over a short period of time, cannot readily be assessed by means of age or grade equivalents.

Grade equivalents are best used with basic skills such as reading or arithmetic. Even with this sort of subject matter, learning will usually take place in a curvilinear rather than a linear fashion, and the learning curve for different subjects will not be the same. To the extent that the increase in performance is not linear, the distance between the points on the scale (grades) will not be the same. In reading, the difference between third and fourth grade will be greater than the difference between seventh and eighth grade. Grade norms are therefore much more like ordinal than interval scales. For this reason mathematical operations should not be performed on grade norms.

Another problem with grade equivalents is that they are affected by differences in variability across subject matter. A child in second grade who obtains a grade equivalent of 5.0 in reading is quite remarkable, whereas a child in fifth grade who obtains an 8.0 in reading is not unusual. At the same time the child in fifth grade who obtains a grade equivalent of 8.0 in both reading and math may be doing much better in math than in reading because reading is characterized by greater variability than is mathematical ability.

When parents are told that their daughter, who is in fifth grade, has obtained a grade equivalent of 8.0 in math, it is natural for them to jump to the conclusion that their child is ready for the eighth grade. This is an erroneous interpretation and it would be better to interpret this grade equivalent as meaning only that the child can do fifth-grade math as well as an eighth-grader can do fifth-grade math, but not that she can actually do eighth-grade math. Fifth-graders are likely to be doing long division and fractions while eighth-graders are doing simple algebra and geometry. The explanation necessary for a parent of a child achieving above grade level is straightforward. Now consider the explanation needed for the parent of a fifth-grader who is at the 3.0 level in math. It really does not make much sense to say that the child is doing fifth-grade work as well as a third-grader because a third-grader presumably cannot do fifth-grade work. The idea that the child is several years behind is perhaps the most that can and should be communicated.

Grade equivalents can be used, perhaps justifiably, in situations where there is a lack of measurement sophistication and where the results of testing must be conveyed to those who are unschooled in measurement statistics. Unfortunately, when the demand for more sophisticated data manipulation is manifested, grade equivalents are sometimes treated mathematically in ways that are entirely inappropriate. The performance of students in September is sometimes subtracted from their performance in June, and the resulting value divided by nine gives birth to the awkward "average grade equivalent gain per month." Such maniplulations are entirely unjustified and will likely result in distortions and bizarre results that make interpretations extremely difficult.

Because grade norms represent the median of a given grade, it makes no sense to talk about bringing every child up to grade level. Once this monumental feat was accomplished, the median would have to be redefined and once again half the children involved would be once again below the grade level. This is true because, by definition, one half of all the children in a given grade are below the median.

With the increased interest in ensuring that all students reach some prescribed minimum level of competency before graduation from high school, there is a temptation to define this level in terms of grade equivalents. This is unfortunate because grade equivalents are insensitive measures of student performance, particularly in high school.

Age Equivalents

This form of derived score is closely related to grade equivalents. Both have the same limitations and their use is not recommended. They were once widely employed as a means of describing level of intellectual functioning, but they have been replaced by more sophisticated methods. Grade equivalents are generally preferred over age equivalents for reporting progress in school because it is much easier to establish norms for them and they are a more meaningful way of describing academic performance.

Percentile Norms

Percentile norms provide a means of describing a student's performance through a comparison with others at the same grade level, rather than by means of a comparison with different levels, as is done with grade and age norms. Percentiles can provide comparision with any group from the classroom, school, district, state, or nation. In interpreting percentiles it is important always to specify the comparison group. Test publishers often provide several percentiles, permitting comparisons with several different groups.

As was the case with grade equivalents, percentiles are generally derived from tables based on norms established by the test publisher, who computes a percentile for each raw score. Percentiles can also be computed by a teacher using the classroom as the norm group.

Computations of Percentiles

Percentiles are computed by dividing a student's rank in a classroom by the total number of students in the class. Rank can be defined in different ways, but the most precise method is to define it in terms of the cumulative midpoint. To determine the cumulative midpoint of a score, count the number of scores below its interval and add to this a value equal to one half of the interval. In Table 3.1 there are six students who obtained scores below 47 and three who obtained scores of 47. The cumulative midpoint of 47 is obtained by adding one half the scores in the interval ($\frac{1}{2} \times 3 = 1.5$) to the number of cases below 6, which yields a cumulative midpoint of 7.5. The percentile is obtained by dividing that value by the total number of cases. In this example the percentile for a score of 47 is 62.5 ($7.5/12 = 62.5$).

Using Percentiles

Percentiles are ordinal-scale data, and for this reason it is inappropriate to use them in mathematical operations requiring an interval scale. The noninterval nature of percentiles results from the fact that, regardless of the shape of a distribution of scores, their percentiles always have a rectangular shape. This means that there are always 10 percent of the cases between the 10th and 20th percentiles, just as there are between the 50th and 60th percentiles. If there are fifteen cases between

TABLE 3.1
Computation of Percentiles

Score	Frequency	Cumulative Midpoint	Percentile
50	0	12.0	100
49	1	11.5	96
48	2	10.0	83
47	3	7.5	62
46	2	5.0	42
45	2	3.0	25
44	1	1.5	12
43	0	.1	8
42	1	.5	4
41	0	0	0
40	0	0	0

the 10th and 20th percentiles, there will be an equal number between the 50th and 60th percentiles. This is illustrated in Figure 3.2.

Because most distributions that we encounter are likely to approximate a normal rather than a rectangular distribution, the intervals between percentiles will be quite different from the intervals between raw scores. This is most dramatically seen on short tests or tests with little variability, where a single raw-score point can cause a large change in the percentile. The change from a normal or nearly normal distribution to a rectangular distribution results in a situation where differences between percentiles at the end of distribution represent more of a distance on the abscissa and presumably more of a difference in the underlying construct than do differences between percentiles in the middle of the distribution. This is because most data are normally distributed and there are relatively few individuals at either end of a distribution, making it necessary to go further along the abscissa to pass the same number that would be required nearer the center of the distributions where there are more subjects.

In Figure 3.3 a set of normally distributed raw scores is presented along with the equivalent percentiles. As can be seen, a change in raw score from 28 to 29

Figure 3.2
Distribution of percentiles.

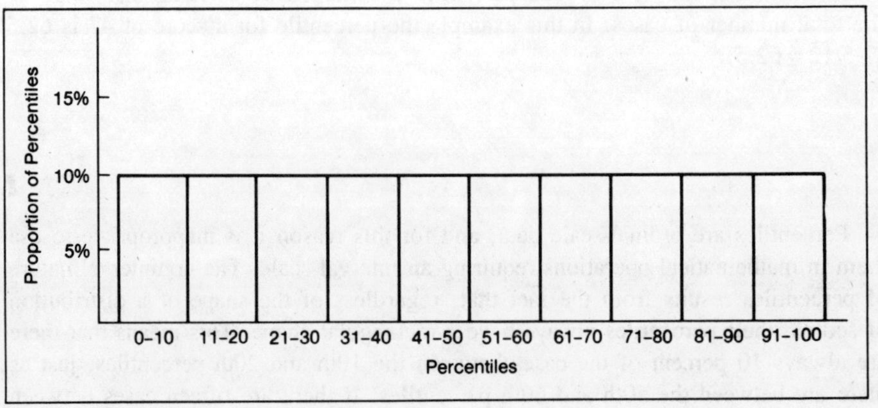

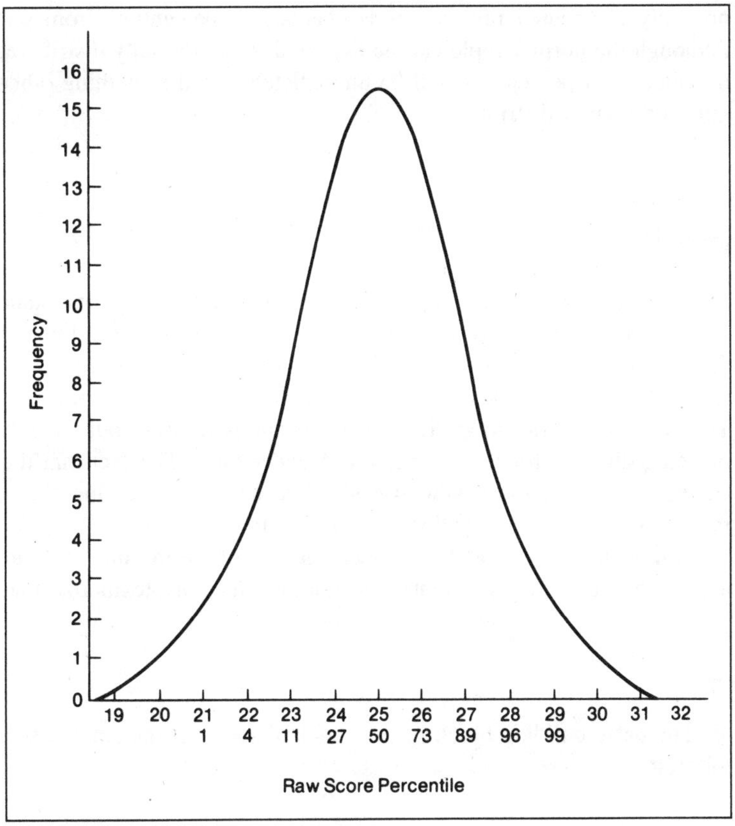

Figure 3.3 Relationship between percentiles and raw-score intervals.

represents an increase in the percentile score of 4, whereas a change in raw score from 25 to 26 represents a percentile change of 23.

The process outlined for computing percentiles involves a nonlinear transformation of scores that effects a change in the scaling properties of the original distribution. For this reason it is necessary to exercise care in interpreting percentiles. They are intended as a means of conveying information concerning an individual's relative rank in a group and should not be used for further computation.

Researchers should be cautioned against the use of percentiles as variables in statistical analyses that require interval data because the nonlinear transformation is likely to introduce distortions into the results. Even though most analysis procedures can be applied to data that deviate somewhat from being of an interval scale, the magnitude of the deviation from interval scale introduced by the use of percentiles, coupled with the complete violation of the assumption of normality that accompanies their use, could render the conclusions of such studies suspect.

When percentiles are derived from published norms, an additional source of distortions is added. When you change raw scores to derived scores, it is usually possible to predict the shape of the ensuing distribution. The new distribution will either be the same as the distribution of raw scores, or it will have been changed to a normal distribution. However, this will not be the case when a set of non-normally distributed raw scores is changed to percentiles from published norms. Although the norm sample can be expected to be normally distributed, the resulting distribution of percentiles will be unpredictable, and something other than a rectangular or normal distribution.

Standard Scores

Standard scores are a type of derived score based on means and standard deviations that have interval-scale properties. They are, for the most part, linear transformations that change the mean and the size of the intervals between scores but maintain the same shape distributions that existed in the scores before they were transformed. They are far superior to grade equivalents and percentiles but have the disadvantage of being difficult for the lay person to understand. The fact that there is a lack of agreement among those who use standard scores concerning the appropriate terminology makes interpretation even more difficult.

Although this textbook provides the set of definitions that are most widely used, the reader may encounter terminology in other textbooks that is different.

The Small z-Score

The basic building block for all standard scores is the small *z*-score. Its formula follows:

$$z = \frac{X - \overline{X}}{\sigma} \qquad [3.1]$$

In words, the small *z*-score is equal to the deviation, or the difference between the mean and the raw score, divided by the standard deviation. This tranforms the score into a value defined by deviations around the mean expressed in terms of standard deviations. By definition, a *z*-score has a mean of 0 and a standard deviation of 1. For instance, if the mean of a test is 55, and the standard deviation is 5; if you obtain a score of 60, your *z* would be +1. If your score was 54, then your *z* would be −.2. The small *z* itself is not often used for reporting scores because it is usually a decimal value and half the time it is negative. It is instead used as the basis for other more easily managed standard scores.

The T-Score

The *T*-score is more often used than the *z* and is defined by the following formula:

$$T = 10z + 50 \qquad [3.2]$$

By definition the *T*-score has a mean of 50 and a standard deviation of 10. It is a useful index for performing mathematical computations because negative values have been eliminated along with one decimal place.

The Normalized T-Score

T-scores, like *z*-scores, are linear transformations that maintain the shape of the original distribution. If a set of raw scores is negatively skewed, it can be expected that the distribution of *T*-scores will also be negatively skewed. There is no way to take such a distribution and make it normally distributed without an unacceptable amount of distortion. But when a set of scores is not exactly normally distributed as a result of measurement error, normalized *T*-scores can be used. These scores transform the raw scores in such a way that the new distribution is normally distributed. Normalized *T*-scores have a mean of 50 and a standard deviation of 10, as do the *T*-scores, and they are computed using the same formula:

$$T = 10z + 50 \qquad \textbf{[3.2]}$$

The difference between the *T*-score and the normalized *T*-score is not in the formula, but in the method used for obtaining the *z*-score. Instead of using formula 3.1, which is based on means and standard deviations, the raw score is first changed to a percentile and then converted to a normalized *z*-score by using a statistical table such as the one in Table A.1, in the Appendix. For purposes of illustration, consider the scores of five students who take a test and obtain scores of 15, 17, 19, 23, and 26. With a mean of 20 and a standard deviation of 4, a score of 15 yields a *T*-score of

$$37.5 \left[z = \frac{15 - 20}{4} = -1.25, T = 10(-1.25) + 50 = 37.5 \right].$$

To compute the normalized *T*-score of 15 we first compute its percentile, which is 10. From Table A.1 in the Appendix (pages 370–372), using interpolation we determine that a percentile of 10 is equivalent to a normalized *z*-score of -1.2816, which yield a normalized *T*-score of 37.18. The normalized *T* and *T*-scores are similar because this distribution of five scores does not stray far from normality.

The computation of the normalized *T*-score, by changing the raw score to a percentile and then to a *z*-score, involves a change from interval to ordinal data. In the process the intervals between the values are stretched or shrunk until the distribution has been made normal. This procedure does not work as well with distributions that deviate markedly from the normal distribution, and this is particularly true of skewed distributions. The normalized *T* transformation is illustrated in Table 3.2. As can be seen, the raw score of 50 when changed to a *T*-score is 62.9. This is near the *T*-score of 49, which is 61.1. However, the normalized *T*-score for a score of 50 is 66.4, which is further from the normalized *T*-score of 49, which is 61.9. Furthermore, although the intervals between *T*-scores are the same (except for rounding error), the intervals between the normalized *T*-scores differ across the distribution.

TABLE 3.2 Distribution of *T*-Scores

Raw Score	Frequency	Percentile	*T*-Score	Normalized *T*-Score
51	1	98.3	64.8	71.2
50	1	95.0	62.9	66.4
49	3	86.7	61.1	61.2
48	3	75.0	59.2	56.7
47	1	68.3	57.3	54.8
46	4	60.0	55.5	52.5
45	0	56.6	53.6	51.7
44	4	48.3	51.7	49.6
43	2	40.0	49.9	47.5
42	0	36.6	48.0	46.6
41	2	33.3	41.2	45.7
40	1	28.3	44.3	44.3
39	2	23.3	42.4	42.7
38	1	18.3	40.5	41.0
37	0	16.6	38.7	40.3
36	1	15.0	36.8	39.6
35	1	11.7	35.0	38.1
34	1	8.3	33.1	36.1
33	1	5.0	31.3	33.5
32	0	3.0	29.4	31.2
31	1	1.7	27.5	28.8

Other Standard Scores

Instead of sticking with *T*-scores with a mean of 50 and a standard deviation of 10, test publishers have selected different scales based on means and standard deviations that can be interpreted in essentially the same way as the *T*-score. Although this proliferation of scores can be confusing, and some writers have argued for the use of only *T*-scores, consumers seem able to differentiate among the different types of scores.

College Entrance Examination Board Scores (CEEB) These scores are used with the SAT and utilize a mean of 500 and a standard deviation of 100. They can be computed using the following formula:

$$CEEB = 100z + 500 \qquad [3.3]$$

Actual scores are reported in increments of 10, so the last digit is superfluous. For these reasons, using three digits instead of two, as with *T*-scores, does not add to the precision of the scale. One can argue that it creates a unique scale not to be confused with other standard scores, but CEEB scores are also used with the GRE, the Medical College Aptitude Test (MCAT), and the Law School Admissions Test (LSAT). These scores can be misleading because they employ such large numbers (a mean of 500 instead of 50 as is used with *T*-scores). This causes small differences in raw scores to yield large scaled-score differences, and this makes small differences appear larger than they really are.

The American College Testing Program (ACT) ACT uses the Iowa Test of Educational Development (ITED) scale, which ranges from 1 to 36, with a mean of 16 for high school seniors in general and 19 for those planning to enter college. It has a standard deviation of 5 and a standard error of 1.

The Normal Curve Equivalent (NCE) The NCE standard score was developed for use with the Elementary and Secondary Education Act (ESEA) projects such as Head Start and Follow-Through. Its purpose is to replace percentiles with a scale that has better mathematical properties. NCEs are computed using the following formula:

$$NCE = 21.06(z) + 50 \quad \textbf{[3.4]}$$

The *z*-scores are normalized using the procedures employed with normalized *T*-scores. The obtained values are then rounded to the nearest whole number. Consider the following five scores used in the example of the computation of the normalized *T*-score: 15, 17, 19, 23, and 26. It was determined that the normalized *z*-score for 15 was -1.2816, so the NCE score for it would be 23 [21.06 ($-1.28.6$) + 50 = 23.0095]. The scale ranges between 1 and 99, with the values of 1, 50, and 99 corresponding to percentiles of 1, 50, and 99. All other values are transformed in such a way that they have equal intervals. NCEs can be interpreted in a manner similar to the way percentiles are interpreted. They have the added advantage of having interval scale characteristics.

The Army General Classification Test (AGCT) The AGCT is used in the classification and selection of army recruits. It has a mean of 100 and a standard deviation of 20.

IQ Scores When Binet constructed the first individual intelligence test in 1905, later revising it in 1908 and 1911, he evaluated intelligence in terms of the discrepancy between mental and chronological age. A child whose mental age was sufficiently behind his or her chronological age was identified as needing special education assistance. William Stern (1914) pointed out that it was more appropriate to use the ratio of mental age to chronological age because absolute differences did not have the same meaning at different ages. A six-year-old whose mental age is one year behind his or her chronological age should cause greater concern than the nine-year-old who is a year behind. The ratio provided a score that was sensitive to these distinctions. This ratio was multiplied by 100 to eliminate the decimals and was later called the intelligence quotient, or IQ. This method of computing IQs is now called the ratio IQ, in order to differentiate it from deviation IQs, which are based on *z*-scores.

Binet was not interested in making discriminations any finer than those available with mental ages. However, when the Binet test was translated into English and revised by Terman in 1916, he adopted Stern's method of computation of IQs. Even though the ratio IQ was a major advance, it has all of the drawbacks of age-equivalent scores. First of all, it is based on the assumption that mental ability increases at a linear rate, although this is obviously not true. The increase in intellectual capacity is more curvilinear than linear. Furthermore, at some point during adolescence, mental ability ceases to increase. The exact point where this occurs is a matter of dispute, and it is likely that different types of intellectual skills reach their maximum point at different ages. This age may also vary among individuals. Another disadvantage of ratio IQs is that when they are used it is necessary to choose items carefully based on their difficulty in order to maintain the same variability across age levels.

With the publication of the Wechsler-Bellevue in 1939, deviation IQs were adopted. They are based on means and standard deviations and are computed in a manner similar to that used with other standard scores. This approach eliminated many of the problems associated with the ratio IQ and is considered an unqualified improvement. Their use was later adopted for the Stanford-Binet when it was revised in 1972. The Stanford-Binet has a standard deviation of 16 and a mean of 100, while the deviation IQ used by Wechsler has the same mean but a standard deviation of 15. It can be computed using the following formula:

$$IQ = 15z + 100 \qquad \textbf{[3.5]}$$

The z-score is normalized—which means that it is derived from a statistical table using percentiles in the same fashion as normalized T-scores.

Stanines Stanines were developed as a method for reporting scores by the Air Force during World War II. The term is derived from the combination of the words *standard* and *nine*. One characteristic, and a reason sometimes given for their adoption, is that their restriction to a single digit facilitated their use on computer cards where each column codes a single digit. Stanines are considered standard scores because they are normally distributed and can be computed using means and standard deviations. They are never reported with decimals and therefore represent a range of scores rather than a single score. They can be computed either from percentiles or z-scores, but if the distribution is not normally distributed, different results will be obtained depending on the method of computation used. If the percentile approach is used, the stanines will be normally distributed regardless of the original distribution. If z-scores are used, the stanines will be distributed in the same way as the raw scores.

To compute stanines using percentiles, you first find the median and assign a stanine of 5 to 10 percent of the scores on either side of the median. Then you assign a stanine of 4 to the next 17 percent of the cases below and a 6 to the next 17 percent of the cases above. The same procedure is used for stanines 3, 2, and 1 below the mean and 7, 8, and 9 using the percentages of 12, 7, and 4. To compute stanines from standard scores the following formula is used:

$$\text{Stanine} = 2z + 5 \qquad \textbf{[3.6]}$$

TABLE 3.3 A Comparison of Stanines with Three Other Types of Derived Scores

Stanine	1		2		3		4		5		6		7		8		9
Percentage of cases	4%		7%		12%		17%		20%		17%		12%		7%		4%
Percentiles		4		11		23		40		60		77		89		96	
z-scores		−1.75		−1.25		−.75		−.25		+.25		+.75		+1.25		+1.75	

The obtained value is then rounded off to an integer. The stanine for a z-score of 1.2 therefore would be 7: [Stanine = 2 (1.2) + 5 = 7 (rounded)]. Also, no matter how small or large the z-score, the stanine can never be smaller than 1 or greater than 9. Table 3.3 provides a summary of the percentile and standard score ranges for stanines.

As can be seen in Table 3.3, each stanine covers a wide range of scores. This imprecision is one of the reasons that this is a popular means of conveying information to parents. The widespread use of stanines is a result of the concern that parents might place too much emphasis on small differences in scores. With stanines there is the apparent assurance that different stanines reflect real differences—that two children with different stanine scores are in fact different. This is of course true only if the scores of both students are in the same relative position in their stanine range. If, for instance, one student is near the top of the fifth stanine with a percentile score of 59 and another student is at the bottom of the sixth stanine with a percentile of 61, then the two scores are really not that much different.

The use of stanines for purposes of evaluation or research is to be avoided because they represent broad bands of performance and convey less information than other standard scores. They should only be used as a means of communicating with parents when precision is intentionally to be avoided. Reporting stanines along with other more precise standard scores makes little sense. Stanines are not easily understood by teachers and parents, and although they have interval properties, their imprecision makes them inappropriate for purposes that involve mathematical computations.

Scaled Scores Another type of derived score is the scaled score, such as is used with the Comprehensive Test of Basic Skills or CTBS (McGraw-Hill, 1982). These scaled scores are based on latent-trait theory, which is described in Chapter 8. This theory provides a method of computing ability scores for students that is more precise than the standard scores described up to this point. For the derived scores discussed so far, performance on a test has been defined in terms of raw-score points based on the number of correct items, which have been transformed into a more convenient standard score. With such an approach, one correct item is considered equal to any other. Two people who each got ten questions correct on a thirty-question test may have correctly answered a different set of ten questions. Using standard scores, they would be considered to have equal ability. However, because the questions they answered were different, they may be quite dissimilar in their abilities. Using scaled scores derived from latent-trait theory, it is possible to obtain an ability score based on the characteristics of each item. Using this methodology items are weighted differently, depending on their characteristics. Ability scores are transformed into scaled scores that can range from zero to a thousand. For each grade there is a different mean and standard deviation. Scaled scores provide an estimate of the ability of students, which can be compared across grades. To illustrate, for reading comprehension on the CTBS, the mean scaled score for the seventh month of the first grade is 456; for the second month of second grade it is 512; and for the seventh month of twelfth grade, the mean scaled score is 803. Twelfth-grade students with greater reading ability will have scaled scores that exceed 803, but their scores could never go above 1,000.

These scaled scores have all the properties of interval-scale data, making them a good choice for research and/or evaluation. Because the scale is continuous across grades, they are also useful for making longitudinal comparison. In their three-digit form, they are not appropriate for reporting test results to parents, but they can be easily transformed to a standard score, such as a *T*-score, at each grade level that then can conveniently be reported to parents.

Scaled scores can only be obtained using a computer, although approximations may be available from conversion tables. Because there is not a direct correspondence between raw scores and scaled scores, confusion about their interpretation may sometimes occur. Consider the scaled scores for two high-achieving students. One missed two items, the other three. It is possible for the student who missed three items to have a slightly higher scaled score than the one who missed two items. This would occur if the two items missed by the first student were weighted more than the three items missed by the second student.

Interpreting Standard Scores

The purpose of measurement is to take attributes and place them on a unidimensional continuum. The nature of most data used in the social sciences and particularly in the fields of education and psychology precludes the identification of endpoints. This is why the data we encounter are usually better described as having interval rather than ratio scale characteristics.

Scores are made meaningful by means of comparisons and they should not be interpreted as absolute. The magnitude of a score is not fixed and it is possible to adjust their magnitude and equalize means by adding or subtracting constants. In a similar fashion, intervals can be equalized by multiplying and/or dividing by constants.

In order to perform these transformations, we must first have interval scale data. This means that the gaps between scores must be the same across the distribution. If you start with only ordinal data, no standard score conversions will make sense.

When interpreting standard scores, it is important to keep the nature of the norm group in mind. Standard scores are based on comparisons with others, using group means as anchors. With each type of standard score there is a different norm group. A student who obtains a 500 on the SAT certainly cannot be expected to have an IQ of 100. On the SAT the student is being compared to high school seniors who intend to go to college, whereas IQ scores are based on a random

TABLE 3.4 A Comparison of Different Methods of Computing Standard Scores

Score	Formula	Mean	SD	Scores															
Raw Score		34	4	27	28	29	30	31	32	33	34	35	36	37	38	39	40	41	42
z-score	$z = \frac{X - \bar{X}}{\sigma}$	0	1		−1.5		−1		−.5		0		+.5		+1		+1.5		+2.0
T-score	$T = 10z + 50$	50	10		35		40		45		50		55		60		65		70
CEEB	$\text{CEEB} = 100z + 500$	500	100		350		400		450		500		550		600		650		700
IQ	$\text{IQ} = 15z + 100$	100	15		77.5		85		92.5		100		107.5		115		122.5		130
ACT	$\text{ACT} = 20z + 19$	19	5		11.5		14		16.5		19		21.5		24		26.5		29
AGCT	$\text{AGCT} = 20z + 100$	100	20		70		80		90		100		110		120		130		140
Stanines	$\text{Stanine} = 2z + 5$, rounded to the nearest whole number	5	2		2		3		4		5		6		7		8		9

sample from a population of all individuals of the same age. The same logic prevents us from making direct comparisons between the SAT and GRE test scores.

Standard scores permit us to take sets of scores that may look very different and put them on the same scale, permitting us to make comparisons. This can be done only with the stipulation that we remember the norm group on which they are based. Table 3.4 presents a comparison between some of the different methods of transforming scores that have been discussed so far.

SUMMARY

1. Derived scores give meaning to raw scores.
2. Student performance can be reported either in terms of absolute or relative performance.
3. Absolute performance is reported using either criterion-referenced or domain-referenced scores.
4. Derived scores are used to indicate relative performance.
5. Although commonly used, grade equivalents are not generally recommended because they provide misleading information about student performance.
6. A major disadvantage of grade equivalents is a lack of stability, which is the result of their use of different grade levels as the basis for comparisons.
7. Percentiles have the advantage of comparing students to students of their own age, but the scale of percentiles deviates so much from being interval that there is a great likelihood of misinterpretation.
8. Standard scores are a better form of derived scores because they have the advantage of having scaling characteristics that permit mathematical computations that are inappropriate with either grade equivalents or percentiles.
9. Standard scores include *z*-scores, *T*-scores, CEEB scores, ACT scores (ITED scale), NCE scores, and IQ scores.
10. A recent advance in the reporting of derived scores involves the use of scaled scores based on latent-trait theory.

SUGGESTED READINGS

ALLEN, M. J., & YEN, W. M. (1979). *Introduction to measurement theory*. Monterey, CA: Brooks/Cole. [This book provides a useful discussion of latent-trait theory.]

LYMAN, H. B. (1978). *Test scores and what they mean*. Englewood Cliffs, NJ: Prentice-Hall. [In Chapter 6 of this brief book about testing is a very complete and useful discussion of derived scores.]

THORNDIKE, R. L., & HAGEN, E. P. (1986). *Measurement and evaluation in psychology and education*. (5th ed). New York: Wiley. [Chapter 4 in this book has a strong presentation of norms and norming that includes a useful discussion of derived scores.]

4

Computer Applications to Measurement

OVERVIEW

The purpose of this chapter is twofold: to provide a description of the different ways that computers can be used to improve the measurement process, and to provide specific directions for using a computer to accomplish measurement-related tasks. Obviously a single chapter cannot provide information about all possible computer applications, but it is hoped that the reader will become aware of the many ways that computers can be used. The chapter also is intended to serve the function of demystification, to emphasize that computers are not magical or mysterious and that their use can be implemented at a fundamental level by those with little experience in their use. By necessity this discussion will take place at a simplified level; it is intended for individuals with little experience with computers.

OBJECTIVES

In this chapter, you will be introduced to the fundamentals of using computers in measurement. Specifically, you will learn the following:

- How to get started on a computer.
- The different methods of entering data into a computer.
- How to use statistical packages.
- How to put data into a form understood by a computer.
- How to enter commands.
- The methods of using a computer to perform item analyses.
- Other computer applications, including test banking, tailor-made tests, automated test scoring, and computer-assisted test interpretation.
- Future developments in the use of computers in measurement.

Introduction

The widespread availability and simplified applications of computer methodology has had an enormous impact on the ways that measurement techniques are used. In the absence of computers, the field of measurement would look vastly different.

Their impact on measurement can be seen in many important areas. They have dramatically increased the level of sophistication of statistical analyses that are performed. At the same time, they have made the computation of all statistical analyses much easier. They also provide the technology to permit sophisticated item analyses, automated test scoring, and tailor made tests. In addition, they can be programmed to perform clinical interpretations of group personality, projective, and individual intelligence tests. Finally, the data processing capabilities of the computer can be harnessed to keep track of the massive amount of data associated with criterion-referenced and minimum competency testing.

Using a Computer to Perform Statistical Analyses

For years an important role of statisticians was to modify computational methods so that their calculations could be performed by hand or on primitive adding machines. Many of the statistical techniques now in use were developed for just this purpose. Those who have used statistics for many years need to reorient themselves to the statistical power of computers. Most statistical computations can be more easily solved by using a computer than by hand or with a calculator.

The most important development in the use of computers for statistical analyses is not the increased power and sophistication of computer hardware, but rather the improvements in software. The consumer no longer needs to be a computer programmer or to employ one in order to use a computer. There are numerous convenient statistical packages that can be accessed, at least on a rudimentary level, by almost anyone. There is a wide range of quality in the documentation of these packages, but the better ones have manuals that beginners can understand. It is possible for anyone with access to a computer to easily perform almost any computation, regardless of its sophistication, including all sorts of permutations of factor analysis, multiple regression, discriminant analysis, multivariate analysis of variance, and so forth. There is no guarantee, however, that an individual lacking the proper background and training will employ the appropriate technique, or that, once the analysis is completed, he or she will be able to interpret the results correctly.

One problem with having these statistical packages so easily accessible and widely available is their potential for misuse. Before the availability of these programs, only the individual well acquainted with an analysis procedure could perform the computation.

Attitudes Toward Computers

Successful use of a computer to analyze data requires the adoption of a special style of completing tasks and solving problems. You must learn to perform certain operatons by rote, without entirely understanding what or why you are doing it. You may find yourself entering commands that make no sense to you. The need to understand every step in a data analysis can act as an impediment to the successful mastery of basic computer operations. There is such a vast amount of knowledge and such a broad breadth of skills that can be possessed, that no one can be expected to understand it all. If a certain command gives you the results you want, you should not insist on knowing why it does, or what every statement, parameter, and argument means. Just be happy that it worked, and focus your energy on understanding the commands and operations that do not give you the desired results.

Getting Started

The best way to learn how to use a computer is just to do it. You do not need to understand the manual completely or take a formal course before you start. If you wait for that to happen, you may never get started. The best way to begin is to have someone show you how to perform a simple operation. The best person to show you is someone who knows just a little more than you do. He or she will be less likely to confuse you by explaining more than you need to know. Soon you will be unsatisfied with your limited knowledge and be ready to use manuals and books and benefit from formal and informal classes.

At this point an important characteristic to develop is a willingness to ask questions. It is possible to spend weeks trying to do something on a computer that someone with experience can show you how to do in a few minutes. He or she can also show you shortcut methods that you have not yet discovered, which can save you enormous amounts of time.

Types of Computers

There are three main types of computers: main-frames, mini-, and micro-computers. The first computers were all of the main-frame type, and at first it took an entire building to contain just one of these. Through the use of microchips they have become much smaller. The smaller versions of the main-frames are called mini-computers. The most recent developments are micro- or personal computers. These take up a small amount of space and can be moved from the classroom to the office or to one's home with varying amounts of ease. The availability of these smallest types of computers have greatly increased the number of people who have access to computer power. It has also permitted much more widespread use of computers to solve measurement related problems.

Entering Data

A computer can help you perform two important tasks: it can store data and it can perform statistical computations in a fraction of a second that it would be impossible or take years to complete by hand. It is this last capacity that is usually considered most important, and computers can perform remarkable feats in this area. Of course it is now possible to purchase hand calculators that can perform many of these computations. It is the data storage that makes the computer superior to the calculator; this capacity is the reason that even simple computations are more easily performed on a computer than a calculator.

With a calculator, every time a computation is performed, the data must be entered. This is not only tedious, but it can be a source of error because it is difficult to avoid entering data incorrectly. This is a problem when the error is undetected because you will obtain erroneous results. Even when the error is detected, you will be forced to reenter all of the data and commands. If you just suspect an error, you will probably feel like you should reenter the data just to make sure.

Test data can be entered into computer memory in several ways. It can be punched onto cards, entered on a terminal connected directly to a computer, or entered by means of a test scorer connected to a computer.

Punched-Card Input In the past the most common method of entering data into a computer was by means of cards on which the data had been stored according to the pattern of punches. Data are entered onto the cards by means of a keypunch machine. Such machines are of comparable complexity to an electric typewriter, and almost anyone can operate a keypunch after a few minutes of instruction. To become proficient requires considerably more practice.

The standard card is the Hollerith 80 column card, on which each column has space for 12 punches. Single-digit numbers are entered by punching a single space representing the number; alphanumerics (letters of the alphabet and punctuation) require that two holes be punched in a column. The cards that have data on them are placed into a hopper and then, following a command from the computer, each card is moved past two sensing stations that detect whether a hole has been punched in each space. The two sensors are employed to provide a means of detecting errors that could occur as a result of the mechanical aspects of the process. The configuration of punches and nonpunches is then converted into a code that can be stored by the computer. Finally, the cards are stacked ready for removal.

The simplest procedure is to submit the deck of cards to the card reader each time a computer analysis is requested. This can become awkward if there is a large amount of data. Not only are you forced to carry bulky and heavy boxes of cards, but the cards are susceptible to damage that can render them unreadable. It also takes a long time for the card reader to process large numbers of cards. An alternate approach is to read the cards into the computer once, and then store them either on a disk or a magnetic tape. The disk has the advantage of being more quickly accessible, but there are usually limits to how much can be stored. They are also more costly. Large amounts of data can be stored on tapes inexpensively. Once you exceed several hundred cards, you should begin to consider one of these alternatives to reading the cards each time you perform a data analysis procedure.

Using a Terminal to Input Data A more modern approach to entering data—and one that is rapidly replacing the use of keypunch machines, cards, and card readers—involves accessing the computer by means of a terminal. The computer is able to work so fast that, even though there may be many others connected to the computer, there is the illusion that you are the only person with which it is communicating. Unfortunately, this illusion can be interrupted by long waits on some computers.

Entering data on a terminal is somewhat more complex than entering data using cards. It requires a knowledge of several computer languages. Each language can call up certain other languages, and each is characterized by its own vocabulary and syntax. To use a computer you will need to use these languages, but do not be intimidated because even with many languages you may need to use only a few commands.

The three most important languages are (1) the monitor language, which allows you to control the computer directly; (2) the language of the statistical package, which is used for manipulating data and performing statistical computations; and (3) an editing language to enable you to create a program and enter data. To start, you can usually get by with a limited knowledge of the monitor language—a few commands may be all that is necessary. Editing systems can be more complex, but they are usually structured so that you can perform some simple operations with a limited knowledge of the language. As you increase your skill, you will learn to operate more quickly, correct errors more easily, and perform a wider range of operations.

Terminals are of two main types: cathode ray tube (CRT) and hard copy. With the CRT, commands typed on the keyboard appear on a screen similar to a television screen; all responses by the computer also appear on it. With a hardcopy terminal, whatever you enter and the computer's responses are printed on paper. Both types of terminals have their uses, and it is nice if you can have access to both. The CRT is less expensive, does not require as much maintenance, and also can operate more quickly. On the other hand, it is difficult to operate with no permanent copy of what you are doing. With most systems it is possible to request a copy of whatever files you wish, to be printed on a high-speed printer. This printer is usually located with the central computer. There may be many jobs waiting to be printed, so that often you will not be able to get your printouts immediately.

Terminals can be either connected directly to the central computer or accessed by telephone through a modem. The telephone-connection means of interface is convenient because it allows you to use a terminal any place that there is a telephone. The "hard-wired" approach permits the terminal to operate at a higher speed because the telephone connection places a limit on how fast the terminal can operate. There are mechanical limitations to the speed with which a hardcopy printer can operate, but CRTs can be set to present material faster than it can be read.

The greatest advantage of terminals is speed. It is possible to request a statistical analysis and then obtain the results almost immediately. A card reader can process a single card quickly, but if you have a large deck of cards or if there are many people waiting to have cards run, this step can take a lot of time. It is when the inevitable errors occur that the speed of the terminal becomes most obvious. With cards, each time you change something, the cards must be entered and you must wait for a printout. This can take quite a bit of time. Several hours or all day would not be unusual. There are delays that can occur when using a terminal because you are sharing the computer with many others, but if the computer is operating correctly, that should not happen. Normally you can correct your errors, rerun the program, and get the results immediately.

Machine-Scorable Answer Sheets As the number of cases you have to analyze increases, data entry can become an expensive and time-consuming bottleneck in your data-processing operation. Entering data either by punching cards or typing on a terminal can be extremely time consuming. This is the reason for the popularity of machine-scorable answer sheets. All student responses are made with a soft pencil and then the responses are scanned either electrically or optically by the machine scorer. With less sophisticated scorers, the results are printed on the user's answer sheet. With more sophisticated scorers, the responses can be both printed on the answer sheet and sent directly to a computer and stored. This is by far the easiest means of entering test data into computer memory where it is accessible for data analysis.

Preparing to Do the Data Analysis

With either the computer terminal method or the machine-scorable answer sheet approach, the data are stored in a file in the computer. To perform a statistical analysis on the data it is necessary to enter commands that will cause these analyses to be performed on the stored data. With cards, the data are not stored; instead, the commands requesting data analysis are printed on cards and placed with the data; then the entire deck of cards is read into the computer for processing.

Statistical Packages At one time most statistical analyses required the services of a computer programmer who would either have to write a special program to do what you wanted done or find a program someplace and copy it. Now statistical analyses are done almost entirely with commercially prepared statistical packages. These are programs that are stored in your computer. All you have to do is to describe your data and then tell the program what to do with it. These programs have become very sophisticated in terms of what they can do; at the same time the better ones are written in such a way that they require limited knowledge and experience in order to get started using them.

There are a number of statistical packages available for mainframe computers: the biomedical package, Biomedical Data Program (BMDP)* (Dixon, 1983); Statistical Package for the Social Sciences, SPSS† (Nie, et al., 1983); Statistical Analysis System, SAS** (1979); and A Statistical Computing Library, STATLIB‡ (Brelsford and Relles, 1981).

* BMDP is the registered trademark of BMDP Statistical Software, Inc.
† SPSS is a trademark of SPSS Inc. of Chicago, Illinois for its proprietary computer software.
**SAS is a registered trademark of SAS Institute Inc. of Raleigh, NC.
‡ STATLIB is a registered trademark of Bell Laboratories and the Rand Corporation.

There is also a proliferation of statistical packages for use with microcomputers. Microcomputers have some advantages over mainframe computers, particularly in terms of accessibility: you own the machine and do not have to share it with other users. You can also work anyplace you can plug your computer in. However, such programs are less powerful, can store less information, and are therefore less appropriate for large data sets and sophisticated analysis. The ideal setup is probably to have a microcompuer with a modem that allows data to be exchanged between the mainframe computer and the micro. This permits the user to perform simple operations on the micro but to do more involved analyses on the mainframe employing its more powerful software.

SPSS is the most widely used statistical program. It has two features that greatly contribute to its popularity: it is very powerful, with the capacity to perform a wide range of statistical operations, from simple descriptive statistics to multivariate analysis of variance; and it is written in such a way that it is easily used, at least at a rudimentary level, even by someone who knows little about computers.

There are many versions of SPSS; each more advanced version is designated by a higher release number. Release 9 is the most advanced form of SPSS, but it is now being replaced by SPSS^x, which is now in Release 2. The discussion that follows is based on SPSS; some modifications will be necessary if only SPSS^x is available to you.* SCSS† is a form of SPSS that can be used interactively. With this system the computer provides prompts to assist in data entry and to request different types of data analysis.

The newest statistical software from SPSS is a program that can be used on a personal computer. This program, called SPSS/PC, has many, but not all, of the capabilities of SPSS and SPSS^x. It was designed to be run on an IBM PC/XT with 320K memory and a 10-MB hard disk. The 8087 coprocessor, which speeds mathematical operations, is also recommended. This statistical package can be used on other computers with similar configurations, such as the Compaq Plus, Zenith 150, Columbia, and Corona. Work is under way to determine if the following microcomputers are compatible: Data General PC, Wang PC, Eagle, Texas Instrument PC, Lee DATA, Leading Edge, Stearns, Seequa Chameleon, Hyperion, and Tava. This is not an inexpensive way to embark on computer statistical analysis. In addition to the need for an expensive personal computer, the SPSS/PC program itself costs around $800.

Putting Data into a Form Understood by the Computer In order to actually perform a statistical computation using a program like SPSS, you must first be aware of certain basic conventions. First of all, data analysis is done in terms of cases. For the most part, a case is the same as a subject or an individual. With each case we have some identifying code or number. Following that number there are fields of data, in the form of numbers, with each field representing a variable. For instance, consider John Jones who is in fifth grade, is eleven years old, has a score of 75 on a reading achievement test and a 68 on a math achievement test, and who obtained this pattern of right and wrong answers on a

* SPSS^x is a trademark of SPSS Inc. of Chicago, Illinois for its proprietary computer software.
† SCSS is a trademark of SPSS Inc. of Chicago, Illinois, for its proprietary computer software.

multiple-choice test assessing his knowledge of the history of the Civil War: RRRWWRRWRRRRWWRRWRRR. This information would be punched onto cards or entered into a file via a terminal as illustrated in Figure 4.1. Notice that each variable is presented in the form of numbers and that right and wrong answers are entered as separate variables, coded with a 1 for a correct answer and a 0 for wrong answers. It would be possible to enter the number of the response made to each multiple-choice question, but additional programming would be required to score each answer as right or wrong.

Whether you have spaces between each field is optional. Spaces between numbers make it easier to tell when you have made an error and can make data entry somewhat easier, but they also take up more space. If you are entering a lot of data and you want to make sure that all of the information fits on a single card, you might consider eliminating the spaces between fields. Although it is possible for the computer to read several cards and know they belong to the same case, this doubles the number of cards. It also means that if one card is lost, all cards following the missing card will be read out of order. With a terminal, each line represents a case and it is much easier to tell at a glance if the data "looks right" when each case is represented by a single line.

The following data for ten students uses the format in Figure 4.1, and are presented as Example 4.1

EXAMPLE 4.1

```
001 11 1 5 75 68 11100110111100110111
002 12 2 5 70 65 11110111111110101111
003 11 1 5 71 72 11101111100011011111
004    2 5 74 71 11111111110011110110
005 12 2 5 66 63 11011011111011111011
006 11 1 5 65 59 11111111111111111110
007  9 2 5 78 67 11101111110001111111
008 11 2 5 77 68 11101100011011101111
009 11 1 5 74 66 11011101110111001111
010 12 2 5 76 76 11101001111110111101
```

The order of the variables is unimportant, but each column should be in the same place for each case. It is possible with some programs to request that the computer define a variable as a field separated by spaces. This simplifies the entry of data and makes it unnecessary for you to worry about where the columns are

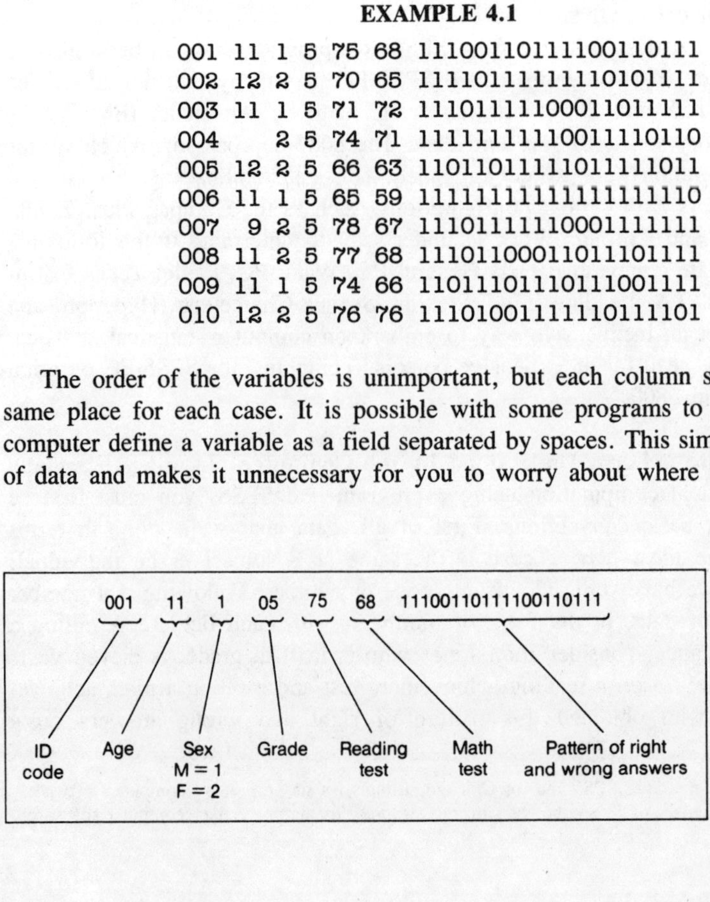

Figure 4.1
Example of data presented in a way that is readable by a computer.

as long as the variables are in the same order. It is also important to keep data for each subject together in the same case. If you have pre- and post scores on a classroom of students, the data for the pre- and post-tests should not be entered as separate cases.

Telling the Computer What You Want It to Do

Whether you use cards or a terminal, you must complete three operations: (1) enter monitor commands, (2) describe your data, and (3) specify what you want the computer to do.

Using Monitor Language You must provide certain administrative information to the computer, such as your name, a billing number indicating to whom the charge for computer use is to be billed, and a password so that the computer knows that it's you rather than some imposter wishing to use your account. Next there are numerical parameters that must be set so that the computer knows how much space you intend to use. Sometimes this is handled by default, which means that these values are set at the level that most users need, and only if there is a need to change the parameters is it necessary to provide special instructions. Finally, the computer must be told what statistics package is to be used.

There are many other commands that can be given in monitor language, but they are for the more advanced user and are specific to the location and type of computer being used. Normally these commands remain the same regardless of the statistical analysis you plan to use. A beginner needs only to learn one set of monitor commands and they can be used each time the individual wants to interact with the computer. The appropriate set of commands, or punched cards, necessary for this stage can be obtained from another user who has employed them successfully.

Describing Your Data Having called up the statistical package, you are ready to begin communicating in the language of that program. Using this language you must convey the following information to the computer before actually requesting that it perform an operation:

1. The number of variables.
2. The name you want to assign to each variable.
3. Where each variable appears on the card.
4. The width of the field defining each variable.
5. Whether there are any decimals.
6. The number of cards associated with each case.
7. The form in which the data are to be entered.
8. The number of cases.

Steps 1 and 2 can be combined because by naming the variable their number is implied. A unique name must be given to each variable. For instance, with the data in Figure 4.1, the following names could be used: ID, AGE, SEX, GRADE, READ, MATH, ITEM1, ITEM2, ITEM3 . . . ITEM20. Using SPSS, they could also be defined as VAR001 to VAR026. This tells the computer that there are 26 variables, that the identification number is stored in VAR001, age in VAR002, sex in VAR003, and so forth. This simplifies the process of naming variables and is particularly useful when you have a large number of them: for instance, if you had a long test with many items, each of which was to be a variable.

Steps 3 to 6 are entered using a format statement. This tells the computer where each variable is stored on a card or a line on a disk file. The specific instructions for writing a format statement are somewhat technical. They can be found in the SPSS manual or other similar sources. Instructions for writing a format for the data in Figure 4.1 is given in the box that follows. It is not necessary for you to be familiar with this information to understand the remainder of the chapter. It is also possible to use a free-field format. With this approach, spaces between variables tell the computer where one variable stops and another starts. However, the use of spaces may cause the data to take up more space than is desirable.

Step 7 involves telling the computer whether the data are stored on cards or magnetic tape. If the data are stored in disk memory, the name of the file on which they are stored is indicated.

Step 8 requires that the computer be told the number of cases. This can be either the exact number or, when permitted, an estimate. In this case the computer counts the cases itself. This is useful with large data sets because you may not know exactly how many cases you have and it would be difficult to count them. An estimate is usually required because the computer must allocate space within the computer core memory for running your program ahead of time. The number of cases is an important factor in deciding how much space to set aside.

Requesting a Specific Analysis Technique After communicating with the monitor program, including an identification of the statistical analysis program that you want, such as SPSS, and after specifying the amount and location of your data,

Writing the Format

The format usually includes the letter *F*, a number, a decimal, and another number. For instance, to enter the identification number for the data in Figure 4.1, the symbol *F3.0* would be entered. The first number tells the computer the number of digits (in this case three), and the second number how many digits there are after the decimal. Because there is no decimal, the second value is a zero. A number placed before the *F*, which is optional, can tell the computer how many sequential variables have the same format. The twenty items on the test from Figure 4.1 could either be represented by a series of F1.0s, or all of them could be indicated by the format 20F1.0. *X*s are used to indicate blank spaces. *A* "/" tells the computer to go to the next card for a continuation of a listing of variables for the same case. This symbol also implies the number of cards associated with each case. If there is no "/" there is only one card per case. For the data in Figure 4.1 the format would be as follows: F3.0, 1X, F2.0, 1X, F1.0, 1X, F1.0, 1X, F2.0, 1X, F2.0, 1X, 20F1.0. There are also other ways this format could be written that would convey the same information to the computer.

you are ready to request the data analysis you want. This also requires that you provide several different types of information. First, you must specify the statistical operation and the variables upon which you want the analysis performed. Using SPSS virtually any analysis can be performed, but the more complicated computations require additional information, all of which is described in the SPSS manual (Nie et al., 1975).

To run an SPSS program on a terminal, you must first enter your account number and your password. This gives you access to the monitor language. Each card is represented by a line in a file sometimes called a card image. The data are stored in one file and the program is stored in another. On the INPUT MEDIUM card image the name of the file where the data are stored is entered instead of the word CARD. The user requests that the SPSS program be run and the program responds with a prompt. The user then provides the name of the file where the SPSS program is stored, along with the name of a file where the results are to be stored.

After the program has run, the file containing the results can be examined. If there are no errors, the file can be printed either on a hardcopy terminal or on a high-speed printer located with the central computer. If the program fails to yield the desired results, the lists of commands in the SPSS program file are modified and the job is run again.

In order to obtain the mean, standard deviation and other descriptive statistics for the variables in Figure 4.1, accessing SPSS from a terminal, the following commands would be listed on a disk file:

```
VARIABLE LIST        VAR001 TO VAR026
INPUT FORMAT         FIXED (F3.0, 1X, F2.0, 1X, F1.0, 1X,
                     F1.0, 1X, F2.0, 1X, F2.0, 1X, 20F1.0)
N OF CASES           10
INPUT MEDIUM         COMP.DAT
ASSIGN BLANKS        -99
MISSING VALUES       VAR001 TO VAR026 (-99)
COMPUTE              TOTAL=VAR007+VAR008+VAR009+VAR010+
                     VAR011+VAR012+VAR013+VAR014+VAR015+
                     VAR016+VAR017+VAR018+VAR019+VAR020+
                     VAR021+VAR022+VAR023+VAR024+VAR025+
                     VAR026
CONDESCRIPTIVE       VAR002, VAR005 TO VAR0026, TOTAL
STATISTICS           ALL
FREQUENCIES          GENERAL=VAR003, VAR004
FINISH
```

The VARIABLE LIST tells the computer that there are 26 variables that are named in order: VAR001, VAR002, VAR003, and so on. The INPUT FORMAT tells the compuer where the data are found on each line. The N OF CASES statement indicates the number of individuals for which you have information. The INPUT MEDIUM statement tells the computer where the raw data are stored. In this case it is in a disk file, COMP.DAT, which contains the data from Figure 4.1. The ASSIGN BLANKS statement tells the computer that when it encounters blanks it should read them as −99s. Without this command it would interpret them as zeros. If you compute the mean age with a zero for one case, as occurs with the data from Figure 4.1, the results would be distorted. Of course, if you only substitute a −99 for blanks, the results would also be misleading, which is the purpose of the MISSING VALUES statement. It tells the computer that any −99s are to be considered missing and are not included in any computations. The particular value the blanks are changed to is arbitrary, but you should select a value that you know does not appear in the input data that the computer is reading. The COMPUTE statement sums across all of the items to create a new variable which is equal to the total score. The CONDESCRIPTIVE statement requests that descriptive statistics be provided for all of the variables except VAR003, which is the sex of the child, and VAR004, which is the grade of the child. These are categorical variables, and the descriptive statistics that are mostly interval data would make no sense. For these two variables, FREQUENCIES are requested and they provide a frequency distribution. The STATISTICS statement that follows the CONDESCRIPTIVE statement tells the computer the specfic statistics that are being requested. By entering ALL, every available descriptive statistic is provided. Alternatively, only those specific statistics in which you are interested could be requested. Any other statistical analyses can be included following the FREQUENCIES statement. The final statement is always FINISH, which tells the computer that it has reached the end of the program. An example of the type of information that is obtained from the printout is provided in Figure 4.2.

When the data are entered using cards, the preceding list of commands is itself preceded by several monitor commands, specific to the location and the particular computer being used. The INPUT MEDIUM card tells the computer whether the data are stored on cards, magnetic tape, or on a disk. If the data are on cards, these would follow the SPSS cards and be introduced by the statement, READ INPUT DATA. The entire deck of cards is then entered for processing by the card reader, which then transfers the information on the cards to the computer for analysis. The results are then printed. If there are any errors, new cards are punched to replace those that are incorrect and the deck is resubmitted for processing.

The preceding set of commands are the minimum necessary to obtain some simple descriptive statistics. There are numerous additional commands that can be used. Once you have tried to run a simple program, you will want to learn more about what you can do. Not only are there many other types of statistical analyses that can be requested, but there are also other useful commands involving the manipulation of data and variables. For instance, logical statements can be used to create new variables. Suppose you want to divide the ten students into two groups by age. Everyone above eleven would go into group 1 and everyone 11 or younger would go into group 2. A new variable would be created that would contain either a 1 or 2, depending on this classification.

Figure 4.2 Descriptive statistics from the SPSS Batch System.

```
              10 CONDESCRIPTIVE VAR002,VAR005 TO VAR026,TOTAL

 ***** GIVEN WORKSPACE ALLOWS FOR  206 VARIABLES FOR CONDESCRIPTIVE PROBLEM *****


- - - - - - - - - - - - - - - - - - - - - - - - - - - - - - - - - - - - - - - - - - - - - - - - - - - - - - - -

SPSS BATCH SYSTEM                                                    28-MAR-85       PAGE   2

FILE    NONAME    (CREATION DATE = 28-MAR-85)

VARIABLE   VAR002

MEAN              11.111            STD ERROR        0.309              STD DEV         0.928
VARIANCE           0.861            KURTOSIS         3.281              SKEWNESS       -1.470
RANGE              3.000            MINIMUM          9.000              MAXIMUM        12.000
SUM              100.000

VALID OBSERVATIONS -        9                MISSING OBSERVATIONS -     1

- - - - - - - - - - - - - - - - - - - - - - - - - - - - - - - - - - - - - - - - - - - - - - -

VARIABLE   VAR005

MEAN              72.600            STD ERROR        1.416              STD DEV         4.477
VARIANCE          20.044            KURTOSIS        -0.708              SKEWNESS       -0.692
RANGE             13.000            MINIMUM         65.000              MAXIMUM        78.000
SUM              726.000

VALID OBSERVATIONS -       10                MISSING OBSERVATIONS -     0

- - - - - - - - - - - - - - - - - - - - - - - - - - - - - - - - - - - - - - - - - - - - - - -

VARIABLE   VAR006

MEAN              67.500            STD ERROR        1.515              STD DEV         4.790
VARIANCE          22.944            KURTOSIS         0.410              SKEWNESS        0.030
RANGE             17.000            MINIMUM         59.000              MAXIMUM        76.000
SUM              675.000

VALID OBSERVATIONS -       10                MISSING OBSERVATIONS -     0

- - - - - - - - - - - - - - - - - - - - - - - - - - - - - - - - - - - - - - - - - - - - - - -

VARIABLE   VAR007

MEAN               1.000            STD ERROR        0.000              STD DEV         0.000
VARIANCE           0.000            KURTOSIS         0.000              SKEWNESS        0.000
RANGE              0.000            MINIMUM          1.000              MAXIMUM         1.000
SUM               10.000

VALID OBSERVATIONS -       10                MISSING OBSERVATIONS -     0

- - - - - - - - - - - - - - - - - - - - - - - - - - - - - - - - - - - - - - - - - - - - - - -
```

SPSS is a trademark of SPSS Inc. of Chicago, Ill., for its proprietary computer software.

Using a Computer to Perform Item Analyses

The vast improvements in standardized tests that have occurred over the last twenty years could not have taken place without the availability of computers and their capacity for performing complex item analyses. Item analysis techniques are employed in order to assess the quality of a test or assessment instrument. Good items can be kept, while poor items are modified or eliminated. Item analyses are usually conducted in either of two ways: through the computation of item discrimination indexes or by means of correlations. With both methods the degree to which an individual item can differentiate between good and poor students is used as a criterion for evaluating items. With the item discrimination approach, good items are those that the best students tend to get right and the poor students get wrong. Bad items are those that both groups do the same on or those on which the worst students do best. The correlation approach is based on the correlation between each item and the total score. The higher the correlation the better the item. With both approaches an index is obtained that can range from -1 to $+1$. The more positive the index the better the item. The item-discrimination approach is practical only for small classroom tests, and even then it can be awkward and time consuming. Item-analysis methods that utilize correlations must be conducted with the aid of a computer. Their use can be expected to proliferate with the increased availability of microcomputers and machine scorers at the school level.

Correlational item-analyses techniques can be used to improve ability tests that are scored as either right or wrong, as well as personality and attitude-rating scales where the examinee responds with a number that indicates his or her agreement or disagreement with a statement.

The first step in conducting an item analysis is to transform the test or attitude-rating-scale data into a form readable by the computer program that is to do the analysis. Test score data can be entered using a code with a 1 if the item is correct and a 0 if it is incorrect. The actual multiple-choice responses can be entered, but this requires that the computer be programmed so that it can score the items as right or wrong.

For personality tests and attitude-rating scales, the numerical response is entered. Any reversed items must be changed so that they are scaled in the correct direction. This is done by subtracting the numerical response from a value equal to the number of steps on the scale plus one. If you have a six-point scale, you subtract each reversed score from 7. In this way a five becomes a two ($7-5=2$) and a six becomes a one ($7-6=1$). This process can be done by the computer using a COMPUTE statement and does not need to take place before the data are entered.

The items are summed to provide a total score, again using a COMPUTE statement, and then each item is correlated with that value. The obtained coefficient provides an indication of how much each item contributes to the overall reliability of the test. The higher the correlation, the better the item. The size of the correlation necessary to make you think that an item is okay the way it is depends on the subject matter and test length. A negative correlation may indicate that the item needs to be reversed.

An example of the computation of the correlations between the individual items and the total score from Example 4.1 on page 86 is provided in Figure 4.3. This would

Figure 4.3 Pearson correlations from the SPSS Batch System.

```
***** PEARSON CORR PROBLEM REQUIRES      240 WORDS WORKSPACE *****



- - - - - - - - - - - - - - - - - - - - - - - - - - - - - - - - - - - - - - - - - - - - - - - - -

SPSS BATCH SYSTEM                                                          28-MAR-85       PAGE    7

FILE     NUNAME     (CREATION DATE = 28-MAR-85)

- - - - - - - - - - - - - P E A R S O N   C O R R E L A T I O N   C O E F F I C I E N T S - - - - - - - - - - - -

              VAR007      VAR008      VAR009      VAR010      VAR011      VAR012      VAR013      VAR014      VAR015      VAR016

TOTAL         99.0000     99.0000     0.0903      0.6019      0.0903      0.0903      0.4466      0.5417      0.3612      0.1605
              (    10)    (    10)    (    10)    (    10)    (    10)    (    10)    (    10)    (    10)    (    10)    (    10)
              P=*****     P=*****     P= .402     P= .033     P= .402     P= .402     P= .098     P= .053     P= .153     P= .329

(COEFFICIENT / (CASES) / SIGNIFICANCE)      (A VALUE OF 99.0000 IS PRINTED IF A COEFFICIENT CANNOT BE COMPUTED)

- - - - - - - - - - - - - - - - - - - - - - - - - - - - - - - - - - - - - - - - - - - - - - - - -

SPSS BATCH SYSTEM                                                          28-MAR-85       PAGE    8

FILE     NUNAME     (CREATION DATE = 28-MAR-85)

- - - - - - - - - - - - - P E A R S O N   C O R R E L A T I O N   C O E F F I C I E N T S - - - - - - - - - - - -

              VAR017      VAR018      VAR019      VAR020      VAR021      VAR022      VAR023      VAR024      VAR025      VAR026

TOTAL         0.1474      0.2408      0.2408      0.1839      0.2408      0.1839      0.2408      -0.0401     0.1605      -0.0401
              (    10)    (    10)    (    10)    (    10)    (    10)    (    10)    (    10)    (    10)    (    10)    (    10)
              P= .342     P= .251     P= .251     P= .306     P= .251     P= .306     P= .251     P= .456     P= .329     P= .456

(COEFFICIENT / (CASES) / SIGNIFICANCE)      (A VALUE OF 99.0000 IS PRINTED IF A COEFFICIENT CANNOT BE COMPUTED)

- - - - - - - - - - - - - - - - - - - - - - - - - - - - - - - - - - - - - - - - - - - - - - - - -

SPSS BATCH SYSTEM                                                          28-MAR-85       PAGE    9

CPU TIME REQUIRED:      0.13 SECONDS


          13 FINISH

     ERROR OPENING USAGE DATA FILE (FORTRAN I/O ERROR:  28,252)
     NOTIFY YOUR SPSS COORDINATOR OF THIS ERROR
```

SPSS is a trademark of SPSS Inc. of Chicago, Ill., for its proprietary computer software.

be obtained by inserting the following command before the FINISH command:

```
PEARSON CORR    TOTAL WITH VAR007 TO VAR026.
```

Notice that the correlations between the total score and items 1 and 2, here labeled VAR007 and VAR008, are 99.0000. This means that no correlations could be computed because all of the students got each of these items correct. The best items were those coded VAR010 and VAR0026. The value in parentheses is the number of cases, and the *p* indicates the significance of the correlation, which would not be of particular importance in conducting an item analysis.

Means and standard deviations should be computed for each item. An inspection of these values will provide clues as to why an item has a low correlation with the total score. With classroom tests the usual problem is that the item is too difficult or too easy. This results in either a low or a high mean and a small standard deviation. On personality tests the variability may be small because all of those taking the test responded in the same way. This lack of variability is likely to result in a low correlation between the item and the total score. The item may need to be rewritten in order to elicit more varied responses.

The correlational approach to item analysis is based on the assumption that the majority of items are effectively measuring the construct being assessed. If this is not the case, then the total score is not a good value to use to evaluate the quality of individual items. Factor analysis could be used to determine if there is more than one factor.

Test Banking and Tailor-Made Tests

Test Banks

As will be emphasized in Chapter 7, "Classroom Testing," objective tests have many advantages over essay and short-answer tests. Their chief disadvantage is logistical. Constructing tests can be a time-consuming and laborious process. Even when the items are already written and are available from old tests, teacher manuals, or 3 x 5 cards, putting a test together can take a long time and involve a major typing effort. The storage of items in computer memory, coupled with word-processing technology, provides a method for constructing tests that is much easier and can make the use of objective tests much more practical. Some publishers are now providing a test-construction service with the textbooks they market. An instructor needs only to provide a list of items and the test publisher mails a test ready for duplication.

Tailor-Made Tests

Traditional test-preparation techniques dictate that a single test be administered to all students at a single sitting. This means that the difficulty of the test must be tailored to the typical student; it also means that if a student needs to take a test at a time other than when the test is scheduled, the instructor is faced with a dilemma. He or she must either create another test, which requires duplicating the effort of constructing the first test, or risk compromising the security of the test administered to the majority of the class. There is no way to prevent students from sharing their recollections of the contents of a test.

Computer technology allows the instructor to construct individual tests tailored to each student. This makes it possible for a student to take a test at any time or to retake a test without fear that the security of the test has been breached. This is possible because the computer is able to select a different set of items for each test. A large bank of items can be stored in a computer and then, according to a predetermined logic, any number of equivalent forms can be generated. It is possible for a student to take a test, receive instruction on the subject matter assessed by the items that were missed, and then be retested over that material.

Of even greater interest, from the perspective of test reliability, is the possibility of tailoring tests to the ability of the student. Tests made up of items selected in such a way that students get half of the items right are likely to have higher reliability than tests with items of higher or lower difficulty. Because there are different ability levels within a classroom, by tailoring a test to the ability level of each student, the reliability of a test can be increased. Traditional techniques must focus on ensuring appropriate item difficulty for those in the middle of the distribution, but tailor-made test technology permits the construction of tests that include items at an appropriate level of difficulty for students at all levels, including the extremes of the distribution.

The appropriate difficulty for a test to be taken by a particular student can be determined in two ways: (1) a locator test can be administered that designates the optimum item difficulty for an individual, for the entire test; or (2) if the test is administered on a terminal, the computer can be programmed to select the appropriate difficulty, item by item. The difficulty of each additional item is determined by whether the student got the previous item right or wrong. Following an incorrect answer, the next item chosen is easier, whereas the item selected to follow a correct answer is more difficult. The result is a test that is of optimum difficulty and is therefore characterized by higher reliability than a test for which items are chosen in a more conventional fashion.

The data-processing requirements for setting up and managing item banks has existed for quite some time. The problem has been to find a method of equating tests of different difficulty levels. The raw scores are clearly not comparable. Latent-trait theory provides a promising approach to weighting items according to their difficulties so that different level tests can be compared. (See Chapter 8.)

Automated Test Scoring and Interpretation

Machine-scorable answer sheets are available for nearly all standardized tests, making the laborious task of hand scoring no longer necessary. A test can be sent to a central location, scored, interpreted, and returned in several days. What was once a convenience has now become a necessity, because modern large-scale standardized tests are usually constructed in such a way that they can not be hand scored. This is true, for instance, for the Strong-Campbell Interest Inventory and the Kuder Occupational Interest Inventory. The Comprehensive Test of Basic Skills can be scored in terms of right and wrong answers, but scaled scores based on latent-trait theory must be computed using a computer.

Test-scoring services now go far beyond merely reporting the number of correct responses or providing various types of derived scores. In the case of achievement tests, information about the performance of individuals, classrooms, and/or school districts can now be provided. This can be broken down in any way a school district desires, including a listing of the types of questions most often missed. These services are intended for the purpose of providing diagnostic information, and the test publishers encourage the utilization of this service because it is a source of additional income.

There also is an increasing availability of computer-assisted interpretation. Machine-scorable answer sheets for psychological tests, including personality and individual intelligence tests, can be sent to scoring centers where they can be processed and returned the same day they are received. In addition to scores, clinical interpretation can be provided.

The most recent development in this area involves the availability of programs stored on disks for use with personal computers that can perform clinical interpretations of personality tests, including projective instruments. Alternatively a central computer can be accessed by terminal and the subjects' responses entered. The results can then be printed at the therapist's location. The availability of such programs can be a great convenience, and the data-processing power of a computer can provide useful analyses.

This methodology is not without its disadvantages. The analyses can be no better than their programming and the information they can access. This is an example of artifical intelligence (AI), where the computer is supposed to replicate the mental processes of the therapist. The state of the art of artificial intelligence has not reached a point where it is possible to program a computer so that it can reproduce the high-level mental processes employed by a psychologist performing a clinical analysis. This sort of cognitive functioning requires the most complex mental processes of which humans are capable. It is possible, however, to program a computer to utilize algorithms for performing computations and to provide interpretation according to sets of decision rules.

In AI studies it has been found that the main advantage that the human brain enjoys in comparison to computers is the ability to scan a large amount of data rapidly, pick out what is important, and disregard the irrelevant. This is what the good clinician does in the process of rendering a clinical diagnosis.

When a clinical analysis is dependent on the initial computation of a great many scores, such as with some approaches to interpreting the Wechsler Intelligence Scale for Children-Revised (WISC-R), then the computer can be of great service. It can perform these computations easily and quickly. It can also generate hypotheses useful to the clinician. The next step is to link such programs with word processors, automate the diagnostic process, and produce a psychological report. This is an inappropriate method of conducting a clinical diagnosis because the computer is not replacing the complex cognitive processes that go into producing a clinical analysis and is instead producing a piece of paper that creates this illusion. It is also possible that the development of such programs will tend to discourage the development of good clinical skills. Why expend the time and energy to interpret a test if it can be done so much easier by a computer?

Future Developments in the Use of Computers in Measurement

There tends to be a large gap between what it is possible to do on a computer and what is actually being done. This is illustrated by the limited degree to which item banks and tailor-made tests are being used. Although technology is available and has been for several years, there are few examples of these applications. The limiting factor is that implementation is expensive—not only in terms of time and money, but more importantly in terms of computer expertise. There are few individuals capable of the high level of programming required for the implementation of these sorts of programs.

Perhaps the most important development in measurement applications for computers is the increased availability of microcomputers. It can be expected that they will soon be widely available at a school or classroom level. This will make feasible measurement techniques presently inaccessible to the classroom teacher. For example, grading procedures based on the use of standard scores are great improvements over the more usual practice of summing across raw scores. Teachers often lack the necessary sophistication to employ these techniques but more importantly, the computations are prohibitively time consuming. A microcomputer, programmed to perform these operations, can greatly simplify these tasks. The use of microcomputers to simplify item-analysis procedures in the classroom requires tests scorers that can be linked directly to the microcomputer, and these are also now becoming available.

A proliferation of new statistical packages is becoming available for microcomputers. Most microcomputers already provide some sort of data-analysis capability, but what exists is somewhat unsophisticated. The main advantage they have over a calculator is the capacity for one-time entry of data. Unfortunately some do not even have this advantage, and data must be reentered for each analysis. Except for the SPSS/PC program available for use with the IBM PC/XT already discussed, most of these packages are still inferior to those available for use with large computers, both in terms of data manipulation and the availability of sophisticated data analysis. They may still be adequate for small amounts of data and less complex analyses, however. In the future it can be expected that any analysis now possible on a mainframe computer will be available on microcomputers. Software is also improving. Instead of using the screen to reproduce card images, different formats will be employed, such as the spread sheet now used in business applications.

Finally, computers can be used to handle the massive amounts of record keeping associated with criterion-referenced and other competency-based systems. These systems often involve a large number of objectives and each must be assessed by a set of items. Computer management of these data represents the only practical approach to using that information. The implementation of such programs in a way that does not take up too much of a teacher's time will probably require tests that are machine scored and the availability of machine scorers in each school.

SUMMARY

1. The widespread availability and simplified use of computers has had an enormous impact on the ways that evaluation and measurement take place.
2. In the area of statistical analysis, computers make complex statistical analyses accessible to a wide range of users.
3. Not only do modern computers have the power to perform complex analyses, but the accompanying software is not overly difficult for inexperienced users to use.
4. The computer can perform two important data-analysis tasks: it can store data and it can perform statistical operations in a fraction of a second that would be virtually impossible to complete by hand.
5. Computers can be accessed either by punched cards or means of a terminal.
6. The use of punched cards to enter data and commands is becoming less and less common and is being replaced by CRT terminals and microcomputers.
7. Statistical analyses are performed using statistical packages.
8. Communicating with the computer requires familiarity with several languages, which enables you to call up packages and initiate commands within the packaged program.
9. There are a number of measurement-related tasks in addition to statistical analyses that are best performed by means of a computer, such as item analyses, test banking, tailor-made tests, and computer-assisted psychological-test interpretation.

SUGGESTED READINGS

AFIFI, A. A., & CLARK, V. (1984). *Computer-aided multivariate analysis*. Belmont, CA: Lifetime Learning. [This book covers multivariate statistics from the point of view of computer application. It includes several different packages but places most of its emphasis on the BMDP series.]

KANTER, H. M. (1985). *Computer applications of educational measurement concepts*. New York: Macmillan.

NIE, N. H., HALL, C. H., JENKINS, J. G., STEINBRENNER, K., & BENT, D. H. (1975). SPSS, (2nd ed.). New York: McGraw-Hill. [This is the basic manual for SPSS. This version is still available on many computers, but it can be expected that it will be soon replaced by SPSS^x. There is a series of manuals for using SPSS^x that is either available now or will be soon: *SPSS$^{x\text{TM}}$* basics, SPSS^x-user's guide, SPSS^x reference handbook, SPSS^x-introductory statistics guide, SPSS^x-advanced statistics guide, and *SPSS^x-graphics*. For use of SPSS on personal computers, there is the *SPSS/PC manual*. All of these manuals are available from McGraw-Hill.]

SCHWARTZ, M. D. (1975). *Using computers in clinical practice: psychotherapy and mental health applications*. New York: McGraw-Hill. [This book describes the use of computers for testing and report writing.]

Educational measurement issues and practice. (Summer 1984). *3*(2), (Entire issue). [This entire issue is devoted to the use of microcomputers in testing. It includes such topics as microcomputers and testing, using microcomputers to develop tests, using microcomputers to administer tests, and using microcomputers to assess achievement and instruction.]

5

Reliability

OVERVIEW

Measurements in the social sciences are of much lower quality than those employed in the so-called hard sciences. Assessments tend to be indirect and to refer to traits for which the precise meaning remains vague and open to contradictory interpretations. The fundamental problem in measurement concerns the fact that a given trait can be measured in many ways that may or may not be comparable or even directly related. There is often no basis for assuming the superiority of one method of assessment over another. Assessing the quality of measurement is a process that takes place in two stages. First of all, without concern for *what* the test is measuring, we must determine if the test is measuring anything. If the responses of students are random then the test is measuring nothing. The more systematic and less random the responses of students, the more the test can be thought to hold together and be measuring a single construct. This characteristic can be called *internal consistency reliability*. Reliability is a statistical quality of test scores that is independent of content. The second stage involves the assessment of validity and is concerned with what constructs a test is measuring, and it is discussed in detail in Chapter 6, "Validity."

Chapter 5 presents a more restrictive discussion of reliability than is usually presented. The stability or consistency of a test or test score is often included as an aspect of reliability. Because stability and internal consistency are independent and separate aspects of measurement, their inclusion together complicates any discussion of reliability. Internal consistency is a statistical characteristic of a test score, while stability is a characteristic of the construct. In this chapter, reliability as internal consistency will be emphasized. The intention is not to minimize the importance of stability. It is very important to know how long after a test has been administered that we can have confidence in a test's results. An aptitude test intended to predict school performance a year after administration is not going to be useful if students change in the degree to which they possess the aptitude. Likewise, an interest inventory will be useful only to the extent that interest patterns remain stable over a number of years.

This chapter begins with an explanation of the definitions of reliability, and is followed by a description of the different factors that affect its magnitude. Included is a discussion of the four major methods of computing reliability coefficients, including parallel forms, internal consistency, and test-retest reliability, as well as the factors that influence the magnitude of a reliability coefficient.

OBJECTIVES

In this chapter you will learn what reliability is, how to compute it, and when to use its various forms. Specifically, you will learn the following:

- How reliability and validity are related.
- The different approaches to defining reliability.
- Factors affecting the magnitude of parallel forms reliability.
- The usefulness of viewing reliability as internal consistency.
- The limitations of test-retest reliability.
- The technical factors affecting reliability.

How Reliability and Validity Are Related

In developing or using tests, it is important to remember that just because a test is labeled as a measure of a specific construct does not necessarily mean that test scores can effectively differentiate among individuals or that inferences made about test scores are legitimate. The methods used for determining whether an instrument has these qualities are reliability and validity.

A test score can be reliable without being valid, but before a test score can be valid it must first be reliable. In other words, reliability is a necessary, but not a sufficient, condition for validity. For example, consider an achievement test intended to assess a student's knowledge of social studies, and the problems that such a test presents. Each school district emphasizes different aspects of this topic and therefore any test that assesses specific knowledge will be unfair to those who weren't exposed to that particular content. The usual solution is to use a reading comprehension format in which a paragraph about some aspect of social studies is accompanied by a series of multiple-choice questions about the paragraph. Such a test is reliable because it is measuring a single construct (probably reading comprehension), and verbal ability items tend to be internally consistent. Reliability is a statistical characteristic of a score and is independent of content. It is validity that is concerned with what a test is measuring. These achievement test scores are an indication of reading comprehension but not social studies ability. Inferences about a student's reading comprehension ability based on the results of the test would be legitimate, but inferences about social studies ability would not. It is therefore reasonable to conclude that the test scores are reliable, and furthermore that they are a valid measure of reading comprehension. The test scores are probably not valid measures of social studies knowledge.

How Reliability and Validity Are Related

Reliability in most cases is expressed by a single value that can be computed in a relatively straightforward manner. For this reason most test manuals emphasize reliability coefficients. Validity is much more difficult to establish, and the argument for its existence often rests on the force of narrative rather than more objectively evaluated coefficients. This makes the process of establishing validity difficult; for this reason there is a tendency for publishers to ignore the subject in their manuals. This is unfortunate because validity is clearly an important characteristic for a test to have.

Test publishers should include detailed information on reliability and validity in their manuals. This information should not be global but should be related to the specific settings and circumstances for which the publisher recommends that the test be used. At the same time the users of a test must take the responsibility for ensuring that the scores from the test they are using are reliable and valid for the settings in which it is being employed.

Measuring More Than One Construct

Throughout this chapter tests scores will be discussed in terms of how well they measure a construct. Of course, most tests are intended to measure more than one construct and this is reflected in their use of subscale scores. Because subscale scores are intended as measures of different constructs, the reliability of each subscale must be computed separately. If a test is measuring more than one construct but this is not reflected in subscale scores, then it can be expected that the reliability of the test scores will be suppressed.

Defining Reliability

Despite its being relatively easy to compute, there are few subjects in the field of measurement more difficult to understand than reliability. This is because reliability is now viewed quite differently from the way it was first envisioned seventy years ago. Often when problems of definition arise in the social sciences we can turn to operational definitions, which in this case, would be the methods used to compute reliability. Unfortunately, each method of assessing reliability tends to measure something different.

Reliability and Measurement Error

Originally the assessment of reliability both conceptually and mathematically was closely related to measurement error. As psychometrists began to refine their measurement techniques at the beginning of this century, there was a need to quantify the degree to which their measurements were imprecise. The concept of measurement error was originally developed by Charles Spearman (1924) for the purpose of determining the degree to which an obtained score would differ from a true score. An obtained score is the raw score from a test or assessment instrument, whereas the true score is what the obtained score would be if there were no error. Because errors are assumed to be random when many measurements are made, obtained scores are expected to be normally distributed around the true score. This distribution is assumed to be the same for each subject, and the standard deviation of this distribution is the standard error of measurement (SEM). The SEM will be discussed in more detail in a later section of this chapter.

Technical Definitions of Reliability

One of the outgrowths of defining measurement error as the relationship between obtained and true scores was the development of classic true-score theory, a formal psychometric theory used to explain reliability and measurement error mathematically. The true score is often operationally defined as the score that would be obtained if all of the items in the domain of observables were administered or as the mean score that would be obtained from an infinitely large number of parallel forms.

Several definitions have been derived from classic true-score theory. For instance, reliability can be defined as the squared correlation between obtained and true scores or the ratio of true-score variance to obtained-score variance where obtained-score variance is the true-score variance plus error variance. This is illustrated in the following formula:

$$\text{Reliability} = \frac{\text{True score variance}}{\text{Obtained score variance}} \qquad \textbf{[5.1]}$$

These theoretical definitions are of little use to the lay person trying to interpret reliability coefficients. They also are not of much use to the practitioner who wants to compute the reliability coefficient.

Parallel Forms Reliability

Parallel forms reliability is a widely favored, although not necessarily often used, method of determining reliability. It is obtained from the correlation between two parallel forms of a test. The two tests can be administered on the same day or the second test can be administered after a period of time. The usual approach is to separate the two administrations by two weeks.

Two tests are defined as parallel if they have the same standard deviation and correlation with the true score and if the variance not explained by the true score is the result of random error (Nunnally, 1968). Again we are faced with the elusive and ephemeral true score. Therefore, the preceding definition is not very useful. For practical purposes we usually consider a test parallel if it was created by the following procedure: (1) a pool of items twice as large as is needed for one test is gathered, and (2) items are assigned to the two tests randomly. One important disadvantage of parallel form reliability is the expense and time needed to develop two forms of the same test.

Factors Suppressing Parallel Forms Reliability

In order to understand what is meant by parallel forms reliability, it is necessary to examine the factors that cause parallel forms reliability to be suppressed. In this section, factors suppressing reliability will be discussed in terms of ability tests where there is a right or wrong answer. The same principles apply to essay tests, where each question may be awarded multiple points, and to personality tests, where there is not a right or wrong answer; instead, different values are awarded to each item, and the items are summed in order to obtain an overall score.

The magnitude of a reliability coefficient is first of all affected by the procedures used to construct the test. These will be discussed at length in Chapter 7, "Classroom Testing." The reliability coefficient is also affected by the stability of the construct when some period of time separates the administration of the two forms of the test, and internal consistency.

Stability

Stability is not a characteristic of the test or test score. It is instead a characteristic of those taking the test. When we say that a test is stable, what we are implying is that those to whom the test is administered are stable with regard to that construct.

While the field of measurement was evolving, most tests focused on ability, a trait that was believed to be stable. It was thought to be stable because it was assumed, at that time, that the major factors determining an individual's possession of an ability trait were innate. Because of the perception that our abilities remain constant, it was not anticipated that subjects were likely to change across the two administrations of the parallel forms of a test, therefore the effect of this factor could be discounted. A more modern view of human characteristics suggests that even though we might not expect a great deal of change, it is certainly reasonable to expect some. One reason for this being true is that an individual's affective state may not be the same on different test days. During one session an individual might be better prepared mentally to take the test—more rested and/or in a better frame of mind—whereas on the other test just the opposite conditions might prevail.

Effect on Ability Tests With ability tests, even following a period as short as two weeks, it is possible that some individuals could increase their knowledge to a degree that would make their score on a second administration of the test somewhat higher. It is also possible that misinformation could be acquired that would have the effect of slightly lowering another individual's score. To the extent that this occurs, measurement error is increased.

Consider a math test, covering simple multiplication, administered to a third-grade class. The test is administered today and then in parallel form in two weeks. We would not expect to obtain different results after two weeks as a result of changes in the subject, but if we did we shouldn't be too surprised. Over the two-week period some students could have improved their knowledge of the multiplication facts. If every student improved to the same degree, this would have no appreciable effect on relative rank or, therefore, on stability. However, if there is a differential effect and some students change more than others, the stability of the test would be affected.

The Stability of Personality Tests The effect that stability has on parallel forms reliability can be expected to be much more important when we examine personality tests. However, because most of our techniques for computing reliability were devised during a period when ability tests were the only assessment instruments employed, changes in the person tested were considered unimportant. This is true even though personality assessment involves constructs that cannot be expected to be particularly stable.

Personality constructs can be classified as either state or trait attributes. Trait attributes are expected to remain stable over time, whereas state attributes are more situational and can be expected to change over time. If you are measuring a state attribute, different results can be expected on separate administrations of a parallel form causing lowered reliability. This lowered reliability may be an indication that the instrument is sensitive in exactly the way that it is intended to be. If the obtained parallel forms reliability is very high for such a test, we should question the validity of the results because a sensitive instrument would be expected to show change over time. For instance, if we develop an instrument to measure situational anxiety, a state attribute, we would expect it to be affected by the circumstances surrounding the test's administration. We would not be pleased to find that we always obtained the same score on an individual no matter how different the testing situation. We would probably be forced to entertain the hypothesis that our instrument was measuring something other than state anxiety.

Internal Consistency

Regardless of how carefully we construct a test, it is highly unlikely that we could develop a test that would yield a parallel forms reliability of 1.0. Even if we administer the parallel forms of a test at the same sitting, to minimize the effect of changes in the subjects, we would not obtain a perfect correlation between the two forms of the test. This is because the two forms of a test, although designated as parallel, would not be exactly the same. This is true even though great pains may have been taken to ensure that the forms were equivalent. The more different the two forms, the smaller the correlation, and therefore the lower our estimate of reliability.

As long as the correct procedures for selecting the parallel forms are followed, the most important factor affecting the degree to which the two parallel forms of a test are dissimilar is the characteristics of the underlying construct and its domain of observables. The most important characteristic of the underlying construct is the internal consistency within the domain of observables.

If we construct two parallel tests by randomly selecting two samples of items from a domain that is characterized by a high degree of internal consistency, it is likely that the two will be more similar than two tests made up of samples selected from a domain that does not have a high degree of internal consistency.

When we say that a test is internally consistent, this means that, for each student, the performance on one item is consistent with the other items. To put this in another way: it is a measure of the intercorrelation among items. As will be learned a little later, intercorrelations among items as low as .25 are considered high and are indications of good overall reliability.

Consider the domain of simple multiplication facts. We would expect the domain to be internally consistent, provided the test was given to a group of students who exhibited sufficient variability in their responses. In a third-grade class where students were first learning multiplication, some students might have completely mastered the task and others might be unable to do any of the problems, while the majority of students fell somewhere in the middle. Under these circumstances this particular task would be internally consistent because knowing how students did on one question would help us predict how they did on others. The most reliable test of multiplication facts would divide the students in two groups: those who got every question right and those who got every question wrong. In this case, every item is a perfect prediction of how a student performed.

Item-Sampling Error Contrast this simple multiplication test with an instrument that measures depression. We can operationally define the construct of depression in terms of a domain consisting of all possible self-report questions that assess the degree of depression of those taking the test. The items from such a domain are unlikely to be characterized by a high level of internal consistency, and a test made up of a sample of such items would similarly lack internal consistency. To Jum C. Nunnally (1968) this is the most important factor in determining reliability. He called this item-sampling error because of the way it could be used to explain why subjects might obtain different scores on two parallel forms of the same test. If the domain is heterogeneous, then it is likely that two samples drawn from the domain would differ by chance alone. Under these circumstances reliability is a function of the internal consistency of the domain.

A test will reflect the internal consistency of its domain only to the extent that it is a random sample from the domain. The usual practice is to construct a test, rather than draw the items randomly from the domain. As a result the reliability of a test may be less a reflection of the internal consistency of the underlying construct it is measuring than the specific procedures used for constructing the test. The normal procedures of item analysis, which use the degree to which items correlate with the total score as a criterion for evaluating items, tend to make tests more internally consistent than their underlying construct.

The Stability and Internal Consistency of Parallel Tests

When the administration of the two forms of a test are separated by a period of time and the reliability is high, it can be assumed that the test is both stable and internally consistent. If the reliability is low it is a good idea to administer the two forms without an intervening time period. If the reliability is increased then we can assume that the test is internally consistent but not stable. If the reliability remains low we might suspect that this is caused by low internal consistency although we have not eliminated the possibility that it also lacks stability. This could be determined directly by computing the internal consistency using one of the methods discussed in the following sections.

Reliability as Internal Consistency

Split-Halves Reliability

One method of assessing reliability that eliminates the time and expense of constructing parallel forms is called split-half reliability. With this method the test is divided into two equal parts that are then correlated.

Although there are a number of ways that this division could be implemented, a test is customarily divided in such a way that the even questions make up one half, while the odd questions make up the other half. The scores from each half are then correlated and the resulting coefficient is used to estimate reliability. The similarity between the split-half approach and the parallel forms method administered without an intervening time period is obvious. The only difference is that with the parallel forms method, the division of items takes place prior to administration, and with the split-half approach the division of items into two forms, or halves, takes place subsequent to administration. This process yields the same information about internal consistency as parallel forms but eliminates the effect of stability when the parallel forms are administered at different times.

Using the Spearman-Brown Formula Because the split-half method is based on a division of the test into two parts, the resulting correlation includes only half as many items as the parallel forms approach. A simplified version of the Spearman-Brown formula is customarily used to adjust for the restricted number of items associated with the split-half method of determining reliability. The formula follows:

$$r_s = \frac{2r_h}{r_h + 1} \qquad \textbf{[5.2]}$$

where

r_s = split-half reliability

r_h = correlation between the two halves of the test.

If the correlation between two halves of a test is .50, the reliability using the Spearman-Brown formula is .66.

$$r_s = \frac{2\,(.50)}{.50 + 1} = \frac{1.0}{1.50} = .66$$

Use of Split-Halves Although the preceding approach provides a good way of estimating reliability, it is not the most widely accepted or used for the following two reasons: (1) although it is mathematically less complex than some of the other methods used to determine reliability, it is not as easy to compute because the division of the test into odd and even parts can be somewhat awkward; (2) it is an indirect method of assessing internal consistency and is therefore not as conceptually straightforward as other methods.

Intercorrelation Among Items

The most direct method of estimating the internal consistency of a construct involves the direct assessment of the intercorrelations among the items on the test. We cannot simply find the average of the intercorrelation, however. When we correlate two items, even if they seem highly related, we will not usually obtain a very large coefficient; consequently, the average of the intercorrelations would seriously underestimate reliability. If the average correlation is adjusted by a factor that takes into account the number of items, it will yield a coefficient equivalent to the value that would be obtained if we correlated test results with a theoretical parallel form of a test (assuming reliability is not affected by stability). The formula for doing this follows:

$$\text{Reliability} = \frac{K(r)}{1 + (k - 1)r} \qquad \textbf{[5.3]}$$

where

K = the number of items on the test
r = the average correlation of the items on the test.

On a test with 40 items, where the average correlation among items is .20, the reliability would be .91.

$$\text{Reliability} = \frac{40\ (.20)}{1 + (40 - 1).20} = \frac{8}{8.8} = .91$$

Notice how a substantial reliability coefficient can be obtained even with the modest average interitem correlation of .20.

Kuder-Richardson 20 (KR-20)

It is of course not easy, even with the use of computers, to compute the average correlation among items. For this reason another formula was designed by the psychometricians G. F. Kuder and M. W. Richardson in 1937 that greatly simplified the computation of reliability. Instead of the average correlation, it requires only the proportion of correct responses to each item. This new formula, however, does require that each item be scored dichotomously as either correct or incorrect. This new formula can be thought of as a computational formula for computing reliability, just as formula 5.3 can be thought of as a definitional formula. It is called Kuder-Richardson 20, or KR-20, to differentiate it from other related formulas developed by these psychometricians. The KR-20 formula follows:

$$\text{KR-20 reliability} = \frac{K}{K-1}\left(1 - \frac{\Sigma pq}{\sigma^2}\right) \qquad [5.4]$$

where

K = the number of items

p = the proportion of correct answers to an item

q = the proportion of incorrect answers to an item ($q = 1 - p$)

σ^2 = the variance of the scores.

In order to compute KR-20 reliability it is necessary to take the decimal value representing the proportion of correct responses (p), multiply it by the proportion of incorrect responses (q), and find the sum of these products. This value is then divided by the variance of the test and subtracted from 1. All of this is then multiplied by a value equal to the number of items divided by the number of items minus 1.

Kuder-Richardson 21 (KR-21)

There is an even simpler formula, KR-21, which, like KR-20, can be used only with a test that has been dichotomously scored. The KR-21 formula requires the assumption that each item has the same level of difficulty. The formula follows:

$$\text{KR-21 reliability} = \frac{K}{K-1}\left(1 - \frac{\overline{X}(K - \overline{X})}{K\sigma^2}\right) \qquad [5.5]$$

where

K = the number of items

$\overline{X}$ = the mean of the test

σ^2 = the variance of the scores.

If a test with forty questions has a mean of 30 and a variance of 16, the reliability would be .54,

$$\text{KR-21 reliability} = \frac{40}{40-1}\left[1 - \frac{30(40-30)}{40(16)}\right] = .54.$$

If the assumption that the proportion of correct answers to each item is the same for all items is not correct, then the KR-21 formula will underestimate reliability.

We are generally less concerned about a procedure that underestimates reliability than one that overestimates it. Whatever the obtained reliability, the consumer knows that the true reliability is at least that high.

How KR-21 Works From just looking at formula 5.4 it may be hard to see its connection with formula 5.3 or with any of the other ways that reliability has been computed up to this point. It seems too simple, being based only on the mean, the variance, and the number of items. It doesn't even include information about the specific items, as do most of the other methods for computing internal consistency. Although it is not based on the use of correlations, it does reflect a separation of the components of variance that forms the basis for correlations.

The formula works conceptually because it reflects the difference between obtained variance and what would have been expected if getting questions right or wrong was merely a function of chance. Reliability increases as the variance on the test increases, over and above what would be expected by chance.

Think of the worst imaginable test, where the response to every question, by each student, was a matter of chance. (Of course you might think that an even worse test would be one on which the best-prepared, most knowledgeable students got lower scores than the least knowledgeable and poorest prepared. If a test consistently yielded such results, it could be inverted, and the highest grades could then go to those with the lowest scores and vice versa). Now consider a second much better test. Both tests have the same number of items and the same mean, but we would expect the second test to have a larger variance. When the items on a test are internally consistent, there will be more of a tendency for a student who gets one item correct to get all other items correct and, similarly, a tendency for the student who gets one item wrong to get other items wrong. This would result in more high scores and more low scores and therefore in more variance. Everything else being equal, the more test score variance exceeds what would be expected to occur by chance, the more internal consistency we can infer.

An Example of KR-21's Computation Two ten-question true-false tests are illustrated in Table 5.1. On test 1 the questions are so poor that whether a student gets an answer correct is a matter of chance. The mean is 4.94 and the variance is 2.55, which you might expect because the scores differ from one another only by chance factors. The reliability of test 1 consequently is .03, reflecting very little internal consistency.

On the second test the opposite picture emerges: there are clearly two distinct groups. Eight students got every question correct and eight got every question wrong. The number of items is the same. The mean is almost the same, 5, but the variance becomes much larger, 25, and consequently the reliability goes from near 0 to 1.0. The reliabilities of actual tests will fall between the two extremes, with the reliability increasing as the variance increases over what could be expected to occur by chance.

The KR-21 formula is simple and straightforward and should routinely be used for any test. A low value will warn the testmaker that something is askew. On a classroom test the first concern should be with the items. The worst items are those for which getting a right or wrong answer is a matter of chance. Items that

TABLE 5.1
Computation of KR-21 Reliability for Two Contrasting True-False Tests

Students	Test 1 Score	Test 2 Score
A	5	10
B	5	10
C	4	10
D	4	10
E	6	10
F	4	10
G	9	10
H	6	10
I	6	0
J	5	0
K	5	0
L	2	0
M	5	0
N	5	0
O	6	0
P	2	0
	$\overline{X} = 4.94$	$\overline{X} = 5$
	$\sigma^2 = 2.55$	$\sigma^2 = 25$
	Reliability = .03	Reliability = 1.0

are either too easy or too hard tend to suppress variance and, therefore, have the effect of lowering reliability.

Determining the Internal Consistency of Tests That Are Not Scored Dichotomously

The two formulas for estimating internal consistency that we have examined so far have required that the data be scored dichotomously. When we want to determine the reliability of a short answer or an essay test on which the student is awarded varying numbers of points depending on the quality of the response or a personality test on which the responses may be given differing values, it is necessary to employ a different formula called coefficient alpha. This formula was developed by Lee J. Cronbach in 1951. Although it was developed subsequent to the KR-20 and KR-21 formulas, it is the most general of the three; the other two can be thought of as special cases of the coefficient alpha formula. In fact, the coefficient alpha formula can be used to compute the reliability of items that are scored dichotomously as well as continuously. Packaged statistical computer programs such as SPSS (Hull & Nie, 1975) use only coefficient alpha because when a computer is used there is no need to worry about computational shortcuts. The formula follows:

$$\text{Coefficient alpha} = \frac{k}{k-1}\left(1 - \frac{\Sigma\sigma_i^2}{\sigma_t^2}\right) \qquad [5.6]$$

where

$$k = \text{the number of items}$$
$$\sigma_i^2 = \text{the variance of each item}$$
$$\Sigma\sigma_i^2 = \text{the sum of the variance of each item}$$
$$\sigma_t^2 = \text{the variance of the entire test.}$$

Test-Retest Reliability

Up to this point, three methods for determining reliability have been discussed: parallel forms, split-half, and other internal consistency methods (KR-20, KR-21, and coefficient alpha). There is another method of assessing reliability called test-retest reliability. With this method the same test is administered twice, with the administrations separated by an interval of about two weeks. The results of the two administrations are then correlated, with the resulting coefficent used as the estimate of reliability. This method of assessing reliability emphasizes stability rather than internal consistency. It is possible to construct a test with almost no internal consistency and still obtain a high reliability coefficent using the test-retest approach. For this reason test-retest reliability estimates usually yield high reliability coefficients; this approach can therefore make a poor test look better than it actually is. Even though it is easier to obtain test-retest reliability than parallel form reliability, it is still more difficult to administer a test twice than just once, as is necessary for the Kuder-Richardson formulas.

Consider a test administered to a fourth-grade student that consists of a long-division problem, a multiple-choice question about American history, and a short-answer question about biology. Such a test would have a little internal consistency, but there is no reason to think that there would be great differences in performance across the two administrations. Those who knew the answers the first time would likely still know them when the test was next administered, and those who did not know the answers the first time would most likely not know them the second time around. For this reason such a test would be likely to yield substantial test-retest reliability while having little internal consistency.

Even with personality tests where the underlying construct is unstable, unrealistically high reliability coefficients can be obtained using the test-retest method because there is a tendency for subjects to remember how they responded to the questions on the first administration and then respond in the same way the second time. One circumstance where the test-retest method of determining reliability is appropriate is when it is necessary to obtain an estimate of the reliability of a speeded test. The reliability of tests on which a student's score is determined mainly by how many relatively easy items can be completed cannot be determined by means of an internal-consistency approach. Under these circumstances test-retest is the only available option.

Technical Factors Affecting Reliability

The technical factors that suppress reliability are independent of the construct measured. They are best thought of as characteristics of the assessment. Good test-development practices should eliminate, or at least ameliorate, their effect. Included as technical factors are the following: quality of items, test length, variability, guessing, and miscellaneous factors.

Quality of Items

If a test has items that are too easy, too hard, poorly written, tricky, or otherwise ambiguous, reliability will be suppressed. Although there may be a myriad of reasons (or excuses) for reliability being low, the quality of the items on a test should be of primary concern and interest to the test maker. The poorer the questions, the more likely it is that a student's score is the result of chance factors or test-taking skills.

Test Length

Another factor that directly affects the magnitude of the reliability coefficient involves the number of items on the test. In general, the more items on a test, the more reliable the test will be, assuming that the items are all of good quality. A longer test with a proportionally greater number of poor items will not have higher reliability than the shorter test with a larger proportion of good items.

Why Short Tests Have Low Reliability The fact that we obtain higher reliability when we include more items on a test makes sense because a few items are likely to represent a poor sample from the domain of possible items. This in turn is unlikely to provide an accurate indication of a subject's capacity to perform on all items in the domain. A short test may emphasize only one aspect of the domain, and there may be an interaction between the particular emphasis of a test and the specific strengths of different subjects taking the test. The student whose aptitudes match the particular facet of content being assessed will do better than the less fortunate student who is being tested over a particular aspect with which he or she is familiar. Luck plays a larger role with a shorter test because a few lucky or unlucky guesses can greatly affect a student's overall score. With a longer test, guessing is likely to have less influence on the outcome. Because they occur in larger numbers, lucky and unlucky guesses are likely to cancel each other.

A Mathematical Explanation It is also possible to take a mathematical approach to explaining how increasing the number of items on a test will improve reliability. We have previously defined reliability as the ratio of obtained to true variance. The more closely obtained variance approximates true variance, the higher the reliability of a test. This is because obtained variance is equal to the sum of true variance and error variance. If true and obtained scores are similar, there must be very little error variance.

According to classic true-score theory, doubling the number of items will quadruple true variance while it only doubles error variance. To illustrate this point consider a test with 30 questions that has a reliability of .60 with an obtained score variance of 25. Suppose we want to determine what the reliability would be if we doubled the number of items. By entering these values into formula 5.7, which is

$$\text{Reliability} = \frac{\text{True score variance}}{\text{Obtained score variance}} \quad [5.7]$$

and solving for true variance, we obtain the value of 15. We also know that error variance must be 10 because error variance is equal to obtained variance minus true variance (25 − 15 = 10). By doubling the number of items, we quadruple the true variance, making it 60. At the same time we only double the error variance, making it 20. The obtained variance then becomes the sum of true and error variance, or 80 (60 + 20 = 80). Because reliability is equal to true over obtained variance, the new reliability is .75. This represents a substantial increase in reliability. This procedure is simplified in the Spearman-Brown formula that follows:

$$r_n = \frac{nr_s}{(n-1)r_s + 1}, \quad [5.8]$$

where

r_n = the reliability of the test lengthened by a factor of n

n = the factor by which the test has been lengthened (for instance, if the test is doubled in length, $n = 2$; if it is tripled in length, $n = 3$)

r_s = the reliability of the shorter test.

Using the previous example, where the test length was doubled, we find that,

$$r_n = \frac{2\ (.60)}{(2-1)\ .60 + 1} = \frac{1.20}{1.60} = .75,$$

which is the same result obtained before. If you look carefully, you will find that this is another form of formula 5.3.

Test Length and Reliability—Practical Considerations Test developers need to be cautioned that this increase in reliability only occurs when the additional items are of a level of quality equal to those on the shorter test. This poses a problem because most test developers are already struggling to get a minimum number of good questions. In many cases, increasing the number of items is not practical or realistic.

A further point needs emphasis. It is not legitimate to report scores in terms of how high the reliability might have been had the number of items been increased.

Test developers are further warned not to make excuses about low reliability by estimating how high it would have been if only more items had been included in the test. That practice is on a par with the student who insists on being evaluated on the basis of the score on a test that he or she would have obtained had an adequate amount of time been spent studying.

The main application of the Spearman-Brown formula is for use with split-halves estimates of reliability, but it also can be used as a way of convincing test developers of the value of increasing the number of items on a test.

Variability

Reliability increases as test-score variance increases. The magnitude of test-score variance is determined directly by the degree of variability among the groups being tested. When there is a great deal of variability among the students taking a test, scores will be more spread out, and therefore the ranking of students will tend to be stable.

Item Difficulty Variability is suppressed when a test is either too easy or too difficult. For this reason, tests of average difficulty are usually more reliable. A test of average difficulty is defined as a test on which the average student gets a score half way between the chance level and the highest possible score. If one must choose between a test that is harder or easier than this, it is probably better to select the easier test because such a test is more likely to have a positive effect on student morale. In addition, with a harder test there is more of a tendency for students to guess, which lowers reliability.

How Variability Affects Reliability Because reliability is based, for the most part, on correlation coefficients, suppressed variance will have the same effect on reliability that it has on the correlation coefficient, which is to lower it. When a group of students all obtain similar scores on one form of a test, their position relative to other students will not likely stay the same on the alternate form of the test. This is because when scores are bunched together, a small change in raw score will lead to large changes in relative position. If scores are spread out (variability is high), it is more likely that the relative position in the group will remain stable across the two forms of the test and the correlation coefficient will be relatively large.

Guessing

The more students guess on a test, the more likely it is that the results of two parallel administrations of a test will not be in agreement simply because a student is likely to be luckier on one test than the other. The fact that some students are more willing to guess than others also adds to this difference. Willingness to guess is particularly important when tests are speeded because not every student has enough time to finish the test. Under these circumstances students who blindly guess on questions that there is insufficient time to answer carefully will do better than students who leave the answer blank.

Controlling Guessing On some standardized tests attempts are made to control for the effects of guessing by means of the correction-for-guessing formula. The method used to correct for guessing in the formula consists of subtracting raw-score points from the score of the person who guesses, equivalent to the gain that can be expected from guessing. On a multiple-choice test with four alternatives, a student can be expected, by chance alone, to get one out of four answers correct by guessing. Therefore, for every three questions a student gets wrong, he or she can be expected to get one right by guessing. In order to operationalize this logic, the following formula is used:

$$\text{Corrected score} = R - \frac{W}{N - 1}, \qquad [5.9]$$

where

R = number of right answers

W = number of wrong answers

N = number of alternatives.

Criticisms of the Correction-for-Guessing Formula The correction-for-guessing formula has been criticized both because its assumptions are difficult to meet and because it does not usually succeed at what it purports to do, which is to correct for guessing. The formula is based on the following two assumptions: (1) that all guesses are blind guesses, with each response having an equal probability of occurring; and (2) that every wrong answer results from guessing. The first assumption rejects the possibility that a student might make an educated guess based on partial information. If this were to happen, the probabilities expressed in formula 5.2 would change. On a four-response multiple-choice test, the probability that a student will obtain a correct answer becomes greater than 1 in 4. Only when you have a highly speeded test, where it is not possible to give a reasoned response to all questions, will you have students engaged in truly blind guessing.

The second assumption rejects the possibility that a student, after careful deliberation, but on the basis of faulty information, could still select the wrong answer. Taken together these two assumptions suggest that a student either knows the right answer or does not—and in the latter case knows that he or she does not know it. For this reason any wrong answers are assumed to be the result of guessing.

Undercorrection On a four-response multiple-choice test, the formula will undercorrect to the extent that a student chooses answers based on partial information or can eliminate responses and guess which of the remaining responses is correct. Under these circumstances the student is well advised to guess: the penalty for guessing is less than the expected increase in score that would be expected to accrue to the student who guessed. If even one alternative can be eliminated, guessing will help the student's score. On the other hand, non-testwise students are likely to be intimidated by the knowledge that the correction-for-guessing formula is being employed, and for this reason they may refrain from guessing.

Overcorrection The correction-for-guessing formula is most likely to overcorrect on tests that emphasize higher-level thought processes. On such a test there will be a larger proportion of students who get items wrong because they were unable to correctly employ the cognitive processes required. For instance, in solving a problem requiring mathematical computations, a student may make arithmetic errors. Although such errors really should not be classified as guesses, they will be when the correction-for-guessing formula is employed, and this causes overcorrection.

When the Assumptions Are Met Even under circumstances where the test is highly speeded and guessing is blind and random, the correction-for-guessing formula does not punish the student for guessing. If individuals get the same number of questions right that would be expected to by chance, they will be brought to the point where they would have been had they not guessed. On a four-alternative multiple-choice test, for every three wrong answers, a student would get one answer correct by guessing alone. Of course it does not happen exactly like that. Some students will be lucky and get more of their fair share of questions right by guessing, whereas others will be unlucky and get fewer than their fair share right. The correction-for-guessing formula can do nothing about these circumstances. The formula corrects for guessing but not for the luck of the guesser.

Technical Limitations Another drawback to the use of this formula is that it does not change the rank order of students if no questions are omitted. Under these circumstances there is a perfect correlation between raw scores and corrected scores. Only when there are omitted responses does the correlation become less than 1.0, and even then it remains in the .90s (Ebel, 1979).

Reliability and validity are increased only if there is a positive correlation between omitted responses and the raw score (Ebel, 1979). Of course this is a circumstance that would not normally be expected to occur because the student who works most quickly and answers the most questions is usually going to be the better student. Additionally, the more testwise students are likely both to answer more questions and also do better on the test overall.

Improving the Formula It would be possible to employ a correction-for-guessing formula that would be even stricter. For instance, on a four-alternative multiple-choice test one point could be deducted for every incorrect answer, rather than one-third point, as is done in formula 5.2.

Students who were made aware of this procedure would be more likely to leave a question blank, unless they were sure of their answer, than risk the large penalty for guessing. Such an approach would certainly diminish guessing, but it is not clear that it would yield a more reliable test because the ability to make educated guesses is an important skill closely related to a student's overall grasp of the subject matter; an increased number of omitted questions would have the effect of shortening the test and lowering reliability. There is little to be gained from discouraging guessing in this way.

Why Is It Used? You might, at this point, be asking why, given the previous discussion, the correction-for-guessing formula is ever employed. The motivation of those employing this procedure does not seem to have as much to do with actually correcting for guessing as it does with intimidating students into not guessing. Because guessing contributes directly to error variance, it is believed that the use of this procedure might increase reliability. Because reliability coefficients are the most easily obtainable and objective evidence of the quality of a test, a great deal of emphasis is placed on these indices, and even slight increases in reliability will be hailed as improvements in a test.

There is a cost, of course, and it involves the fact that while the correction-for-guessing formula might result in a somewhat lower measurement error, it increases the importance of testwiseness. The testwise student guesses to his or her advantage, whereas the non-testwise student is afraid to guess and ends up with a lower score. Because it is anticipated that testwiseness correlates with the total score on the test, the introduction of this factor enhances rather than subtracts from reliability. This would occur to the degree that test-wiseness was internally consistent and correlated with the construct being measured. Validity might be lowered because, instead of being a pure measurement of the intended construct, the score is contaminated by test-wiseness.

Scorer Reliability

The degree to which reliability is affected by test scoring is called scorer reliability. When several scorers are used, scorer reliability can be determined from intercorrelations. If only one scorer is used, the extent of this cause of measurement error is not easily determined. Just because it is not easily assessed does not mean that it does not exist, however.

Scorer reliability does not typically play an important role in determining the size of the coefficient when objective tests are used, but it may be important in the determination of the reliability of more subjectively scored tests. This factor places a limit on the possible reliability of a test because the overall reliability of a test cannot exceed the reliability of the scorers.

Sample Size

Another factor that can affect reliability involves the number of subjects in the group taking the test upon which reliability is being computed. The larger the sample, the more stable the correlation coefficient will be. Smaller samples will typically yield coefficients that are either too high or too low. For this reason it is wise to not place too much credence in coefficients based on small samples.

Physical Conditions

The physical conditions of testing can also affect the size of the reliability coefficient. Poor heating, lighting, and/or seating arrangements can have a differential effect on student performance, with some students affected more than others.

The effect is even greater when these conditions differ across the parallel administrations of the test. In addition to these physical characteristics, distractions such as loud noises or outbursts can be expected to affect reliability. The manner in which instructions are presented and the degree to which they are kept standardized may also have an impact on the size of the reliability coefficient. Finally, errors in the computation of the test scores and/or errors in machine scoring will suppress the magnitude of the reliability coefficient.

Standard Error of Measurement (SEM)

The standard error of measurement (SEM) is intended to convey the same information that is provided by the reliability coefficient and it can be computed directly from that value using the following formula:

$$SEM = SD\sqrt{1 - \text{reliability}} \qquad [5.10]$$

In words this means that, to obtain the standard error of measurement, we subtract the reliability coefficient from 1, compute the square root of this value, and multiply the result by the standard deviation. If the reliability of a test is .91 and the standard deviation is 10, the SEM would be 3 (the square root of 1 − .91 = .3, which, when multiplied times 10, yields 3).

The main use for the SEM is to construct confidence bands around a test score. For instance, if, on a classroom test, a student obtains a score of 36 and the test has a SEM of 3, it can be said that, if we repeated the measurement many times, 68 percent of the time the true score would be between 33 and 39, and 95 percent of the time between 30 and 42. It is, however, not accurate to say that the range of 30 to 42 represents a 95 percent confidence zone (Cronbach, 1970).

The probability associated with the width of a confidence band is derived from the relationship between the standard deviation and the normal curve, which was explained in Chapter 2. In that chapter it was shown how the probability that a score would occur between two raw-score points could be computed from Table A.1 in the Appendix.

The standard error is in the same scale as the data on which it is computed. For a classroom test it would be in raw-score form, and for an IQ test it would be in IQ points. This means that we cannot evaluate standard errors independently of their scale. The reliability coefficient was devised in order to provide a standard measure of the consistency of a test independent of its scale.

For instance, the SAT has a standard error of 30, whereas the American College Test (ACT) has a standard error of one. This difference in a standard error size is the result of the much larger standard deviation associated with the SAT, and not because the ACT is more reliable. The reliability coefficients of the two tests can be directly compared.

SUMMARY

1. Reliability and validity are the two major criteria for evaluating an assessment instrument.
2. A test can be reliable without being valid, but before a test can be valid it must first be reliable.
3. Reliability is easy to compute but difficult to define and interpret.
4. Validity is difficult to compute but relatively easy to define and interpret.
5. Most test manuals include far more information about reliability than validity.
6. Reliability can be defined either in terms of technical mathematical definitions or by means of operational definitions.
7. There are four main methods of determining reliability: parallel forms, split half, internal consistency, and test retest.
8. The main factors affecting reliability are changes in those tested and item-sampling error.
9. Parallel forms reliability assesses both changes in subjects and item-sampling error.
10. Coefficient Alpha, KR20, and KR21 are measures of item-sampling error assessed by means of internal consistency.
11. Split-half reliability provides an indirect estimate of internal consistency, which appears simple and straightforward but is more difficult to compute than the more direct methods of assessing reliability.
12. There are a number of technical factors that affect the magnitude of reliability coefficients: the quality of items, test length, variability, item difficulty, guessing, scorer reliability, and the physical conditions of testing.

SUGGESTED READINGS

ALLEN, M. J., & YEN, W. M. (1979). *Introduction to measurement theory.* Monterey, CA: Brooks/Cole. [This is a clear but mathematical description of reliability from a true-score theory prospective.]

CRONBACH, L. J., GLESER, G. C., NANDA, H., & RAJARATNAM, N. (1972). *The dependability of behavioral measurements: Theory of generalizability for scores and profiles.* New York: Wiley. [This is the basic source of information on generalizability theory, which represents an extremely sophisticated method of examining reliability.]

NUNNALLY, J. C. (1978). *Psychometric theory* (2nd ed.). New York: McGraw-Hill. [This is perhaps the most complete and thorough discussion of reliability available. It also includes a discussion of the relationship between classic true-score theory and domain-sampling theory.]

6

Validity

OVERVIEW

When tests and other measurements are used, there is a need to separate the good from the bad. The two major criteria for making this distinction are reliability and validity. The complexities surrounding the establishment of reliability have already been discussed in Chapter 5. Although the definitions of validity are somewhat more accessible than those for reliability, establishing validity is difficult because we often need a variety of types of information and cannot always depend on the availability of concrete numerical coefficients. For this reason there is a lamentable tendency for test publishers either to avoid mention of validity or to include it in only a cursory fashion. This is unfortunate because validity is the most important trait that scores from an assessment instrument can have.

The validity of test scores is established through three approaches: criterion-related, construct-related, and content-related validity. Validity should be thought of as unitary; each of these approaches is used to provide evidence to support the validity of a test. One of these approaches may be more appropriate than the others for a specific test, but the strongest case for validity will result from employing all three.

The purpose of this chapter is to give the reader an understanding of when each approach to determining validity should be used, along with information about the strengths and weaknesses of each.

OBJECTIVES

In this chapter you will learn how validity is established using three different approaches. Specifically you will learn the following:

- The definition of validity.
- When and how to employ the criterion approaches to establishing validity.
- The steps required for the implementation of the construct approach to validity.
- The situations where the construct approach to establishing validity is most necessary.

- The methods of using the analysis of a test's content to establish validity.
- The reasons that a unitary view of validity is more useful than the categorical approach.
- The special case of face validity and the conditions in which it is important.

Objectives

Introduction

When we examine a test score we generally assume that its magnitude provides an indication of the degree to which an individual possesses a construct. Validity provides a means of evaluating whether that assumption is justified. It therefore refers to the legitimacy of the inferences that we make about a score.

We need to remember that it is not the test itself that is either valid or invalid. It is the interpretation of the results in the form of scores and the degree to which they assess the construct being assessed that should be evaluated in terms of their validity.

Because we may want to make many different types of inferences, it is possible for the results of a test to be valid for one purpose and invalid for another. The results of an interest inventory might accurately indicate which individuals are interested in a specific job; they might be valid for that purpose but be invalid for selecting those likely to be successful on the job. Therefore, before we can know whether the results of a test are valid, we must know how the test is to be used. We should never flatly state that a test is valid, we should instead specify the degree of the validity of the results of a test under different circumstances.

Methods of Assessing Validity

In the past, validity was divided into categories based on the method of its computation. This resulted in three or four types of validity, depending on whether face validity (which will be discussed at the conclusion of this chapter) is included or not. This categorical approach is espoused in most measurement textbooks and is the point of view supported by the 1974 version of the *Standards for Educational and Psychological Tests*. This document has been revised (1985) and now takes the position that validity is unitary, and that each of what used to be considered types can now be better thought of as approaches to establishing validity.

The reason that this view of validity has changed, as pointed out by Samuel Messick (1981), is that the use of separate types of validity gives the impression that the different methods are equal and that the test developer needs only to select one and use it to establish validity. During the 1970s, a time of considerable litigation over testing, the courts began to use the 1974 standards, with their emphasis on types of validity, as the basis for testimony concerning the validity of tests. This caused problems because the different approaches are not equivalent and do not provide equal evidence for the validity of test results.

It is better to think of validity as a unitary trait with each approach providing evidence for validity. Furthermore, establishing validity is relative rather than absolute, and the accumulation of as much evidence as possible, through the use of all three approaches, is desirable. In the following sections, the different types of evidence used for establishing validity are described.

Criterion-Related Validity

The criterion approach to establishing validity involves the demonstration of a relationship between test scores and a criterion that is usually, but not necessarily, another test. Correlational techniques are generally employed to accomplish this.

The criterion approach is most often used to evaluate the scores from aptitude tests because these instruments are intended to predict concrete behaviors. The objectivity of criterion validity makes it attractive for such applied settings as evaluating civil service tests, employee selection procedures, and tests used for making educational decisions. These can range from instruments used to decide which child should be placed in preschool to who should be accepted into law or medical school. It would be desirable to have criterion evidence to evaluate the validity of all tests, but usually no acceptable criterion exists.

Types of Criterion-Related Validity

Concurrent Criterion-Related Validity Concurrent criterion-related validity is employed when an accepted method of assessment already exists. Of course the existence of a method of assessment so widely endorsed that it would be accepted as a criterion might argue against the need for the development of new ways of assessing a construct. In addition, the fact that we have gone to the trouble to develop a way to measure something suggests that an acceptable method of assessment does not already exist.

The criterion is usually a test, but this is not the only form it can take. For instance, the results of a self-report inventory intended to assess an individual's medical history could be validated by actual medical records.

The criterion approach is most appropriate when the development of a test results from the need or perceived need for shorter or more efficient methods of measuring a construct. The validity of the results of the new test is assessed by computing the correlation coefficient between it and the new test. For many years now the Stanford-Binet fulfilled this role for intelligence tests. All new intelligence tests are compared against this standard. If a reasonably high correlation could be established with the Stanford-Binet, the new test was said to have concurrent validity. A good example of this is the Kaufman Assessment Battery for Children. Before it appeared on the market, studies of its relationship with the Stanford-Binet had already been conducted.

It is usually not possible to assess the validity of the results of personality tests using concurrent validity because existing personality tests have not acquired sufficient acceptance to warrant their use as a criterion.

The Predictive Approach The predictive approach is the most often-used type of criterion-related validity. It involves an evaluation of a test score's capacity to make predictions about future performance. Scholastic aptitude tests, tests for identifying individuals with special talents, and job aptitude tests are examples for which the predictive approach to establishing validity would be particularly useful.

The Difficulty in Obtaining Criterion Measures

Although the criterion approach appears to be ideal, it is in fact not always easy to establish validity in this way. The biggest problem with this approach stems from the lack of good criterion measures. In most cases either no criterion is available, or it is seriously flawed.

It is quite difficult to obtain high validity coefficients for tests intended to predict who will be successful on a job and who will not. This is because there are few good measures of job success. Production measures, such as amount of inventory produced in a manufacturing setting, or amount of a product sold in a sales position, appear to be good criteria; however, in actual practice they do not work well. Production in a factory or dollar amount of sales is often too dependent on the actions of more than one person or on factors other than competence.

Ratings are a more often-used criterion for establishing the validity of job-related tests. As explained in Chapter 16, ratings have important limitations, particularly their poor reliability. When the reliability of the criterion measure is low, high validity coefficients are unlikely to be obtained because the correlation between two tests cannot exceed the reliability of either.

Restricted Range

The ideal procedure for validating the results of a job-related test is to administer the test to a large pool of candidates, obtain scores, place all the candidates on the job, and evaluate their performance at some later date. The correlation between test scores and job performance can be used to determine the degree to which the test was effective in discriminating between those who were successful on the job and those who were not. There is of course an obvious problem with such an approach. It would be difficult to find employers willing to hire large numbers of employees, many of whom obviously would not be successful workers, for the sole purpose of validating the results of a test. Instead, a different procedure is almost always used. Tests are administered to a large pool of candidates, and the best are selected on the basis of their test performance and on any other criteria that might be deemed appropriate. After an appropriate amount of time, the test scores are correlated with a measure of job performance.

This approach is unsatisfactory because the obtained correlations only evaluate the capacity of the test results to discriminate among different levels of success. Because the test is presumably intended to determine who should be hired, the emphasis should be on how effectively the test scores can discriminate between those who will succeed on the job and those who will fail.

It is more difficult to obtain high validity coefficients when differentiating among levels of success because the range of performance on both the test and the criterion is restricted. The result may be an underestimate of the validity of the test's results.

The Validity of the Scholastic Aptitude Test (SAT) Problems associated with the determination of the validity of academic aptitude tests can be illustrated by the controversy that has surrounded the Scholastic Aptitude Test (SAT) published by ETS. Much of the concern about the SAT involves the validity of the scores obtained. Establishing the validity of the test seems straightforward. One needs only to compute the correlation between a sample of students' scores on the SAT and their grade-point average (GPA) after they have been in school. Unfortunately, establishing validity is not quite as easy as it might first appear.

Thousands of such studies have been conducted, and the coefficients obtained range from almost zero to the high .70s. The median value for the multiple correlation of both Verbal and Quantitative sections yields coefficients of around .40. The first problem of interpretation involves the issue of whether this is a high or low validity coefficient. For those who favor the use of the test, this appears to be a substantial coefficient, while for those who opppose its use, it is too small. Actually the obtained correlations are unlikely to be accurate indicators of test-score validity. This is because they are likely to be underestimates of the relationship between the test scores and GPAs. This is caused by restrictions in the range of grades because of grade inflation, and in the range of SAT scores because schools generally accept students from a narrow range of scores. Selective schools are unwilling to admit students who are poor risks. At the same time, those schools that do accept students with low scores probably don't admit many students with high scores.

Higher-education policy is now changing as a result of declining enrollment. More and more colleges and universities are being forced to accept students with lower SAT scores, which leads to a wider range in scores and, consequently, to higher validity coefficients. We are now faced with the irony that, as SAT test scores become less important, their validity is increasing.

In Chapter 15 the technical problems and controversies that have surrounded the procedures used to determine the validity of the scores obtained from the SAT are discussed in more detail.

Which Is the Predictor and Which Is the Criterion?

The relationship between the predictor and the criterion needs to be kept in mind because the two are sometimes confused. There is an often-told story in higher education about the student who is accepted into a graduate program despite low aptitude-test scores. The student is successful in the program, but later his or her degree is withheld until satisfactory test scores can be obtained. This is illogical because the results of the aptitude test are intended only as a predictor of academic performance; if the two are not in agreement, it is the aptitude test that should be questioned.

How Large Should the Validity Coefficient Be?

The magnitude of the coefficient obtained should not be evaluated in terms of its deviation from a perfect correlation of 1.0. As was emphasized in Chapter 2, there are many factors that suppress the magnitude of the obtained correlation. A more reasonable criterion would be the improvement in prediction an aptitude test provides when compared to the prediction obtained when either a different aptitude test is used or the prediction is made without the use of an aptitude test.

Academic aptitude tests are intended for use in schools that have a limited enrollment and are selecting those to be admitted from a large pool of students. If there are no restrictions on enrollment and the test is administered in order to eliminate those students at the lower end of the scale who are least likely to succeed, it is important that the validity of the test scores be established for these purposes.

Construct-Related Validity

Our language is rich in words used to describe classes of behaviors, such as *intelligence*, *self-confidence*, *creativity*, and *reading comprehension*. These terms refer to entities with no objective reality that exist only as descriptors. They are called constructs, and psychologists, along with other social scientists, have a large investment in their use.

A major purpose of measurement is to take these constructs and quantify them on scales, with numbers corresponding to the amount of the trait that the individual possesses. For instance, psychologists might describe self-concept as a trait that the subjects of an experiment possess in varying degrees. The usual procedure for assessing such a construct would be to employ an instrument that yields a numerical value to indicate the degree to which individual subjects in the experiment possess the trait. Such an instrument would usually consist of a series of statements relevant to the construct, self-concept. Subjects would be asked to endorse or not to endorse the series of statements. A score could be obtained by summing across the responses. This score is intended to reflect the amount of the construct the subjects possess.

The purpose of construct-related evidence of validity is the determination of the degree to which the scores on such an instrument are a true reflection of the construct. Just because a test or instrument has a title that implies the measurement of a specific construct does not mean that the test actually measures it. Whether the results of a test accurately reflect the degree to which an individual is characterized by a construct must be established in an empirical fashion through the use of construct-related evidence of validity.

Establishing Construct-Related Validity

With construct-related evidence of validity we do not enjoy the convenience of a single validity coefficient. Instead we must develop a logical validation, based on empirical data, which takes the form of an extended argument. This means that before we can accept the view that a test measures what it purports to measure, a logical case for why inferences about a construct derived from scores on a particular instrument must be established.

The accruing of construct-related evidence of validity takes place in three phases: first, by determining whether a single entity is being measured; second, through a description of the theory on which the construct is based; and third, by means of an examination of empirical data to determine whether the construct interacts with other variables in a predictable fashion.

Unidimensionality For a test to be unidimensional, it must have two characteristics: (1) it must be measuring *something*, and (2) it must measure one and only one trait. It is measuring something if its variability exceeds what could be expected to occur by chance. Factor analysis can be used to determine if a single trait is being measured; the stronger the factor, the more sure we can be that something is being measured. Internal consistency reliability also provides evidence that something is being measured. Furthermore, if more than one trait is being assessed, the size of this coefficient will be relatively small. Although high internal consistency indicates that one factor is being measured and that it is being measured well, a small coefficient may leave us unsure of whether the test is measuring more than one construct or is measuring nothing very well.

If a test cannot meet these two conditions, it is not measuring the construct it is intended to measure. However, just because a test measures a single trait and measures it well does not mean that it measures the right trait. For example, Allen Edwards (1953), in a now classic study, demonstrated that, on self-report personality tests, subjects tended to endorse items according to how socially desirable they perceived the items to be, rather than on the degree to which they described the trait they were intended to measure. It is possible to obtain sizable internal-consistency reliability coefficients with such instruments. This is because the test is reliably measuring the subject's social intelligence or ability to make good judgments about the social desirability of items, but not necessarily the aspect of personality it is supposed to assess.

Description of Theory The second step in accruing construct-related evidence of validity is more difficult to accomplish than the first because it is less concrete than the statistical determination of internal consistency or factor analysis. It requires the description of the theory that underlies the construct being measured. For instance, construct-related evidence of validity for the results of a test intended to assess field dependence would include a detailed explanation of what is meant by "field independence." The theory should encompass, as much as possible, a definition and a delineation of the domain of observables that define the construct. In this particular case, it would be necessary to include the ways the trait is manifested and the various tests that might be used to assess its existence. In addition, the correlates of the construct would need to be described. This would include the way other measures are related to the construct, which variables would show a positive relationship with the construct, and those for which the correlation would be negative. It also is necessary to list variables that could be expected to have only a minor relationship to the construct under consideration.

Empirical Analysis The third stage in accruing construct-related evidence of validity requires the use of empirical evidence. This is usually done in an ex post facto fashion. The first step would be to compute correlations with other relevant measures. Construct-related evidence would result from the demonstration that the obtained correlations were in the expected direction, as outlined in the theory of the construct.

Construct-related validity can also be established using an experimental approach. This provides more precise evidence of construct-related validity, but it is usually time consuming and expensive. It also may violate accepted conventions concerning the appropriate use of human subjects. One example of an experimental approach to obtaining construct-related evidence of validity would involve artificially inducing anxiety in an experimental group, but not in a control group, and then assessing both with an instrument intended to measure anxiety. It would be expected that much higher scores for anxiety would be obtained in the group where anxiety was induced. If this did not occur, the validity of the scores on the instrument would be impugned. Even though such an approach might provide strong evidence for construct validity, test developers might feel uncomfortable about inducing anxiety and the ethical questions such an approach would raise.

Content-Related Validity

Content-related validity is defined as the degree to which the set of items included on a particular test are representative of the entire domain of items that the test is intended to assess. If you were planning to assess a student's ability to multiply single-digit numbers and you intended to include less than the one hundred possible number combinations, it would be necessary to select your sample of number pairs in such a way that they would be representative of the entire universe of possible items. If the test were not representative, perhaps because it included a disproportionate amount of low numbers, it would not be possible to legitimately infer from this one test an understanding of the student's overall grasp of simple multiplication.

The most important step in establishing content-related validity is to specify the domain of all possible items that could be included on the test. In the case of a simple math test, it is easy to delineate the domain of items, to specify a procedure for selecting a representative sample from this domain, and to evaluate the effectiveness of the item-selection process. This is unusual because the domains of most tests are large and diverse, which complicates the process of their definition and renders the process of ensuring representativeness in the test sample difficult. The number of items in most domains is nearly infinite. For instance, we cannot begin to describe all possible items that might be included on an intelligence test, achievement test, or personality adjustment scale.

Another impediment to the precise description of a domain is the use of item analysis. When only items with appropriate characteristics are included on a test, which is the purpose of item analysis, the representativeness of the items is further limited. Direct evidence about whether the domain has been adequately sampled is difficult to accumulate. Therefore, in practice, evidence for content-related validity tends to focus on the processes employed in test development and on a determination of whether they are likely to lead to a test that is representative of the domain of all possible items.

A further step in establishing content validity involves the use of a table of specifications, such as is illustrated in Table 6.1. As can be seen, the content is listed in column form along the left margin, and the levels of the items are listed across the top of the table. The numbers in the matrix represent the percentage of each category of items included.

The Legal Implications of Content-Related Validity

In recent years the importance of content-related evidence of validity has been increased by state and federal courts that, in cases where the legitimacy of a test is at issue, have tended to accept and have even encouraged the provision of evidence concerning content-related validity. This is an example of the misuse of the categorical approach to validity, which permits the defenders of a test's use to select the easiest type of validity to establish. All that is necessary is the provision of evidence that the content is appropriate. This approach to validity provides little indication of whether inferences about test scores are legitimate; it resembles face validity, which is a dubious form of validity (face validity is described on page 132).

Examples of the use of content validity in legal settings include civil service and employment screening tests. Content validity has now become a crucial element

TABLE 6.1 A Table of Specifications for a Test in a Course in Human Development and Learning, Showing the Percentage of Items in Terms of Content and Question Level

	Question Levels			
Content Area	**Recognition**	**Comprehension**	**Application**	**Total**
Introduction	5	10	5	20
Biological bases of behavior	7	7	6	20
Infant development	3	14	3	20
Child development	4	10	6	20
Adolescent development	6	9	5	20
Total	25	25	25	100

in court cases involving minimum competency testing (see Chapter 11, "Minimum Competency Testing").

The legal implications of content-related validity are best illustrated by the challenges to Florida's minimum competency test. The instrument used in Florida, which is called a functional literacy test, was first administered in the fall of 1977.

In the series of court cases that followed, a major issue was the content validity of the test. While the original court upheld the content validity of the test, it was demonstrated to the appellate court that a test could have content validity and still be unfair because content validity is only an indication that the test adequately assesses the items associated with a set of objectives. It does not address the issue of whether the objectives are fair—that is, whether the objectives of a state's mimimum competency testing (MCT) program are the same as the local school district's and whether the content assessed is actually taught to students in school.

Because of the limitations of content-related validity as it relates to MCT, the concept has been broadened to include both curricular validity and instructional validity. Curricular validity refers to the degree to which a test measures the curriculum of a school system; instructional validity is the determination of whether what is included on a test is actually taught to students. This subject is discussed in more detail in Chapter 11, "Minimum Competency Testing."

These reconceptualizations of content-related validity push it even further from the realm of validity as the term is usually used. Instructional validity seems almost completely divorced from any connection with a determination of the degree to which a test measures a construct. James Popham (1983) prefers "adequacy of preparation" to instructional validity. Although the fairness of a test is important, it is an altogether different concept from validity as it has been defined up to this point.

The Limitations of Content Validity

Measurement specialists (Messick, 1981; Guion, 1977) have questioned whether content validity should be considered a form of validity. Validity refers to the legitimacy of inferences made about the existence of constructs based on test scores, but content-related validity focuses only on the content of the test. It is possible to present convincing evidence for content-related validity for the results of a test on which inferences about the test scores cannot easily be made.

First of all, a test that includes all of the relevant content could be so technically deficient that it fails to measure the intended construct. It is also possible for a test to have both good content validity and good reliability and yet still not have construct validity. This could happen because the process of making items fit into the objective format of a standardized test may cause them to be written in such a way that they assess cognitive processes that differ in subtle ways from what is intended. For example, there is probably no testing procedure as pervasive as the weekly spelling test used in the typical American elementary school classroom. An achievement test cannot use the usual format in which the words are read aloud by the teacher and are written by the student. On standardized tests a different approach must be employed, such as requiring the student to pick out the correctly spelled from among several misspelled words, or the incorrectly spelled word from among correctly spelled words. Such a procedure utilizes different cognitive processes than the usual spelling test format.

Although good content-related validity practices require that the underlying psychological processes be considered along with the content, in actual practice this is not easy to accomplish. A student can get the correct answer to an item for a myriad of different reasons, and it is difficult to examine an item and make a determination of just what it is assessing. This is because we cannot anticipate, with any degree of accuracy, the cognitive processes that take place in the brains of those responding to the item. For this reason most attempts to establish content validity focus on the items on a test rather than on the behaviors they elicit and the underlying cognitive processes with which they are related. The solution is not to eliminate the content-related approach to establishing the validity of test results, but to recognize its limitations and utilize it as one of several sources of evidence rather than the sole basis for validation.

Improving Content-Related Validity

A method of providing evidence of content-related validity that promises to be an improvement over current practices is the domain-referenced approach to criterion-reference testing advocated by Popham (1981). This approach is described in more detail in Chapter 10, "Criterion-Referenced Testing." Briefly, domain-referenced testing defines instructional objectives in terms of how items are generated to assess them. This informs users about what a test is measuring in terms of specific behaviors. Although there are practical as well as theoretical disadvantages to this approach, it does show promise as a useful direction for future developments in establishing content validity.

Limitations of the Categorical View of Validity

Earlier views of validity emphasized a categorical approach that divided validity into different types, with each type assigned to a different kind of test. With this approach, aptitude tests are evaluated using criterion validity, achievement tests are evaluated with content validity, and instruments assessing personality are evaluated with either criterion or construct validity.

With the publication of the 1985 version of the *Joint Technical Standards for Educational and Psychological Testing*, the interpretation of validity shifted to a unitary view. The goal of test validation is no longer the selection of the single best type of validity to apply to a given test. Instead, validity is now thought of as being relative, and the more evidence gathered from as many possible sources, the stronger the case for validity. The categorical approach to validity is convenient for test publishers because evidence of content validity in the form of information about test-development procedures is easily accumulated. Content-related validity is a much weaker form of validity than the other two and cannot easily stand alone.

Combining Different Approaches To Validity

Just as content validity, in isolation, does not provide sufficient evidence for the validity of test results, criterion-related validity can seldom stand alone as evidence of validity. In addition, the establishment of the criterion-related validity of the results of a test provides a justification for using the results only for predicting that particular criterion; it does not establish validity for all possible test uses.

The strongest case for validity would emerge from the use of all three approaches. Just because one type of validity is available does not mean that no other evidence should be sought. Construct validity should probably be employed for all tests, not just for those that neither construct nor content validity seems feasible. Similarly, the use of content-related validity should not be restricted to achievement and classroom tests. A thorough understanding of the content included on aptitude and personality instruments can provide useful information about exactly which constructs are being measured by an instrument.

A good illustration of the limitations of criterion-related validity emerges from the controversies that surround the use of scores obtained from the Wechsler Intelligence Scale for Children–Revised (WISC-R) for placing children in special education classes. David Wechsler never actually discusses validity in his manual, and there is no attempt to build a case for why this test measures those constructs that Wechsler equates with intelligence. Although he discusses the use of the test for diagnostic purposes, he does not try to establish its validity for this purpose. He never discusses the use of the test as a predictor of academic ability, and in fact disavows this use by saying that the test "appraises educational, vocational and other competencies only to the extent that it establishes and reflects whatever it is one defines as overall capacity for intelligent behavior" (Wechsler, 1974, p. 1).

Throughout this chapter the emphasis has been on establishing the validity of test scores, rather than on the test itself because it is the uses of a test that have validity. The validity of a test must be established for whatever the use of the test scores will be. The burden of proof of validity rests on those using a test for a particular purpose. For instance, if we want to use an individual intelligence test, such as the WISC-R, as a basis for placing children into special education classes, we should be able to ensure that the test will predict academic performance in school. This is done assuming that the prediction that a child is unable to benefit from continued enrollment in regular classes provides a good basis for assignment to special classes.

A wealth of information concerning the predictive validity of the WISC-R in academic settings exists (Matarrazo, 1972; Jensen, 1980). Such information is much less available in the specific area of special education placement; in general, however, a strong case for the validity of the test scores in these settings can be made. If one wants to determine the degree to which the test measures the construct of intelligence, no suitable criterion measure of intelligence can be found. Validating the test scores against the results of other intelligence tests leads to uncertainty regarding which results are most valid. We need to use construct-related validity to determine whether the WISC-R really measures the construct of intelligence. It is possible for a test's results to have good criterion-related validity for certain purposes but not necessarily be measuring the construct we want it to measure.

There is a further politically sensitive aspect of the use of the tests. It involves the fact that minorities, and particularly blacks, perform poorly on the test in comparision with nonminorities. If the test scores have construct validity—if the test measures what David Wechsler defines as *intelligence*—then the results of studies comparing the performance of minorities and nonminorities say something very profound about ethnic differences in intellectual functioning. We are also placing a great deal more importance on these differences than we would if we accepted the more conventional view that those tests measure academic potential, a construct much more sensitive to the effects of environmental and cultural differences. Because evidence for the construct validity of the test is not compelling, it is reasonable to say that the test has criterion validity for the purpose of assessing academic performance, but that it does not necessarily have construct validity for broader definitions of intelligence.

The Special Case of Face Validity

Face validity refers to the degree to which a test *appears* to be measuring the construct it is supposed to be measuring. Descriptions of face validity are often not included in measurement textbooks because it is not believed to be a legitimate form of validity. Despite this, face validity can have a remarkable amount of political and social importance. For instance, you might speculate about how long a state could continue to administer a driver's license test, no matter how good its criterion-related validity, if the test did not contain the kinds of questions people have grown to expect on such a test. Those who take such tests expect to see questions about the distance it takes to stop when traveling at a given speed, to be able to identify different traffic signs by their shape alone, and to know when certain types of turns are allowed and whether they are prohibited. Whether some other types of questions actually sort drivers into those who are poor risks and those who are not is of secondary importance, compared to the issue of whether the test appears to be measuring what it purports to measure. Those who construct such tests must keep face validity foremost in mind.

A similar problem emerges on civil service and job-related tests, particularly as they are related to affirmative action programs. If a test is to be constructed to determine who, from among a pool of applicants, should be selected for admission to a training program for firemen, the test must be job related. Because it is extremely difficult to construct a standardized test whose results can be easily shown to have predictive validity in such a setting, the criterion often used is a determination of the degree that the test looks like it is job related. Translated into practice, this usually means that, instead of assessing reading comprehension using paragraphs on just any topic, the paragraphs used deal specifically with fire fighting. Although the test is still just measuring reading comprehension, which may or may not be a crucial skill for firemen, it appears to be a fairer test. These cosmetic changes do not alter the nature of the test and its criterion-related validity. It is still a test of academic aptitude, but it has face validity.

SUMMARY

1. Validity is best assessed using a combination of criterion, construct, and content validity.
2. Validity is best thought of as being unitary rather than categorical.
3. It is the test scores that have validity not the tests themselves.
4. Criterion-related validity involves establishing a relationship between test scores and a criterion.
5. Criterion-related validity is most effectively used with aptitude tests and when a good criterion exists.
6. Criterion-related validity can be used either concurrently or predictively.
7. A restricted range in either the test scores or the criterion will suppress the size of the validity coefficient.
8. Construct-related validity involves the determination of whether a test measures the construct it is supposed to be measuring.
9. The three types of evidence used to demonstrate construct validity include the establishment of unidimensionality, the description of theory, and the use of empirical tests.
10. Construct-related validity is particularly useful for personality tests, but it really should be applied to all tests.
11. Content validation provides an indication of the degree to which items on a test are representative of the item domain of the construct being measured.
12. Content validity has played an important role in litigation involving testing.
13. Content validation is probably not as legitimate a form of validity as are the criterion- and construct-related approaches.
14. Face validity is an indication of the degree that a test looks like it is measuring what it is supposed to measure.

SUGGESTED READINGS

MESSICK, S. (1981). Evidence and ethics in the evaluation of tests. *Educational Researcher 10*(9), 9–20. [In this article the author provides a useful description of construct validity and argues that all forms of validity can be subsumed under this general heading.]

NUNNALLY, J. C. (1978). *Psychometric theory*. New York: McGraw-Hill. [This book provides some of the clearest and most readable explanations of validity. Of particular interest and importance are the descriptions of construct validity.]

YALOW, E. S., & POPHAM, W. J. (1983). Content validity at the crossroads. *Educational Researcher, 12*(8), 10–14, 21. [This is an excellent discussion of recent changes in the way that content validity is being used, particularly its relationship with court decisions in the area of minimum competency testing.]

7

Classroom Testing

OVERVIEW

The purpose of this chapter is to provide teachers with suggestions for creating good classroom tests. There is a general consensus among testing experts concerning what it takes to make a good test, and the information needed to accomplish this goal is included. It also needs to be emphasized, however, that this knowledge is necessary but not sufficient to ensure good test construction. The teacher also needs to have a commitment to constructing good tests because it takes a great deal of time and effort to do so.

The specific instructions for constructing test items are divided into supply and selection items. The supply items include essay and short-answer formats, and the selection items include matching, true-false, and multiple-choice-item formats. These are described in terms of their advantages and disadvantages, along with suggestions for writing better items.

OBJECTIVES

From this chapter you will learn the basic rules for constructing achievement tests. Specifically, you will learn the following:

- The basic considerations that lead to the construction of good tests.
- The advantages and disadvantages of essay tests.
- How to improve essay-test questions.
- How to improve the scoring of essay tests.
- How to write better short-answer items.
- The advantages and disadvantages of objective items.
- How to write better matching items.
- How to write better true-false items.
- How to write better multiple-choice items.

Introduction

Constructing, administering, and evaluating classroom tests are extremely important activities for teachers. They also are activities that consume a great deal of time. Unfortunately, there is a tendency for this process not to be done well. The general poor quality of classroom tests is unfortunate because this is the one area of measurement that is characterized by a consensus concerning correct and incorrect methods. There is a set of practices that, when followed, can be expected to result in the construction of a good test.

There are a number of reasons why teachers fail to apply this test-development technology effectively. One is that teachers are not often well trained in this area. Considering its importance and the amount of time teachers must devote to this activity, there is a lamentably small amount of course work on the topic in most teacher-preparation programs. Another factor that prevents good classroom tests from being developed is that the agreed-on methodology and procedures to be followed are not easy to implement—and even if they are well understood, they require a great deal of time. Item-analysis procedures and reliability computations require that the teacher understand and be capable of performing difficult computations. With the increased availability of microcomputers in the school and classroom, it may be possible to automate some of these procedures. However, this will not take the place of good teacher-training programs and appropriate inservice activities.

Separate procedures for constructing tests for the classroom and standardized tests need not be delineated. The basic techniques for test construction are the same for both and have been carefully developed over a number of years, are generally accepted, and can be applied correctly with minimum training.

The techniques of test construction used for norm-referenced tests also can be applied to criterion-referenced tests with some modifications. The writers of items for criterion-referenced tests are generally seeking homogeneous items. They do not usually try to increase variablity in scores by means of greater item difficulty, as is done with norm-referenced tests. Items on criterion-referenced tests therefore are generally easier than those found on norm-referenced tests.

Time Commitment

Constructing a classroom test can take time, and teachers too often just want to complete the task as soon as possible. Procrastination is also a problem because when test construction is put off to the point that it has to be rushed, the teacher's main objective becomes having something ready at the designated time. It is unlikely that the test that is so prepared will do a good job of assessing student performance. It is very important that time and effort go into planning, as well as actually writing, the items for tests.

Planning the Test

The first step in planning is to establish the instructional objectives that are to be measured. In the past there has been considerable interest surrounding behaviorally stated instructional objectives, and these will be discussed in detail in Chapter 10. At this point, it is not the specific form of the objective that is important, but just that objectives exist, whatever their form. They may be explicitly written or exist only in the memory of the test preparer. Too often, classroom tests are just groups of items haphazardly thrown together unrelated to any objectives.

One of the easiest ways to plan a test is to begin with a list of the content to be covered derived from the instructional objectives of the course. Then items can be matched to the content. It is not necessary to have an item for every topic, but you would not want to have all of the items come from only a couple of topics while others were ignored. The next step involves a concern for the level of sophistication of the items. Some items measure only recall or recognition of facts, whereas others tap into higher-level thought processes. For example, using Benjamin Bloom's taxonomy from the *Taxonomy of Educational Objective: Handbook 7, Cognitive Domain* (1956), the emphasis is on comprehension, application, analysis, synthesis, and evaluation. This is a popular approach for categorizing items and has been widely adopted by test publishers. There are other systems for classifying items that are more sophisticated—for example, Robert Gagne's learning hierarchies (1977).

As a means of establishing content validity, test publishers typically construct a table of specifications. This is a matrix consisting of a list of topics on one side and the levels of Bloom's taxonomy (or some other system) across the top. The test can then be evaluated to see that there are items covering all of the content and that for each topic there are items at the appropriate level of sophistication. Although such methods are widely used for standardized tests, they are not often adopted by teachers. As involved as these procedures are, they are quite simplistic compared to the methods advocated by James Popham (1980) for constructing criterion-referenced tests. These also will be discussed in Chapter 10.

Item Writing

The methods for developing items for classroom tests are essentially the same as those used for constructing nationally normed standardized achievement tests, and the item-writing skills used for norm-referenced tests are easily transferred to criterion-referenced tests.

Making good tests requires knowledge, training, and the willingness to put forth effort. It is not easy to construct a good test, and there is the temptation, for those who are ideologically opposed to testing, to register this protest through an unwillingness to commit an adequate amount of time to test preparation and construction. This is of course unfair to students and has a deleterious effect on their evaluation.

Items on educational tests can be classified into the categories of either supply or selection. Supply items include both short-answer and essay questions, whereas selection items include objective test items such as multiple choice, true-false, and matching.

Essay Tests

Since objective testing was first introduced, there has been considerable debate in the field of educational measurement concerning the relative merits of essay and objective tests. Among psychometrists this issue has been resolved in favor of objective tests, which are believed to be superior to essay tests.

The Disadvantages of Essay Tests

Virtually all nationally distributed standardized tests use an objective format because of the limitations of essay tests. Chief among these is the fact that there is no easy way of accurately or reliably grading an essay test. In a now classic study, James D. Falls (1928) had 100 English teachers grade an essay written by a high school senior. The raters were to grade the essay from 0 to 100 and assign a grade level. The ratings ranged from 60 to 98 percent and the grade level from fifth grade to junior in college. Similar results were obtainted by W. E. Coffman (1971).

The best test is believed to be the one that is the purest measure of the instructional objectives of a course. A good test should be measuring a single trait, and the score should not be confounded by unrelated variables. The score obtained on an essay test tends to be a composite of extraneous factors, in addition to the central purpose of assessing the student's performance in mastering instructional objectives. Such factors as penmanship, spelling, writing style, and general knowledge tend to determine the score on the essay test. Even when graders are told to ignore these factors, the grades assigned have been shown to be affected by their presence (Marshall, 1967). Even with experienced graders, 40 percent of a subject's grade is determined by who the grader is and 10 percent by when the paper is read (Ashbury, 1938). The reliability of essay tests is not only a function of the inconsistency among graders, but also a result of the fact that such tests contain only a relatively few questions—which prevents them from adequately sampling the subject matter. In general, the fewer questions on a test, the lower its reliability.

Another major disadvantage of essay tests is the time required for grading. Grading lengthy essay tests for a large class presents teachers with a dilemma. Although the teacher may want to do a good job and grade the papers fairly, a careful reading of the essay-test answers may require a half hour to an hour per test. With more than a small number of students, this can become a monumental task. There is a strong temptation, to which teachers too often accede, to grade papers quickly and superficially. This is a root cause of the low reliability and validity of essay tests.

At the college level, graduate assistants are sometimes used as graders. Unless there is consistency among the grading, a student's grade will be determined by the graduate assistant to whom it is assigned.

Essay tests are not an efficient method of measuring factual material. Students are given too much latitude in answering questions, and it is simply not fair to expect them to produce specific facts. Another problem with essay tests is that they are subject to student bluffing. Many students have a gift for appearing knowledgeable on an essay test although they have prepared little and lack any real knowledge of the course subject matter.

The Advantages of Essay Tests

There must be advantages to essay tests because they remain a popular form of classroom testing. They do require the student to construct his or her answers, which minimizes guessing, and they assess the ability of a student to bring disparate knowledge together into a meaningful whole. Such tests allow the student to choose the material that is most important and gives him or her a wide range in which to respond. Even though it may take some time to write each question, because there are fewer questions, test preparation is greatly simplified, as compared to an objective test.

If only a few students need to be tested, it is much easier to use an essay test. The preparation of an objective test for three or four students may be impractical, and grading this many essay tests would not be difficult.

The argument that is most often advanced in defense of essay tests is that they are essential for the development of good writing skills. The importance of developing these skills is undeniable, but it remains to be proven that essay tests are the best means of accomplishing this purpose. Under the pressure of the exam atmosphere and accompanying constraints of time, students do their worst writing. Having students practice poor writing habits under these circumstances is not going to make them better writers. The types of experiences that lead to the development of good writing skills involve careful, thoughtful writing, the opportunity for proofreading, and second, third, and even fourth drafts. Being able to read what you have written and see how it could be improved is also essential to the development of good writing skills. These are obviously not the experiences of the student taking an essay test.

Improving Essay Tests

Although essay tests are not recommended for general use, there are some suggestions that, when applied, can lead to better assessment of students. The most important thing to remember is preparation. One reason that essay tests are used so often is the short amount of time needed to prepare these tests. However, the essay test prepared in a short amount of time is likely to be poor. Essay tests should not be merely the last resort for the procrastinator. Essay tests, like all tests, need to be the product of a logical process involving consideration of what is most important and, therefore, what should be tested. The following are some specific instructions about how to write essay tests.

1. Write concise and explicit items and endeavor to have many items to which the student can make a brief response, rather than a few requiring lengthy responses. The more explicit the description of the task that you want students to accomplish, the less likely it is that students will go off on a tangent—either because they did not understand the focus of the question or because they are trying to avoid answering it. Broadly stated questions allow ill-prepared students to produce answers that are plausible, but quite different from what you intended. Increasing the number of questions also enhances the reliability of the test.

Poor **1.** Discuss the events leading up to Columbus's voyage in 1492.

Better **2.** What was the cause of Queen Isabella's initial hesitancy in financing Columbus's voyages?

2. Make the questions novel, so that the student can go beyond the familiar. Such a process forces students to think instead of merely regurgitate a set of memorized facts or phrases. It also makes the test-taking procedure more interesting and challenging to students.

Poor **1.** Describe the problems faced by General Washington at Valley Forge as he attempted to build the Continental Army into an effective fighting force.

Better **2.** Imagine that you are a lieutenant stationed at Valley Forge preparing a report for General Washington on what is needed to prepare the army for its battles with the British. What recommendations would your report contain?

3. Make clear in the question the limits to the response. If students perceive no limits to their responses, the only restrictions on length may be the students' physical limitations—in the form of arm cramps. It is better to encourage students to construct good answers that are well thought out and concise. They take less time to grade and can be assessed much more objectively.

4. Use terms such as* explain, compare, contrast, *rather than "Tell all you know about . . . " or "Review . . . ." The former instructions focus the student's response, making it easier for knowledgeable students to produce a good answer. Bluffing may be somewhat minimized, and the answer is more easily graded.

5. Do not give students a choice of questions to answer. Such a procedure makes grading more difficult because student responses are not directly comparable. If students answer different combinations of questions, the grader will be forced to make difficult judgments. He or she will have to decide how to compare the student who writes a good answer to an easy question with the student who writes a less adequate response to a harder question.

6. Provide an indication of how much time should be spent on each question. This can be done either by time limits or by an indication of the number of points to be awarded for each question. Such procedures prevent students from either spending too much time on an unimportant question or too little time on one that is more important.

7. Consider a take-home test. If good writing is an instructional objective, then a take-home test should be considered. Such an approach eliminates time pressure and gives students an opportunity to practice good writing habits. A disadvantage to this approach is the difficulty in ensuring that the answers produced are solely the work of the students who submit them. Such an exam is unproctorable; it requires the instructor to place some trust in the students taking the test.

Improving the Scoring of Essay Tests

Much of the unreliability of essay tests stems from the difficulty encountered in their evaluation. The following are suggestions for improving their scoring.

1. Cover the names before scoring the responses. This procedure prevents personalities from interfering with objectivity. This may stop the teacher from saying to him- or herself that, despite how poorly the response is written, "Mary Jane must really know the answer," or "Johnny Jones just thinks he is smart, but I don't think his answers are so great."

2. Score each question for all students before going to the next question. This procedure allows the grader to concentrate on each question separately and provides a clearer idea of how students' responses compare. There is also less chance for the instructor's evaluation of one answer to generalize to other answers.

3. Decide on your scoring method before you start grading. There are two main approaches to grading essay tests. The *analytic approach* requires the grader to outline what will be considered a correct answer, prior to seeing how the students have responded. The number of points each type of response is to receive is then determined. Tests also can be graded using a *global approach.* With this approach, the grader reads all of the papers quickly, to get some general impressions, and then divides them into categories according to the overall impression of how good they are. Second, and even third, readings are used to verify and adjust the obtained ratings obtained (Hopkins and Antes, 1978).

The analytical approach is systematic and conveys to the students the idea that their grades are not being determined capriciously. This approach has the disadvantage of being time consuming both to set up and to implement and may also result in an overemphasis on the trivial. The reliability of the global approach has been shown to be satisfactory, and it can be used with a large number of essay tests with some savings in time. It is a difficult approach to defend to students who usually like their teachers to be specific about why their exams were graded the way they were.

4. Either reread the test papers a second time—before returning them—or have someone else read them. One limitation of essay tests is the difficulty in maintaining consistency across a large number of papers. Responses that get low marks when they are the first graded may become quite acceptable after the grader has waded through a great many papers. You might be outraged at the inadequacies of one of the first papers read and grade it accordingly, only to find that the rest of the class did little better and end up giving higher marks to the later papers.

Another thing that happens is that you start out with great energy and resolve to read carefully, but when it's late at night and the papers must be returned the next day, it is easy to succumb to the temptation to read less carefully. The less attention we are able to give to a test, the more willing we may be to give the student the benefit of the doubt. This causes grading to be less consistent. A final rereading of all of the papers can help increase fairness in grading.

5. Put comments on the exams. This forces you to actually read students' responses and provides proof to students that you have done so. There is something very disconcerting to the student about having a paper returned with a grade but without any indication of why that particular grade was assigned.

Short-Answer Tests

On short-answer tests the student is required either to construct a short answer to a question or to determine what word or phrase is missing in a fill-in-the-blank or completion format. This approach measures the student's ability to supply, rather than merely to select, correct answers. This seems like an attractive alternative to multiple-choice tests because it is not as impersonal and is less likely to be "tricky." It also seems less subjective than an essay test. On closer examination these advantages become illusory, however. The scoring of such tests involves a great deal more subjectivity than you might expect, and they can measure only the recall of facts. It is really not possible to assess higher levels of understanding using this format. Speed of test construction would appear to be another advantage of this format. However, to construct a good short-answer test takes a considerable amount of time and effort. It is easy for such a test to end up measuring only the most trivial information or being unscorable because of the multiplicity of plausible answers with which students could respond. It is also difficult to know ahead of time just how difficult an item will be. As a result, such tests are often either too easy or too hard. Such tests have more of the disadvantages than the advantages of both the essay and objective tests.

Improving the Short-Answer Test

Although there are some clear disadvantages to the use of the short-answer test, there are some circumstances in which they are appropriately used. This is usually when the teacher is interested in assessing the students' recall of specific facts. The following section includes suggestions for constructing good short-answer items.

1. Word items so that a single brief answer can be established as correct. One of the purported advantages of the short-answer format is that it allows the teacher to construct a test that he or she believes is straightforward and easy to score. However, when the marking of papers begins, it is often discovered that students are responding with answers that, although quite different from what was intended as correct, are plausible and cannot legitimately be scored as wrong. Even though this is an inherent problem with this sort of item, careful item construction can make the problem less severe.

Poor **1.** Where does Congress meet? (Plausible answers: in the capital, the District of Columbia, Washington, in a building, in the East, etc.)

Better **2.** In what U.S. city does Congress convene?

2. It is usually better to use direct questions rather than incomplete sentences. Incomplete sentences tend to be more vague than direct questions. Using a direct question permits the test writer to specify in more detail the limits of the question being asked, which is not always possible in the case of incomplete sentences or fill-in-the-blank types of questions.

3. Blanks for answers should not provide clues to the correct answer. With any type of testing, it is important that students get credit for a correct answer because they know the answer—not because they are clever at second guessing the test preparer.

Poor **1.** Which institution of government has final say concerning the constitutionality of laws? ________ ________

Better **2.** Which institution of government has final say concerning the constitutionality of laws? ________________

The two spaces would cue the student that the answer is the Supreme Court, rather than the president or Congress.

4. If you use completion questions do not use more than one blank.

Poor **1.** In ________ the first permanent English ________ was established at ________________.

Better **2.** The first permanent English settlement was established at Jamestown in the year ________.

Objective Tests

Professionals who specialize in educational testing generally favor objective tests over essay tests. This does not mean that essay tests are in any real danger of disappearing, but rather that their adherents are unlikely to find much support in standard texts on testing.

The Advantages of Objective Tests

Objective tests have numerous advantages over essay and short-answer tests. They are excellent for measuring a students' knowledge of facts and allow a broad sampling of subject matter. They present students with a highly structured testing situation that prevents them from bluffing. Students, through cleverness, cannot convey the impression that they know more than they really do, as they can on an essay test. Written carefully, multiple-choice questions can measure knowledge at any level, from the simple recall of facts to the most complex of formal operations. Perhaps the biggest advantage of objective tests is the simplicity and objectivity of scoring. Not only does this save a great deal of time, but, coupled with the fact that objective tests can include many questions, it greatly increases the reliability of the test. The myriad of problems surrounding essay tests also are avoided by the use of objective tests.

The Disadvantages of Objective Tests

Objective tests also have some disadvantages. First, there is the time and effort required to construct this sort of test, which can be truly formidable. The difficulty in constructing the tests means that the test items must be used more than once, which can have several unhappy consequences. Students cannot be allowed to keep their tests, which deprives them of an aid to understanding and gaining insight into the kind of errors they are prone to make. Going over a test in class helps, but it is just not as good as releasing the test to the student. The instructor must always be concerned about the security of the test. A student with a good memory who passes questions on to other students in subsequent classes can compromise the test.

One charge often made against objective tests is that they place too much emphasis on trivial subject matter. Some objective tests do this either intentionally or unintentionally, but objective tests can be constructed in such a way that they measure a wide range of levels of comprehension from simple associations to the most complex problem-solving and synthesis skills. Questions can be written that are very sophisticated in terms of the kind of understanding they measure, but they are difficult to write. They are also hard to construct in such a way that they are not trick questions.

Objective tests also provide students with the opportunity for guessing, which can distort the results of the test. As long as students are not evaluated on the basis of the absolute number of correct answers, guessing does not have much effect on a student's performance. To the extent that everyone does the same amount of guessing, its effect tends to be random, and good guesses tend to be canceled by bad guesses. This is true as long as there is a sufficient number of questions on the test and it has an adequate level of difficulty. If the test is too easy, a student's grade may be determined by only a few items, and guessing is more likely to affect a student's score.

The big problem with guessing is that the degree of guessing a student does is an inherent personality trait that can be characterized by considerable variability. If some students do a lot of guessing and others are reluctant to record an answer about which they are unsure, then a student's score becomes, to some degree, a function of his or her own willingness to guess, which adds an unwelcome source of test score variance.

On standardized tests students are sometimes warned not to guess because a correction for guessing formula is being employed. The intention is to frighten those being tested by the threat of punishment for guessing so that they will refrain from it. This is done because it is believed that guessing will add unwanted error variance and lower reliability. An alternative approach is to suggest that all students taking the test guess. This may not work because there will always be some students who will not guess even if urged to do so. Apparently it is easier to intimidate someone who is prone to guessing into not guessing than to convince nonguessers that they should. For a more thorough discussion of the correction for guessing formula, see Chapter 5, "Reliability."

Matching Tests

The matching test is an objective test that is closely related to the multiple-choice test. A series of items is listed down the left-hand column of the test paper and a series of options is listed down the right-hand column. The student then picks the option that goes with each item.

When the student's acquisition of associations is of most interest, this approach is more efficient than a series of multiple-choice tests. The major disadvantage of this approach is that it is only suitable for measuring associations and not for use in assessing higher levels of understanding. An added disadvantage of this method is that such a test cannot easily be machine scored because the number of options exceeds the five spaces allocated to each item on machine-scorable answer sheets. Of course answer sheets could be tailor-made for this type of item.

Constructing Better Matching Tests As is true with all tests, the construction of good matching tests is the product of ample time and care and the application of a set of rules that define good items. This section contains suggestions for writing good matching items.

1. Use only homogeneous subject matter. If there is a great deal of heterogeneity in subject matter on a set of matching items, students may be able to figure out the correct answer by just matching categories, without having a real knowledge of the subject matter. Making the set of items more homogeneous forces students to have a better understanding of the relationships that are being assessed.

2. Do not have the same number of items and options; allow students to use a response once or twice or not at all. The goal of test writing is to construct items in such a way that they are pure measures of students' mastery of objectives. If there are the same number of items as options and each option is used only once, the clever student will get some questions right through a process of elimination. This makes the test more a measure of testwiseness than an indication of the mastery of instructional objectives.

3. Arrange the list of responses in logical order. If the list of items is not in a logical or systematic order, the order may provide clues to the correct answer.

4. Keep the list of items brief.

5. Always place the entire task on the same page.

True-false tests owe much of their popularity to objectivity in scoring and ease of construction. Their use also permits the inclusion of a larger number of items than do other item formats. Even though it is easy to generate a larger number of statements to be used on a true-false test and the responses can quite easily be marked as correct or incorrect, the true-false test is not considered to be a sound method of assessing student performance. This is because it is hard to write items that are not too easy, too difficult, or so ambiguous and tricky that they provide a poor assessment of knowledge. There is only a relatively limited type of course material that lends itself to this approach, and in many fields there are no statements, except for the trivial, than can be said to be unambiguously true or false. Guessing is another major limitation. Corrections for guessing methods do little more than intimidate the less assertive student while they reward the student willing to gamble on hunches.

Writing Better True-False Items There are serious limitations to the true-false test format, and its use is not recommended. However, there are rules that, when applied, can result in better true-false items.

1. Avoid statements that are too general. The major problem with true-false tests is the difficulty in generating statements that are absolutely true or false. Vague or general items make this problem even more severe. The more specific the statement, the more confident the test maker can be that the students' scores reflect knowledge rather than luck.

Poor **T or F** **1.** Slavery was the cause of the Civil War.

Better **T or F** **2.** The president of the Confederate States was Jefferson Davis.

2. Do not use negatives or double negatives. The use of complicated sentences on a true-false test makes the test a measure of cognitive ability rather than knowledge of the material—which is supposedly the focus of the assessment.

Poor **T or F** **1.** At no time during the Revolutionary War were the French not willing to provide assistance to the American colonies.

Better **T or F** **2.** The French government provided assistance to the American colonies during the Revolutionary War.

3. Do not use long, complex sentences. Involved and complex sentences make the task mainly an assessment of reading comprehension rather than knowledge of subject matter.

Poor **T or F** **1.** Charles II was the monarch against whom Oliver Cromwell rebelled in the period that was subsequently labeled the Reformation.

Better **T or F** **2.** Charles II was the king of England during the Reformation.

4. Do not include more than one idea. If one idea is true and the other is false, the item becomes artificially difficult and it will favor the more testwise students.

Poor **T or F** **1.** By one year the majority of babies can say two words and take at least three unaided steps.

Better **T or F** **2.** By one year the majority of babies can say at least two words.

5. If you are using an opinion, indicate the source.

Poor **T or F** **1.** Aggression is an innate human characteristic.

Better **T or F** **2.** According to Konrad Lorenz, aggression is an innate human characteristic.

6. There should not be a difference in length between true and false statements. The testwise student may figure out that longer statements are more likely to be associated with true statements.

7. Include the same number (approximately) of true and false statements. Teachers often include more true than false statements because they believe that the student might remember the false statements and thus be learning material that is incorrect. If this is done, then clever students will answer, "True," whenever they do not know the answer.

***8. Do not use specific qualifiers such as* always, never, all, none, usually, sometimes, occasionally, may, *or* could.** Such absolutes cue the students as to the correct answer. No statement couched with absolutes is likely to be true, and any statement could "sometimes," or "occasionally" be true.

Multiple-Choice Tests

The multiple-choice item consists of a stem, usually in the form of a completion task or a question, three or four alternative responses, and one correct answer. The student must select the correct answer from among the options. Multiple-choice items are extremely versatile and can be used to assess different ability levels across a wide range of subject matter. The breadth of multiple-choice test items is limited only by the creativity and cleverness of the author of the test.

It should be noted that not all multiple-choice test items are good, and that it takes a great deal of time and skill to write good questions. Perhaps the most important characteristic of the multiple-choice test is the way that alternative responses can be changed and manipulated. This gives the test author flexibility in adjusting the difficulty of the test item. In this way tests can be constructed that are at the optimum difficulty level, to ensure maximum reliability.

The major disadvantage of multiple-choice tests involves the excessive amounts of time and skill required to construct good items. When not well constructed, they can end up measuring only trivial subject matter or become dependent on the testwiseness of the person taking the test.

Good items once developed can be used over and over, as long as their security can be maintained. One good technique for storing items is to place them on cards along with pertinent item characteristics obtained from item analysis (which is discussed in the following chapter). One approach that works well is to use computer cards. These are long enough to hold items cut from existing tests, which can be taped to them. The construction of a new test involves arranging the previously used questions, revising individual items where appropriate, and adding other new questions. With increased availability of personal computers, it is now possible to store items in computer disk memory and, through the use of computer technology, greatly simplify the process of test construction. (See Chapter 4, "Computer Applications to Measurement.")

Suggestions for Writing Better Items As was previously emphasized, writing good multiple-choice items takes time, skill, and creativity. It can be an agonizing process. The avoidance of bad items takes both practice and a knowledge of the rules for writing good items. These rules have been developed over many years, and they are well known and accepted.

The rules for writing multiple-choice items can be placed into two categories: first, the rules that have the goal of making the test items more straightforward, a consequence of which is that the test is a more direct measure of the type of knowledge and skills emphasized in the instructional objectives; and second, rules that emphasize the avoidance of item characteristics that tend to give the answer away.

Constructing Items That Are Straightforward

1. Use good English at an appropriate level for the students taking the test. Unless you are constructing a reading test, you want to make sure that reading comprehension is not all that your test measures. If the wording is such that only the best readers do well, then the validity of your test is imperiled.

2. Make sure that the stem contains an entire idea. It is inefficient for students to spend time trying to figure out what is being asked. One goal is to so construct the stem that it could be used as a short-answer question, without the provision of any alternatives.

Poor **1.** The constitution:
- a. does not provide protection for the independence of the press.
- b. was written by Thomas Jefferson.
- c. provides for separation of powers.
- d. is a brief document.

Better **2.** The Bill of Rights in the Constitution protects which of the following rights?
- a. Freedom from usury.
- b. Right of states to set tariffs.
- c. Freedom of the press.
- d. Establishment of state religion.

3. Avoid unnecessary words in the responses. Extra words make the students' task more difficult and more dependent on reading ability. When the test maker wants to increase the difficulty of an item, the alternatives should be made more tempting. It is not a good practice to accomplish this by making the response hard to read.

Poor **1.** What aspect of learning did B. F. Skinner emphasize?
- a. The importance of reinforcement.
- b. The importance of practice.
- c. The importance of identical elements.
- d. The importance of contiguity.

Better **2.** What aspect of learning did B. F. Skinner consider most important?
a. Reinforcement.
b. Practice.
c. Identical elements.
d. Contiguity.

4. Questions are usually better than fill-in-the-blanks items. This question format is more straightforward and less dependent on reading ability. It also provides a task that is more natural.

Poor **1.** ________ is the process of cell division leading to the formation of the gamete.
a. Mitosis.
b. Meiosis.
c. Entropy.
d. Parthogensis.

Better **2.** What is the process of cell division that results in the formation of the gamete?
a. Mitosis.
b. Meiosis.
c. Entropy.
d. Parthogensis.

5. Avoid trick questions. There are much better ways of adjusting the difficulty of a test than including trick questions. It is not only unfair, but it affects reliability and validity negatively while introducing an irrelevant variable into students' scores.

Poor **1.** Which type of laboratory research did Piaget conduct?
a. Stimulus-response studies.
b. Naturalistic observations of children.
c. Maze studies using rats.
d. None of the above.

Answer *d* is correct. Strictly speaking, Piaget did not work in a laboratory, so response *b*, the answer that would seem most reasonable to students with some knowledge of Piaget, is wrong. This item clearly measures more than a student's knowledge of Piaget.

6. Do not ask for the students' opinion; instead, specify authorities. This is particularly important when you are dealing with subject matter that is somewhat controversial. If you ask for an opinion, it is hardly fair to count wrong a response that reflects students' (or someone else's) points of view, even if they conflict with your own.

Poor **1.** The structure of intelligence is best explained as:
a. consisting of a single unitary trait.
b. being made up of a number of separate factors.
c. a global entity.
d. consisting of a *g* factor and more specific factors.

Better **2.** According to J. P. Guilford, the structure of intelligence is best explained as:
a. consisting of a single unitary trait.
b. being made up of a number of separate factors.

c. a global entity.
d. consisting of a *g* factor and more specific factors.

7. Try to avoid negatively stated items. Negatives introduce complexities into the questions, making the task more difficult to understand. Test-wiseness and reading ability then become unwanted extraneous variables. Sometimes it is just not possible to avoid their use. If they must be used, make sure that you underline the negative word so that it is not missed by students.

8. Make the alternatives parallel and avoid unnecessary words. Such practices will make the task more straightforward and keep it independent of students' reading ability.

Avoid Clues that Give Away the Answer

9. Eliminate clues that allow a student to get an item correct without really knowing the subject matter. The purpose of any test is to be a pure measure of students' acquisition of the sort of skills and knowledge described in the instructional objectives. It is best to avoid situations where students get questions right through testwiseness and cleverness. This introduces an extraneous variable into students' performances that makes the interpretation of the score difficult.

Poor **1.** Which of the following statements about chromosomes is true. They:
a. are made out of DNA.
b. are not made of DNA.
c. are the building blocks of the gene.
d. contain the information acquired by the organism.

Clever students will be able to conclude that either *a* or *b* must be the right answer because both cannot be false. Students can then ignore options *c* and *d*.

10. Make all alternate responses plausible and give them some logical relationship to the stem. The difficulty of a multiple-choice test is dependent on the alternate responses provided. If they are unrelated or implausible, they can be eliminated even by students with little knowledge.

11. Avoid items for which clues are provided in other questions on the test.

12. The length of the option should not provide a clue to the correct answer. There is sometimes a tendency to have the correct answer be longer than the incorrect options. Clever students may realize this and use it as a basis for guessing. Such a practice gives test-wise students an unfair advantage.

Conclusions

The construction of a good achievement test is a demanding, difficult task that is not always easily accomplished. Knowledge of good test-construction practices is a prerequisite, but it is not enough to guarantee the creation of a good test. There must also exist the belief in the importance of constructing high-quality tests and a willingness to put forth the necessary effort. Once the test is completed and administered, there are also techniques of item analysis that can be employed to evaluate items and to determine those that should be eliminated, those that should be improved, and those that are acceptable as is. Instructions for conducting item analyses can be found in the next chapter.

SUMMARY

1. To construct a good test it is necessary not only to have a knowledge of test-construction rules; one must also possess a willingness to put forth an adequate amount of time and effort.

2. Poor tests are usually the result of a lack of training and an unwillingness on the part of test constructors to put forth sufficient effort.

3. The basic rules for constructing good tests are applicable to both classroom and standardized tests.

4. With some modifications these rules can be applied to criterion-referenced tests.

5. The construction of a good test requires planning and must start with a firm idea of what the test is intended to measure.

6. Test items can be categorized as measuring either recall or recognition ability. Essay and short-answer tests are made up of recall items, whereas matching, true-false, and multiple-choice tests consist of recognition items.

7. Measurement specialists generally favor objective tests over essay tests because essay tests are characterized by a greater amount of scorer error.

8. The scorer error associated with essay tests is partially a function of subjectivity and partially a function of the length of time required to grade them.

9. The major advantage of essay tests is their capacity to assess the student's ability to synthesize large amounts of information.

10. The belief that the use of essay tests promotes the development of good writing skills is probably incorrect because they require the student to practice bad habits.

11. Essay tests can be improved by careful construction with an emphasis on having the task for each student be the same.

12. The scoring of essay tests can be improved by ensuring the anonymity of the student, by developing a preset criterion, and by scoring all of the answers to one question before moving to the next.

13. Short-answer tests seem to have the advantages of both essay and objective tests, when in fact they appear to have more of their disadvantages. They are as subjective as essay tests and tend to emphasize only the recall of facts.

14. Objective tests are time consuming to construct; it requires skill to prevent them from assessing only trivial subject matter.

15. It is possible, using objective tests, to assess cognitive functioning at any desired level.

16. Matching items are an efficient method of assessing a student's knowledge of a large number of relationships or associations.

17. The main thing to remember when constructing matching items is to make certain that the structure of the items does not give the answer away.

18. True-false items are not recommended because it is hard to control their difficulty, they tend to emphasize trivial information, and guessing can play a large part in scores.

19. Multiple-choice items are preferred because they permit the assessment of knowledge and ability at any cognitive level and it is possible to control difficulty by carefully selecting the detractors.

20. In the construction of good multiple-choice questions, there are two main considerations: (1) they need to be constructed in such a way that they do not merely measure reading ability, logical thinking, or some other construct that is not the focus of the test, and (2) they need to be constructed in such a way that the student cannot obtain the correct answer by second guessing the test constructor.

SUGGESTED READINGS

EBEL, R. L. (1979). *Essentials of educational measurement*. Englewood Cliffs, NJ: Prentice-Hall. [This is a classic textbook that covers the application of measurement principles to classroom testing. The coverage of true-false tests is particularly well done and provides a spirited defense of the use of this method.]

GRONLUND, N. E. (1982) *Constructing achievement tests*. Englewood Cliffs, NJ: Prentice-Hall. [This is a small book (148 pages) covering the rudiments of test construction from test planning to suggestions about how to write various item types.]

GRONLUND, N. E. (1985). *Measurement and evaluation in teaching* (5th ed.). New York: Macmillan. [This comprehensive textbook focuses on the type of testing and measurement skills that a teacher needs to have. It also contains a wealth of examples unequaled in other books on the subject.]

NITKO, A. J. (1983). *Educational tests and measurement: An introduction*. New York: Harcourt. [This textbook is notable in that it provides a particularly up-to-date description of classroom testing. It also includes more of an emphasis on criterion-referenced testing.]

8

Improving Achievement Tests

OVERVIEW

The purpose of this chapter is to provide information about methods of improving achievement tests, whether they are constructed by the classroom teacher for his or her use alone or they are intended for administration throughout a school, across a school district or for national distribution. The focus is on techniques of item analysis, the contributions of latent-trait theory, and the problems of test bias. The various methods that are used to eliminate, or at least ameliorate, test bias are described, and their strengths and weaknesses are discussed.

OBJECTIVES

From this chapter you will learn about the various ways that achievement tests can be improved. Specifically, you will learn the following:

- The three main considerations in the construction of good tests.
- The purposes of conducting an item analysis.
- The basic assumptions on which item analyses are based.
- How to use the item-discrimination method to conduct an item analysis.
- How to use the correlational method to conduct an item analysis.
- The advantages and disadvantages of using these two methods.
- The theoretical and practical significance of latent-trait theory.
- The various applications of latent-trait theory.
- Methods of identifying test bias.
- Methods of eliminating test bias.

Steps in Improving Achievement Tests

No achievement test, whether it is a classroom or standardized test, should be considered to be in final form as long as there is the possibility of making it better. The good test author should spend the bulk of his or her time improving old tests, not constructing new ones. Not only does such a policy lead to better tests, it makes it possible to avoid the need to construct a new test each time one is needed.

There are three steps to improving a test. First and foremost, content validity must be ensured. Unless the test is measuring what it is supposed to measure, there is no reason to progress further. Second, the rules for constructing a good test must be followed. Finally, statistical techniques for evaluating the characteristics of items should be implemented in order to determine which items to keep, which to reject, and which to improve. This process is called item analysis.

Content-Related Validity

The most relevant form of validity for the classroom test is content-related validity. As was emphasized in Chapter 5, this form of validity is concerned not only with the coverage of content, but also with the process that was used to select the particular items included on a test. A test may be constructed of what appear to be outstanding items, each meeting the highest standards of test-writing excellence, but if what the items measure is irrelevant to the purposes of the test, it will be flawed. The test scores will lack validity and be incapable of giving the user the sort of information that is needed.

The test author should avoid the situation where the test-construction process is viewed in terms of product rather than process. *X* number of items are needed; that many are written or borrowed until the goal is met, and then the process stops. There are aspects of any subject matter for which items can easily be constructed and others that seem to defy assessment. The ease with which an item can be constructed to measure a particular aspect of a curriculum and the importance of that aspect are not necessarily connected. There is also no guaranteed relationship between course goals and the availability of existing items from borrowed tests of the teachers manuals that accompany textbooks. Goal-oriented test-construction methods that emphasize just getting the task done can rapidly deteriorate into the unhappy circumstance where the dog is wagged by the tail. The content of the test becomes a function of convenience in acquiring items, rather than assessing the avowed purposes of the test. An important side effect of this practice is a distortion in instruction. The teacher may begin to tailor what is taught to what is covered on the test at the expense of what is most important.

For these reasons it is important that the items on a test be chosen because they match course objectives. This means that the goals of a class must be established first and the test constructed to determine if the student has reached the goals. Although this may seem obvious and perhaps overly simplistic, it is emphasized because tests are too often constructed and revised without sufficient consideration of test validity. Regardless of how scrupulously the rules of item construction are followed, or how elaborate the item analysis is, a good test must first and foremost measure the purposes of the instruction it is intended to evaluate.

Following the Rules for Good Item Construction

Once the match between course objectives and test content is established, the test author can turn his or her attention to the refinement of items. The first step is to make sure that the rules of good item construction have been followed. (These are outlined in Chapter 7.) There is little controversy about these rules because test specialists have reached a degree of consensus concerning what should and what should not be done in the way of constructing items. Of course most of the rules emphasize what is to be avoided, rather than what is to be done. Once you have eliminated all items that are clearly poor, your test will not be terrible, but you will not necessarily have a good test.

Good tests are the result of a combination of hard work and creativity. The teacher who wants to improve his or her test-writing skills needs to go beyond the elimination of bad items. Of most importance is the willingness to spend time and put forth effort. The procedures outlined in the following section will enable the test constructor to know which items work and which do not. Experience will help in the formulation of better items when tied to a feedback system based on item analysis.

Item Analysis

Having constructed, administered, and graded a test, you need a method of determining which items to include on your next test, which to modify, and which to eliminate. Your students will be all too happy to point out the bad items by providing a convenient operational definition. A bad item will be defined as one they got wrong. If they got it correct, it will be considered a good item. But these are not particularly useful criteria. It is possible to have items that many students miss that are assessing something useful and should be retained, whereas an item that everyone gets right is usually not a good item. It contributes nothing to the understanding of how students compare to each other. However, if the item covered a particularly important point you may be pleased that everyone got it correct. Students can also give useful information about items that have problems, and their suggestions should not be discounted.

Categorizing items as good and poor by inspection is also of limited value. Other than for purposes of identifying clearly flawed items, this practice provides little insight into their usefulness.

The Reasons for Conducting Item Analyses Item-analysis procedures are generally associated with large-scale standardized tests where the test publishers have sizable resources that can be devoted to elaborate item analyses. In that setting they are indispensable. The use of item-analysis procedures by classroom teachers is somewhat less common. These procedures are seldom used because not many teachers know how to conduct an item-analysis themselves, nor do they possess the expertise necessary to interpret the results of an item analysis if they are provided. In addition, even when the necessary skills and knowledge are possessed by the teacher, the amount of effort necessary to accomplish this task may be too great. The teacher, however, should not be intimidated by the amount of work required. Some of the techniques that follow can be implemented without an unreasonable amount of effort. Furthermore, the logistical problems offer some hope for remediation. As microcomputers and inexpensive test scorers increase in availability, it will become possible for a teacher to use them to conduct item analyses with a minimum of effort.

As has already been emphasized, good testing practice requires the reuse of test items. This is necessary because the amount of work involved in generating items is so great that this is the only practical method of test development. Of course if the same tests are used over and over with no change, there will be no improvement and there will be an increase in the probability that the security of the test will be breached. It is only through the modifications achieved through item analysis that better tests evolve.

In addition to communicating to the test developer which items need to be improved or eliminated, item analysis gives the teacher feedback concerning his or her item-writing skills. This enables the test writer to enhance his or her test-writing competency. Through this practice the number of poor items should decrease. The item-analysis process also can provide feedback to the teacher concerning misinformation that students might have acquired. If a large number of students provide the same wrong answer, a flaw in instruction should be suspected.

Item-Analysis Assumptions Item-analysis procedures are intended to maximize reliability; their use is based on the assumption that the test is measuring what it is supposed to measure. Because item-analysis procedures focus on comparisons between items and the total score, it is necessary to assume that the total score represents what you want it to represent. If the test is not measuring what it is supposed to measure, the total score will be a poor criterion against which to compare items. It must also be assumed that the best criterion for evaluation is internal consistency reliability. This is the result of the emphasis on the relationship between individual items and the total score. There are three methods of conducting an item anaslysis: (1) the discrimination method, (2) the correlation method, and (3) through an application of latent-trait theory. The first two methods will be discussed in the following section; the latent-trait method will be discussed in a later one.

The Item-Discrimination Method of Item Analysis In using the item-discrimination method, each student's test is scored and is rank ordered. Twenty-seven percent of the students at the top and a like number at the bottom are then identified. This percentage is selected because it is desirable to have as many students in each group as possible to increase stability; at the same time the two groups should be as different as possible in order to make the discriminations clearer. It has been determined through the use of calculus that the use of 27 percent maximizes these two considerations. In actual practice if you have between twenty-five and thirty-five students in your class, it is probably better to place ten student tests in each group; this simplifies the mathematical computations without any undue negative effects on the stability of the discrimination index.

The item-analysis process is accomplished mathematically by subtracting the number right in the lower group (*RL*) from the number right in the upper group (*RU*) and dividing by the number in each group (*N*). The formula follows:

$$\text{Discrimination index } (D) = \frac{RU - RL}{N(\text{each})} \quad [8.1]$$

For example, suppose that seventy-four students took a test. Twenty-seven percent of that number is twenty (*N*), so you would select the twenty students who did best on the test and the twenty who did poorest. The responses of the students to one item are shown in Table 8.1. Fifteen students got the item right in the upper group (*RU*) and only three in the lower group (*RL*). The difference between the two is twelve; and when that is divided by twenty you obtain a *D* of .60. This analysis procedure is used to compute discrimination indexes for each item.

The higher the *D*, the better the item because this is an indication that the item discriminates in favor of the upper group, which should get more items correct. A question that everyone gets right or everyone gets wrong will have a *D* equal to zero. If more students get a question right in the lower group than in the upper group, then the question will have a negative value and is probably flawed. This can happen with an item covering complex material written in such a way that it is possible to select the correct response without any real understanding of what is being assessed. A poor student may make a guess, select that response, and come up with the correct answer. Good students may be suspicious of a question that looks too easy and will take the harder path to solving the problem and may end up being less successful than those who guess. In general, high *D*s are better than low *D*s, but items should not necessarily be rejected on the basis of low discrimination indexes alone. Items with low *D*s could be measuring something important that is not closely related to what is being measured by the total score. However, negative *D*s indicate the need to modify or eliminate an item.

TABLE 8.1
Item Discrimination Analysis for a Sample Item

	Responses			
	A	B	C[a]	D
Twenty best students	3	2	15	0
Twenty poorest students	12	3	3	2
Difference			12	

$$D = \frac{RU - RL}{N} = \frac{15 - 3}{20} = .60$$

[a] Correct response.

Correlation Item Analysis The preceding method is a straightforward approach to conducting an item analysis on a classroom test. But even with thirty students and a fifty-item test, it will be necessary for the person conducting the item analysis to examine 1,000 items (20 students × 50 items = 1,000). This is more work than most teachers are likely to be willing to put forth. To conduct an item analysis using the correlation method, it is necessary to employ a computer and enter each student's response to every item. This is an arduous task. If a machine scorer is available, the students' responses can be made on machine scoreable answer sheets and be read directly into the computer memory. This greatly simplifies the item-analyses process. The data can be analyzed using available item-analysis packages, a special program can be written, or an existing statistical-analysis program can be used. The outcome that is of most interest is the correlation between the item and the total score, but it is also possible to have item difficulties, item means, standard deviations, and the frequencies of responses to the detractors produced. The correlations are interpreted in the same way as the discrimination index.

Item Difficulty Item difficulty is computed by dividing the number of students getting an item correct by the total number of students attempting the item. This value is then multiplied by 100, to eliminate the decimal. A difficulty level of 50 indicates that, on the average, students got half of the items right and half wrong. The lower the difficulty index, the more difficult the item. In general the difficulty of a test should be halfway between the number of items a student could get correct by guessing and 100 percent. For a multiple-choice test with four options, the discrimination approach would favor items with a difficulty of 62.5; for a true-false test, the best level of difficulty would be 75.

Of course a test made up of items of this level of difficulty also can cause morale problems. Most students are conditioned to believe that a good student should get a high percentage of questions correct, and the student who does not get much more than half of the questions on a test correct is not likely to think of him- or herself as average. It is difficult to convince students otherwise. The best compromise is probably to educate students in terms of the optimum psychometric properties of a test and try to ensure that the difficulty is not so low as to cause problems with morale or so high that the reliability of the test is impaired.

Comparing the Discrimination and Correlational Methods Some test specialists believe that there is an important difference between item analyses conducted by means of correlations and those based on the discrimination approach. Both measure the same thing (the degree to which a given item is consistent with the total score) and both lead to tests with internal consistency. One difference between the two is related to the effect of item difficulty. The discrimination approach favors items with a level of difficulty halfway between a chance score and 100 percent. Correlational approaches favor items in the same range of difficulty, but they do so to a lesser degree. This difference is sometimes used to argue for the superiority of the discrimination approach; the logic is that if multiple-choice items with difficulties around 62.5 are better, then the discrimination approach, which is more sensitive to that characteristic, must be a better method for evaluating items. This is an incorrect conclusion because the discrimination approach emphasizes the categorization of the students taking the test into two groups, a high and a low. Under such circumstances, an item difficulty of 62.5 becomes optimum, but those are not the only important discriminations. It is also important to be able to make discrimination all along the scale. It is best to have a median difficulty of 62.5, with a range of difficulties, in order to make the test appropriate for all students.

An Analysis of Detractors The item-analysis process is also enhanced by a listing of the number of students responding to each detractor for each question. This allows the test developer to understand why an item is not working. A detractor that is selected often because it appears to be correct may cause an item to be too difficult and may need to be replaced. Detractors that are so unattractive that they are never selected may need to be replaced with detractors that are more likely to be chosen. This will make the item more difficult, increase variability, and enhance the capacity of the item to make good discriminations.

The Size of the Sample Item analysis is best conducted with large samples. Interpreting item analyses of locally constructed tests with small samples must be done with caution because such analyses tend to be unstable. An item might be effective with one class and not work with another. Subtle differences in the presentation of material, or the response by the instructor to a specific question in class, can alter the difficulty and effectiveness of an item.

Conclusions

Improving the achievement test is a three-step process. It involves ensuring content relevance, following the rules of good item construction, and employing appropriate item-analysis procedures. Of course the use of these three steps does not guarantee good items or a good test, but it certainly provides the foundation for accomplishing these goals.

Latent-Trait Theory

One of the most important recent developments in the field of measurement involves the development of latent-trait theory. This theory has many applications, including the development of better derived scores, improved test-development techniques, and improvements in norming procedures. It is also called *item response theory*. In Chapter 12, "Achievement Tests," this is the term used to describe the methods employed in the development of the Comprehensive Test of Basic Skills.

Up to this point we have referred to the attribute measured as a construct, graphically described as the distance along a continuum. The amount of the attribute possessed by an individual is sometimes referred to as the true score, but it may be better to avoid this term because it suggests that something real and concrete is being measured rather than just a construct. An alternative way of describing what is measured is as a latent trait. The term *latent trait* refers to the underlying attribute estimated by means of the scores on a test. The applications of this theory are relevant for a diverse range of testing and assessment instruments; for the purposes of this discussion, however, we will consider cognitive tests on which the items are scored as right or wrong, with the raw score based on the number of items correct. The discussion that follows, with some modification, also is relevant to tests not scored dichotomously.

The development and derivation of latent-trait models can only take place at a sophisticated mathematical level. Because any in-depth treatment of the subject would go beyond the intended level of this textbook, it will be treated narratively and proceed, as much as possible, at a nonmathematical level.

One purpose of this discussion of latent-trait theory is to remove the mystique that is likely to surround such a new and compex technique. It is not intended to provide the reader with enough information actually to apply these methodologies. Once he or she gets past the initial shock of its highly mathematical nature, then latent-trait theory can become comprehensible.

The Limitations of Standard Scores

The purpose of measurement in the social sciences is to quantify human attributes, a process that normally takes place by means of an instrument, or a test, yielding a score. The more items scored correct, the higher the raw score, and the more of the attribute the subject is believed to possess. Of course this is true only if the test is measuring one, rather than many, attributes.

Standard scores have been suggested as the best ways of placing different scores on the same continuum for purposes of making comparisons. But there is an important limitation to the use of the linear transformations associated with standard scores. With these approaches every item is assumed to be equal to every other item. For each additional item scored as correct, the student is believed to have to have an additional unit of that attribute. Because the items on a test are unlikely to be equalivalent, either in terms of difficulty or the degree to which they are related to the underlying construct, chances are that scales produced in this manner will not be exactly interval.

The Advantages of the Latent-Trait Approach

Latent-trait theory was developed as a means of addressing the sort of problems outlined above. It provides a way to analyze a set of test scores so that information concerning the amount of a latent trait possessed by an individual can be estimated very precisely. To compute ability scores, it utilizes information about item difficulty and the degree to which each item measures the underlying construct. It also provides information about individual items. This item-characteristic information is particularly useful because it is not dependent on the characteristics of the norm sample from which it is computed. This is in contrast with tests developed using traditional methods that must employ a carefully selected norm group that has the same characteristics as the group with which the test is to be used. This can be avoided using latent-trait theory, which makes it a valuable technique for test development.

The Assumptions Necessary for the Model

Latent-trait theory is based on the following three assumptions: unidimensionality, independence, and the item-characteristic curve. *Unidimensionality* means that all items on a test measure the same attribute, construct, or latent trait. In general this is an easily met condition for intelligence and academic aptitude tests. The methodology employed in their construction tends to emphasize internal consistency, which ensures their unidimensionality. The existence of unidimensionality is somewhat more problematic in the case of achievement tests, where items are selected according to their match with a table of specifications rather than their correlation with the total score on the test. Under such conditions the assumption of unidimensionality is difficult to satisfy. Despite this, the latent-trait model has been used extensively in the development of achievement tests.

The assumtion of *independence* simply means that one item does not affect the probability of a student answering other items. The assumption will not be met if the answer to one item is found in a second, or the response to an item interferes with obtaining the correct answer to another item.

According to the *item-characteristic-curve* assumption, the probability that a student will get an item correct increases as the student's ability increases. This assumption will not be met if an item is constructed in such a way that the poor student can guess the correct answer; or by avoiding guessing and trying to work out the correct answer, the better student is likely to get the item wrong. The assumption would also be violated if a distractor were particularly attractive to the student with greater ability. Basically this assumption requires that, for every item, students with more of the latent trait have a higher probability of getting the item correct than those with less of the trait.

The Basic Model

Although he did have some predecessors, Frederick Lord (1952, 1953) is generally given credit for the early development of latent-trait theory. There are a number of different approaches to latent-trait analysis, generally classified as one-, two-, or three-parameter models. The model proposed by Lord had two parameters: item difficulty and item discrimination. This is referred to as the *normal ogive model*. Item difficulty, which has previously been defined as the proportion of students who get an item correct, in latent-trait theory is redefined as the point on a scale where the item is most effective in discriminating among students. For every item there is a level of student ability for which that item attains maximum discrimination. For more difficult items the level of ability of students must be higher, whereas easy items discriminate better among students with lower ability. With this method of measuring item difficulty, the greater the magnitude of the item-difficulty score, the more difficult the item. Item discrimination is an indication of the degree to which an item discriminates among subjects in terms of their ability.

Although the probability that an individual will get an item correct is dependent on the subject's ability, there is not a linear relationship between the two. The relationship instead is best represented by a cumulative normal-, or ogive-shaped curve. This curve is illustrated in Figure 8.1.

This particular curve shape is obtained because students with very low ability also have a uniformly low probability of correctly answering the question. The probability curve reaches its lower asymptote at this point, which means that it has become nearly parallel with the horizontal axis. At the other extreme, students with very high ability have a uniformly high probability of successfully answering the question, and at that point the curve reaches its upper asymptote. There are many different variations in this shape that still fit the general ogive form.

The actual shape of the curve for a specific item is determined by item difficulty and discrimination. The greater the discrimination, the steeper the curve. The location of the curve along the abscissa is determined by the difficulty of the test. The effect of varying the magnitute of the parameters is illustrated in Figure 8.2. The shape of the item characteristic curve can also be affected by the size of the units used in the scale, on which both ability and the probability of getting an item correct are measured.

Other Models

The model we have discussed so far has been Lord's *normal ogive model*. Because of its mathematical complexity, it has generally been replaced by Allen Birnbaum's *two-parameter logistic model* (1968), which yields the same results as the normal ogive model but is somewhat more mathematically manageable.

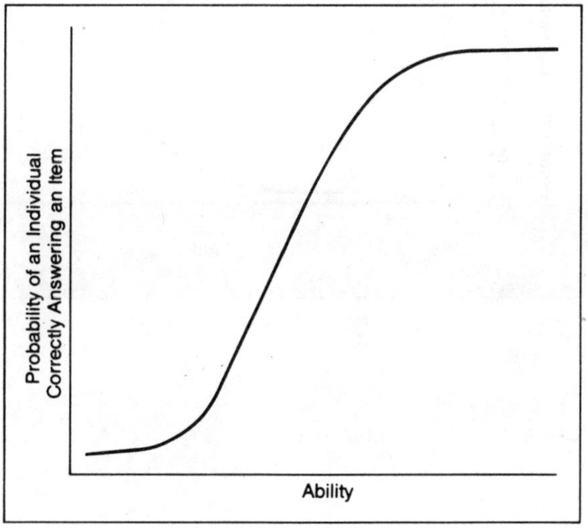

Figure 8.1
The characteristic curve for an item.

Figure 8.2
The effect of varying the magnitude of difficulty and discrimination parameters on the characteristic item curve.

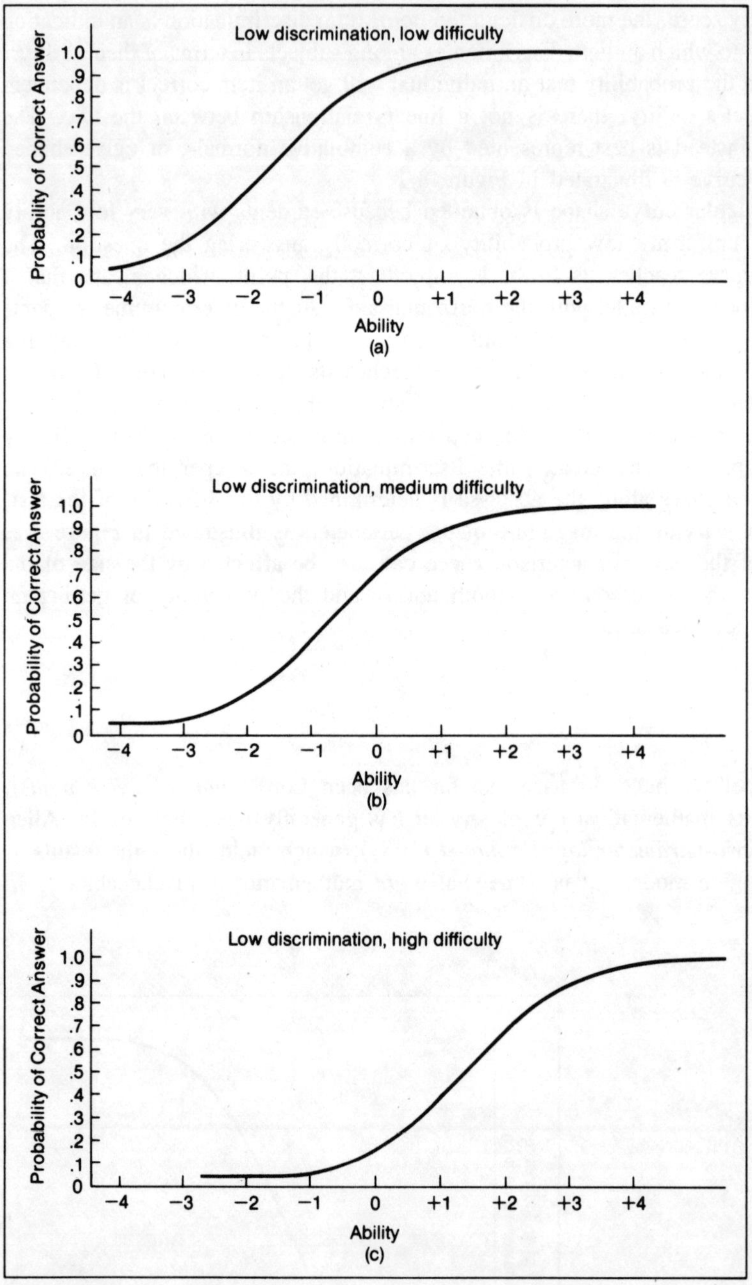

Figure 8.2 *(continued).*

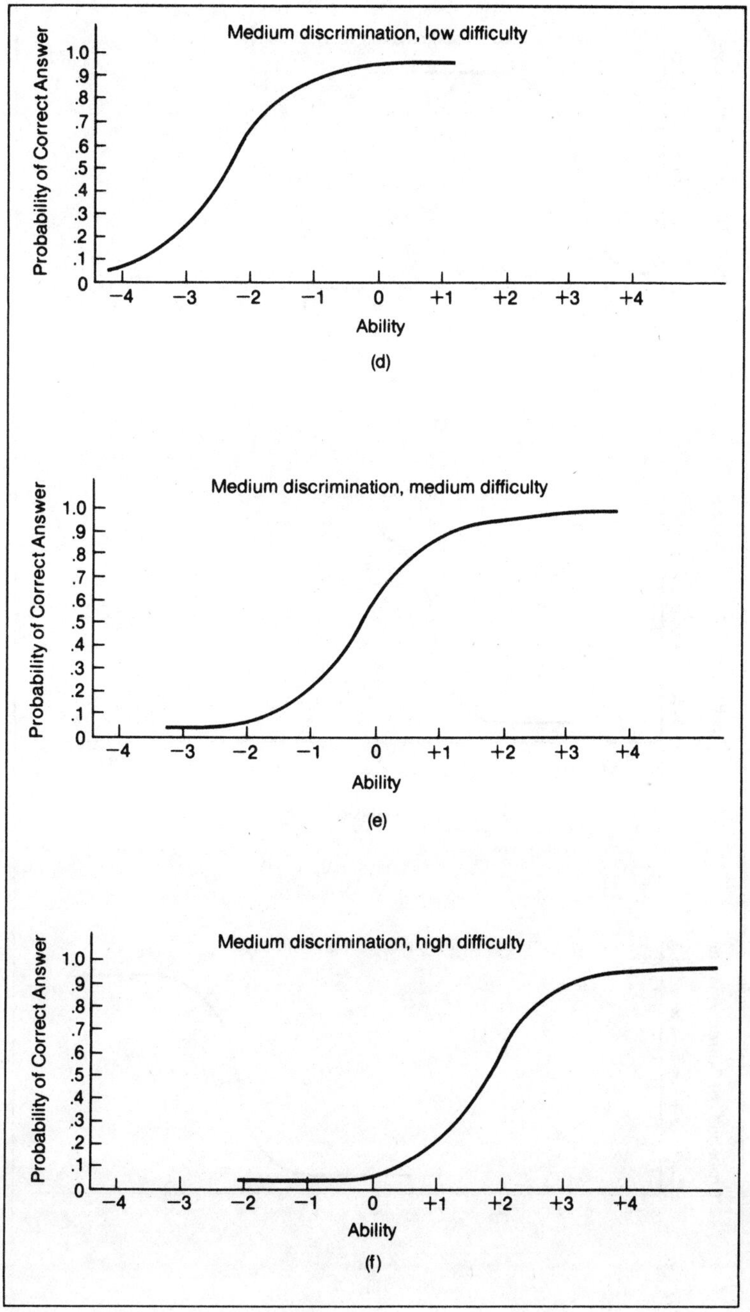

Figure 8.2
(continued).

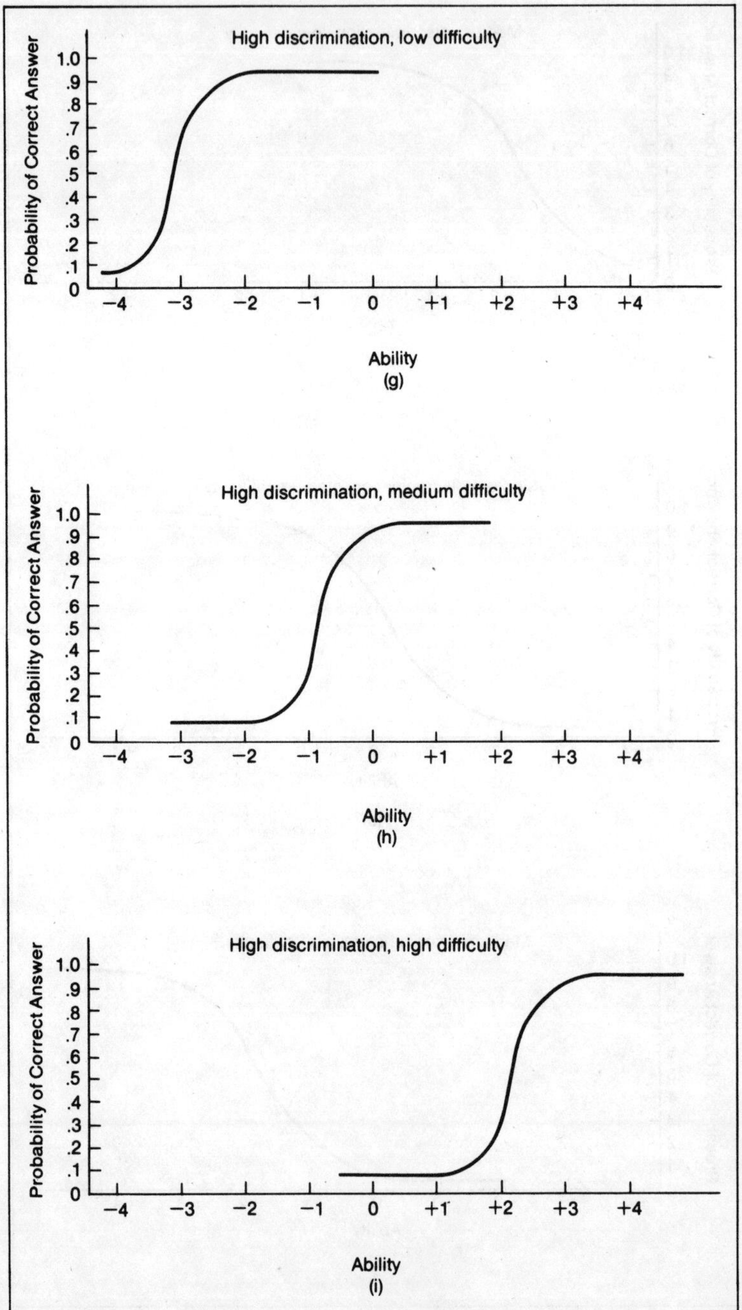

The Three-Parameter Model The model that has gained most acceptance is the three-parameter logistic model (Lord & Novick, 1968). The additional parameter is intended to control for the fact that even the student with the lowest ability does not have a zero probability of obtaining a correct answer. He or she can always guess and have some chance of getting the question correct. Interestingly, this parameter is not set at the chance level because these students typically obtain lower scores than would be anticipated if they were guessing blindly. This is a result of the cleverness of the item writer, who makes incorrect alternatives appear appealingly correct. For this reason Lord and Novick refer to this as the "pseudo chance level," rather than the "chance level" or "guessing level." The problem with using this parameter is that it requires a substantial number of subjects of very low ability for its estimation; often the norm sample used will not contain enough subjects with ability low enough for its estimation.

The Rasch Model Still another latent-trait model developed independently of the logistic model is called the Rasch model (Rasch, 1960). It is a one-parameter model in which the discrimination of all items is assumed to be the same. This model has the advantage of being simpler than the others, and when the assumptions on which it is based are met, the ability scale appears to have ratio scale characteristics. The major limitation of the Rasch model is that the assumption of equivalent discrimination among items seems difficult to defend. On the other hand, the mathematical methods used to estimate the parameters used in the other models have caused even greater problems. If these parameters cannot be accurately estimated, models that require them will also be difficult to defend.

Applications

After deciding on the particular latent-trait model to be used, it is necessary to estimate ability scores and item parameters. This is the most difficult part of latent-trait analysis procedure. The most often-used technique for obtaining this information is the *maximum likelihood estimate*. There are many permutations of this technique, as well as other related approaches, that can be employed. Because of the large amount of data and the complexity of the approach, this analysis must be conducted with the aid of a computer. There are several computer packages available for this analysis. The one most prominently mentioned in the literature is LOGIST (Wood, Wingersky, & Lord, 1976). With this approach the parameters are set initially using an a priori estimate of each student's ability. The standard score, based on the number of correct items, is most often used for this purpose. Next the item parameters are estimated for each item; ability scores are then computed for each student using these parameters. New parameters are estimated, and the process is repeated until the equation stabilizes and new iterations fail to improve on the estimates. This process yields a set of parameters for each item and an ability score for each student. The ability score is initially on a scale similar to the small z-scale score. This score can then be linearly transformed (multiplied or divided by constants and/or added to constants) into a convenient scale.

This approach finds a diversity of possible applications, but at the present time it is being used mainly in test development. The value of the data obtained through the application of latent-trait theory results from the stability of the shape of the item curve across different samples of subject. As a result, the item parameters also have a high degree of stability.

Test Development In the process of test development, it is necessary to generate a pool of items and then try them out on a sample of subjects. With traditional methods it is desirable to use a "try out" group that is as similar as possible to the population with which the test will eventually be used. Accomplishing this can entail a considerable commitment of resources, but failing to do it can lead to errors in item selection that result from the inadequacies of the try-out group. There is always the possibility that the item chacacteristics of the try-out group will differ from the population with which the test is eventually to be used.

Through the use of latent-trait theory, it is possible to use a small number of items selected from a standardized test that has been nationally normed and from which parameters have been derived. By including some items from the nationally normed test with try-out test items, it is possible to gain enough information to adjust the parameters of the try-out test in such a way that it takes on the same characteristics as the nationally normed tests. This not only saves money, but can lead to the development of a better test.

Item Analysis The parameters obtained through latent-trait analysis can also be used to conduct item analyses. Needless to say, the implementation of such an analysis requires a great deal of measurement knowledge and computer sophistication. Right now it is mainly being used by commercial test companies that are employing it in overall test development.

Latent-trait methods have several apparent advantages over standard item analyses. First of all, they are less sample dependent. Conventional methods such as discrimination indexes and item total-score correlations tend to change across samples. An item might prove to be a good discriminator with one group but a poor one with another. Because latent-trait parameters are based on an underlying trait, presumably independent of the sample, they promise greater stability.

It is also possible to determine not only how well an item fits with the overall test, but how well it works with different subsets of students. An item that over all does not appear to be a good item might be shown to be effective with high-functioning students and be retained for this reason.

It needs to be pointed out that the use of this approach to item analysis is in its early stages of development. To this point, there is a lack of clear evidence that tests developed using this approach are in fact superior to those developed using more conventional item-analysis techniques.

Test Equating Similar techniques to those used in item analysis can be used to equate tests both horizontally and vertically. *Horozontal equating* refers to the process of developing equivalent forms. By including common items in two tests, it is possible—by means of multiplying, dividing, and/or adding constants—to make the parameters for the two tests equivalent. This does not necessarily mean that the two tests are of equivalent difficulty, and scoring based on number of right answers may not produce an equivalent test. However, when the test is scored using a computer program based on the latent-trait model, it is possible to produce ability scores for students that have the same meaning for students regardless of which test is taken.

Vertical Equating Vertical equating is used when a test is developed that has different levels to correspond to different grades. The approach used by Wendy Yen in the development of the Comprehensive Test of Basic Skills (CTBS, 1982) was to develop linking tests that included items from adjacent levels and then have subsets of the norming population take both the level of the test appropriate for their grade as well as the two adjoining linking tests. It was then possible to go step by step through the levels of the test, and, by making adjustments; arrive at a final set of parameters that were meaningful across the entire range of grades.

Test Bias Another area where item characteristics derived from latent-trait analyses can be useful is in the construction of nondiscriminatory tests. The more precise item-characteristic data can be used to determine whether individual items are equally fair for all subpopulations being assessed. By determining whether the difficulty of items differs across subgroups whose overall ability level has been equated, it is possible to learn which items are biased. This has the advantage not only of stability across different samples, but it is also more theoretically sound than other methods.

Test Banks and Tailor-Made Tests Latent-trait theory can also be used in the development of test banks. This requires the storage of large numbers of items in computer memory along with their parameters. Tests are constructed from this pool, and the scores obtained from two students taking different tests can be made comparable, even though the two tests had no items in common. It is possible to construct tailor-made tests in this fashion; this enables students to take tests on an individual basis, at any time. The fear that the security of the test will be compromised is eliminated because every student gets a different test.

Criterion-Referenced Tests Finally, there is work being done in the area of using latent-trait theory as the basis for constructing criterion-referenced tests. This permits the construction of items that maximize the probability of discriminating between students who have mastered and those who have not.

Conclusions

Latent-trait theory is a new and exciting aspect of measurement, and its uses and applications can be expected to multiply in the future. The increased availability of microcomputers can be expected to make these techniques more readily accessible.

Bias in Achievement Tests

Much of the criticism of standardized testing during recent years has had bias as its focus, and much of this concern has centered on the perceived unfairness of such tests for minorities, particularly for blacks. These tests are believed to be unfair because, as a group, black students obtain average scores that are lower than those of white students. This discrimination is often labeled bias. Unfortunately this is not an easily defined term, and one of the most important impediments in obtaining an understanding of bias results from the variety of meanings associated with it. In the press and for the general public, the term is used to describe unfairness in testing. Any test that yields results other than those anticipated or desired is labeled biased. There are many reasons why test results may end up being other than what we want, and the reasons do not always center around faults in the test themselves.

Bias can be described either in terms of the relationship between the test and a criterion variable or in terms of individual items. Individual items, in turn, can be evaluated either by judges (who presumably are able to detect bias by inspection), or through the examination of their psychometric characteristics.

To distinguish between perceptions of unfairness and the technical measurement characteristics of a test, testing specialists divide bias into two types. *Vernacular bias* describes circumstances where a test appears to be unfair, whereas *statistical bias* is associated more with the psychometric characteristics of a test. The difference between the two is illustrated by the following example.

Suppose you administer a math aptitude test and a math achievement test to a group of seventh-graders, and suppose the boys do better on the aptitude test than the girls. One response might be to say that the test is biased against girls. This would be vernacular test bias. If it turned out that the boys and girls performed equally on a math achievement test, or that the girls did better than the boys, then the math aptitude test would be underestimating the ability of the girls, and we would say that the aptitude test was statistically biased against the girls. On the other hand, if performance on the math achievement test is at the level predicted by the aptitude test even though the performance of the boys is higher than that obtained by the girls, then the test is not considered *statistically* biased because the aptitude test is accurately predicting achievement.

Understanding bias through examination of the relationship between a test and a criterion has some limitations. It is first of all only appropriate when a suitable criterion exists and this tends to restrict its applicability to aptitude tests. Achievement tests cannot easily be evaluated in this fashion. Such analyses also fail to tell us what aspects of a test are biased; furthermore, there are technical limitations to the approach that can make the results equivocal.

The usefulness of the distinction between vernacular and statistical bias also has limitations. Issues of bias are not merely an esoteric measurement issue, but are the basis for widespread concern about testing. Individuals that are concerned about test bias, even if what they are identifying is only vernacular test bias, are not likely to be mollified by explanations of the meaning of statistical bias. Test publishers find themselves under pressure to avoid the appearance that their tests are unfair and must therefore be concerned with vernacular bias whenever the scores of minority and nonminority students differ. If the differences among subgroup mean scores on a test are small, it is possible to manipulate the item content to eliminate those differences. This is what is usually done with mental ability tests, to erase differences between the sexes. When the differences are large they cannot be eliminated in this fashion without seriously degrading the overall validity of the test. Unfortunately, some publishers have done this to increase the marketability of their tests.

Another popular approach is to employ judges to determine whether items appear to be unfair to different minority groups. Other than as an exercise in public relations and as a way to show that the publisher is working hard to eliminate bias, this is not particularly useful. It is quite difficult to determine how an item is functioning in a test or whether it is fair by inspection alone. Not only do judges tend to identify items as being biased when psychometric evidence shows them to be unbiased, but more puzzlingly, they fail to identify items that other evidence indicates are biased.

More empirical approaches to understanding bias include examinations of such characteristics as item discrimination and item difficulty. Comparing ethnic groups on the basis of the discrimination of items does not work very well because item discrimination is distorted by the existence of group differences in mean test scores. This can cause the resulting discrimination indexes to be unstable. A more straightforward approach is to rank order items in terms of their difficulty, across different ethnic groups. Items that are more difficult for a particular group might, on the basis of this evidence, be considered biased. This conclusion, although more sound than one based solely on the opinion of judges, is not entirely satisfactory. Its acceptance rests on the same shaky ground as the case for vernacular bias—the assumption that the specific skills or knowledge tapped by an item is the same across groups, and that any differences in the ranking of item difficulty proves that bias exists.

The use of item characteristics that are derived from latent-trait theory seems to be a more sound approach because item characteristics obtained in this fashion can be made statistically independent of the group from which they are obtained.

The concern about test bias and fairness has spawned a large amount of research into the relationship between test scores and items and how the interpretation of tests should be altered by group membership. The results of this research are unlikely to be applied because there appears to be an inverse relationship between vernacular and statistical bias. By lessening statistical bias in a test, it is likely that you will increase group differences and the appearance of vernacular bias. Because test publishers are primarily interested in eliminating these differences in order to increase sales, the new knowledge that is being acquired about test and item characteristics, as they relate to bias, is unlikely to ever be applied (Linn, 1984).

SUMMARY

1. There is always the possibility of improving any achievement test.
2. The three approaches to improving these tests include ensuring content validity, following good test-construction practices, and employing item-analysis techniques.

3. Item analysis can be conducted in three ways: (1) by means of item discriminations, (2) item total-score correlations, (3) and item characteristics based on latent-trait theory.
4. Latent-trait analysis provides a powerful measurement technique for obtaining more precise derived scores, better item-analysis techniques, improved item banking, and better methods for constructing tailor-made tests.
5. Test bias can be categorized as being either vernacular or statistical.
6. Eliminating bias is difficult because methods of correcting statistical bias tend to increase vernacular bias.

SUGGESTED READINGS

ALLEN, M. J., & YEN, W. M. (1979). *Introduction to measurement theory*. Monterey, CA: Brooks/Cole. [Chapter 11 of this relatively small book is a very readable and useful description of latent-trait techniques.]

EBEL, R. L. (1979). *Essentials of educational measurement* (3rd ed.). Englewood Cliffs, NJ: Prentice-Hall. [This book contains a good description of methods of conducting item analyses.]

GRONLUND, N. E. (1985). *Measurement and evaluation in teaching* (5th ed.). New York: Macmillan. [This book provides excellent descriptions of the best ways to improve tests.]

HAMBLETON, R. K., SWAMINATHAN, H., COOK, L. L., EIGNOR, D. R., & GIFFORD, J. A. (1978). Developments in latent trait theory: Models, technical issues, and applications. *Review of Educational Research*, *40*, 467–510. [This is an up-to-date, readable review of what is being done in the area of latent-trait theory.]

LINN, R. L. (1984). Selection bias: Multiple meanings. *Journal of Educational Measurement* *21*(1), 33–47. [This article provides a sophisticated discussion of methods for understanding test bias as a function of prediction. The author makes the interesting point that the elimination of bias may have unexpected results. Individuals with low scores who believe that their scores are low because of bias may find their scores are even lower when corrections for bias are made.]

LORD, F. M. (1980). *Applications of item response theory to practical testing problems*. Hillsdale, NJ: Erlbaum. [This is a primary source for information on latent-trait theory. The presentation is technical and requires a fair level of reader sophistication.]

LORD, F. M., & NOVICK, M. R. (1968). *Statistical theories of mental test scores*. Reading, MA: Addison-Wesley. [With the additional contributions of Allan Birnbaum, this can be thought of as a classic book on the topic of latent theory. The mathematical basis for the three-parameter method of understanding latent traits is presented.]

SHEPARD, L., CAMILLI, G. & WILLIAMS, D. M. (1984). Accounting for statistical artifacts in item bias research. *Journal of Educational Statistics*, *9*, 93–128. [This is an excellent discussion and description of item-analysis methods of assessing test bias. The emphasis is on item-response-theory techniques.]

9

Assigning Grades

OVERVIEW

An important task that teachers are expected to accomplish is that of reporting on student learning progress. This process begins with testing, which provides the teacher with an indication of student performance in the form of raw scores. Next, the teacher must take those data and turn them into a form that parents and others who need to know about a student's progress can understand. The usual method for accomplishing this is by converting performance into grades. It is not easy to transform raw scores from a test into grades, but the process is often treated as though it were. This entire process deserves to be examined thoughtfully, and decisions concerning how it takes place need to be made carefully. This chapter begins with an explanation of why we need grades. The different methods of evaluating scores and transforming them to grades are discussed next. A preferred model for accomplishing this is presented, and the chapter concludes with explanations of the best ways to combine inputs from different sources and the problems of grade inflation.

OBJECTIVES

From this chapter you will learn about the various methods of assigning grades—the methods that are recommended and those that are not. Specifically you will learn

- The five methods of assigning grades, which include intuitive approaches, ipsative methods, reference-to-perfection approaches, criterion-referenced evaluation, and norm-referenced evaluation.
- A basic recommended method for assigning grades.
- The best ways of combining inputs so that a single grade can be assigned.

Introduction

Evaluating students and assigning grades is generally viewed as one of the most unpleasant aspects of the educational process. Not only are the mechanical aspects of the process difficult, but there are many educators who oppose the entire process on philosophical grounds.

As much as we may oppose the grading process philosophically, and as troublesome as it is, we cannot eliminate grades. Experimental attempts to operate public schools on a grade-free basis have been unsuccessful. This is largely because parents and students end up directing hostility toward teachers, who, it is felt, are not doing their job.

The assignment of grades involves the making of comparisons, and comparisons are generally odious. There are few students who genuinely enjoy the grading process. For teachers, grading is an activity that requires a great deal of time and effort; it is one for which the payoff is often a sizable number of dissatisfied students.

Most of us tend to weave a fantasy about ourselves in order to maintain our self-image. Grades constitute an unwelcome form of reality testing. Grades are stark and often traumatic, and they operationalize and legitimize the practices of our meritocracy, allowing those who achieve the most or who have the most ability to reap the greatest rewards.

At one time, when social class was the most important determiner of success, the systematic assessment of ability was considered a force on the side of democracy because it allowed the poor child with ability a chance to succeed regardless of family background. We have now reached the point where an emphasis on grades is considered elitest and undemocratic.

The Need for Grades

Grades provide feedback to the student. Most learning theorists from behaviorists to cognitivist-gestaltists have emphasized this as a necessary component for learning. It is hard to improve unless you know how you are doing, but the feedback also must be honest. Because the natural inclination of most teachers is to be helpful and supportive, they tend to dislike giving feedback that is not positive. However, when every child gets high praise, no one is getting useful feedback.

The process of growing and developing involves the testing of limits. Children need to know how they stand in relation to peers. If they only receive erroneously positive feedback, their movement toward maturity is likely to be stunted. If students are to improve, they need to know when improvement is needed.

Parents also need to know how their child is progressing in school. There are a number of possible means of fulfilling this need: anecdotal records, teacher conferences, and/or lists of objectives mastered or not mastered are possible means of communication. Experience has shown that parents know, understand, and respond best to the traditional methods of assigning grades. In order to institute an alternate system, a tremendous amount of parent education would be necessary. Up to this point, the attempts to substitute alternate methods of reporting student progress have met with strong parental objections.

Parents have a right to the accurate reporting of their children's progress in school, in language they understand. Avoiding the anguish of assigning grades by only giving high grades also must be avoided. Nothing is more damaging to parent-school rapport than to have parents erroneously believe that their child has no academic problems. The school does no one a favor by shielding the child in this manner.

The school also has a responsibility to certify that students know the material in the courses they have taken. If a student receives a satisfactory grade in a course, it should be reasonable to expect that the prospective employers or schools to which the student is applying can have confidence that the grade means something. Clearly this is not a school's only responsibility, or even its first responsibility, but it is a responsibility nevertheless.

Standards Used to Compare Students

All grading methods are based on comparisons, or references to some standard. This is necessary because tests, whether they are teacher-made or standardized, start off as a raw score. This can either be in the form of the number of questions right, as is the case with an objective test, or points, which are often used on more subjective tests. Although these scores may have some intrinsic meaning, they do not tell us much about absolute performance, and they require further interpretation before they can be used for assigning grades. There are five approaches, or references, that can be used: intuitive, ipsative, reference to perfection, norm-referenced, and criterion-referenced. These terms are used to distinguish between different types of tests, but it is more accurate to think of them as representing different methods of interpreting the results of tests. Although the tests and the items on which they are based may all look the same, it is the interpretation of their meaning that may differ.

The Intuitive Approach

The teacher who uses the intuitive approach believes that there is no need for a careful delineation of course requirements and grading policies because he or she knows how a student should perform in order to receive a certain grade. This approach has the flavor of norm-referenced testing because the teacher is generally making a subconscious comparison with all of the other students with whom he or she has had experience.

The intuitive approach is most often used at the elementary school level. This approach can be justified under some circumstances, but it does require an inordinate amount of experience, and it permits extraneous factors to affect the decision. Sometimes such approaches have subjective testing for their basis, which calls for a great deal of judgment. If such informal evaluation procedures are used, the designation of good and poor performance is a subjective decision made by the teacher. If you choose to use such an approach and you have the experience and the nerve to pull it off, you might be successful, but the odds are against you.

Ipsative Methods

When a student's performance is evaluated by making comparisons with his or her own performance, the process is referred to as an ipsative evaluation. There are two ways that this approach can be used to assign grades: on the basis of effort, and the amount of improvement. The two are clearly related. The child who starts the year behind but shows improvement gets a higher grade than the child who is ahead at the beginning of the year but shows no improvement. The usefulness of such an approach is dependent on the accuracy of preinstructional test scores. This approach, therefore, could not be used with sophisticated students because there is the possibility that they might fake a low-entry skill level.

When final performance in a class is dependent on incoming level of ability, teachers face particular problems. For instance, on the first day of art and music classes, some students can perform at a level that exceeds that of other students with less ability when they have finished the course. There is an understandable reluctance to ignore the degree of improvement over the year. The student gifted in art who does nothing for a semester probably does not deserve an A, despite the fact that at the end of the course he or she can produce the best project. Conversely, it seems only fair to give credit to the student who starts with little ability but who, through the expenditure of great effort, shows considerable improvement.

Another use of ipsative scoring is in diagnostic testing, where the focus is on intrasubject variability. Diagnostic testing is predicated on the assumption that within each individual there are strengths and weaknesses that can be identified and can serve as a focus for instruction. Diagnostic testing is discussed further in Chapter 12, "Achievement Testing."

In general the use of ipsative methods for the assignment of grades is strongly discouraged. Grades based on this approach are not useful for purposes of certification. No one would want to be operated on by a surgeon who was awarded his or her medical degree on the basis of effort, or fly in an airplane guided by a pilot who showed great improvement in his training. As teachers we have no right to certify students as literate and knowledgeable on the basis of ipsative comparisons.

Reference to Perfection

When a teacher walks into a classroom and places the following scale (or some other permutation) on the chalkboard, he or she is evaluating students using the reference to perfection approach.

A	95–100
B	88–94
C	80–87
D	70–79
F	Below 70

It is the method that is most often used for communicating the meaning of a student's score on a teacher-made test. This method is not used with standardized tests because it is inconsistent with accepted psychometric practice. Many textbooks discuss this approach as a historical curiosity that is no longer being used. However, it is often used by teachers because it is simple and because it has a long tradition. It even has been institutionalized by entire school systems. The reason for its unpopularity with measurement experts stems from the fact that the assumptions on which it is based are unlikely to be met.

Assumptions The primary assumption underlying this approach is the requirement that a score of 100 percent represent a meaningful entity. That is, we must know what 100 percent means when applied to a specific test. Consider a test administered to third-graders consisting of a series of single-digit multiplication problems. Such a test (albeit a prohibitively long one) would consist of all hundred "facts." In this case the test encompasses the entire domain of possible items. A perfect score would mean that the student knew all such facts. A score of 80 percent would indicate that the student got 80 percent of the facts correct. In this case the score is meaningful in comparison to complete mastery.

In most cases a score of 100 percent means only that the student got all of the questions correct. There is a big difference between getting all of the questions on a test correct and getting all questions correct within a domain, such as was illustrated with the multiplication test.

To use the reference-to-perfection approach, we need to know how the items on a test are related to the domain of all possible questions that could be asked on a given test. We also need to know what it means to get no answers correct. In other words, we need to be able to define absolute zero.

In the context of the discussion of scaling that appears in Chapter 2, for reference to perfection to work, the scores must be of ratio-scale level. The multiplication test mentioned earlier might be of a ratio scale because the child who gets no questions right might be considered to have no knowledge of multiplication facts. Of course no child would be likely to get a zero score because by chance alone, with some guessing, the child is always going to get some answers correct even if he or she knows none of the facts.

Because this approach is based on one hundred points, there is the false impression that scores can legitimately be combined as long as the total number of possible points adds up to one hundred. The fallacy of this assumption is explained in the section on combining scores in this chapter.

Now consider a test of fifty multiple-choice questions about the Civil War administered to a fifth-grade class. Getting all of the questions right does not tell us that the child knows everything there is to know about the Civil War; nor does it tell us everything that a fifth-grader should know about the Civil War. At the same time it is not clear what it means if a child gets every question wrong. We cannot comfortably say that the child knows nothing about the Civil War. As a matter of fact, the score of a student on such a test tells relatively little about a student's absolute knowledge.

For the reference-to-perfection approach to work, we must assume that all tests are of equal and appropriate difficulty. This is an assumption so absurd as to need no refutation. If various tests differ in terms of difficulty, which they must, we are not measuring a student in any absolute sense; the grade a student gets is more a function of the chance factors that go into determining the difficulty of a test than anything else.

Additional Problems with This Approach The meaning of an acceptable percent correct also differs according to the subject matter with which it is used. The student who gets 80 percent of the questions on a test about the Civil War correct might be thought to have accomplished some minimal level of competence in the subject, but the child who only knows 80 percent of his or her multiplication facts is probably deficient in knowledge of this topic. It would be necessary to set up a different set of percentages for grades for each subject matter if the reference to perfection approach to student evaluation were to be adopted.

Real-World Applications Despite its obvious limitations, this is the most often-used method of assigning grades. Teachers that use this approach quickly learn that, as a result of variability in test difficulty, they are likely to obtain grade distributions contrary to their expectations. This leads to adjustments in the grading system. They start out with a grading scale that specifies the raw score necessary for different grades, they construct and administer the test, and finally they examine the resulting grade distribution. If the test proves too difficult, and an unacceptable number of low grades seems imminent, then some sort of adjustments are made. The usual method of adjusting the scale is either to award extra credit in some way, or to make the next test easier. Similarly, if the test is too easy, the teacher will have to grade harder or make the next test more difficult. The goal is to bring the distribution within the limits of the expected range of acceptable grades. In this way the best students still get the highest grades, the poor students still get the lowest grades, and the distribution of grades is kept within acceptable limits.

Your first reaction might be that such adjustments are dishonest and that students should get the grade they deserve. The reference to perfection approach, however, does not tell us the grade a student deserves, which is its big promise and major failing. There is simply nothing innately revealing about the ratio of the number of questions a student gets right and the total number of questions on a test.

Comparisons with Other Methods The reference-to-perfection approach has some of the characteristics of norm-referenced and some of criterion-referenced assessment. It resembles norm-referenced testing to the extent that a teacher makes a decision about a student's grade based on the goal of obtaining a fixed distribution of grades for the students in a class. It resembles criterion-referenced tests by endeavoring to set absolute standards. In comparison to these two approaches it is awkward and forced, which results in a lack of precision. Even though it may produce a grade distribution similar to what would be obtained with a norm-referenced approach, the results are not identical. When the approaches yield different grade distributions, we need to ask which provides the best assignment of class grades. The degree to which grades obtained by means of the reference-to-perfection approach differ from those obtained using the norm-referenced approach is a function of error resulting from the violated assumptions surrounding the reference-to-perfection approach.

Why This Approach Is Used Students are usually quite happy with explanations of grading policies based on the reference-to-perfection method because they are familiar with them. In the event that they begin thinking about more than just the surface characteristics of this approach, they are likely to be less satisfied. Because the reference-to-perfection approach is so indirect and misleading, it cannot easily be explained to students or peers. The forced adjustments to obtain acceptable distributions of grades are not easily justified either.

The decision concerning where, within the culturally imposed bounds of a grade distribution, a teacher want to be is much more capricious when the reference-to-perfection method is used. It is better for a teacher to make a conscious decision about how hard a grader he or she wants to be than to allow this to occur in the more indirect ways it will be manifested under the reference-to-perfection approach.

The use of this method of student evaluation continues unabated, largely as a result of ignorance. Students demand an explanation of grading policies and they get one. The use of this approach to evaluation continues as a result of the gap between what is known about the best ways of conducting educational evaluation and what teachers believe can reasonably be applied in the classroom.

Criterion-Referenced Evaluation

Although teacher-made tests are usually evaluated by means of a reference-to-perfection approach, criterion-referenced testing has increased in popularity. It is being used for assigning grades as well as many other evaluation purposes. Defining and describing criterion-referenced testing are much more formidable tasks than describing any of the other methods. Criterion-referenced testing is a relatively new method, and there is little agreement concerning just what it is. Briefly, and according to the most often-used definition, criterion-referenced tests are those for which the interpretation of the results provides information concerning *what* a student has learned, rather than how he or she did in relation to someone else, as is done with norm-referenced tests. The criterion-referenced results of a math test, for instance, might indicate that a child can add columns of figures eight high but cannot do so if carrying is required, or that he or she can do simple subtraction that does not require borrowing. This is, of course, awkward to communicate, so the process is simplified by defining the content in terms of objectives and then describing the child's performance in terms of objectives mastered and not mastered.

There are two types of criterion-referenced test situations: those where we measure performance absolutely and those where it is measured relatively. Popham (1981) distinguishes between criterion as a level and criterion as a desired behavior, with the former being relative and the latter being absolute. In the case of solving math problems or conducting chemistry experiments, successful mastery is absolute. Unfortunately, most subject matter taught in schools cannot easily be evaluated in an absolute sense. The acquisition of most subject matter must be evaluated in a relative sense. For instance, a person does not either understand or not understand the motivation of Hamlet or the causes of the Civil War. Understanding is a question of degree. The use of criterion-referenced tests is awkward under these circumstances.

One suggested solution to this problem is to employ much more detailed descriptions of performance than behavioral objectives. This forces us to face the question of what true criterion-referenced testing is. We must decide whether the common practice of assessing performance in terms of the mastery of objectives deserves to be called criterion-referenced testing, or whether much more sophisticated descriptions, as advocated by Popham (1981), are required before a given practice can be called criterion-referenced testing. These issues will be discussed in detail in Chapter 10, "Criterion-Referenced Testing."

The use of criterion-referenced methods of assigning grades is also awkward. Strictly speaking, there are only two states relative to instructional objectives when using this method: mastery and nonmastery. It is difficult to decide whether the student who masters should get an A, B, or C. Of course it is possible to devise a system based on partial mastery or the mastery of a given proportion of objectives. The major problem encountered with such systems, however, is devising a rational basis for accomplishing this. What generally happens is that such decisions become entirely subjective and one finds him- or herself with a system quite similar to the reference-to-perfection approach. A set of arbitrary standards must be set up to designate the number of items that must be correct before we can say that a student has mastered an objective. Likewise, the proportion of objectives necessary for each grade must be designated. Unless the items measuring an objective were randomly selected from the domain of all possible items, the grades a student gets are determined by item difficulty and the cut-off scores that have been set by the teacher. A pass-fail system is probably the only acceptable form of grading with this method. The all too common practice of assigning an A to students who master, results in rampant grade inflation and a general denigration of the grading process.

Norm-Referenced Grading

This method of evaluating students is perhaps the best way for the classroom teacher to assign grades. It compares an individual's score with a reference group in order to determine what grade to assign. The simplest form of norm-referenced comparison is ranking. If you look at the results of a test and rank the students in your class from highest to lowest, you are using a norm-referenced approach. Of course if you merely rank students, a great deal of information provided by the test scores is lost. The difference between the student who got fifteen out of twenty questions correct and the one who got sixteen correct is much less than the difference between the student who got ten correct and the student who got fifteen correct. Ranking masks those differences. Ranking implies ordinal-scale data, with their inherent limitations on computation. For this reason, it is best to utilize more elaborate systems for interpreting scores, such as the standard scores discussed in Chapter 2.

Grading on the Curve The use of test scores to rank students has always been a big part of the grading procedure, but the difficult aspect of grading does not involve ranking but the determination of how many students should receive each grade. Grading on the curve involves basing the decision on the normal distribution, awarding as many A's as F's and proportionally more C's than any other grade. Grading on the curve is a special case of norm-referenced grading, and it is quite possible to interpret scores through a norm-reference process without "grading on the curve."

A Basic Model for Grading

The biggest problem with grading practices as they exist today is that they remain unexamined. Teachers tend to grade the way they have always graded, the way their peers grade, or the way their own teachers graded. They often look with disfavor on any rational discussion of their methods because they cannot easily defend what they are doing. This tendency is exacerbated by the fact that those involved with administering tests and assigning grades are likely to have had minimal training in this area. The result is a high degree of defensiveness that manifests itself in an unwillingness to talk or even think about what is done or why it is being done.

Bringing teachers to the point where their methods are correct, from a textbook point of view, is not a realistic goal. The most important consideration is whether after due deliberation they can evaluate their own policies and procedures and feel comfortable about what they are doing.

Assigning grades involves two distinct procedures: (1) a determination of approximately how many of each grade to assign—that is, how many A's, B's, C's—and (2) who should get which grades.

Deciding How Many of Each Grade to Assign

This procedure may seem strange to you. The idea of determining how many of each grade to give ahead of time may seem like an unusual practice. You might be thinking that it is better to construct the test, administer it, and then assign the grades earned, with the distribution of grades determined by the performance of the students. Such a procedure would have to be based on the naive assumption that a grade is an inherent property of a test score: if the construction of a test is subjective, the grade distribution would be determined by the difficulty of the test.

It is much more reasonable to view a grade as a subjective categorization conferred by the instructor, and to rank order the students and determine the cutoffs between grades on the basis of how many of each grade you intend to assign. It needs to be emphasized that this anticipated grade distribution must be approached with flexibility. It should be viewed as a set of general guidelines that can and should be modified when the instructor feels that this is appropriate.

Grades as a Cultural Artifact The determination of how many of each grade to assign is a difficult process; we are forced to rely on subjective decisions that themselves depend more on the cultural milieu in which we are operating than on any other factor. Wherever you teach there will be rules governing the number of each grade you can assign. These rules may be written down explicitly or involve an implicit understanding. No one may ever tell you, but you will know and follow the rules anyhow. Rules are in the form of acceptable ranges of grades. These differ from institution to institution; some will be liberal and allow many high grades while others are more conservative and mandate that teachers give low grades. You might choose to be at the high end of the range, giving a lot of high grades and being labeled an easy grader; or you might choose to function at the low end of the range, giving out more low grades and being labeled with terminology unprintable here. If you violate the limits, you will most likely hear from your supervisor. You also will be likely to feel peer pressure. The enforcement of the rules varies depending on the setting. The important point is that there are rules, you will know what they are, and most likely you will stay within their limits.

Setting Your Cutoff Points The cutoff points that determine the number of each grade you are to assign should be determined by three factors: (1) the limits imposed by the setting in which you are teaching; (2) whether you choose to be an easy, hard, or middle-of-the-road grader; and (3) your perception of the general functioning of the class. If a specific class seems particularly bright, you will be inclined to give more A's and B's and fewer lower grades. If its your perception that the class is performing below standards, you likely will assign more lower grades.

Who Should Get Which Grade

Once the number of each grade assigned is known, decisions must be made concerning who is to get each. This is easier than determining how many of each grade to assign because we can call on the resources of a long tradition of testing and evaluation to aid in the process. The principles of test construction and administration are well known, if not universally applied.

The best method for making these decisions is to use the norm-referenced approach. This means that grades are based on tests that permit students to be rank ordered: the highest grades are assigned to students with the highest rank, and lower grades are assigned according to each student's position in the hierarchy.

Tests can be constructed in many different ways as long as they yield a score because the score is what is used to rank order the students. Testing needs to be based on the assumption that grades are intended to reflect a pure measure of knowledge or accomplishment. Extraneous factors such as behavior and attitude should not be allowed to intrude into the grade-assignment process.

Combining Scores

Quite often it is necessary to combine scores from several inputs in order to obtain a single score for determining a grade. For instance, the instructor may want to combine performance on a midterm, a final exam, a term paper, and class participation. The teacher might want the midterm to count 30 percent, the final exam 40 percent, the term paper 20 percent, and class participation 10 percent. These inputs are usually incorrectly combined by means of a point system, such as having each of 60 questions on the midterm count a half point and each of 80 questions on the final exam count a half point and to award up to 20 points for the term paper and up to 10 points for class participation. In that way there is the possibility of a total of 100 points. It is assumed that, by allocating points in this way, the desired weighting of each factor will result. This will usually not be the case. The total possible number of points is only partially related to the weight of a given factor. It is the amount of variability that determines how much an input is weighted.

Why Adding Raw Scores Does Not Work

Consider a simplified situation where a grade is to be determined by an exam, which is to count 90 percent, and class participation, which is to count 10 percent. This might be implemented by having each question on a 45-question multiple-choice test count 2 points and then assign from 1 to 10 points for class participation. The desired weighting will only occur if there is a 9:1 ratio in variability between the two, which would be very difficult to achieve. Suppose that the test is fairly easy, and everyone gets a score between 80 and 90. In that case the test and class participation contribute nearly equally to a student's grade, as long as the class participation scores are distributed between 0 and 10.

As already stated, the total number of points that a student can receive is not related to the weight of a factor. If a certain number of points are awarded to everyone, then they do not contribute to variability or to how a student does in relationship to peers. It is only variability that is important in determining how much each input is weighted.

Making Sure That Input for Grades Is Properly Weighted

Consider the earlier example in which a teacher wants to count a midterm 30 percent, the final 40 percent, a term paper 20 percent, and class participation 10 percent. Suppose there are 60 questions on the midterm, 80 on the final, 20 possible points on the paper, and 10 possible points for class participation. A typical but incorrect method for obtaining a ranking of students from which grades can be determined would involve summing across the raw scores. Test lengths of 60 and 80 items would be selected because, by awarding a half point for each correctly answered item, the total possible number of points would be 30 and 40, respectively; when added to the 20 for the paper and the 10 for class participation, this yields a total possible number of points of 100. This has two purposes: it creates the illusion that each of the inputs is correctly weighted, and it fits nicely into a reference-to-perfection system of grading. Table 9.1 provides the raw scores, points, and ranking based on raw scores for ten students.

If you are combining several tests that you want to count equally, as long as

TABLE 9.1 Computation of Grades by Summing Raw Scores

Student	Midterm		Final		Paper		Class Participation			
	Raw Score	Points	Raw Score	Points	Raw Score	Points	Raw Score	Points	Total	Rank
Bob	58	29	70	35	3	3	1	1	68	10
Alice	56	28	64	32	12	12	6	6	78	4
June	54	27	60	30	13	13	7	7	77	5
Joe	54	27	68	34	9	9	5	5	75	6
Al	56	28	70	35	4	4	2	2	69	9
Betty	50	25	60	30	19	19	10	10	84	2
Jean	52	26	60	30	20	20	9	9	85	1
Jerry	54	27	66	33	10	10	4	4	74	7
Bill	56	28	68	34	6	6	3	3	71	8
Mary	54	27	62	31	15	15	7	7	80	3

the tests are of about the same length and difficulty, the variability will probably be similar enough for you to be on fairly safe ground. When you start combining inputs such as test scores and term papers that are not based on a common scoring system, or when you want to weight inputs differently, raw scores should not be merely totaled. Before they can be combined in a meaningful way, they must be placed on the same scale. The best way of doing this is to compute T-scores, as was explained in Chapter 3, "Derived Scores." These T-scores can be multiplied by a weighting factor and treated mathematically with confidence that the intended weighting is the weighting that actually occurs.

Table 9.2 lists the same students and their raw scores but has changed each to T-scores and then weighted them by the appropriate percent using the following formula: weighted T-score $((((\text{raw score} - \text{mean}) \div \text{standard deviation}) \times 10) + 50) \times \text{weighting}$. The formula is written in this linear style because this is the way that it would be programmed onto a computer or programmable calculator. Take Bob's score on the midterm, for example. To obtain his weighted T-score you would subtract 54.4 (the mean for the midterm) from 58 (Bob's raw score on the midterm), which would give you a value of 3.6. This would be divided by 2.15 (standard deviation of the midterm), giving you a value of 1.67. This would be multiplied by 10 and the result added to 50, which would yield a T-score of 66.7. Multiplying this times the weighting of 30 percent, or .30, gives you a score of 20.02 rounded off to 20.0. This process would be repeated for each raw score. Obviously, to do this by hand for a large class with several grade inputs would be quite cumbersome. But the preceding formula can be entered onto a programmable calculator or computer and the process made fairly simple.

An examination of Tables 9.1 and 9.2 reveals a sharp contrast in the obtained ranking. They are nearly opposites. This is an extreme case for purposes of illustration, where those who do well on the tests do poorly on the paper and in class participation while those who do poorly on the tests do well on the other inputs. This would be unlikely to occur to this degree in a real-world example. However,

TABLE 9.2 Computation of Grades Using Weighted *T*-Scores

Student	Midterm		Final		Paper		Class Participation		Total	Rank
	Raw Score	Weighted *T*-Score	Raw Score	Weighted *T*-Score	Raw Score	Weighted *T*-Score	Raw Score	Weighted *T*-Score		
Bob	58	20.0	70	25.3	3	7.1	1	5.4	55.8	1
Alice	56	17.2	64	19.2	12	10.3	6	5.2	51.9	4
June	54	14.4	60	15.1	13	10.7	7	5.6	45.8	9
Joe	54	14.4	68	23.3	9	9.2	5	4.9	51.8	5
Al	56	17.2	70	25.3	4	7.4	2	3.8	53.8	2
Betty	50	8.9	60	15.1	19	12.9	10	6.6	43.5	10
Jean	52	11.6	60	15.1	20	13.2	9	6.3	46.2	8
Jerry	54	14.4	66	21.2	10	9.6	4	4.5	49.7	6
Bill	56	17.2	68	23.3	6	8.2	3	4.1	52.8	3
Mary	54	14.4	62	17.1	15	11.4	7	5.6	48.5	7
	$\overline{X}$ =	54.4	$\overline{X}$ =	64.8	$\overline{X}$ =	11.1	$\overline{X}$ =	5.4		
	σ =	2.15	σ =	3.91	σ =	5.55	σ =	2.8		

we would never expect them to be perfectly correlated either. That is why a variety of assignments is required.

Table 9.3 provides the intended and expected weightings for both the point and the weighted T-score method. Notice that the weightings obtained with the T-score method are the same as those intended, whereas the use of the point method yields weightings that are quite different.

Should You Go to This Much Trouble?

It might strike you at this point that this procedure is complex, overly mathematical, and time consuming. You might argue that you have not used such procedures in the past and the sky has not fallen, so why should you start now. It is certainly fair to question the cost of not applying these methods and to ask what will happen if we ignore this issue.

TABLE 9.3 A Comparison of Weightings Using a Point System and *T*-Scores

Inputs	Desired Weightings	Actual Weightings Using *T*-Scores	Actual Weightings Using Points
Midterm	.30	.30	.15
Final	.40	.40	.27
Paper	.20	.20	.39
Class participation	.10	.10	.19

Factors Affecting Weighting

The loss of validity that results from combining scores without considering variability increases with the following four factors. They are discussed in terms of test scores, but it should be understood that the same principles apply for any numerical input used for determining grades. Points used for crediting term papers, projects, or class participation are subject to the same considerations and in fact are even more likely to differ in variability when compared with other sources.

Discrepancies in Variability If a grade is to be determined by tests, with each test to be weighted equally, then each needs to have the same variability before the raw scores can be added. The less similar the variability, the farther we stray from our goal of counting each equally. In the same fashion, if one test is to count twice as much as another, then it needs to have twice the variability. Any time this condition does not exist, the actual weightings will be different from what is intended.

Cause of Variability If two tests are believed to be equivalent but one test has a greater variability because some students have done very poorly as a result of not studying, then a correction to equalize variability will make the poor prformance seem not as bad. It might be argued that the full weight of the poor performance should be reflected in the students' grades.

Correlations Among Tests If tests are highly correlated, the same results will be obtained no matter how the scores are combined. Of course when this is true, there is no need to give more than one test.

Fineness of Discrminations If every student is to get the same grade, it really does not matter what method for combining scores is used—or whether any tests are given and evaluated for that matter. If a teacher gives mostly A's and only a few B's, the fine distinctions provided by sophisticated systems of combining and evaluating scores are probably wasted. In the case of a teacher who gives out a range of such scores, these considerations take on greater importance. This is true because the possibility of misclassification of students is dramatically increased.

Pass-Fail Grading

At one time there was a movement in the United States toward the general adoption of pass-fail methods of grading in colleges and universities. The implementation of this system had two purposes. First of all, it was viewed as a means of avoiding the nonegalitarian aspects of traditional grading procedures. A secondary purpose was to encourage students to enroll in courses that they might otherwise avoid for fear of receiving a bad grade. Although this practice still exists, its use has declined for several reasons. First of all it makes the process of evaluation much more difficult. Under such a system there are only two categories in which to place a student: either passing or failing. Second, it defeats a major purpose of education, promotion of excellence. Third, graduate schools tend to discount grades earned on a pass-fail basis because there is no way to know what the P or F means. Did the student who passed just pass, or is the student reasonably competent? There is no way the reader of a transcript can render a decision.

Grade Inflation

Elementary and high schools typically place strict limits on teachers concerning the number of each grade that can be assigned. The assignment of too many high or low grades can lead to censure in that setting. College instructors are typically given much more latitude because the assignment of grades is construed to fall under the heading of academic freedom. This free hand in assigning grades frequently results in the assignment of high grades. The assignment of too many low grades can lead to student unrest and to the inconvenience of numerous student grievances.

According to Isaac I. Bejar (1981) grade inflation is the increase in grades without a concommitant increase in ability. He states that the grade-inflation phenomenon was most evident between 1964 and 1974 and that since then there has been a leveling in the number of high grades assigned in colleges and universities.

In addition to making an instructor more popular, there are other reasons for the grade-inflation phenomenon. The Vietnam War is often cited as one of them. During the manpower buildup in the Armed Services in the latter half of the 1960s caused by that conflict, poor grades for males could result in the loss of a student deferment, in being drafted, and in an eventual assignment to combat duty in Vietnam. Because colleges and universities were often the center of opposition to the war, many professors bent over backward to avoid assigning low grades to students in danger of being drafted. When grades were raised for one group, in the interest of fairness, they needed to be raised for all groups. Furthermore, our society as a whole and particularly the colleges and universities, became greatly influenced by egalitarian sentiments during that period. Because grades are believed to perpetuate hierarchies, the awarding of uniformly high grades was seen as a blow struck for egalitarianism.

SUMMARY

1. Grading is unpleasant because it is an example of an often unwelcome form of reality testing.
2. Grades provide necessary feedback to students and parents and provide needed certification information for the community.
3. Students are compared and grades derived in five ways: intuitively, with ipsative methods, by means of reference to perfection, normatively, and through criterion-referenced tests.
4. Although commonly used, the reference-to-perfection method is not recommended because the assumptions upon which it is based are so difficult to meet.
5. Grades should be based on a student's academic accomplishments.

6. The first step in assigning grades should be to decide how much of each grade to assign and second the rank order of students should be determined.
7. The number of each grade to assign is not based on psychometric considerations but is, rather, a cultural phenomenon.
8. When combining scores it is necessary to remember that the weighting of an input is a function of variability, not the available number of points.

SUGGESTED READINGS

BIEHLER, R. F., & SNOWMAN, J. (1982). *Psychology applied to teaching*. Boston: Houghton. [This is a nicely done, readable discussion of the techniques and methods of grades and grading.]

GRONLUND, N. E. (1985). *Measurement and evaluation in teaching* (5th ed.). New York: Macmillan. [This book contains an informative chapter on grades and marking.]

HILLS, J. R. (1981) *Measurement and evaluation in the classroom*. Columbus, OH: Merrill. [This is a basic measurement text intended for teacher-preparation programs. It includes six chapters on grades and grading.]

10

Criterion-Referenced Testing

OVERVIEW

One of the most prominent innovations in the field of educational measurement over the last twenty years is criterion-referenced testing. It arrived with great promise and the strong support of those who thought it could eliminate the problems surrounding educational assessment. The historical events that have led to this view are included in this chapter. Unfortunately, in addition to this great promise, this testing methodology is characterized by a number of technical problems. Those problems are outlined along with various approaches to eliminating, or at least ameliorating, them. Finally, the mechanics and methods of setting cutoff scores and computing reliability and validity are included.

OBJECTIVES

From this chapter you will learn about criterion-referenced testing. Specifically you will learn the following:

- The historical development of educational technology and how it eventually led to the development of criterion-referenced testing.
- The reasons for the widespread acceptance of criterion-referenced testing.
- The difficulties associated with setting cutoff scores.
- How to determine the reliability of criterion-referenced tests.
- How to determine the validity of criterion-referenced tests.
- The use of the domain-referenced approach to criterion-referenced testing.

Introduction

Criterion-referenced testing is a form of evaluation that reports results in terms of what a student has learned, rather than how the student compares to others. The purpose of this approach is to describe as accurately as possible what test results mean in terms of specific behaviors. The most common practice is to describe the results of such a test in terms of instructional objectives mastered; a more modern approach is to use amplified objectives, or domain specifications.

Since the widespread adoption of standardized tests following World War I, nearly all testing has been norm-referenced. In fact, norm-referenced testing was never named as such until the need to contrast it with criterion-referenced testing emerged. Although there have been and still are technical problems associated with norm-referenced tests, over the years many of them have been solved. Unfortunately, this is not the case with criterion-referenced tests. Measurement experts are only at the beginning stages of understanding and effectively using criterion-referenced testing. There are problems with their implementation that seem almost unsolvable. There is also a broad gap between the practitioners, who have already implemented this method of testing, and the measurement experts, who are interested in the best ways of implementing this approach. The criterion-referenced testing experts have high expectations concerning the way these tests should be used and tend to be critical of present practices. On the other hand, practitioners do not feel that they can wait for all of the issues to be settled before beginning. They are employing instructional methods that require this sort of testing and prefer to put tests together as best they can, ignoring the unanswered questions about the best ways of using criterion-referenced tests.

Educational Technology

The history of criterion-referenced testing is closely related to the history of educational technology. Educational technology refers to a procedure that employs a reductionist approach to school learning that is roughly based on behaviorist psychology. In practice, this is an instructional approach characterized by the articulation of an overall educational goal followed by a listing of the specific objectives that would permit a student to reach that goal.

Historical Antecedents

Block (1971) describes some of the early attempts to apply these methods in a school setting: the Winnetka plan developed by Carleton Washburne and his associates in 1922 and the Morrison approach developed by Professor Henry C. Morrison in 1926. Both plans involved the setting of terminal objectives, the specification of enabling objectives, and diagnostic testing to monitor progress. The results of this monitoring were to be used as a basis for providing feedback and giving diagnostic assistance. Although these approaches met with some moderate success, their popularity waned, and it was not until World War II that use of the methods enjoyed a resurgence. At that time the military services began hiring psychologists to improve their educational programs, they chose educational technology techniques because such approaches seemed particularly appropriate for use in a military setting. In most cases terminal objectives are easily identified, and there is an adequate control structure to ensure that the programs are carried out correctly.

Programmed Instruction

The movement toward the development of an educational technology approach to learning gained new impetus with the emergence of the programmed instruction movement in the 1950s. Programmed instruction has its roots in the works of many, but the publication of B. F. Skinner's article (1954), "The Science of Learning and the Art of Teaching," was the event that signaled the beginning of this movement. The basic method was not new. Other theorists had already advanced the idea that the learning of any subject matter, no matter how complex, could best be taught if it were first broken down into its smallest components and then sequenced in an optimum fashion (Block, 1971). The new idea that Skinner proposed was that the existing knowledge about how animals learned, derived from laboratory studies, could be applied to human learning in a systematic way, and that this could be best facilitated by means of mechanical devices called teaching machines. For a short time programmed instruction seemed to be the wave of the future. It proved to be effective with some students and some subject matter but never became a dominating force in education, to the dismay of its exponents and the relief of its critics. There was another characteristic of programmed instruction that proved to be extremely important. The early developers of programmed instruction were insistent that its objectives be stated behaviorally (Anderson & Faust, 1973). The introduction of behavioral objectives into the repertoire of educators was an extremely important event.

Behavioral Objectives

The writing of behavioral objectives begins with the identification of an overall goal that is intended to represent the purpose of the educational experience and can be stated in general terms. Next, all knowledge and skills necessary for the mastery of this goal are listed as enabling objectives. When they are written in a precise form, they are referred to as behavioral objectives. The purpose of this process is to have instructional goals stated in such a way that there is no ambiguity concerning whether an objective has been mastered. A behavioral objective must be stated in such a way that different judges could easily agree on whether the objective has been mastered. Robert Mager (1962, p. 12), a strong supporter of the use of behavioral objectives in the 1960s, provides these guides for writing behavioral objectives:

First, identify the terminal behavior by name; you can specify the kind of behavior that will be accepted as evidence that the learner has achieved the objective.

Second, try to define the desired behavior further by describing the important conditions under which the behavior will be expected to occur.

Third, specify the criteria of acceptable performance by describing how well the learner must perform to be considered acceptable.

The use of behavioral objectives to describe instructional goals progressed from being a useful instructional technique to becoming a widely adopted educational practice. Articles appearing during the early to the mid-1960s, arguing the merits of their use, tended to be intemperate. Bumper stickers were seen emblazoned with the battle cry "Stamp out nonbehavioral objectives." In one of the more popular books on the methodology of writing behavioral objectives, Mager's *Preparing Instructional Objectives* (1962), the author zealously advocates their use and manages to instill guilt in anyone who would harbor impure thoughts about stating an instructional goal in other than behavioral terms.

Mastery Learning

Mastery learning began in the late 1950s. It utilized techniques developed for programmed instruction and was adopted by such theoreticians as Carroll (1963) and Bloom (1968). They advocated an approach to teaching that assumed that maximum learning would occur when each student was given the optimum amount of time to master objectives.

As is the case with related instructional techniques, mastery learning requires the articulation of an overall instructional goal. Following this, a series of enabling objectives, believed to be most likely to lead to the successful mastery of this objective, is constructed. The mastery-learning approach is characterized by a greater sophistication about how these enabling objectives should be sequenced than earlier approaches, calling on the instructional models developed by Bloom (1956) and Gagné (1977). Evaluation plays an important role in this approach, with students pretested to determine which objective should be taught next and then post-tested to determine if mastery occurred or recycling was necessary.

The most important contribution of mastery learning is the deemphasis on individual differences and the articulation of the view that all students can progress up to an acceptable level of functioning, regardless of ability, as long as the instructional materials are correctly constructed and adequate time for mastery is provided. Mastery learning was introduced in the 1960s when concern about inequalities in our society was at its peak—as was the belief that this problem could be solved through education. Here was a well-thought-out educational technique that promised that all children could learn, that had the support of behavioral psychology (the natural enemy of most programs of this sort). There was a further bonus: using mastery learning, students are evaluated in terms of whether they have mastered objectives, not in comparison with each other. This approach lessened the emphasis on establishing hierarchies and the negative self-concepts associated with failure.

The Use of Educational Technology

In addition to the advantages already mentioned, educational technology is attractive because it is logical and breaks the learning process down into more easily comprehended components. Educational researchers have met with little success in explaining how learning takes place or how it can be facilitated, but by breaking the process into its smallest components there is a promise of clarity. It has a great attraction to those who believe that there is a simple explanation for even the most complex issues.

Educational technology began in the armed services, spread to the public school sector, and then took root in the medical education field. Here was an area ripe for the approach: it had long been characterized by traditional methods of teaching and was now anxious to modernize. Much of the subject matter is either performance oriented or concrete enough to facilitate the writing of behaviorally stated objectives, it is an empirically oriented field, and it had the resources to make the conversion. As a result, educational psychologists were hired and medical education in a short time has become the showplace for instructional technology.

The Limitations of Educational Technology

Educational technology, although it has gone largely unexamined, has had an enormous impact on the way all of our educational establishments, from the armed services to the public school, are operated. The uncritical acceptance and the speed with which these approaches have been adopted are the result of the various factors already mentioned that happened to occur at the appropriate time to maximize their impact. All of this success cannot be attributed to the demonstration of successful learning by students.

The instructional-technology approach is one of many instructional techniques that can be very effective for teaching some subject matter under certain conditions and be totally inappropriate for others. This is why it works well for math classes but is less appropriate for a course in English literature. For this approach to be effective, the subject matter must be concrete, and the expected educational outcomes must be clear and unambiguous. This is the reason for the success that this methodology has had in the armed services. Such success has not always been realized in public school settings. In public schools the subject matter is often not concrete or easy to specify, and the organizational structure of public schools is quite different from the army. Instructional decisions in public schools have traditionally rested in the hands of teachers, whereas in the armed forces, there is an authoritarian structure in which decisions are made by those with the highest rank.

Critics of the use of behavioral objectives based approaches to instruction have pointed out that such programs are characterized by rigidity, suppression of spontaneity, and an unhealthy emphasis on the more trivial aspects of a content area that lend themselves to neatly written objectives. They also point out that while some subject matter may work well with such an approach, others may not work at all. It is extremely difficult to get a group of teachers to reach consensus regarding the overall educational goal for a specific course, and without that consensus, objectives cannot be written effectively. Behavioral objectives need to be written in such a way that there is no ambiguity concerning whether or not they have been mastered. Different teachers should be able to read the objectives, observe the child's performance and make a decision as to whether the objective has been mastered. Each teacher should arrive at the same decision regarding mastery. The more abstract the behavior to be measured, the more difficult this is. Determining whether fifth-graders can solve long division problems is easy but deciding whether high school students have mastered an objective assessing their knowledge of economic theory is almost impossible. Under these circumstances, mastery is usually defined as correctly answering a previously defined number of multiple-choice items. What this does is shift the subjectivity of the grading process to the item writing process.

Every summer teachers are paid to meet with their peers and write curriculum guides utilizing behavioral objectives. In most school systems there now exist lists of objectives for every course offered. They exist mainly for the purpose of being dutifully trotted out for the benefit of visiting supervisors and acrediting boards, but they are not always used for instructional purposes.

In summary, behavioral objectives and instructional technology are useful and appropriate for some subject matter, and skill in their use should certainly be a part of any good teacher's repertoire; however, they are not the only instructional technique with which a teacher should be familiar.

Criterion-Referenced Testing

Criterion-referenced testing was developed as a means of evaluating behavioral objectives based instructional methods. The use of the term *criterion-referenced* is generally traced to an article published by Robert Glaser and D. J. Klaus in 1962, "Instructional Technology and the Measurement of Learning Outcomes: Some Questions." They felt that norm-referenced tests were inappropriate for use with behavioral objectives based instruction.

The Limitations of Norm-Referenced Tests

The inadequacy of norm-referenced tests is particularly obvious when standardized tests are used to evaluate instruction based on behavioral objectives. Nationally distributed standardized tests are specifically constructed to have content validity across a wide range of instructional methods and philosophies. The more specific they are made, the less marketable they become. For this reason they do a poor job of assessing specific objectives. Glazer (1963), and later others—in particular Popham and Husek (1969)—called for testing methods that were more appropriate and better able to exploit the needs of the instructional-technology movement.

In order to make their product more saleable in a market atuned to criterion-referenced testing, some achievement test publishers have endeavored to match the items on existing tests to sets of behavioral objectives. When an existing norm-referenced achievement test is converted into a criterion-referenced test the resulting scores are not particularly useful. Criterion-referenced tests must be built from the ground up. Criterion-referenced tests can assess far fewer objectives than a norm-referenced test, if each objective is to be assessed by a sufficient number of items. On a criterion-referenced test a separate score must be reported for each objective, and reliability should be computed separately for each score. Since the reliability of a score is partially a function of the number of items used to measure it, measuring many objectives can result in low reliability for each. In trying to make a norm-referenced test function as a criterion-referenced test, the publisher has three choices: (1) to restrict the number of objectives assessed; (2) to make a very large increase in the number of items; or (3) to report objectives mastered at a low level of reliability. It is the third option that is usually chosen. Some publishers report criterion-referenced scores for objectives measured by only one or two items.

Implementing Criterion-Referenced Tests

For criterion-referenced testing to be effective, the instructional objectives must be prepared first. Someone, preferably a committee within a school district, must determine precisely what students should learn. Ideally that group should be broadly based, with representation from all segments of the school community. An important unresolved question concerns whether entities outside of the school district should impose instructional objectives. This is already happening in many states through minimal competency testing. When the state specifies objectives that must be mastered before graduation from high school, they are deciding what is to be taught.

Most criterion-referenced testing takes place at the local school district level, where a set of instructional objectives is adopted and criterion-referenced tests are developed to evaluate students based on those objectives. The tests are either written by local personnel or the task is delegated to outside consultants or a test publishing company.

The Response to Criterion-Referenced Testing

Criterion-referenced testing has met with widespread acceptance because it fits nicely with, and is a necessary adjunct to, instructional technology. All of the factors already discussed that led to the proliferation of objectives-based instruction also encourage criterion-referenced testing. There are so many criticisms and negative feelings toward traditional testing that criterion-referenced testing is viewed as a panacea. This is a mistake. Criterion-referenced testing not only fails to eliminate all of the problems of norm-referenced testing, it introduces many new ones.

The Limitations of Criterion-Referenced Tests

The development of instructional-technology methods has taken place over a long period of time and is based on the application of widely accepted theories of learning and instruction. There are many studies that argue for its effectiveness under proper conditions. Criterion-referenced testing has existed for a much shorter amount of time, and the methodologies surrounding its use are less well developed.

Norm-referenced tests are intended to tell us how much a student has learned in relation to others, whereas a criterion-referenced test is intended to tell us specifically what a student has learned. If the test fails to provide this sort of specificity, it is something other than a criterion-referenced test. The most obvious way of accomplishing this goal is to evaluate a student's performance in terms of objectives mastered. This becomes quite awkward when we are talking about aggregates of students such as are found in classes, schools, and school districts. Such an approach requires the listing of each student along with an enumeration of which objectives have been mastered. If there are 100 objectives to be mastered in a grade, which is conservative, then a teacher with 35 students has 3,500 objectives with which to be concerned. Of course for every objective there must be items. At least 10 per objective is recommended, and this means there might be as many as 35,000 items a year for one teacher. Multiply this by the number of teachers in a school, and classes in a school system, and we are faced with a massive clerical problem.

Not only does this represent a clerical problem, but this mass of data is much too large for any sort of assimilation. Programs for use in micro-computers are becoming available that can assist in these record keeping chores. Before they can be of much help, they will need to be coupled with electronic test scorers and made more sophisticated. The temptation is to start using summary statistics to describe students or make comparisons. Once this is done, the essence of criterion-referenced testing is lost, and all that is left is a hybrid approach to evaluation that lacks the advantages of either criterion- or norm-referenced testing. The psychometric and mathematical characteristics of the average number of objectives mastered is poor, and knowledge of what is learned, which is the critical element of criterion-referenced tests, is lost.

Unresolved Issues in Criterion-Referenced Testing

The usual method of setting up a criterion-referenced testing program is to begin with instructional obejctives and then generate a set of items to measure the students' ability in relation to the objective. A cutoff score is set to determine how many items must be correctly answered before the objective is considered to be mastered.

This procedure might be thought of as first-generation criterion-referenced testing. Despite its attractiveness at a conceptual level, it is characterized by many unresolved issues that tend to manifest themselves after such programs have been implemented. Among the most important are the following: cutoff scores, reliability, and validity.

For criterion-referenced testing to become an important and useful means of testing, its methodology needs to be improved and refined. If this does not happen, it may prove to be just one more educational fad that, having had its moment in the sun, fades into one more tired old educational cliché.

Cutoff Scores

The setting of cutoff scores is one of the most important considerations in utilizing criterion-referenced tests. Unfortunately, most discussions of the subject place little emphasis on this aspect of testing, even though the legitimacy of any program of criterion-referenced testing is dependent on how these decisions are made.

Approaches to solving the problem of establishing cutoff scores are largely determined by which of two assumptions about the nature of criterion-referenced testing is accepted: the *state model view*, which describes the mastery of an objective as an all-or-nothing proposition, or the *continuum model*, which is based on the assumption that the trait being measured is continuously distributed, and defines mastery as performance at the upper end of the continuum.

State Model Methods

With this model, mastery is viewed as absolute, and it is therefore believed to be illogical to place qualifications on it. The model seems to work best with performance objectives where mastery is inferred directly from observable behaviors; it is most easily applied to the type of subject matter that the armed services and the health sciences emphasize. Although it can be applied to some types of school learning, such as math and science, it is not a reasonable way to describe most school learning, where mastery of an objective is inferred from performance on test items.

We cannot walk into a classroom and divide the class into those who can read third-grade vocabulary and those who cannot. There is always a range: some know the material well, some do not know it at all, and the rest are in between. To draw an arbitrary line and say that those above a certain point have reached mastery while those below have not is nonsensical. The problem is exacerbated by the fact that the performance of a group of students in a class can be expected to be normally distributed. When this is the case, the majority of students are in the middle, where we probably want to distinguish mastery from nonmastery. This means that the number of decision errors is maximized.

Using the state model we might expect that the students who have mastered an objective should correctly answer all of the items used to assess the objective. Given the imperfectability of testing, this is an unlikely occurrence and such an absolute criterion is unrealistic. To take measurement error into account, the cutoff score is reluctantly set below perfection. Exactly where it is set is intuitive, but 80 percent is typical. If the student correctly answers 80 percent of the questions, he or she is believed to be in a state of mastery. Sometimes one might even hear the following rationale for the use of 80 percent as the cutoff: 90 percent is too high and 70 percent is too low.

Underlying this approach is the further assumption that the items used to assess an objective represent a random sample from the domain of all possible items. This assumption is best supported by the use of the domain-referenced method of selecting items (to be discussed later in this chapter). In the absence of this or a similar methodology it is quite difficult to justify the arbitrary assignment of a cutoff score. Such an approach fails to take either the item difficulty or the consequences of the decision into consideration. This approach bears a resemblance to the reference-to-perfection approach described in Chapter 6. All of the problems that are associated with reference-to-perfection methods are present with the state model methods of determining cutoff scores.

One approach to dealing with the problem of item difficulty is to conduct pilot tests and use the results to determine this characteristic. Item difficulty is then adjusted to obtain the correct proportion of those designated as having mastered and those who have not mastered. Using this methodology changes criterion-referenced testing into something that more clearly resembles norm-referenced assessment. This approach combines the worst aspects of both criterion and norm-referenced tests.

There are other more sophisticated methods of setting cutoff scores that are based on the state model. They are based either on complex computations of measurement error to determine how far below perfection it is reasonable to go, or on the cost of making errors in classification.

Continuum Model Methods

With the continuum model method there is no assumption of absolute mastery. Instead the goal is the determination of where along the continuum it is most reasonable to set cutoff scores to differentiate mastery from nonmastery. One advantage of this approach over the state model approach is that it is somewhat less important to have the items represent a random sample from a domain.

All of these methods depend on the use of judges to rate individual items. Even though they may seem like objective psychometric procedures, they depend on subjective decisions. With the Nedelsky method (1954), judges decide for each item how many detractors the lowest passing student should be able to eliminate. The minimum passing level (MPL) is the reciprocal of the remaining choices. On a multiple-choice test with four choices, for an item on which the minimum-level student could be expected to eliminate two items, the MPL would be one half or .5 (the reciprocal of 4 ÷ 2 is ½ or .5). The MPLs are then averaged across judges and items to obtain a cutting score for the entire test. Robert Ebel's method (1972) involves the setting up of a 3 × 4 matrix based on three levels of difficulty (easy, medium, and hard) and four levels of relevance (essential, important, acceptable, and questionable). Judges place each item in the appropriate cell and also decide the minimum percentages of questions in each cell that a student should get right. Then the number of questions is multiplied by the percentages in each cell. This is summed and divided by the total number of items to yield the minimum passing score.

A simpler approach was proposed by William Angoff (1971). He suggests that judges estimate the probability that the minimally acceptable student would pass each item. These are then summed to set up a passing score.

Gene Glass (1978) reviewed studies that endeavored to determine which of these methods works best. He concluded that one can obtain widely divergent results depending on which method is selected, and that in the absence of a strong rationale for deciding which method to use, none should be considered acceptable.

Another approach that might be useful is to have a series of objectives arranged in a hierarchy and show that one cannot pass a particular objective until the preceding objectives have been mastered. Then a determination of how well the preceding objective must be mastered to allow success with the following objective could provide the basis for setting the cutoff score. If students who have mastered objective 4 at an 80 percent level can master objective 5, but those who mastered 4 only at a 70 percent level cannot, it should be clear that the appropriate criterion level is 80 percent. This approach is seldom used, perhaps because it is difficult to establish the existence of fixed hierarchies of learning tasks.

The lack of a satisfactory method for setting cutoff scores poses a major impediment to the use of criterion-reference tests. The criterion-reference approach places so much emphasis on separating mastery from nonmastery that, in the absence of an appopriate method for setting cutoff scores, the theoretical rationale for using criterion-referenced testing can be called into question.

Reliability

The assessment of reliability is one of the most important steps in evaluating educational tests. In the case of norm-referenced tests, their computation is relatively simple and straightforward. Unfortunately, the same methods used for assessing the reliability of norm-referenced tests cannot routinely be applied to criterion-referenced tests. The goal of criterion-referenced tests used to assess mastery learning is to differentiate between mastery and nonmastery, whereas norm-referenced tests are intended to maximize differences among students. Under conditions where most students master, variability among students is restricted, which tends to make the usual estimates of reliability low. For this reason, alternate methods have been developed to assess the reliability of criterion-referenced tests.

Decision Consistency Reliability

When it is possible to adminster two forms of a criterion-referenced test, a reliability coefficient can be computed that is easily obtained and understood. As suggested by Ronald Hambleton and Melvin Novick (1973, p. 168), reliability can be determined by computing the proportion of individuals correctly classified as masters or nonmasters (P_o). Using the data in Table 10.1, a reliability coefficient of .80 is obtained:

$$P_o = \frac{30}{50} + \frac{10}{50} = \frac{40}{50} = .80$$

This method of computing reliability, while being computationally simple and easy for the practitioner to understand, has two limitations: (1) developing two

TABLE 10.1 Mastery-Nonmastery Outcomes on Two Parallel Criterion-Referenced Tests

	Form 2		
Form 1	**Mastery**	**Nonmastery**	**Total**
Mastery	30	6	36
Nonmastery	4	10	14
Total	34	16	50

forms of a test may be impractical, and (2) the resulting coefficient may be unstable because it varies as a function of different proportions of masters to nonmasters. Although the coefficient obtained is called a reliability coefficient, it is not the same as the correlation-based reliabilities discussed in Chapter 5.

If almost all students master on both forms (or less commonly if most students fail), the P_o coefficient will always be fairly high. For instance, if ninety out of one hundred students reach mastery on each of two forms of a criterion-referenced test, even if the two forms are totally unrelated, the smallest value that can be obtained for P_o is .80. This point is illustrated in Tables 10.2 and 10.3. In Table 10.2 there is complete agreement between the two forms, and the P_o value is 1.00. In Table 10.3 all ten students who failed to master on form 1 mastered on form 2, and all students who failed to master on form 2 mastered on form 1. This represents the greatest disagreement possible. With a 90 percent passing rate, the P_o value in this case is .80. This is a matter of concern because in many cases an .80 reliability coefficient would be considered acceptable.

The level of P_o that can be expected by chance (P_c), given the preceding considerations, can be computed by summing the products of the marginals. For example, the P_o level that could be expected to occur by chance with the data from Table 10.1 is .58:

$$P_c = \frac{36}{50} \times \frac{34}{50} + \frac{14}{50} \times \frac{16}{50} = \frac{1448}{2500} = .58$$

Swaminathan, Hambleton, and Algina (1974) view the elevated P_o coefficient resulting from a high percentage of passes as a major disadvantage. They suggest that the chance agreement be removed from the P_o coefficient using Cohen's (1960) coefficient:

$$K = \frac{P_o - P_c}{1 - P_c}$$

Applying the correction formula to the data from Table 10.1 yields the following:

$$K = \frac{.80 - .58}{1 - .58} = .52$$

TABLE 10.2 Mastery-Nonmastery Outcomes on Two Forms of a Criterion-Referenced Test Where Both Obtain the Same Results

	Form 2	
Form 1	Mastery	Nonmastery
Mastery	90	0
Nonmastery	0	10

TABLE 10.3 Mastery-Nonmastery Outcomes on Two Forms of a Criterion-Referenced Test That Are in Complete Disagreement

	Form 2	
Form 1	Mastery	Nonmastery
Mastery	80	10
Nonmastery	10	0

Both Subkoviak (1980) and Berk (1980) criticize the use of K. Although K corrects the bias in favor of criterion-referenced tests on which most students pass (or fail), K is biased in favor of tests that are of average difficulty; Berk (1980) also cites other factors that can suppress the value of K and make it a less acceptable estimate of reliability.

In summary, even though P_o yields high reliability coefficients, this is a function of the fact that what is being measured is the degree of agreement-disagreement; this should be interpreted differently from traditional reliability coefficients. Agreement is simply easier to obtain if most students pass. The introduction of K increases the computational complexity and, consequently, problems of interpretation. Correcting for this one type of bias introduces additional biases.

There are three methods for computing P_o or K using a single test administration: the Huynh method (1976), the Subkoviak method (1975), and the Marshall-Haertel method (Marshall & Haertel, 1976). These are all computationally complex and require the use of a computer.

Validity

The most obvious type of validity needed for a criterion-referenced test is content related validity. For educational tests in general, the case for content validity tends to be made indirectly; for criterion-referenced tests, this characteristic is made more concrete through the use of objectives. The introduction of domain-sampling introduces a heightened level of content-related validity.

The most important issue surrounding the validity of criterion-referenced tests is the extent to which it is necessary to go beyond content-related validity. Hambleton (1980) takes the position that content-related validity is not enough, and that even a domain-referenced approach does not ensure this type of validity. To him the use of amplified objectives provides an a priori type of validity, but an a posteriori evaluation of validity is also necessary. He urges that judges be used to enhance the case for content-related validity.

In addition to content-related validity, construct (logical) validity is also recommended. The techniques already described for measuring reliability through agreement-disagreement indices would provide some evidence for construct validity. Additional evidence for construct validity could be obtained using the methodology described in Chapter 6.

Amplified Objectives

The introduction of instructional objectives, particularly when stated behaviorally, represented an advance in the precision with which the content of a course could be described. To the degree that the tasks are such that a decision concerning mastery-nonmastery is easily resolved they tend to work well. For instance, for instruction in the armed services, where a trainee is being taught to disassemble a weapon, it is not difficult to decide whether the task has been accomplished. Similarly in math, a decision concerning whether a student can solve simultaneous equations can be rendered with a minimum of difficulty. In such cases, mastery of an objective is easily assessed because we are focusing on overt behaviors and it is desirable that instructional objectives describing these educational goals be written as behavioral objectives. This is not the case with most subject matter taught in school. The tasks are more likely to involve understanding and cannot easily be thought of on an either-or basis. One doesn't either understand or not understand the motivations of Hamlet. There are degrees of understanding.

The usual practice of choosing a set of items to measure an objective is not satisfactory both because of the difficulty in setting an appropriate cutoff score, and because the selection of items tends to be unsystematic. This can be a major problem because of the crucial importance of item difficulty in determining who does and who doesn't master. Because the focus is no longer on overt behaviors, the use of behavioral objectives is less easily justified. We must infer mastery of an instructional objective from the successful responses to a series of items, thus the instructional objective must emphasize the procedure for generating the items that measure the targeted behavior. These are sometimes called amplified objectives.

Domain-Referenced Testing

Popham (1980) has suggested a method of writing amplified objectives that addresses the issue of how the items that define an objective are selected. He calls the procedure domain-referenced testing. It involves a lengthy and complex description of educational goals in a way that presents an unambiguous view of the targeted behavior and leaves no room for uncertainty concerning what was mastered. Included is a process for generating a set of items that is representative of the entire domain of possible items associated with the construct under consideration.

Popham does not view domain-referenced testing as a procedure separate from criterion-referenced testing; he states that "A criterion-referenced test is used to ascertain an individual's status with respect to a well defined domain" (1980, p. 16). This is different from the way we have described criterion-referenced testing up to this point and presents a definitional conflict. One way of resolving this conflict would be to discontinue the use of the term *criterion-referenced* in favor of the term *domain-referenced*. However, this would be impractical because so many years have been devoted to urging educators to adopt criterion-referenced testing as an evaluation technique; the suggestion that what is being done in its name is wrong would not be happily received by those already utilizing this methodology. Instead, Popham would like to adjust the definitions so that the haphazard practice of associating items with objectives would no longer be called criterion-referenced testing and would instead be called objectives-referenced testing. Only measurement procedures characterized by reference to well-defined domains of behavior would be deserving of the name criterion-referenced. It is hard to be optimistic about changing the perceptions of such a wide range of educators.

Implementing Domain-Referenced Testing

Domain-referenced testing is an evaluation technique that goes beyond behavioral objectives in describing student performance. It also conveys a much better understanding of what a student has accomplished; it is an approach consistent with the domain-sampling theory described in Chapter 1.

According Popham, instructional objectives should focus on the item rather than the objective, behavioral or otherwise. When using the domain-sampling approach, the items must be homogeneous and measure a single skill, a characteristic described as unidimensionality. Furthermore, the procedure for selecting items must be specified, and the items themselves described to a degree that we really know what is being measured. The goal is to have the items used to assess an objective or amplified objective be representative of the entire domain. With this approach a smaller number of instructional objectives is targeted. The test specifications have the following characteristics: general description, sample items, stimulus attributes, response attributes, and an optional specifications supplement (Popham, 1980).

General Description Specifications include one or two sentences describing what the test is intended to measure. Its purpose is to give those who choose not to go through the details provided by the remainder of the specifications an idea of what is being measured.

Sample Item The sample item is an example of an item similar to those appearing on the test. It provides a quick description of how the construct is being measured for those who neither need nor want to delve into the complexities of stimulus and response attributes.

Stimulus Attributes Because tests generally consist of stimulus materials to which the subject responds, it is important to describe just what sort of content is appropriate and what is not. This is the question part of a multiple-choice test. The writer of such specifications must steer a careful course between being overly detailed and being so general that the specifications lack meaning.

Response Attributes If we are using an objective test format where the student selects his or her answer, we need to specify the characteristics of the correct answer. It is not enough to merely say that the other answers will be wrong. The characteristics of the detractors in a multiple-choice test determine the character of an item and control the difficulty of the item. Their precise nature must be described. For constructed responses the delineation of response attributes is more difficult because it is necessary to delineate the characteristics of all responses that are correct from those that are incorrect.

Specification Supplement The specification supplement is an optional section to be used in those cases where it is more effficient to list the specific content eligible for testing, instead of including the information in the stimulus- and response-attributes sections, which can then be reserved for general rules. For example, on a spelling test the specification supplement might include the source for a list of acceptable vocabulary words.

Domain-Referenced Reliability

When we want to make generalizations, whether our test is norm- or criterion-referenced, we must assume that the items on the test represent a sample from the domain of all possible items that define the construct being measured. On a norm-referenced test, as long as the results of the test place students in the proper rank, the necessity that this sampling procedure be actual rather than theoretical is not absolute. This is true because item difficulty is not of crucial importance. On criterion-referenced tests, where absolute standards are set, the deleterious effect of any deviations in the item difficulty of the sample from the item difficulty of the domain can result in an entirely different proportion of masters and nonmasters. For this reason, the requirement that the items on a test represent a random sample from the domain of the construct is much stronger. The methods for computing reliability under these conditions has been described in the previous section.

When a test is best characterized as being based on a continuum model, reliability can be computed in a manner similar to that used for norm-referenced tests. Reliability can be explained in terms of item-sampling error. Parallel forms of a test are expected to yield different results, mainly because the items on a given test are a sample from the construct domain and two samples will not be exactly the same (Nunnally, 1967). The more heterogeneous the items in the domain, the greater the likelihood that two samples will be different. Measures of internal consistency reliability assess this characteristic.

When a domain-referenced approach is employed, standard internal consistency methods can be used to compute reliability, and the resulting coefficient can be interpreted as being descriptive of the underlying construct. Such an approach would be a major contribution to the understanding of the underlying domain construct.

Conclusions About Domain-Referenced Testing

Domain-referenced testing which represents a clear advance in the precision with which instructional objectives can be described, has some disadvantages. First of all, it involves prodigous amounts of work. Curriculum writers, who have long complained about the lengthy amounts of time required for writing behavioral objectives, are likely to be overwhelmed by the work required by this approach. Some course content may be so broad that it is almost impossible to delineate all of the possible stimuli and responses. This is an approach that would seem to work best with convergent content, such as mathematics or perhaps science.

A major advantage of this method is that it provides a very sophisticated means of establishing content-related validity. Next to this approach, the conventional methods of establishing content-related validity, such as tables of specifications, seem meager. Although domain-referenced methodology is intended for use with criterion-referenced tests, it could provide important contributions to the field of norm-referenced testing.

SUMMARY

1. Criterion-referenced tests report results in terms of *what* a student has learned rather than how they compare to others.
2. What a student has learned is generally defined in terms of instructional objectives.
3. Most of the technical problems associated with the implementation of norm-referenced tests have been solved, but the technical problems associated with criterion-referenced tests remain unresolved.
4. Criterion-referenced testing is an outgrowth of educational technology based on the principle of breaking the learning process down into its smallest components.
5. Programmed instruction is a form of educational technology that introduced the use of behavioral objectives.
6. Mastery learning is a form of educational technology that emphasizes the sequencing of the instruction and the idea that it is time, rather than ability, that is the most important determinant of who is successful in an academic setting.
7. Although educational technology is widely accepted, it has some limitations: it works well only with concrete subject matter, and it tends to promote an inflexible approach to education.
8. Norm-referenced tests are often not appropriate for evaluating educational technology; criterion-referenced tests are often used for this purpose.
9. There are serious clerical problems associated with keeping track of a large number of objectives for a large number of students.
10. The use of criterion-referenced tests is also limited by the unsolved problems associated with setting cutoff scores and determining reliability.
11. One approach to dealing with the limitations of criterion-referenced tests is through the use of domain-referenced testing techniques.

SUGGESTED READINGS

BERK, R. A. (1984). *A guide to criterion-referenced test construction*. Baltimore: Johns Hopkins University Press. [This book includes a wide selection of articles about criterion-referenced testing, including such topics as domain-referenced testing, item analysis, reliability, validity, and the relationship between criterion-referenced tests and generalizability theory.]

BLOCK, J. H. (1971). *Mastery learning: Theory and practice*. New York: Holt. [This book includes the basic rationale for why criterion-referenced testing is necessary and how it relates to mastery learning.]

GRONLUND, N. E. (1985). *Measurement and evaluation in teaching* (5th ed.). New York: Macmillan. [This book contains useful instructions for developing criterion-referenced tests.]

——— (1985). *Stating educational objectives* (3rd ed.). New York: Macmillan. [This book provides detailed but practical instructions for the writer of educational objectives.]

HAMBLETON, R. K., SWAMINATHAN, H., ALGINA, J., & COULSON, D. B. (1978). Criterion referenced testing and measurement: A review of technical issues and developments. *Review of Educational Research*, *48*, 1–47. [This article provides a great deal of information about the technical problems associated with criterion-referenced testing, such as setting cutoff scores and computing reliability.]

MAGER, N. F. (1962). *Preparing instructional objectives*. Palo Alto, CA: Fearson. [This short book provides useful directions for how to write behavioral objectives correctly.]

POPHAM, W. J. (1981). *Modern educational measurement*. Englewood Cliffs, NJ: Prentice-Hall. [This general measurement textbook is intended for teacher-preparation programs. It is perhaps the only such book that has criterion-referenced testing as its major emphasis. It is also one of the best sources of information about how to actually go about constructing and using domain-referenced tests and includes excellent examples and descriptions of criterion-referenced testing.]

11

Minimum Competency Testing

OVERVIEW

The following chapter describes the minimum competency testing (MCT) movement in the United States. Its historical development is discussed, including the factors that have led to its becoming such an important trend in present-day education. Legal issues are presented from the perspective of several key court cases, emphasizing the point of view of students in general, minorities, and handicapped children. In addition, the limitations of MCT are described, along with suggestions of ways that these programs can be improved.

OBJECTIVES

From this chapter you will learn about the evolution of minimum competency testing and problems with its implementation. Specificallly you will learn the following:

- The reasons for the rapid and widespread implementation of minimum competency testing.
- The legal issues that characterize this movement.
- The problems associated with minimum competency testing.
- Ways of improving minimum competency testing.

Introduction

One of the most important educational trends during the 1970s and early 1980s involved an increasing interest in the importance of basic skills. A major manifestation of this trend was the enactment of laws in nearly every state requiring minimum competency testing (MCT), although each state has a unique approach to the problem. The movement stems from the perception by the public that the nation's schools are failing to educate properly the students they teach.

It is felt that establishing a clear differentiation between those students who have learned what they are supposed to have learned and those who have failed to do so can be an important step in improving our educational system. It is a political movement supported by editorial writers, state legislatures, candidates for governor, recommendations of blue-ribbon citizens' committees studying education, and public opinion polls. The attitude of educators tends to range from open hostility to a willingness to acceed to public and political pressure. Occasionally educators have even expressed strong support.

The Reasons for the Growth of the MCT Movement

Since the days of Horace Mann and John Dewey, a strong faith in the value of education has existed in this country. During the great migrations from Europe, education was believed to be the best means for preparing large numbers of immigrants for their role in society. Attendance laws were passed to ensure that the children of immigrants received a solid grounding in what it meant to be an American. Our education system was believed to be the greatest in the world, and we had won wars and had the most powerful industrial and technological systems to prove it. All children who were willing to take advantage of the education that was offered were believed capable of becoming whatever they or their parents wanted them to become.

Such high expectations are bound to be tempered by disappointment when the system fails to provide all that it promises. These disappointments cause public concern, and as a result, politicians begin to seek solutions. The solution that is often chosen is MCT. The rapid and general acceptance of MCT is the result of two factors: (1) the perception that there is a decline in the quality of education provided by public schools, and (2) an unwillingness to spend more money to improve the quality of education.

Decline in the Quality of Education

The history of education in this country over the last thirty years has included many disappointments that led its citizens to question some of their basic beliefs in the effectiveness of our educational institutions.

Sputnik The explosion of atomic weapons by the Soviet Union in the early 1950s caused a great shock, as did its successful orbiting of an unmanned satellite, Sputnik, before the United States could launch theirs. The preeminence of the United States in science and technology began to be questioned, and the public schools were held responsible for much of the failure of our national scientific programs. They had failed to produce enough skilled scientists to maintain our technological lead over the rest of the world. Congress responded by allocating large amounts of money to improve the teaching of science and math in the schools. As we shall see, this expenditure was not entirely successful in reversing the perception that we were facing a downward trend in educational quality, particularly in such basic skill areas as science, math, and reading.

Declining Test Scores In the mid 1970s there was another series of events that called into question the efficacy of our educational institutions. Reports from diverse test publishers began to show declines in standardized test performance. The test that received the most publicity was the SAT. It is the single-most widely administered standardized test and the closest thing we have to a national achievement test. Like most standardized tests, scores had increased steadily since the introduction of the test in its present form. But, beginning in the 1960s, the scores began to decline. The decline continued into the 1970s but has now leveled off. The reasons for the decline are not known, although in all likelihood there are many causes. There seems to be a general belief that the decline is indicative of the failure of our schools to teach the fundamental skills that are prerequisites for success in both academic and nonacademic settings. This view is maintained despite the fact that the SAT measures higher-level functioning rather than basic skills, and student performance in the early grades did not show a decline.

The meaning of these test-score declines seems to have become secondary to the perceptions they have generated. Primary among these is the view that the declines indicate a failure of the public schools to teach students basic skills. In Chapter 15, the SAT will be discussed in more detail, along with the issue of declining test scores.

Societal Changes Although young people always seem to be in a state of rebellion against their elders, the late 1960s and early 1970s were times when the rebellion was particularly in evidence. Sometimes the result was severe societal disruptions. The schools were the institution often blamed for these problems.

That was also a time when the predominant educational philosophy emphasized flexibility rather than structure. Students were given more choices in determining their curriculum, and courses often became less rigorous as they were tailored to be more attractive to students.

Desegregation The 1970s was also a time of increased school desegregation, which resulted in students of different abilities being placed in the same schools. At the same time state and federal courts were ruling that tracking and/or grouping students was illegal. As a result of these two factors, children of quite different abilities were often placed in the same class. These practices tended to make the inequalities in academic preparation among students more noticeable. As a result, the inability of the schools to educate all students up to the same level became too obvious to ignore.

Technological Threats from Other Countries Finally, in the 1970s a general awareness that American technological superiority was waning began to emerge. Japanese products, which were once sneered at as being shoddy imitations, began to dominate the market and set the standard for quality in automobiles, electronics, heavy industry, and other fields. The public began to believe that our educational systems were once again failing to do the job.

Unwillingness to Solve our Educational Problems Through a Greater Allocation of Funds

As president, Lyndon Johnson was intent on establishing what he called the Great Society. The cornerstone of this philosophy was the elimination of poverty and racial inequality. Because this was to be accomplished without alienating the existing power structure, education was seen as the best means of accomplishing the goal (Hodgson, 1973). Johnson, as a former schoolteacher, reflected the common wisdom that education was the key to success in our society. He believed that by providing additional funds to schools, the result would be a better-educated citizenry and a narrowing of the gap between society's rich and poor.

In the Civil Rights Act of 1964, the commissioner of education was ordered by Congress to conduct a study of educational opportunity in the United States, with the goal of establishing that inequalities exist and are the cause of differential educational performance and, ultimately, social class difference. James Coleman was given the task and fully expected to find data to support these views. However, when his massive study was published (Coleman, 1966), the conclusions were surprising. It was found that there were no vast differences in the physical characteristics of schools and/or the quality of teachers, and that it is differences in family background that explain most of the differences in performance among students. The conclusions provided little support for the view that additional funds for improving student performance would be successful.

In 1972 Christopher Jencks published *Inequality: A Reassessment of the Effects of Family and Schooling in America*, which provided a second look at the data Coleman had amassed. Jencks took an even more negative position regarding the effectiveness of improving student achievement by means of altering school programs. The Coleman and Jencks reports, coupled with the dismal results of attempts to initiate new and innovative programs in schools, led social scientists away from their previous faith in the efficacy of schools. At the same time, the general public perceived the outlay of large amounts of money for programs that had an emphasis on affective rather than cognitive education as being wasteful.

In times of prosperity it is not difficult to justify the expenditure of funds for improving the lives of those who are at the lower end of the socioeconomic continuum because money for such programs can come from the expansion of the economy. Toward the end of the 1970s, however, there was a recession and a need to trim all budgets. Extra money for projects to benefit special student populations became unavailable. MCT is attractive because, compared to many suggested solutions for improving education, it seems inexpensive. However, such programs are not cheap and often end up costing more money than anticipated.

The Ascendancy of MCT

There has been a series of events—from Sputnik to failures in compensatory education programs, and from declining SAT scores to the ascendancy of Japanese technology—that has tended to erode faith in the nation's educational system. This disapppointment soon became translated into political action as politicians came to recognize that this was an issue that could garner widespread support.

Legislators and governors sought solutions. What they wanted was a strategy that, in effect, would make it illegal for a student not to learn in school. Those who failed to learn would then be punished by the denial of a diploma.

If this movement had occurred prior to the 1960s, it probably would not have gotten very far. The existing norm-referenced testing technology does not lend itself easily to MCT. It does not make sense to say that all students must be above average, or above a predetermined percentile. Such assessments are relative, and it is absolute standards that are needed.

The Application of Criterion-Referenced Testing Methods

Criterion-referenced testing has provided what appears to be the perfect technology. This method of testing is predicated on the assumption that it is possible to determine which students have mastered and which have not mastered a given set of objectives. Remediation, or at least the opportunity to retake the test, is provided; those who fail to reach the prescribed level are ultimately denied a diploma and instead given a certificate of attendance.

The capacity of criterion-referenced tests to provide the sort of information required has generally been uncritically accepted. This has occurred despite the general agreement among those who specialize in criterion-referenced testing that there are important technical issues surrounding its use that remain to be solved.

The widespread acceptance of the criterion-referenced methodology resulted from the series of historical occurrences outlined in Chapter 10. It met a need that many have to remove the mystery from the learning process and turn it into somethng mechanical and more easily understood. Individuals from other fields who have successfully used such techniques as management by objectives, tend to see criterion-referenced testing as a way of describing the educational process that finally makes sense. Students are put into a school, they are educated, and what they have learned is evaluated as a concrete product. Those students who are imperfect can be plucked out and discareded like a bad transistor. It is not easy to convince those who see this as a panacea that the educational process fits imperfectly into this paradigm.

The Proliferation of MCT

Interest in MCT seems to have touched nearly every state in the United States. The particular manifestation in each has differed as a result of uncertainty about the best way to implement MCT and because such programs are the result of a political process. There are many forces within a state pulling a program in different directions: local school boards may want to maintain control, the legislature may want to assess functional literacy, and the governor may want to focus on basic academic skills.

MCT programs range from centralized programs, where instructional objectives and tests are developed at the state level, to those where the state permits the local school district to take responsibility or requires it. Remedial programs are sometimes funded at the state level or made the sole responsibility of the local school board. Some states have created their own tests, whereas others have contracted with outside agencies. Most states use criterion-referenced tests, but a few use norm-referenced achievement. There are some programs that focus on academic skills whereas others emphasize the skills needed in everyday life. There are also programs that combine all of these. The inconsistency in terminology and variability in programs makes it difficult to describe with any certainty the status of MCT nationwide. It is also difficult to categorize the programs because each is unique. Summaries of state activities are often inaccurate because the response obtained may be dependent on who provided the information at the state level.

Pipho (1978) states that there are thirty-three states with mandated standards for promotion, while the rest of the states have legislation pending. Baratz (1980) found that there were over thirty states that had either enacted or considered legislation mandating MCT, whereas Ross (1982) could locate only four states that had neither adopted nor considered minimum competency legislation.

Legal Issues Surrounding MCT

Since the introduction of MCT, concern has arisen about the legality of its various aspects. The crucial issue is how test results are to be used. If they are strictly for the purpose of determining which students need remediation, then the concern about legal challenges is less pressing. It is when test results are to be used for making critical decisions, such as determining if a child will be given a diploma, that the legality of MCT comes into question. This concern is heightened by the fact that minorities generally do not perform as well as nonminorities on standardized tests, so it can be anticipated that their failure rate on MCT will be greater. This has in fact happened in some states, and legal challenges of such programs has followed.

When the MCT movement began in the 1970s, there were many questions raised about the legality of these tests—particularly their use for denying diplomas to students. Now most of those issues have been resolved, generally in favor of MCT. Much of this legal clarification took place in Florida because of its statewide program utilizing a single test for determining which students could graduate. The other feature that caused Florida to take the lead in the resolution of legal questions was the fact that their program started before those in most other states. In addition, Florida's program came closest to matching what educators and the general public expcted MCT to be.

Florida's mandatory literacy test (which is what they call it) was announced in 1977 and was slated to go into effect in 1979. It was challenged in a class action suit brought by a group of parents whose children had failed the test. In *Debra P.* vs. *Turlington* (1979) Judge George Carr of the federal district court ruled that there must be a sufficient amount of time between the announcement of such programs and the date when diplomas are actually denied, in order to allow students to remedy deficiencies. In this ruling it was specified that the test could not be mandatory until the 1982–83 school year. In addition, the court held that competency tests could not perpetuate past racial discrimination, and that it must be shown that disproportionately high failure rates by minorities are not the result of past school segregation. In *Anderson* vs. *Banks* (1981) it was held that the school system must wait until students who attended segregated classes had graduated before implementing such programs.

In 1981 the *Debra P.* vs. *Turlington* case was appealed to the Court of Appeals for the Fifth Circuit. Judge Carr was upheld on the issue of fair warning and the requirement that MCT not carry forward the effects of segregation. The Court of Appeals added one further condition: the test must have content validity. In the case of MCT, content validity is usually divided into two types (McClung, 1979). First of all, there is *curricular validity*, which refers to the match between the competency test and the curriculum. To establish curriculum validity it is necessary to demonstrate agreement between the curricula of the various school districts and the state curriculum and compare them with what is on the test. Because competency tests are generally built from sets of instructional objectives that are developed to provide guidance concerning curriculum, it is not difficult to establish this sort of validity. The biggest problem is that teachers may not be teaching exactly what is listed in the curriculum. This leads to a concern about a more stringent type of validity—*instructional validity*. Instructional validity requires the establishment of a match between what is assessed on the minimal competency instrument and what happens in the classroom. This is the sort of content validity that the Fifth Circuit Court required, although that was not the term used. It was a controversial decision among other members of the Fifth Circuit Court because it had implications for all testing conducted by a school system and because the courts have traditionally left such judgment in the hands of educators.

In 1983 Judge Carr found that Florida had met all required conditions, including content validity, and the injunction was lifted, allowing students who did not pass the test to be denied diplomas.

Special Education and MCT

The implementation of MCT poses a "no-win" situation for children enrolled in special education classes, particularly those whose disability results in lowered overall academic performance. This is true of students enrolled in classes for the educable mentally handicapped (EMH) or for the learning disabled (LD) and, to a lesser extent, students enrolled in other special classes. If special education students are forced to take the test, LD and EMH students will be likely to fail. On the other hand, if they do not take the test, they can be stigmatized. In Georgia, all special education students are required to take the tests, and any student who fails the test can be denied a diploma. In *Anderson* vs. *Banks* (1981) the court upheld the view that handicapped students could be required to pass such a test in that state before obtaining a diploma.

Vermont provides one means of avoiding this dilemma. In this state there are 66 competencies that must be mastered. Determinations of mastery take place at the school district level. In South Burlington High School, the teachers do the testing. When a student fails a competency, he or she is given remediation and is retested. The remediation program is titled, Interactive Model for Professional Action and Change for Teachers (IMPACT). At the beginning of the program, on the average, special education students had mastered 27 percent of the competencies, but at the end of the project, all special education students had mastered all the competencies (Maheady, 1983). One might question the validity of the results of a program where the assessment was done strictly by the teachers. Of even greater concern is the legitmacy of an MCT program based on a set of instructional objectives that all special education students can pass.

The Problems Associated with MCT

The purpose of MCT is twofold: (1) to prevent the awarding of degrees to students who are not functioning at an appropriate level, and (2) to serve as a prod for students and teachers that will encourage them to perform at a more acceptable level. The ultimate goal of the programs does not seem to be so much on educating students—although that is a hoped-for effect—as it is on ensuring that students below a certain level do not obtain degrees. As Larry Cuban (1980, p. 71) states, "in the next few years there will be large numbers of minority students who will have to pay directly the cost of ineffective schooling." But we should not worry. The younger brothers and sisters of these students may do better as a result of school practices that will improve because of "the whip of minimum competency testing and the prodding that will stem from test results on annual display for the community" (Cuban, 1980, p. 71).

There are additional disadvantages to the use of these tests that makes the sizable financial investment difficult to justify: they can have a negative effect on the learning process because instruction may begin to focus only on the specific skills that will lead to high performance on such a test. Rather than improve overall performance, it will tend to pull everyone down to one mediocre level.

The most important limitations of MCT are methodological. Given what is known about testing at the present time, it is simply not possible to accomplish all that the advocates of MCT have promised.

The Advantages of the Criterion-Referenced Approach

The biggest problem with MCT as it is now being used is its heavy reliance on criterion-referenced testing. The approach does have benefits, some of which follow:

1. It is congruent with the management models used in business and industry (management by objectives) and it demystifies the education process.
2. It creates the illusion that competence is discrete and that performance by students can be divided into the categories of mastery and nonmastery.
3. It avoids some of the stigma that can be associated with failure on a norm-referenced test because students are compared to an absolute standard, not to each other. This also makes the test appear more fair, because minorities do not seem to be compared to nonminorities.

The Disadvantages of Criterion-Referenced Testing

One disadvantage of the use of criterion-referenced testing with MCT is that criterion-referenced testing is a new approach and there has not been sufficient time to determine the best means of implementing it. In addition, its use with MCT is based on the false assumption that academic achievement can be divided into states of competence and noncompetence

Methodological Problems The methodolological problems of criterion-referenced testing are exacerbated when applied to MCT. When a procedural error leads to a teacher misclassifying a student as not having mastered a competency, the main consequence is that the student may receive additional instruction or a lower grade than is deserved. When procedural and methodological errors creep into the MCT process, the results are much more severe. A student who ends up with a certificate of attendance rather than a diploma is having to pay an enormous price for the mistakes of those who developed the test.

The Assumption that Academic Achievement Can Be Viewed as a State The assumption that academic achievement can be viewed as a state provides a theoretical basis for MCT programs and makes them politically acceptable. To be avoided is the circumstance where one student is declared noncompetent and the other competent, when there is really no difference between them. This is the problem with using norm-referenced tests for MCT. If on a reading test we declare that everyone above the 30th percentile has reached minimum competence and everyone below has not, any student at the 29th percentile who fails is going to yell "Foul." Failing students will claim that there is no real difference between them and the student who obtains a score of 30, and they would be justified in their complaint. With criterion-referenced testing, those who pass are assumed to be qualitatively different from those who have not.

The assumption that the criterion-referenced testing approach is capable of assessing absolute levels of performance and making a distinction between mastery and nonmastery is fundamental. The legitimacy of using criterion-referenced testing as a means of implementing MCT depends on the legitimacy of this assumption. Unfortunately, existing evidence does not support the view that this is a reasonable assumption. The types of skills typically assessed in these testing programs exist on a continuum and are not discrete. Students cannot be neatly categorized as knowing how to read or not knowing how to read; some children can read better than others, with most students falling somewhere in between. There is no evidence that cutoff scores can make absolute distinctions.

Cutoff Scores In Chapter 10, three techniques for setting cutoff scores were discussed: the Nedelski method (1954), the Angoff method (1971), and the Ebel method (1979). Only the Nedelski method has been used extensively, and there is no evidence to show that it, or either of the two other methods, can legtimately set a cutoff score. The method also may yield different cutoff scores for different tests. If a school district administered both a math test and a reading test, it might have a cutoff score at 83 percent for math, whereas for reading it might be set at 72 percent. When the test is revised, an entirely different set of cutoff scores must be set. This can prove confusing and difficult to explain to the public.

The most common method of setting a cutoff score is to employ a system similar to that used in Florida, where a student is required to answer 70 percent of the questions correctly on both the math and communications tests (reading and writing). The decision to use this particular cutoff score was made by the Florida Department of Education staff, after conferring with local school districts and hearing the advice of consultants. The decision was made before examining the actual items that were to be on the test. Setting a cutoff score in this manner requires an act of great faith. It is hoped that the items are all of the appropriate level of difficulty.

Thomas H. Fisher (1980), Director of the Assessment Section in the Florida Department of Education, provides the following rationale for the method of setting a cutoff score used in his state:

> Much has been written about the development of criterion-referenced tests, but the literature is still fluid, showing great diversity of opinion about what approaches to take in developing cutoff scores, creating test items, determining test reliability, and so forth. The department staff considered the current literature and made the best decisions it could, given the state of the art (p.224).

This constitutes a rather remarkable admission of ignorance, considering that in 1983 three thousand seniors in Florida were denied diplomas. Despite the fact that there is no indication that Florida students have a different level of ability in math than in communications, after the first administration of the test, 10 percent of the students failed the communications section of the test, and 35 percent failed the math section. The difference in performance occurred because the Educational Testing Service (ETS)—the consultants who actually wrote the questions—obviously did not include items of similar levels of difficulty in the two sections of the test. It is extremely difficult, if not impossible, to look at an item and decide how difficult it is for a student in a specified grade.

Difficulty Level and Standard Setting Gene Glass (1978), in a very revealing article about the problems surrounding the Florida test, provides two examples to illustrate how hard it is to set standards, as a result of uncertainty about the difficulty level of items. Consider two items from the Stanford reading test that are intended to measure the same objective and appear to be of similar difficulty. The first item asks the student to distinguish the word *firm* from *firm, form* and *farm*. On the second item the student is asked to distinguish the word *girl* from *goal, girl* and *grill*. On item 1, 56 percent of the students obtained the correct response, whereas 88 percent correctly responded to item 2. He also found that, on the task of adding the same series of digits, 86 percent of the students could correctly add them vertically, whereas only 46 percent were successful when the numbers were horizontal. Under these circumstances, success or failure becomes an arbitrary function of the item-writing process.

Setting the Standard for Minimum Competency MCT programs usually begin with a set of competencies, in the form of instructional objectives, for which students are responsible. The fact that there are many competencies to master makes decision making difficult. We are faced with the question of whether students should be required to master all or some proportion of competencies, or whether competence should be determined by the total number of questions correctly answered, as was done in Florida. Of course, once competencies are no longer individually assessed, the essence of criterion-referenced testing is lost.

Finally, the methods of conducting item analyses with criterion-referenced tests are inferior to these available for norm-referenced tests. Generally the individuals who do the actual item writing are given item specifications, and all that can be done is to examine the test items to make sure that they actually match the specifications. Judges can also evaluate the items to determine if they are biased against any specific cultural or ethnic groups. This methodology is unlikely to lead to a good test.

Improving MCT with Norm-Referenced Methods

Norm-referenced methods have not generally been used for MCT for two reasons: (1) they destroy the illusion that competency is discrete because norm-referenced tests place individuals on a continuum, and (2) norm-referenced tests do not make the sort of absolute statements about a student's performance that are made by criterion-referenced tests. However, if those who decide the format of minimum competency tests understood the lack of validity in the assumptions underlying the choice of criterion referencing as a methodology for use with MCT, they might find norm-referenced methods more appropriate.

If MCT is to be used, norm-referenced tests have some clear advantages over criterion-referenced test methods. First of all, they do not require the unobtainable assumptions associated with criterion-referenced tests. They are backed by a long tradition of well-established technology, and there are excellent methods for conducting item analyses and establishing the reliability of the tests. This makes it possible to develop tests that improve through use.

The utilization of norm-referenced testing techniques also makes the selection of commercially prepared tests a viable alternative in the test selection stage of MCT. Because criterion-referenced tests are developed directly through instructional objective, it is difficult to use an "off-the-shelf" test because it would be unlikely to be based on the specific set of objectives adopted by a state or local school district. Of course, this can also pose a similar problem for norm-referenced tests. They also need to be in agreement with a state's or school district's instructional objectives, but the match is not as critical.

Most MCT programs focus on math and reading. These are areas in which there is much more consistency across states than other topics. Existing commercially prepared tests might be used to assess these two areas, although changes in those tests might be required because modern test-development practices emphasize the development of achievement tests that are broadly generalized across curricula. This means that they are likely to place more emphasis on ability than achievement.

If a state or school district wants to develop its own test, it should probably focus on such topics as science and social studies because these are subjects for which the content varies a great deal from locality to locality. Commercially prepared tests either do not assess these topics or assess them so broadly that the results are not useful to school systems wanting to understand how their students are actually performing.

SUMMARY

1. The MCT movement is primarily politically motivated educational reform.
2. The MCT movement is a response to the perception that the educational process in this country is declining.
3. This decline can be seen in test scores and in terms of a widening technological gap between this and other countries.
4. There has been an unwillingness to solve these problems through greater expenditures of money.
5. The courts, with some reservations, have supported the states' right to use MCT as a criteria for determining who will receive diplomas.
6. The use of criterion-referenced testing techniques with MCT has many disadvantages.
7. One of the biggest problems with MCT concerns the difficulty in setting cutoff scores.
8. Those intent on implementing such programs would be wise to consider the use of existing standardized norm-refernced texts.

SUGGESTED READINGS

Dick, W., Watson, K., & Kaufman, R. (1981). Deriving competencies: Consensus versus model building. *Educational Researcher, 10*(8), 5–10,13. [This is a description of the procedures used in Florida to choose the competencies to be assessed by that state's minimum competency test.]

Glass, G. V. (1978) Minimum competence and incompetence in Florida. *Phi Delta Kappa, 59,* 602–605. [This article provides an interesting account of the problems encountered by the state of Florida in its implementation of a minimum competency testing program.]

——— (1978). Standards and criteria. *Journal of Educational Measurement, 15,* 237–261.

[This article examines the technical problems associated with setting cutoff scores for minimum competency tests.]

JAEGER, R. M. & TITTLE, C. K. (Eds.) (1980). *Minimum competency achievement testing: Motives, models, measures, and consequences*. Berkeley, CA: McCutchan. [This book of readings contains broad coverage of the issues surrounding minimum competency testing.]

MCCLUNG, M. S. (1979). Competency testing programs: Legal and educational issues. *Fordham Law Review, 47,* 652. [This is an excellent account of the legal problems surrounding minimum competency testing.]

12

Achievement Testing

OVERVIEW

This chapter focuses on standardized educational achievement tests. The contrasts and comparisons between achievement and aptitude tests are outlined with an emphasis on correcting the misconceptions concerning the manner in which these two types of tests should be used. The similarities and differences between teacher-made and standardized achievement tests also are discussed. The development of the modern day achievement test is outlined, including such topics as the use of test batteries, diagnostic tests, and criterion-referenced tests. One particular standardized achievement test, the Comprehensive Test of Basic Skills (CTBS) is described in detail.

OBJECTIVES

From this chapter you will learn about achievement tests, their historical development, and the best ways to use them. Specifically, you will learn the following:

- The relationship between achievement and aptitude.
- How standardized achievement tests differ from teacher-made tests.
- The various developments in standardized achievement testing.
- The available standardized achievement tests.
- The problems with standardized achievement tests.

Introduction

The development of modern achievement tests is the direct outgrowth of the methods developed for measuring intelligence in a group setting. Although the first recognizable achievement tests predate the development of group intelligence tests, their widespread use and acceptance occurred after the introduction of the group intelligence tests. The first standardized achievement test is generally recognized to be Rice's spelling test, developed in 1894.

Arthur Otis is believed to have initiated the use of multiple-choice items and the objective scoring format for testing (Robertson, 1972). This methodology was adopted by the Committee on the Psychological Examination of Recruits when they constructed the Army Alpha and Beta tests that were used to classify recruits during World War I. In 1918 the World Book Company published the Otis Group Intelligence Scale. Otis introduced such innovations as the use of multiple-choice questions, answer sheets, test booklets, simplified scoring methods, better and more sophisticated norm-sampling procedures, and improved ways of translating raw scores into meaningful information. These developments led to the introduction of increasingly more advanced achievement tests. The modern era of achievement testing was ushered in by the publication of the Stanford Achievement test in 1923.

Achievement and Aptitude

Traditional Views

The development of separate group tests to assess intelligence and achievement occurred as a result of the way cognitive functioning was viewed at the time. A clear distinction was drawn between aptitude, as measured by the intelligence tests, and achievement. Intellectual ability and aptitude were considered to be fixed at birth and determined almost entirely by heredity. It was believed that the intellectual prowess with which we arrive on earth could neither be increased nor lost through environmental intercession. The immutable nature of this faculty was believed to make it a good predictor of future performance. The use of test behavior as an indicator of intellectual capacity was justified by the assumption that all subjects came into the testing situation having had an equal opportunity to learn. For this reason, differences in performance were believed to indicate innate capacity. Achievement was believed to be determined more by environment, mainly schooling, and was limited by the amount of innate potential possessed by the student. Discrepancies between the two scores were then interpreted at either signs of over- or underachieving.

Modern Interpretation

Modern views of cognitive abilities are somewhat more sophisticated. It is now generally believed that both types of tests measure nearly the same thing. If items from both types of tests are mixed, it is difficult to sort them according to test.

The assumption that all children have the same opportunity to learn is of course fallacious, and performance on any test is mainly determined by differences in the acquisition of skills. Discrepancies between performances on the two types of tests are often better described as measurement error than over- or underachievement.

The difference between the two tests is mainly in terms of specificity, degree of abstraction, and method of validation. Achievement tests measure narrow aspects of behavior, whereas aptitude tests measure broader areas. Because the best predictor of future performance is present performance, knowledge of present achievement test scores are the best predictor of future achievement. The use of the mental aptitude test becomes important when we are endeavoring to predict a broad range of skills, where the administration of a great many separate achievement tests would be impractical. A single mental ability test can be used, in that case, to predict a wide range of performances.

Increased Blurring of the Distinctions

Achievement tests also emphasize more concrete measures of ability, whereas aptitude tests focus on more abstract thinking. In determining the validity of achievement tests content-related evidence of validation is of primary importance, whereas criterion and construct-related evidence of validity are more important for establishing the validity of aptitude tests.

There is a trend in modern test development to blur the distinction even further. Tests that were once called intelligence tests are now having their names changed. The publishers are apparently seeking to avoid the controversy and negative connotations surrounding the term *intelligence*. For instance, the Lorge-Thorndike Intelligence Test is now the Cognitive Abilities Test. At the same time, achievement test publishers are moving in the direction of measuring more general abilities. They want to avoid the narrow aspects of content that might favor one school district over another.

Another important difference between aptitude and achievement tests concerns the number of subscale scores provided. Mental ability tests usually provide only a few scores. For instance, the Cognitive Abilities Test provides a verbal, nonverbal, and quantitative score. Achievement tests, on the other hand, provide many subtest scores.

Standardized Achievement and Classroom Tests

Teacher-made tests are constructed by the teacher for the purpose of assessing students within the classroom; they have for their focus the specific learning taking place in the classroom. Their strength is their relevance and applicability in the setting in which they are used. They are, however, characterized by technical deficiencies associated with the limited amount of time and resources available to teachers.

Because standardized achievement tests cover a broader range of behavior than classroom tests, they are unsuitable for evaluating the specific progress of a student in a particular class. They are appropriate for assessing and comparing classes, schools, and school districts.

There is a generally accepted process for constructing an achievement test. When these procedures are followed, uniformly good tests are constructed. As a consequence, there are few differences in quality among the most widely used achievement tests. The technical weaknesses of teacher-made tests are the strengths of standardized tests. The money, time, expert input, and large norm samples associated with standardized tests allow them to achieve a level of technical sophistication unavailable to the classroom teacher. The large commitment of resources associated with standardized tests results from the fact that such tests are commercial ventures intended to be administered to large numbers of students. Pilot testing and complex item analyses are not only easily justified, they are mandatory. The specific techniques for conducting item analyses are covered in Chapter 8.

Standardized tests are administered to large numbers of subjects, which enables the test publisher to provide norms. These permit comparisons with all other students of the same grade or other demographic categorization. This enables standardized tests to fulfill evaluative needs that could not be met with locally constructed tests. With teacher-made tests, students can only be compared within the same class, or across semesters when the same test is used.

The quality of the norm sample is largely a function of how much money the publisher is willing to spend. Because norm samples may include hundreds of thousands of subjects, they can indeed be expensive. When reading a standardized achievement test manual, it is easy to be impressed by the effort and expense that goes into ensuring a large representative sample. It is, of course, not possible to obtain a truly random sample because the test publishers must do their testing in those school districts where they can obtain permission. This usually turns out to be the school districts that have adopted their tests (Baglin, 1981).

The requirement that standardized achievement tests be constructed in such a way as to be useful for the widest possible audience is a major weakness. They must avoid measuring subject matter unique to one location and must instead emphasize general subject matter. This detracts from their usefulness.

To this point, tests have been characterized as either standardized or teacher-made. There are other types of tests that are neither. These tests are constructed to evaluate several classes in school or for an entire school district. They cannot focus on the specific learning taking place in a classroom, and they are not characterized by the kind of technical sophistication enjoyed by the large standardized tests. Their chief advantage is that they allow comparisons to be made that go beyond the individual classroom. An English supervisor, for instance, can get a grasp of the performance of all such classes in a school district. Locally constructed tests are often used when criterion-referenced evaluation methods are adopted by a school district.

Developments in Achievement Testing

Test Batteries

The first achievement tests measured performance in specific areas. A school district that wanted to measure the achievement of students in reading, spelling, math and social studies would have to administer four different tests. Such a procedure was expensive and time consuming, and teachers needed to become familiar with the administration procedures for each test. Test batteries, which include different subjects, can be administered as a package at one sitting, using a single test booklet. This provides a far more efficient means of administration and still permits coverage of the major topics about which a school district is interested.

In addition, the fact that the same norm group is used makes it possible to compare performance in different areas. With separate tests the use of different norm samples makes such a comparison unworkable.

Diagnostic Tests

Another trend in achievement testing involves an emphasis on diagnostic testing. There are standardized tests, particularly in reading and math, that are constructed for the sole purpose of providing diagnostic information. This means that, instead of just providing summary information, about how a child is progressing in a particular subject matter area, the focus is on specific details of weaknesses. Such tests should not be confused with the more common standardized achievement tests. Diagnostic tests emphasize unitary component skills rather than overall performance, and the assessment of the component skills must have high reliability. At the same time, these subtests should not be highly correlated and need not emphasize norms.

Because scores on achievement tests can be expected to approximate the normal distribution, most students fall into the middle range, and standardized tests are constructed to be most reliable for assessing students in this part of the distribution. In contrast, diagnostic tests are intended for use with students who are performing poorly in a given subject matter area; these tests must be constructed in such a way that the finest distinctions are made at the low end of the scale.

Obtaining Diagnostic Information from Achievement Tests The usual method for using a general achievement test diagnostically is providing details about student performance on each item. Computer scoring and analysis make providing the information easy. It also provides additional income for the test publisher, who charges extra for this information.

Such data are of limited diagnostic value because of poor test reliability at the low end of the scale, and because achievement tests are not constructed in such a way as to isolate component skills. Furthermore, each component skill is measured by only a few items. This makes their reliability unacceptably low. Such a procedure can also compromise the security of the test. These diagnostic procedures may tell the teacher specifically what the children in a class have missed. For example, the teacher will be informed that a given student, or the entire class, has not performed well on the language arts section. Then the teacher will be told that the problem is in capitalization, specifically the capitalization of states and in particular the capitalization of Minnesota. If the teacher responds by increasing the time spent teaching capitalization, improves the quality of instruction, or even emphasizes the need to capitalize the names of states, this is probably acceptable; however, when the teacher simply tells a student always to capitalize Minnesota, the validity of the test has been compromised.

Despite the vast differences in qualities necessary for the two types of tests, achievement test publishers have in many cases claimed that their tests were useful as diagnostic tests as well as measures of overall performance. From a marketing standpoint, such an approach makes sense; in an era of widespread opposition to testing, it helps to describe an achievement test in ways that make it seem more acceptable. The purpose of the test shifts from overall performance to a focus on specific skills, the understanding of which can be of direct educational benefit to the child. Unfortunately, it is not possible to construct a test that can effectively measure overall educational achievement and function as a diagnostic test as well. Such claims should be viewed with suspicion.

Criterion-Referenced Tests

The enthusiasm surrounding the introduction of criterion-referenced approaches to classroom tests has generated interest in the application of these methodologies to standardized achievement tests. This need can be met in two ways: (1) objectives can be associated with the items from existing norm-referenced achievement tests to give the appearance of a norm-referenced test; or (2) achievement tests can be constructed from the ground up as a criterion-referenced test. Although the first approach is being employed on a widespread basis, the availability of criterion-referenced achievement tests of the second type is more limited. In the immediate future it can be expected that more of these will be developed because there is a market for such tests.

Examples of Criterion-Referenced Achievement Tests The Psychological Corporation has introduced two different forms of the Metropolitan Achievement Test. One form is a survey battery similar to other norm-referenced survey achievement batteries, and the second is made up of three criterion-referenced instructional tests covering reading, language, and mathematics. SRA has available 34 criterion-referenced diagnostic tests covering instructional objectives included in the curriculum for children in grades one to four. Houghton-Mifflin, in its School Curriculum Objectives-Referenced Evaluation (SCORE), provides five thousand items that can be put together for criterion-referenced tests to meet the specific needs of teacher and classroom settings.

Problems with Criterion-Referenced Standardized Achievement Tests In general, standardized testing and criterion-referenced testing are not very compatible because such tests need to be tied closely to the specific instructional objectives of a classroom or school district. The publishers of nationally distributed achievement tests must avoid any objectives that are not relevant to the broad spectrum of school districts. This means that this approach is most practical for the early grades in the areas of reading and math, where there is the greatest consensus among school districts concerning which objectives should be emphasized. The demand for criterion-referenced achievement tests has led some test publishers to associate objectives with existing items and to claim that these tests have the properties of, or can be used as, criterion-referenced tests. As pointed out in Chapter 10, such tests are better described as objectives-referenced tests and are considered a poor form of assessment. The criterion-referenced approach to assessment is attractive because it seems to avoid some of the negative associations that surround testing by avoiding the labeling of students as failures. There are just some students who have not as yet mastered the objectives.

There is another problem with the criterion-referenced approach to achievement testing. In order to reliably assess a large number of objectives, it is necessary to administer many items. For instance, the Metropolitan Reading Instructional Test includes over two hundred items but assesses some objectives with only three items. The Metropolitan Survey Achievement Test, on the other hand, uses only sixty items to assess reading. Each time you want to report an additional score on a test, you must also increase the number of items or the reliability of the score will decrease. If, instead of reporting ten subscales, you want to report performance on fifty objectives, the number of items must drastically increase or reliability will drop below acceptable levels.

Available Standardized Achievement Tests

There are six major large-scale achievement test batteries. These include the California Achievement Test (CAT) published by McGraw-Hill; the Comprehensive Test of Basic Skills (CTBS), also published by McGraw-Hill; the Iowa Test of Basic Skills (ITBS), published by Riverside Publishing Company; the Metropolitan Achievement Test (MAT), published by the Psychological Corporation; the SRA Achievement Series, published by Science Research Associates, Inc.; and the Stanford Achievement Test (SAT), published by the Psychological Corporation. These tests are all apppropriate for use from kindergarten through twelfth grade, except for the ITBS, which stops at the ninth grade. However, the Riverside Publishing Company also publishes the Iowa Test of Educational Development, which is for students in grades nine to twelve. All of these tests include reading, language, and math, but the CTBS, MAT, and the SAT also cover science and social studies.

These tests are similar in terms of the time and effort that has gone into their development and their general overall high quality. They cover the same ranges of students and have similar content areas. The test-development and norming procedures are generally exemplary. The tests differ in terms of specific items, subscales, and techniques of test development. What is of greatest importance is that the specific objectives they assess are different. Anyone involved in the process of making decisions concerning which test to use needs to compare tests carefully along this dimension to determine which test's objectives are most appropriate.

The Comprehensive Test of Basic Skills (CTBS) will be discussed in detail in the following section. It was selected because it is widely used, although the California Achievement Test (CAT) actually has the most adoptions (the CTBS is a close second, with the other tests fairly far behind). It is the most recently developed, and it incorporates the most sophisticated techniques of test development and test-score reporting.

The Comprehensive Test of Basic Skills (CTBS)

When McGraw-Hill wanted to develop an achievement test that incorporated recent advances in achievement test construction, they chose not to modify the existing CAT. They instead developed an entirely new test that they titled the Comprehensive Test of Basic Skills (CTBS). The term *achievement* was not included because they wanted to emphasize the broad focus of the test.

The purpose of the CTBS is to measure basic skills that are developed from exposure to varied curricula. It is intended to be independent of the particular course content taught in a given school district. However, the test cannot be made entirely independent of the effect of the year that subjects are introduced. Students not yet introduced to a topic are unlikely to do as well on a test covering that material as students who have already been exposed to the subject matter.

The CTBS does not endeavor to measure specific knowledge or content directly. The emphasis is instead on more general skills. Although modern curriculum methods are given consideration, items were rejected if they would be failed by students enrolled in traditional programs.

The forms of the CTBS currently in use are U and V, published in 1981. These are revisions of forms S and T published in 1973 and 1976, respectively. Form V is an alternate form with the purpose of preventing a student from being required to take the same test two years in a row. If the test is administered to each grade, every year, repetition would occur without the two forms. As can be seen in Table 12.1, there is more than one grade associated with a given level.

TABLE 12.1 Levels and Corresponding Grades

Form U only	Level A	K.0 – K.9
	Level B	K.6 – 1.6
	Level C	1.0 – 1.9
Forms U and V	Level D	1.6 – 2.9
	Level E	2.6 – 3.9
	Level F	3.6 – 4.9
	Level G	4.6 – 6.9
	Level H	6.6 – 8.9
	Level J	8.6 – 12.9

Determining the Appropriate Level Where more than one level is appropriate, decisions concerning which to administer should be made according to the following rules. For average students, the lower of the two levels should be given during the first half of the year and the higher level during the second half. Bright students should be given higher levels and below-average students lower levels. The test is normed so that several grades can be given the same level, but the better the match between difficulty level and where a child is functioning, the higher the reliability of the test.

This procedure also reduces the frustration students experience when given a test that is too far above or below their level of achievement. Locator tests consisting of twenty vocabulary and twenty mathematics items are available to assist in the selection of the most appropriate test level.

Content Covered The test is divided into seven content areas, each of which has one or more tests associated with it. Each content area and test is not administered to every level. Table 12.2 provides a list of content areas, tests, and the levels to which they are administered. The technical manual for the CTBS provides the objectives that are associated with each test. Some tests have only one objective, others as many as eleven.

Norming The CTBS was developed to provide fall and spring norms and was based on the school population of the entire United States. The total sample included approximately 250,000 students selected from public, Catholic, and private schools. A stratified random sampling procedure was employed that takes into account geographic region, size, and past achievement test performance.

The test publisher spent a great deal of money to ensure a representative sample.

TABLE 12.2 Content, Tests, and Levels of the CTBS

Content Area	Test	Level
Reading	Visual Recognition	A
	Sound Recognition	A
	Oral Comprehension	AB
	Word Attack	BCDE
	Vocabulary	ABCDEFGHJ
	Reading Comprehension	CDEFGHJ
Spelling	Spelling	DEFGHJ
Language	Language Mechanics	DEFGHJ
	Language Expression	BCDEFGHJ
Mathematics	Mathematics Computation	CDEFGHJ
	Mathematics Concepts and Applications	ABCDEFGHJ
Reference skills	Reference Skills	FGHJ
Science	Science	DEFGHJ
Social studies	Social Studies	DEFGHJ

As a further check on sample characteristics, a questionnaire was sent to all 858 schools participating in the norming process. Examples of the type of information collected are the percentage of single-parent families, the number of homes in which a language other than English is spoken, and ethnic group status. The results of this procedure support the view that the norm sample is representative of the school population in the United States.

The item analysis and scaling of the CTBS is based on a highly sophisticated latent-trait approach, which is referred to in the CTBS manuals as item response theory (IRT), to emphasize its application to test development. The methods used represent the state of the art of standardized test development.

Reporting Results The use of the IRT approach to test scoring necessitates the use of a computer to interpret the results. This interpretation must be done either by McGraw-Hill, the test's publisher, or by programs leased from that company. This computer-based test scoring makes available a wide array of derived scores, such as normal curve equivalents, scaled scores, grade equivalents, and percentiles based on local, state, and national norms. Figure 12.1 is an illustration of the type of information available from McGraw-Hill for each student taking the test.

The Reliability of the CTBS The Preliminary Technical Report (McGraw-Hill, 1982) does not report any reliability data other than standard errors of measurement (SEM), although internal consistency reliability is promised for the final technical manual. The SEM data are impressive in their detail because the use of IRT permits the computation of SEMs for every possible score, whereas traditional methods provide only overall SEMs. The tables of SEMs reported make clear the degree to which the SEM is smaller at the midranges of performance and larger at the floor and ceiling of the test. They also illustrate the advantage of IRT over "number right" approaches to computing scaled scores. The complete reporting of data on the SEMs also is useful in the interpretation of individual test scores because it permits the quantification of the reliability of an individual's test score. This information demonstrates why we can place more confidence in the score of a student in the midrange of performance than at upper or lower levels. It is not useful for comparing the reliability of the CTBS with other comparable achievement tests. Any conclusions about this aspect of the test will have to await the availability of more complete data.

Validity of the CTBS The *Test Coordinator's Handbook* (McGraw-Hill, 1982) states that the content-related validity of the CTBS must be determined by a comparison of a local district's instructional objectives with those on which the CTBS is based. Implicit in this definition is an evaluation of how items are selected to match the stated objectives of the CTBS. The manual lists the instructional objectives the test purports to measure, labeling them "categorical objectives," to indicate that there may be more than one skill or even many skills subsumed under a single objective. The objectives are selected in such a way that they represent the most commonly stated curriculum objectives from across the country. This of course poses an obvious limitation because by implication only objectives that are broadly shared can be included. Items are then written to indicate mastery of

Figure 12.1 Individual test record for the CTBS.

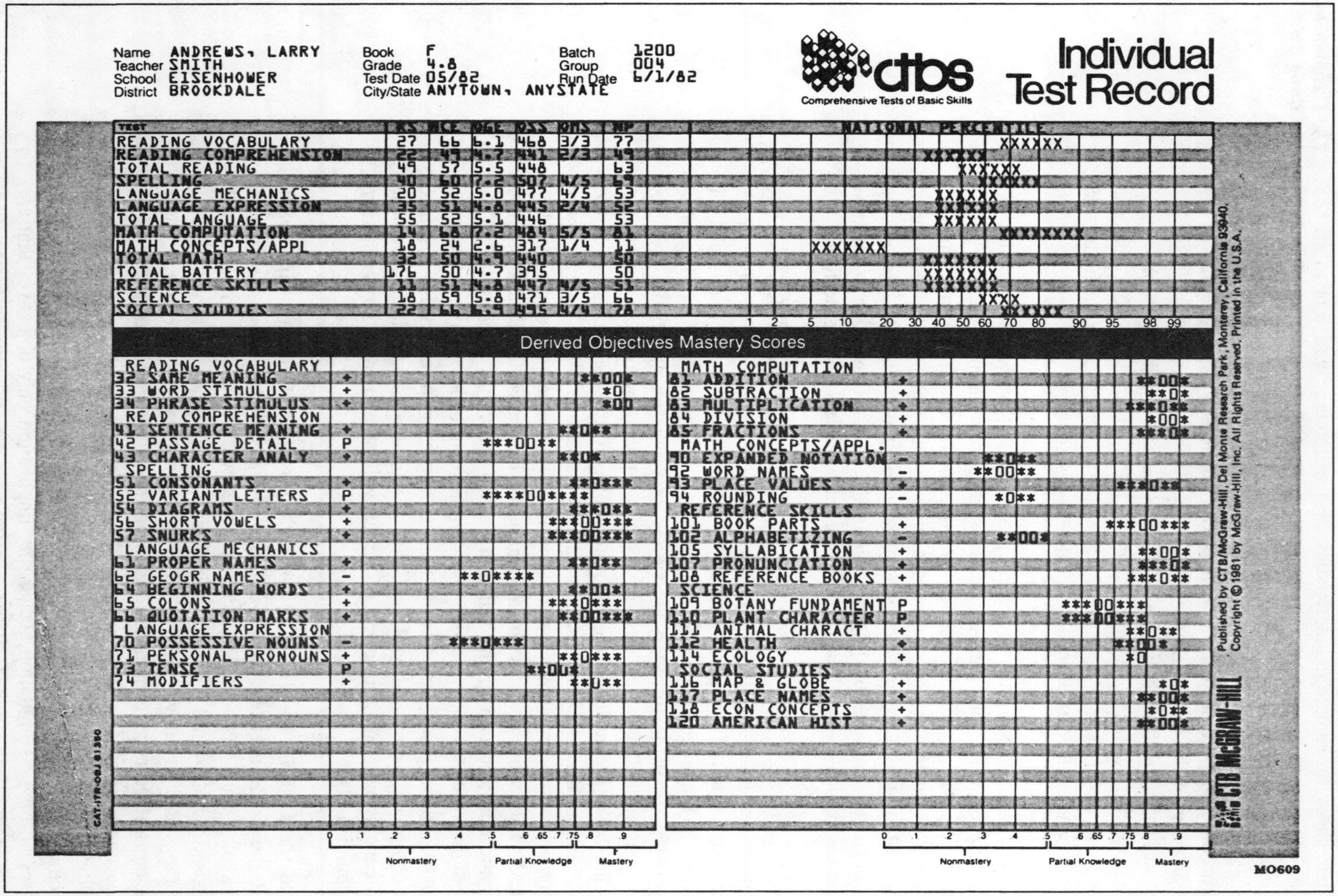

Name ANDREWS, LARRY · Teacher SMITH · School EISENHOWER · District BROOKDALE

Book F · Grade 4.8 · Test Date 05/82 · City/State ANYTOWN, ANYSTATE

Batch 1200 · Group 004 · Run Date 6/1/82

ctbs Comprehensive Tests of Basic Skills

Individual Test Record

TEST	RS	NCE	GE	SS	OMS	NP
READING VOCABULARY	27	66	6.1	468	3/3	77
READING COMPREHENSION	22	49	4.7	441	2/3	49
TOTAL READING	49	57	5.5	448		63
SPELLING	40	60	7.2	507	4/5	69
LANGUAGE MECHANICS	20	52	5.0	477	4/5	53
LANGUAGE EXPRESSION	35	51	4.8	445	2/4	52
TOTAL LANGUAGE	55	52	5.1	446		53
MATH COMPUTATION	14	68	7.2	484	5/5	81
MATH CONCEPTS/APPL	18	24	2.6	317	1/4	11
TOTAL MATH	32	50	4.9	440		50
TOTAL BATTERY	176	50	4.7	395		50
REFERENCE SKILLS	11	51	4.8	447	4/5	51
SCIENCE	18	59	5.8	471	3/5	66
SOCIAL STUDIES	22	66	6.9	495	4/4	78

NATIONAL PERCENTILE: 1 2 5 10 20 30 40 50 60 70 80 90 95 98 99

Derived Objectives Mastery Scores

READING VOCABULARY	
32 SAME MEANING	+
33 WORD STIMULUS	+
34 PHRASE STIMULUS	+
READ COMPREHENSION	
41 SENTENCE MEANING	+
42 PASSAGE DETAIL	P
43 CHARACTER ANALY	+
SPELLING	
51 CONSONANTS	+
52 VARIANT LETTERS	P
54 DIAGRAMS	+
56 SHORT VOWELS	+
57 SNURKS	+
LANGUAGE MECHANICS	
61 PROPER NAMES	+
62 GEOGR NAMES	−
64 BEGINNING WORDS	+
65 COLONS	+
66 QUOTATION MARKS	+
LANGUAGE EXPRESSION	
70 POSSESSIVE NOUNS	−
71 PERSONAL PRONOUNS	+
73 TENSE	P
74 MODIFIERS	+

MATH COMPUTATION	
81 ADDITION	+
82 SUBTRACTION	+
83 MULTIPLICATION	+
84 DIVISION	+
85 FRACTIONS	+
MATH CONCEPTS/APPL.	
90 EXPANDED NOTATION	−
92 WORD NAMES	−
93 PLACE VALUES	+
94 ROUNDING	−
REFERENCE SKILLS	
101 BOOK PARTS	+
102 ALPHABETIZING	−
105 SYLLABICATION	+
107 PRONUNCIATION	+
108 REFERENCE BOOKS	+
SCIENCE	
109 BOTANY FUNDAMENT	P
110 PLANT CHARACTER	P
111 ANIMAL CHARACT	+
112 HEALTH	+
114 ECOLOGY	+
SOCIAL STUDIES	
116 MAP & GLOBE	+
117 PLACE NAMES	+
118 ECON CONCEPTS	+
120 AMERICAN HIST	+

Scale: 0 .1 .2 .3 .4 .5 .6 .65 .7 .75 .8 .9 — Nonmastery · Partial Knowledge · Mastery

CTB McGRAW-HILL · CAT-ITR-OBJ 81380 · MO609

selected educational objectives. The test authors realize that the use of broad educational objectives does not provide much guidance for the writers of the items. Furthermore, it is understood that items can be written on a number of different levels to reflect varying degrees of abstractness and different cognitive functions. For this reason, each item is categorized as assessing one of four processes. The processes are derived from Bloom's *Taxonomy Of Educational Objectives* (1956), which seems to be a popular adjunct to many content analyses. The processes include the following:

Process I	Recall	The student answers from memory alone.
Process II	Identification or translation of explicit information	The student is required to locate material embedded in the text or in a chart.
Process III	Inferential reasoning	The student must be able to draw on divergent pieces of information to make a general conclusion. For instance, to answer questions about a subject's character, the student would be expected to use information about behavior, motives, and/or traits, etc.
Process IV	Evaluation	Given information, the student must be able to draw conclusions.

A chart is provided in the *Test Coordinator's Handbook* that lists the objectives in an abbreviated form, by number, with the full objective provided in the appendix of the manual. Each item at each level of the test is then listed beside the objective under the appropriate heading for the process.

Items are written by teachers in the appropriate subject matter field under the direction of test specialists. From a pool of possible items, the final items to appear on the test are selected by means of complex statistical item-analysis procedures.

The *Test Coordinator's Manual* devotes little space to building a case for content-related validity. It simply states that the school districts that purchase the test will have to decide whether the CTBS adequately assessed their instructional objectives. In order to do this, a school district must complete two tasks:

1. It must make a determination of how well the school system's objectives match the objectives of the CTBS. Of course if the school system possesses explicity stated objectives, this is relatively easy.
2. The school district then must determine the degree to which the items on the CTBS adequately measure the instructional objectives of the test. This can be quite difficult because other than providing broad categorizations of items, little information about their content is presented in the manuals.

If the prospective test purchaser requires more detail about content-related validity, he or she will be forced to examine the items and subjectively decide if they provide an acceptable match.

The selection of objectives to be assessed on the test is restricted by marketing considerations. Each objective to be included must be common to all school districts. A school district obviously would not select a test that included objectives not in their curriculum. It is a less serious concern when there are school district objectives that are not covered by the test. This need to restrict a test to a common core of objectives does not present problems in reading, language, and mathematics because most school districts cover similar subject matter in these areas. It is a major problem in such areas as science and social studies. There is a tremendous variability in the coverage of these topics across states and school districts.

This was the dilemma faced by McGraw-Hill when they wanted to include these topics on their achievement test. The way they dealt with this problem was to assess these areas with items that measured vocabulary, reading comprehension, and chart reading using science and social studies as the subject matter. The student taking such a test needs to know very little in terms of specific facts in order to be successful on the test. The test only looks like it is measuring science and social studies. The sections of the test covering these topics has face validity at best.

For science there are six objectives listed for the CTBS. All are written in the same format. The first objective is as follows: "The student will demonstrate knowledge of the language, concepts, or methods used to communicate and inquire about botany." The same statement is made about zoology, ecology, physics, chemistry, and land, sea, and space sciences. The focus is on communication rather than facts. Because our major method of communication is through the written word, the focus of this part of the test is on reading. The questions in this section require the student to interpret paragraphs, charts, and/or diagrams. Seldom does the student need to know any specific science content. The ability to read and understand what has been read is enough to allow a student to get any question correct. The social studies section of the test takes the same approach and also measures reading ability and the capacity to interpret charts and pictures. The only difference is that the content of the reading paragraphs and charts emphasizes social studies rather than science.

Evaluating the Usefulness of Standardized Achievement Tests

The popularity and public acceptance of standardized tests seems to come in cycles. In the 1950s standardized testing was one of the most uncritically accepted public school activities; however, during the late 1960s and 1970s, questions about its legitimacy began to appear in both professional journals and in the popular press. Much of the opposition was focused on mental ability tests, but calls for the elimination of those tests were generalized to all standardized tests, including achievement tests.

Education is now in a period when the belief in the importance of accountability seems to have reached its zenith. This has led to the increased use of standardized achievement tests, as well as diagnostic and locally constructed tests that can be used to assess minimum competency. This has stimulated interest in assessing the quality of achievement tests.

Reliability

Reliability is an important consideration because without it a test cannot possibly be valid. Rather than report overall reliability, separate coefficients should be reported for each subscale. Because items within a subscale can be expected to be measuring the same constructs, and because the item-analysis procedures employed eliminate items that do not enhance reliability, standardized achievement tests usually are characterized by good reliability. Coefficients in the .90s are typical.

Validity

It is difficult to establish the validity of the scores from an achievement test. Superficially, it can be established by means of content-related validity through a determination of the degree to which the test objectives are represented by the test items. Unfortunately this approach tends mainly to serve the purpose of fulfilling the requirement that the test manuals provide validity data. As was emphasized in Chapter 6, content-related validity is a weak form of evidence for validity. Tests can be constructed that meet all of the requirements for this sort of validity but that fail to measure accurately the constructs they are intended to assess. Evidence for the validity of standardized achievement tests needs to be bolstered by criterion- and construct-related validity along with content-related validity.

The Limitations of the Objective Test Format Items must be written in such a way that they can be objectively scored. With some subject matter this can be done with a minimum degree of distortion of the desired educational outcome, whereas with others the behaviors that we want students to exhibit may be quite different from those we assess.

When the statement is made that students should be good spellers, this presumably means that they should be able to write with a minimum of spelling errors. Although teachers may evaluate this ability by checking for spelling errors in a student's written work, more often the ability is assessed through the venerable tradition of the weekly spelling test. The teacher reads a list of words that the students must then write down. Spelling ability is measured by determining the number of words correctly spelled. This cannot be done on an achievement test because the task must be accomplished with a multiple-choice format. In the spelling content area of the CTBS, for instance, the student is required to identify the correctly spelled word from among four words where three are misspelled. This represents a marked abstraction from the original instructional objective. The same problem occurs with reading comprehension, where this most important skill has been reduced to a series of measurable competencies such as identifying the main idea in a short paragraph. Even though this is an important skill, it is quite different from the capacity to understand and evaluate lengthy passages, chapters, and entire books.

Making Objectives General Another factor that limits the validity of standardized achievement tests is the requirement that they be nonspecific, in order to ensure that they are appropriate across all school districts.

As was pointed out in the case of the CTBS, restricting achievement tests to a common core of objectives does not have much of a negative effect on validity in the areas of reading, mathematics, and language development because all school systems tend to teach content that is not that different. Other subject matter, particularly that taught in high schools, seldom can be validly assessed by standardized tests because nationwide curriculums are too diverse to expect any one test to be appropriate for all.

Using Standardized Achievement Tests to Evaluate School Systems

An important reason for schools to administer standardized achievement tests is to serve the purposes of evaluation by comparing school districts, schools, classes, and/or grades in terms of student achievement. Furthermore, because of the difficulty of the task of evaluating how good a job a school system is doing, there is a tendency for the public, politicians, or state legislatures to use test scores as the major criterion for assessing the effectiveness of a school district. This emphasis can lead to distortions. Testing procedures are sometimes adopted because they promise higher scores, rather than because they are justified for purposes of increasing student learning.

If standardized tests are to be used for the purpose of evaluation in such a way that school districts can legitimately be compared, then the testing will have to be conducted by a body other than the school district itself. For instance, when students are given the SAT, they must present identification to ensure that the correct person is taking the test. A new test is developed for each administration, and the forms of the tests administered are varied within the testing room to prevent students from copying answers from those sitting next to them. Furthermore, access to items before the test is administered is severely restricted. None of these cautions is employed with standardized achievement tests.

Frequencies of Test Revision and Test Security Instead of using a new test for each administration, there is often more than five years between revisions. This means that, year after year, teachers are administering the same test to their students. Because the results are disseminated in such a way that the school, grade, and/or classroom can be compared, it is not surprising that teachers are under pressure to have their students do well. Teachers can very easily find out the content of the test and emphasize spelling and vocabulary words that appear on the test. The school system is tempted to look the other way in the face of such breaches of test security because such practices serve to increase the overall performance of the school district.

Excluding Students from Taking the Tests

School districts also are able to choose who will be exempted from taking the test. In some districts, membership in a special class results in exclusion from having to take the test. In others, students who have been referred for possible placement are also exempted. Such practices can greatly limit the number of low-scoring students taking the test and artifically inflate overall scores.

Examiners' manuals also permit the invalidation of tests when it is felt that the student is marking randomly, is losing time—or because of some other irregularity in testing procedures. This is, of course, a subjective decision made by the examiner. If the teacher is the examiner and he or she is under pressure to improve test-score performance, the temptation to invalidate more tests, particularly those of low-performing students, may be too much to resist.

The Diagnostic Use of Standardized Achievement Tests

Another use for standardized achievement tests is the determination of specific areas of strengths and weaknesses. What this usually involves is a form of error analysis whereby teachers are informed of the types of errors individuals or classes of children are making. Unfortunately this is not very effective because it is not practical to include a sufficient number of items to make the measurement of these errors reliable. The unintended result is that it becomes tempting for teachers to teach to these errors, which results in the students' scores being artifically inflated.

The Time of Test Administration

For standardized achievement tests to be of maximum value to teachers, they need to be administered early in the year so that they can be scored and returned in time to be used for evaluating individual student progress. At one time this was difficult because most of these tests were standardized so that they could be administered in the spring. However, as a result of the increased use of the tests for evaluating federal programs such as Head Start and Follow Through, which require pre-and post-data, both fall and spring norms are being made available. Despite the fact that these norms are available, and even though a fall administration would have the advantage of providing test results to teachers early enough that they could make use of the results, this is seldom done. This is because the spring administration seems more appropriate for evaluation purposes and because of the perception that, by testing late in the year, students will obtain higher scores and the school district can be made to look better. As a result, the test results are seldom returned soon enough for them to be useful to teachers.

Achievement Tests Commonly Used for Individual Educational Assessment

Over the last twenty years there has been an increased interest in individually administered achievement tests for use with special populations. This is the result of increases in enrollment in special education classes and the concomitant need for appropriate methods for determining which children can benefit from regular classroom placement and which can only be expected to maximize their potential in an adapted educational setting. Individually administered tests are of particular importance in this setting because when a child performs poorly on a group test, it is not easy to determine the cause. It could be the result of inattention, poor motivation, a misunderstanding about directions, or a myriad of other factors. Many of these can be detected during the administration of an individual test. Once the child has been identified as needing special educational adaptations, there is a further need to have diagnostic information that can lead to the formulation of the educational plan that would be most beneficial.

The need for more appropriate assessment tools increased after PL 94-142 (the bill of rights for exceptional children) became law. Although it did not mandate specific tests, it did require more thorough assessment procedures and the collection of test data beyond individual intelligence scores. At the same time that special education services were expanding, there was an increase in the concern for children who were functioning at a low academic level. This was the result of increased school desegregation, declines in the use of grouping, and campaigns to discourage students from dropping out of school.

There are a large number of instruments that can be used for the purpose of individual assessment of academic achievement, but there are four that are the most often encountered: the Wide Range Achievement Test, the Peabody Individual Achievement Test, The Woodcock Reading Mastery Test, and the KeyMath Diagnostic Arithmetic Test.

None of these four instruments require extensive special training, but they are most effectively used by professional educators who are familiar with the instruments and who are experienced in their use.

The Wide Range Achievement Test

The Wide Range Achievement Test (Jastak & Jastak, 1978), often included as part of a standard psychological assessment battery, is individually administered and takes twenty to thirty minutes. There are two levels of the test, with level I for use with students ages 5–0 to 11–11, and level II for students aged 12–0 through adulthood. There are different sets of items for each subtest within each level, and for each level there are three subtests: Spelling, Arithmetic, and Reading. The items for each subject are presented in order of their difficulty from easy to difficult. The beginning items for the Spelling subtest require the student to copy geometric shapes and write their name. The remainder of the test consists of dictated words that the student must write down on the answer sheet. The student receives one point for each correctly spelled word. The Arithmetic subtest consists of a series of computation problems presented on a sheet of paper that the student must solve by writing his or her answers on the sheet with a pencil. There are 43 items in level I and 46 in level II. The student's score is determined by the number of items that can be correctly answered in ten minutes. Young children and older children who do not correctly answer the easiest problems are asked simple oral questions requiring counting and recognition of numbers. The Reading subtest consists of a list of words. The student is asked to pronounce each word, starting with the easiest. Younger students and those who cannot pronounce the first words are given easier tasks, consisting of the identification of two letters in their own name followed by a series of letters not presented in alphabetical order.

Raw scores on each subtest can be converted to age equivalents, percentiles, or standard scores with a mean of 100 and a standard deviation of 15. Reliability using the split-halves method is in the .90s. Given the homogeneity of the subject matter, such high reliabilities should be expected. The validity of the scores from these tests is determined by content-related validity and concurrent criterion-related validity. Content-related validity is assessed through a determination of whether the test covers the content that it should. This is a subjective process, but in the case of an achievement test there is general agreement concerning what should be covered. The content-related validity of the Spelling and Arithmetic subtests seems to be good. These two subtests are clearly measuring what one would expect such tests to measure. There is an expected set of competencies in math, and this test covers them. The Spelling subtest is superior to similar subtests found in most standardized achievement tests. Such tests usually assess spelling in one of two ways: either by determining if the student can identify misspelled words from among distractors that are spelled correctly, or if he or she can identify correctly spelled words from among those that are misspelled. These approaches to assessing spelling are concessions to the necessities of objective scoring, but they weaken the construct-related validity of a test because such procedures result in a test that is not really assessing what we usually think of as spelling ability. The WRAT approach, which requires the child to actually write down dictated words, is superior to these more conventional approaches. The Reading subtest, on the other hand, provides an unsatisfactory assessment of reading ability because the student is required to do no more than decode and pronounce the words. The ability to decode and pronounce words is a necessary condition for reading, and good readers can be expected to be proficient in this. The problem is that it is possible for a student to be quite good at pronouncing words without really knowing what they mean and without possessing any capacity for reading comprehension.

As might be expected from the observations, concurrent criterion-related validity for Spelling and Arithmetic are in the acceptable upper .70s, but the Reading subtest is in a not very acceptable lower .60 range (McLoughlin & Lewis, 1981). Jerome Sattler (1982) also points out that the WRAT tends to underestimate functioning when compared to other standardized achievement tests.

The WRAT remains a popular and often used measure of school achievement because it is easy to use and because it can be quickly administered. It also provides scores in the three areas that are of usual interest. It is certainly useful as a quick screening device. In two areas it provides useful and valid scores, as long as the person using the results is aware of the test's proclivity to underestimate scores. The reading subtest is not as useful, although the scores obtained are related to scores that might be obtained on other reading tests.

The Peabody Individual Achievement Test

Like the WRAT, the Peabody Individual Achievement Test (Dunn & Markwardt, 1970) (PIAT) is an individually administered achievement test most often used for the purpose of screening in grades K through 12. Administration of the test takes thirty to forty minutes and requires a minimum of training on the part of the examiner.

About half of the items are multiple choice, requiring the student to point to the correct answer from four possible choices; the other half of the items require verbal responses. There are five subtests: Mathematics, Reading Recognition, Reading Comprehension, Spelling, and General Information. On the Mathematics subtest items are read to the student and he or she must respond by pointing to one of four alternatives. The content is diverse and includes such operations as adding, subtraction, multiplication, division, time, measurement, mathematical vocabulary, geometry, and trigonometry. The easiest items on the Reading Recognition subtest require the student to read individual vocabulary words aloud. On the Reading Comprehension subtest, the student selects the best depiction of a sentence from among four pictures. The Spelling subtest requires the student to choose the correct answer from among four alternatives. The subtest begins with the identification of symbols that are different; then the student must identify the correct letter after it is presented orally, identify words, and finally identify the correctly spelled words from among those that are misspelled. The General-Information subtest requires the student to reply orally to questions covering knowledge of science, social studies, the arts, and so on.

The PIAT yields both a total score and subtest scores. Scores are reported by means of age equivalents, grade equivalents, percentiles, or standard scores with a mean of 100 and a standard deviation of 15. Percentiles and standard scores are available for both age and grade norms. Normally we are most interested in grade norms, but if a child is either older or younger than other children in his or her class, the age norms might be preferred.

The reliability of the test was determined using a test-retest method. Coefficients are in the .60s, .70s, and .80s. Information on internal consistency should have been provided because test-retest coefficients do not tell us what is most important about reliability (see Chapter 5, the section on internal consistency, p. 106).

The content validity of the test for Mathematics, Reading Comprehension, and General Information seems adequate, but the Reading-Recognition subtest is like the Reading subtest of the WRAT—it measures only the ability to pronounce words. This is not a major limitation because of the availability of the Reading-Comprehension subtest. The Spelling subtest has the same limitations as the spelling subtests on most standardized achievement tests on which the task of spelling is abstracted from what we normally think of as spelling ability in order to facilitate standardized scoring. This is unnecessary on an individually administered test, and it is hard to justify the decision not to just have the student write down words presented orally, as does the WRAT and virtually every elementary schoolteacher. That would have made scores on the spelling test more closely relate to what is conventionally thought of as spelling ability: the ability to perform well on a conventional spelling test. The concurrent validity of the PIAT, when compared to other achievement tests, in the words of Sattler (1982), is "excellent."

The PIAT, like the WRAT, is a good screening test for use in circumstances where a quick estimate of academic functioning is needed. Because it covers a wider range of skills, and because it measures reading better, the PIAT seems like a better choice than the WRAT. Except for situations where time is a consideration or the student to be tested has characteristics that prevent a group test administration, a standardized group achievement or a diagnostic test in specific areas where the student is experiencing difficulty is preferred.

The Woodcock Reading Mastery Test

The Woodcock Reading Mastery Test (Woodcock, 1977) is an individually administered reading test that requires between thirty and forty minutes to administer. It is often used in conjunction with the diagnosis of children referred for special education placement. There are two forms of the test, A and B. The test is appropriate for administration from grades K to 12. Responses to all items are made orally by the student. There are five subtests: Letter Identification, Word Identification, Word Attack, Word Comprehension, and Passage Comprehension. The Letter-Identification test, as its name suggests, requires the student to identify letters. This task is made difficult enough to be appropriate for children beyond the first couple grades by using different and unusual styles of type. The manual suggests that this subtest not be administered to students beyond sixth grade, but its results are not very useful beyond second grade. The Word-Identification test includes 150 words ranging from those one might expect in a beginning reader to those that a twelfth-grader might find difficult. The student is required to name as many as he or she can. The Word-Attack test contains fifty items consisting of nonsense words that the student is asked to pronounce correctly. This task requires the student to apply phonic and structure-analysis skills. The Word-Comprehension test contains seventy items that utilize an analogy format; it assesses a student's vocabulary and ability to see the relationship between words. The items are presented in the following format:

cow – calf   cat – ________

The student must first of all determine the relationship between the first pair of words and then demonstrate his or her understanding by filling in the missing word to form the second pair. The Passage-Comprehension test contains eighty-five items consisting of phrases or sentences that have had a word removed. The student reads the item silently to him- or herself and then states which word is missing. The first eighteen items include illustrations to help the student understand what the sentence means. There are only two figures used with the remainder of the items, a circle in one case, a ball in another.

Derived scores are computed for each subtest and for the total score, and this score is called the Index of Total Reading. A basal-ceiling approach is used to avoid asking the student questions that are either too easy or too difficult. Tables are then used to transform the raw score into a mastery score that in turn can be used to determine the grade equivalent and to obtain percentiles. To extend the grade equivalents below 1.0 or above 12.9, superscripts (small numerals above the line) are used to indicate a child's percentile rank. Mastery scores are derived using the Rasch-Wright approach, which results in a scale that has interval properties and that is based on both the difficulty of the task and the probability that a student will succeed at a task. This type of scale has better psychometric characteristics than grade equivalents or percentiles, and because it is not a linear transformation, as is a standard score, it might provide slightly more precision than standard scores based on *z*-scores. However, they are not as precise as the scaled scores derived from the three-parameter latent-trait model described in Chapter 8. Mastery scores do not seem that much better than *T*-scores, but they were a technical innovation in 1973. Unfortunately, the authors, in seeking even greater technical virtuosity, chose to add a criterion-referenced perspective to their test. Rasch-Wright scores are purely norm-referenced, and nothing could be more incompatible with criterion-referenced assessment. In order to accomplish the task of combining such opposites, the authors introduced what they call joint norm-referenced/criterion-referenced interpretations. As laughable as this is, it can probably be excused by the immaturity of the criterion-referenced field in 1973. The authors went on to provide a bewildering array of additional scores predicated on the concept of "relative mastery." Of course mastery is an absolute, and relative mastery makes no more sense than saying something is "partially unique." The user is best advised to stick with the grade equivalents and percentile scores that are provided.

Split halves and parallel forms methods were used to assess reliability. As should be expected with a reading test, the reliabilities are uniformly high in the upper .90s, with one exception. The reliability for Letter Identification at grade 7.9 is reported to be an astoundingly low .02. This should not be a source of concern because the subtest need not be administered beyond the second-grade level.

The content-related validity of the test seems acceptable. The subtests generally cover those aspects of reading that one would expect. However, it would have been useful if a subtest had been included that required the student to answer questions about short passages. This is closer to what is usually thought of as reading comprehension. The Letter-Recognition test could easily be eliminated, and some letter-identification tasks could be included at the beginning of the Word-Recognition subtest for those children who cannot name any words. The identification of letters in different type styles cannot be considered an important reading skill. The manual does not include information about concurrent criterion-related validity. This is an important source of evidence for validity because the user needs to know if the reading scores obtained are similar to those that would have been obtained if a longer standardized reading test had been administered. Such data would have been easy to obtain. Instead, the authors include data about the intercorrelation of subtests and the correlation between different forms under the heading of validity. This is interesting but it more appropriately belongs under the heading of reliability than validity.

In conclusion, this is a useful test to administer when one wants to obtain a quick estimation of a student's overall reading level, in addition to some information about strengths and weaknesses. It is unfortunate that the authors chose to attach so many needless and questionable technical gimmicks to what is basically a sound screening instrument.

The KeyMath Diagnostic Arithmetic Test

The KeyMath (Connolly, Nuchtman, & Pritchett, 1976) is an individually administered test used for assessing mathematical skills that is often administered in conjunction with special education diagnoses. It is intended for use with children from preschool to sixth grade and takes about forty minutes to administer. There are fourteen subtests grouped into three areas. The structure follows:

Area I: Content—Basic arithmetic concepts

A. Numeration—Recognition of numbers and counting (24 items).

B. Fractions—Finding and recognizing fractions and recognizing the relationships among fractions (11 items).

C. Geometry and Symbols—Recognition of geometrical shapes and mathematical symbols and recognition of parallel and perpendicular lines (20 items).

Area II: Operations—Basic mathematical operations

D. Addition—Three problems using pictures and 12 written computations solved using a pencil (14 items).

E. Subtraction—Three problems using pictures and 11 written computations solved using a pencil (14 items).

F. Multiplication—Two oral word problems and 9 written problems solved using pencil (11 items).

G. Division—Two oral problems using pictures and 8 written problems using a pencil (10 items).

H. Mental Computations—A series of mathematical operations presented orally, such as "1 plus 2, minus 1, times 3" (10 items).

I. Numerical Reasoning—Solving visually presented equations (12 items).

Area III: Applications—Application of mathematical principles

J. Word Problems—Orally presented word problems, the first seven of which are accompanied by a picture (14 items).

K. Missing Elements—Word problems for which the student must provide the critical information that is missing, rather than the numerical answer (7 items).

L. Money—Counting money, familiarity with different denominations, reading checks, and understanding budget items (15 items).

M. Measurement—Use of ruler, scales, and thermometer and general knowledge measurement concepts (27 items).

N. Time—Reading clocks and understanding time intervals, alarm clock settings, holidays, and seasons.

Scores can be reported for subtest, areas, and total scores. Unfortunately only grade equivalents are available. The manual could have easily provided tables to derive percentiles and some other standard score but does not. Furthermore, means and standard deviations are not provided, so users cannot compute their own standard scores. This simplistic approach to reporting scores seems strange because the scaling of the test is based on the sophisticated latent-trait Rasch-Wright technique. To go to such trouble to obtain latent-trait scores and then to make available only grade equivalents with all of their limitations is indefensible.

The manual does provide a table that can be used to convert raw scores to *W*-scores. Although these are not readily interpretable in terms of understanding a child's performance, they can be used as an interval measure for purposes of research. Grade equivalents of course are not interval-scale data and cannot be used in computations that require such a scale.

Across grades K through 7, the reliabilities for the fourteen subtests are generally in the .60s and .70s. This is not very high, but these moderate coefficients are likely the result of the small numbers of items included in the subtests. More troubling are the sporadically low reliabilities for several subtests at specific ages. The low reliability for kindergarten and first-graders on the Fractions subtest was probably the result of the task being too difficult. But one must question why there is .65 reliability for fifth-graders and a .74 reliability for seventh-graders on the Geometry and Symbols subtest but a .28 reliability for sixth-graders. Likewise with Word Problems: a .37 for fifth-graders sandwiched between .60s for fourth- and sixth-graders. The same type of problem occurs with Subtraction and Addition for second-graders. We do not know if there is something inappropriate in the difficulty of the subtests for these particular grades or if there was something anomalous in the norming population. The manual reports these results without comment. The reliability of the total score across all grades is in the middle to upper .90s, which is very good.

The content-related validity of the test appears to be satisfactory. The test certainly covers a wide range of mathematical skills. If anything, it tries to cover too many for what is intended to be a brief test. It would have been better to have concentrated on fewer skills and included more items in their assessment. This would have enhanced reliability and resulted in a better diagnostic instrument. Evidence for concurrent criterion-related validity is spotty. Kratochwill and Demuth (1976) obtained a correlation of .63 between the KeyMath and math scores on the Metropolitan Achievement Test. Price and Rogers (1981) conclude that there is a dearth of validity data to demonstrate that the KeyMath should be used as a diagnostic instrument for special education children.

The KeyMath test yields a total score that can be useful in assessing the overall math functioning of children in grades K through 6 or 7, however, the subtest scores need to be interpreted with a great deal of caution. The test materials are easy to use and attractive, but the lack of any derived scores other than grade equivalents is a major drawback of the test.

SUMMARY

1. The development of standardized achievement tests was an outgrowth of methods developed for measuring intelligence in a group setting.
2. At one time it was believed that there were clear differences between aptitude and achievement tests; at the present time it is generally understood that they both are measuring acquired ability and that there is considerable overlap in content.
3. Standardized achievement tests differ from teacher-made tests in terms of specificity, norming, and technical sophistication.
4. Important developments in the field of standardized achievement testing include the use of test batteries and diagnostic tests, as well as criterion-referenced testing principles.
5. There are six major standardized achievement tests. The CAT is the one that is most often administered.
6. The effectiveness of standardized achievement tests is limited by the need to modify content so that it will fit into an objective test format and the requirement that no objective be assessed that is not common to all school districts.
7. There are four individually administered achievement tests: the Wide Range Achievement Test, the Peabody Individual Achievement Test, the Woodcock Reading Mastery Test, and the KeyMath Diagnostic Arithmetic Test.
8. These four tests do not require extensive training for their use, and they are useful as screening instruments or in circumstances where group administration is not practical.

SUGGESTED READINGS

GRONLUND N. E. (1985). *Measurement and evaluation in teaching* (5th ed.). New York: Macmillan. [Chapter 1 of this book provides useful descriptions of standardized achievement testing and describes those that are most commonly used.]

MCLOUGHLIN, J. A., & LEWIS, R. B. (1981). *Assessing special students*. Columbus, OH: Merrill. [This book contains extensive descriptions of individually administered achievement tests in all areas, with particular emphasis on those that are most appropriate for the special education student].

SHERTZER, B., & LINDEN, J. D. (1979). *Fundamentals of individual appraisal: Assessment techniques for counselors*. Boston: Houghton. [This book is a good source for brief descriptions of commonly used standardized achievement tests.]

13

Mental Ability Testing

OVERVIEW

From the start, the mental ability testing field has been the center of controversy, which is the theme of much of this chapter. A good starting point for a discussion of the controversy involves the difficulties in arriving at a workable definition of intelligence. The definitions provided emphasize the differences between functional intelligence and academic ability. Next, the differences between single-factor and multiple-factor theories of intelligence are discussed, along with the other ways in which intelligence has been conceptualized. One of the most contentious aspects of mental ability testing concerns efforts to determine the relative contributions of heredity and environment. This is discussed in terms of its relationship to population, genetics, ethnic and cultural differences, and sex differences. The chapter concludes with a discussion of bias and the use of culture-fair tests.

OBJECTIVES

In this chapter you will learn about the theoretical and definitional problems that characterize mental ability testing. Specificallly you will learn the following:

- The various and somtimes conflicting definitions of intelligence.
- How different scientists have evaluated the relative contributions of heredity and environment to intelligence.
- The extent of differences among cultural and ethnic groups in terms of mental ability.
- The extent of sex differences in intelligence.
- The degree to which mental ability tests are biased.

Introduction

There are many types of ability that come under the heading of mental ability. There is intelligence, which can be assessed either individually or in a group setting; academic aptitude, as assessed by the SAT, the Graduate Record Exam (GRE), Miller's Analogies Test; multiple aptitude tests, which are used for assisting students in selecting a college major or occupations; and achievement, which is assessed by instruments discussed in Chapter 12. The differences among tests intended to measure these abilities are not always apparent from an examination of test items because of the overlap in content. The most important difference among types of tests concerns the ways they are used and validated.

Intelligence

Intelligence was first used in its modern sense by Herbert Spencer in 1895, although the term itself can be found in use as far back as the writings of Cicero. Spencer believed that humans differed in terms of intelligence, whereas animals differed in terms of their instincts.

From the beginning, the assessment of intelligence has faced strong opposition that has often been characterized by an almost visceral revulsion. This is partially because much of what has been learned about intelligence in the last eighty years conflicts with Western liberal tradition and partially because of the way intelligence tests have been misused.

Those who oppose the testing of intelligence sometimes deny the existence of intelligence. Of course, intelligence is just a construct, and therefore it does not exist as a physical entity. If we were to deny the existence of all human characteristics that do not have a physical reality, our language would be greatly impoverished. In addition, few other constructs are measured as well as intelligence.

Definitions of Intelligence

One possible starting point for the development of a definition of *intelligence* is through the writing of Alfred Binet. Although he never provided a formal definition, he did emphasize higher-order mental functioning. He did not believe that intelligence was an attribute itself but instead emphasized that it was an attribute of behaviors. He wanted to avoid the then-favored view that intelligence was inherited, permanent, and impervious to change. He likely would have been displeased with the widespread adoption of IQ scores that occurred after his death.

Wechsler (1944) provides the following definition: "intelligence is the aggregate or global capacity of the individual to act purposefully, to think rationally, and to deal effectively with his environment." E. G. Boring (1923), an early psychologist specializing in the study of intelligence, gives a definition so operational as to sound facetious, stating that intelligence is the "measurable capacity to do well on an intelligence test." Wechsler's definition is so broad that it threatens to encompass all behavior; it also has led to an overemphasis on the importance of intelligence. Boring's definition is so operational it lacks useful generality.

In defining intelligence it is useful to distinguish between *functional intelligence*, which is the way the term is used in the vernacular, and *academic ability*, which is the type of intelligence emphasized on intelligence tests.

Functional Intelligence A person who can operate effectively in his or her environment is generally labeled intelligent. Different cultures have different views of what it means to operate effectively within an environment; therefore, they have their own views and perceptions of what they consider intelligent behavior. In a sense, like beauty, functional intelligence is in the eyes of the beholder.

Consider the owner of a gas station who is very successful. He knows how to handle people and money, he's a good businessman who certainly does not appear unintelligent, yet he has minimal reading skills and only finished the eighth grade. Without question he would fare poorly on an intelligence test and similarly have considerable difficulty in a college freshman English class. In this case a scholastic aptitude test might be a good predictor of academic performance but a poor indication of functional intelligence.

Is this person intelligent? That depends on how we define intelligence. The definitional confusion about intelligence is the source of much controversy. The problem is abetted by test constructors, who are unwilling to give up the idea that they are measuring functional intelligence when they are really measuring academic aptitude.

Academic Aptitude Makers of intelligence tests tend to develop tests that measure intelligence in a manner consistent with their own philosophy, emphasizing those things that they consider important. There is one rule concerning the creation of an intelligence test that is seldom violated: no one creates an intelligence test on which he or she would do poorly. Because the authors of intelligence tests typically come from academic settings, it should come as no surprise that considerable emphasis is placed on the sort of verbal skills favored by higher education.

Furthermore, the developers of early intelligence tests were interested in solving practical problems rather than in developing theoretical definitions of intelligence. Binet wanted to create an intelligence test that could differentiate between children who were mentally retarded and those who were normal. The items that worked best were those that required mental processing—thinking and problem solving. Later, when he wanted to create a test that could differentiate among normal children, he looked for items that were related to age—items that older children would get correct but that younger children would fail. Again, items that required higher-level thought processing seemed to work best, as did school-related items. Because each higher grade represents the accumulation of another year of schooling, items that were related to academic material tended to differentiate among children of different ages. This practice was also adopted by Terman in the 1916 version of the Stanford-Binet. The relationship between school experiences and test performance also served to enhance the predictive validity of the test. One would expect that children who obtained higher scores on tests constructed this way would also obtain higher grades. The Stanford-Binet became so well established that the author of any new intelligence test had to demonstrate that it measured the same things as the Stanford-Binet or it would not be accepted. Therefore, subsequent tests also tended to measure academic ability.

This does not mean that all intelligence tests had to be verbal, and in fact the Stanford-Binet contains many nonverbal items. But when nonverbal items are selected from the pool of all possible nonverbal items, only those that demonstrate a substantial correlation with school performance are used. For instance, nonverbal memory tasks tend not to correlate well with either school performance or other test items, so they are likely to be eliminated in favor of items that are better predictors of academic performance.

Comparing Functional Intelligence and Academic Aptitude The distinction between functional intelligence and academic aptitude is not always made clear, and there has been a tendency to assume that there is only one type of intelligence (encompassing both). The view that there is only this one type of intelligence, and that it is what is measured by intelligence tests, makes the explanation of the variability in mental ability test scores across ethnic groups difficult to explain. It is suggestive of overall inferiority, rather than a lack of educational development.

Unitary Versus Multifaceted Views of Intelligence A major issue confronting those seeking a definition of intelligence concerns the question of whether intelligence is a single trait or is made up of many separate entities that should be labeled intelligence. Although Binet did not believe that intelligence was unitary, the intelligence test he created yielded a single score. This did not set well with those who advocated a multifaceted view of intelligence and who were anxious to claim Binet as one of their own. Apparently Binet was able to suppress any philosophical reservation he may have had about espousing a unitary view of intelligence for the obvious practical advantages that accrue from the use of a single score to categorize students according to their academic potential.

Charles Spearman is credited with an early empirical defense of the unitary view of intelligence. Using newly developed techniques of correlation, he showed that a variety of different mental ability tests were correlated. He believed that the reason for this correlation was that they shared a common factor, which he labeled the general factor, *g*. He also pointed out that, to the extent that two tests are not perfectly correlated, and are therefore not measuring only *g*, they are assessing specific factors, or *s*. Spearman rejected the view that tests could be grouped to make up factors that were secondary to the *g* factor. This view of intelligence, which was introduced prior to the publication of the Stanford-Binet in 1916, serves as a justification for the method of item selection used with that test. Thurstone (1941) challenged Spearman's view of intelligence, also by using factor analysis. He identified numerous separate factors that he believed operated independently of *g*. J. P. Guilford (1967), a more modern exponent of this view of intelligence, developed an elaborate three-dimensional model of the structure of intelligence, using factor analysis, that yields 120 separate facets.

The decision concerning whether to side with those who view intelligence as unitary or those who view it as multifaceted becomes very much a function of one's own perception. As Jean Piaget has so elegantly asserted, one of the most impressive capacities of humans is their ability to take in information and change it into a form that is familiar and thus more easily comprehensible. The way we ultimately perceive data to be organized is more a function of our cognitive experiences and what we bring to the setting than the innate characteristics of the data. When researchers examine the responses of a large number of subjects to various tests of cognitive functioning, it is very reasonable that there would not be unanimity concerning the optimum organization of the data. For this reason some researchers have concluded that intelligence is unitary, whereas others are committed to a multifaceted view.

Fluid Versus Crystallized Ability Another way of categorizing intellectual functioning is to divide it into fluid and crystallized abilities (Cattel, 1968; Horn, 1979). Fluid ability involves the capacity to function on tasks that are so constructed as to be independent of culture and learning and represent innate intellectual abilities. Tests used to assess this ability are typically nonverbal and novel.

Fluid intelligence is related to the way that Spearman believed *g* should be measured. He advocated the primacy of tests that assessed a subject's ability to educe relationships. For example, a subject might be given the words *apple* and *orange* and then be required to state how the two are the same. The subject's reply that they are both fruit indicates that he or she recognizes the relationship between the two. The words themselves are called fundaments, and when they are recognized, the process is called *apperception*. Eduction could also be assessed by providing the word *fast* and asking for the subject to provide its opposite. In this case, one fundament is provided along with the relationship, and the subject is asked to provide the second fundament. A popular method of assessing eduction ability combines the two. A series of geometric shapes is provided in such a way as to suggest a pattern. The subject is then asked to select from a group of similar geometric shapes the one that follows next in the pattern. The subject is therefore required to educe the pattern and then show that he or she understands it by indicating the next appropriate geometric shape. (See Figure 13.1.)

Crystallized ability involves the capacity to perform tasks that are dependent

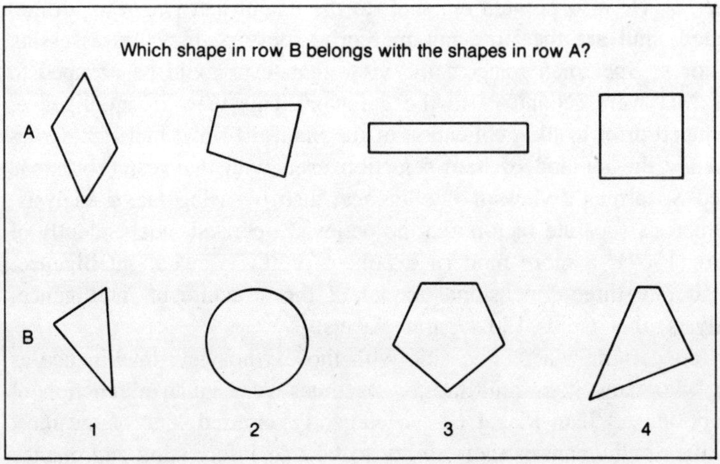

Figure 13.1
An item that assesses eduction ability.

on learning. The recall of facts and information is an example of items that measure crystallized ability. Crystallized ability is not believed to function independently of fluid ability because crystallized ability is acquired to a large extent through the use of fluid ability.

Eduction problems measure fluid intelligence only when the recognition of the fundaments does not require much learning, which is why geometric shapes are used. It is assumed that geometric shapes provide a novel task, and therefore no child has an advantage as a result of greater experiences. Of course when a child has had such experiences and, after all, much of our early experience activities for children involve such exposure, what were once measures of fluid intelligence become contaminated with crystallized intelligence. This is an even greater problem with verbal questions because our vocabularies are a function of experience. Consider the following two verbal items.

1. In what way are *large* and *heavy* alike?
2. In what way are *Darwin* and *Wallace* alike?

The fundaments in item 1 are easily recognized, but understanding their relationship would be somewhat difficult for a young child because the problem requires an understanding of volume and displacement. Item 2 is also difficult, but for a different reason. If the subject knows who Darwin and Wallace are, that is, if the fundaments are recognized, understanding that they are similar because of their roles in the development of the theory of evolution comes easily. While the second item does not require the utilization of much eduction, the initial recognition of the fundaments requires the eduction skills associated with reading comprehension.

The need to distinguish between fluid and crystallized ability emerged from an interest in developing culture-fair tests. Culture-fair tests emphasize fluid ability because crystallized ability is clearly related to the particular culture in which an individual is located.

Evidence for the existence of fluid and crystallized abilities is based on correlational and factor analysis studies, but there is additional evidence of their existence. It appears that the two abilities reach their peak at different ages. Crystallized intelligence can continue to develop far beyond the age when fluid intelligence begins to level off. The growth curve for fluid ability is similar to the growth curve for physical characteristics such as lung capacity and brain weight, which reach their peak in late adolescence, level off in adulthood, and finally decline in one's later years. Crystallized ability, on the other hand, while leveling off in the early twenties continues to increase, albeit slowly, throughout a person's life (Cattell, 1971). Brain injury has also been shown to have a differential effect on the two, with a tendency for fluid ability to be reduced more than crystallized ability when there has been an injury to a specific part of the brain. It has been hypothesized that crystallized ability is generalized across the brain, whereas fluid ability is located in more specific areas (Cattell, 1965).

Differential Hemispheric Functioning of the Brain Paul Broca (Restak, 1979) is credited with the discovery that brain damage to a specific site in the brain would have a different effect on verbal functioning depending on the hemisphere involved. Damage to the left brain, in what is now referred to as Broca's area, affects speech much more than similar damage on the right side. This hemispheric specialization appears to be more noticeable and permanent in males than in females. It is now generally accepted that the processing of verbal material, along with sequential thinking, takes place in the left brain, whereas simultaneous thinking (the perception of gestalts and the ability to process data simultaneously) is located on the right side.

This is a new field, and there is still much to be learned about brain functioning. The results of different studies of brain functioning are not always in agreement. There has been some effort directed toward the categorization of items in terms of which hemisphere they assess. Verbal tests such as vocabulary, synonyms, and verbal analogies are examples of tests that appear to assess left-brain functioning. Nonverbal tests requiring the apperception of geometric shapes and the recognition of human faces are examples of tests that appear to assess right-brain functioning. This distinction is made difficult because it is impossible to control for the amount of verbal mediation that may be taking place when nonverbal problems are being solved.

The effect of left-handedness cannot be explained simply in terms of a reversal of hemispheric functioning. About 56 percent of left-handed people still process verbal information in the left brain, leaving 44 percent of left-handed people processing verbal material in the right side of the brain (Restak, 1979). Those left-handed individuals who process verbal material in the left brain are distinguished by an inverted writing style, where the pen or pencil goes over and around the top of the page (Levy, 1976). Left-handed people who process verbal material in the right hemisphere of the brain, except for the fact that they use their left hand, write the same way that right-handed people write.

Evidence exists to support either the position that cognitive functioning is localized, or the position that it is more generally spread throughout the brain. We are still far from having anything approaching a complete understanding of the localization of specific cognitive skills. This is because there is no way of directly observing brain functioning. At this point, our understanding must come from accidents or brain surgery, which allow us to isolate specific parts of the brain to gain an understanding of how cognitive functioning is affected.

A second important impediment to understanding the relationship between cognitive functioning and specific parts of the brain results from the fact that most of the intelligence tests that we use were developed without much awareness of brain functioning.

There have been attempts to use the Wechsler tests and other psychological instruments as means of understanding psychoneurological functioning, but because the items tend not to be pure measures of either right- or left-hemisphere functioning this has not been particularly successful. With the introduction of the Kaufman Assessment Battery for children (1982), we now have a psychological instrument developed with this purpose in mind. It is Kaufman's contention that an understanding of brain functioning from this perspective has significance for our understanding of educational problems (Kaufman, 1983). For instance, learning-disabled (LD) children appear to function best on tasks requiring simultaneous, or right-brained, abilities and poorest on sequential, or left-brained, activities. The implications of this knowledge for remediation are somewhat difficult to establish. It is unclear whether we should focus our remediation efforts on strengthening the deficit or emphasizing the strength. Empirical studies intended to answer this question have not provided much support for either position, or in fact even supported the view that a knowledge of brain functioning is valuable for developing strategies for the remediation of educational problems (Arter & Jenkins, 1979).

Learning Disabilities Brain functioning, as it is related to intelligence and academic performance, has been of particular importance in the study of learning disabilities. Initially, children with a learning disability were believed to be suffering from some type of minimal brain damage because they exhibited symptoms similar to children with known brain damage. These were labeled neurological soft signs and included such behaviors as hyperactivity, perseveration, inability to recognize gestalts, and so on. Learning disabilities no longer focus on these characteristics. First, attempts at remediation that focused on central nervous system dysfunction tended to be unsuccessful. Second, the term *learning disability* was so much more attractive than other special education labels, particularly the label mentally retarded, that there was great pressure to increase the number of children diagnosed as having a learning disability by broadening the definition.

The emphasis in identification switched to discrepancies in performance, particularly but not exclusively discrepancies between intelligence and achievement. Identifying children in this fashion is unreliable because a considerable amount of variability in performance is normal, and the same problems that lower academic performance in an area will also depress performance on an intelligence test.

As a result, functional definitions of learning disabilities are no longer tied either to neurological dysfunctions or anything very concrete. Shepard et al. (1983) found that less than half of the children in LD classes in Colorado had characteristics that met federal and/or professional definitions of learning disabilities.

Heredity Versus Environment

Since psychologists first began to consider the construct of intelligence, the most volatile issue surrounding intelligence and its assessment has been the question of the relative influences of heredity and environment. With Binet as a notable exception, most of the early writers and researchers in the area of intelligence have had a strong belief in the genetic basis of intelligence. To them, a child's intelligence was determined almost in its entirety by the genetic contributions of the parents. This view was maintained despite the fact that little was known about the mechanics of genetics.

Accompanying this belief in the importance of heredity was the idea that intelligence was best understood as a physical entity, and that its assessment could be undertaken in the same manner as the measurement of such physical characteristics as height and weight. In addition, intelligence was also believed to be fixed. Whatever score an individual obtained as a child, he or she could be expected to maintain as an adult. This dogmatic hereditarian view, which was supported by Galton, Terman, Goddard, and many others, had consequences for sociopolitical decisions. For example, it was used as a rationale for restrictive immigration policies and to support eugenic practices. Associated with this view was a philosophical position labeled social Darwinism. It asserted that those who were successful in a society deserved to reap the reward of the society because of their superior genotype (genetic characteristics affecting behavior). Those who failed were believed to be genetically defective. The social Darwinists sought changes in public policy based on this fixed hereditarian view of intelligence. Because poverty, insanity, and criminal behavior also were believed to be genetically based, they advocated that such individuals be sterilized.

There were many strong reactions against this rigid hereditarian view. The behaviorists were particularly influential, espousing the belief that a person's entire being—character, personality, and intelligence—was strictly the result of environmental factors and, specifically, what a person had learned in his or her lifetime. They believed that all infants entered the world as a blank slate, and that whatever they became as adults could be explained in terms of some variant of learning theory.

Debate over the relative influences of heredity and environment, although it sometimes waned, has never died out. In the 1960s attention focused on the differences in performance on standardized tests among cultural and ethnic groups. There is a great deal of overlap among the different groups, but the average scores of blacks tends to be lower than those of nonminority groups. These tests are used at many decision points in our society, from placement in special education classes to admission to highly desired professional and graduate schools. In the 1960s there was increasing concern that blacks were being systematically denied such opportunities.

Unfortunately, attempts to emphasize the heritability of standardized test performance have been interpreted as an argument in support of the existence of innate differences among cultural and ethnic groups and a justification for discrimination. Concern about such issues is certainly justified by the sad history of the misuse of such information in Western society.

The nature-nurture issue has staunchly resisted any sort of resolution over the nearly one hundred years that it has been the focus of interest. It does not appear that it is any nearer to resolution today than it was fifty years ago, despite the fact that so much more is known about the nature of intelligence and genetics.

Social scientists and geneticists provide two distinct points of view on the subject.

The Social Scientists' View

Although some social scientists believe in the importance of genes as determiner of behavior, most have tended to reject the idea that genes have much of an effect on behavior at all. This rejection can be traced to a number of causes.

1. The social sciences have tended to reflect a Western humanistic view of mankind, which stresses equality among individuals and a general disapproval of hierarchal societal structures. This position, it is believed, can be undermined by an emphasis on the importance of heredity.
2. An optimistic view of the possibility for change in the human condition is much more likely to prevail if behavior is controlled only by the environment.

3. Knowledge of genetics has been misused in the past in ways that social scientists find repugnant, from the establishment of eugenics programs and social Darwinism to the views on racial purity espoused in Nazi Germany.
4. Up until recently there has been a lack of knowledge about genetics. It is ony now that biologists have begun to understand how genes actually work. Many of the present-day theories of social science were established when very little was known about genetics.

Social scientists have tended to view the usefulness of heredity as a means of explaining differences in mental ability in the general population in a manner analogous to Pascal's wager. Blaise Pascal was a seventeenth-century philosopher much interested in the development of logical proof of the existence of God. After becoming frustrated in this attempt, he finally decided on the resolution of the issue in favor of the existence of God based on the following logic: (1) given that no definitive proof exists on either side of the issue, (2) after considering all of the positive outcomes of the decision that God does exist, (3) and considering all of the advantages of the opposite conclusion, (4) it is, therefore, best to assume God's existence. Social scientists, in the absence of definitive proof concerning the effect of genes on intelligence, have decided that it is much better to believe that they have little effect.

The Geneticists' View

Geneticists believe that the relative contribution of heredity and environment is a legitimate scientific question. They tend to criticize their opponents as ideological and unscientific.

Because the geneticists are scientists, there is a tendency to assume that they are objective in their approach to these issues. However, it is reasonable to ask just how objective they are. It is somewhat difficult to imagine a geneticist coming to the conclusion that genes are not particularly important. The conclusion that genes play a minor role in human behavior would not enhance the stature of the field of genetics.

Should We Study the Effects of Heredity on Behavior?

Heritability studies involve attempts to determine the relative importance of heredity and environment. The evaluation of the validity of such studies is not easy. Their validity is based on complex mathematical formulas that focus on procedures for accounting for proportions of variance in intelligence across populations. This is a difficult area because of the myriad of factors that come into play when we consider correlations and variances.

Attacking such studies because they are evil, or because we are better off not knowing the answers, will not resolve the issue. We find ourselves caught between the sad history of the misuse of such information in the past and the dangers of Lysenkoism. Lysenko was a Russian geneticist who proposed a theory that emphasized the heritability of acquired characteristics. This is in contrast to the views of Gregor Mendel, who asserted that acquired characteristics could not be inherited. In the West, Mendel's view of genetics was accepted, whereas Lysenko's theory became dogma in the Soviet Union, where it was more compatible than Mendelian genetics with Marxism.

In the belief that wheat could develop a resistance to cold and pass this characteristic on to succeeding generations, Russian agricultural scientists spent years exposing wheat to the Russian winter, with the anticipation that a cold-resistant strain could be developed. Such a strain would greatly increase the productivity of their farms. Large amounts of money and the productive lives of scientists were spent on the venture, which had no chance of success. This is one reason why Russian agriculture has such a long history of failure. Scientists who did not embrace this view, or those who opted for the Mendelian heresy, became victims of Stalin's purges or were relegated to the gulags. There is an important lesson here. The mere fact that a given theory of genetics, or any other scientific theory, is incompatible with existing and popular perceptions of human behavior does not mean that it should be rejected.

Heritability Studies

Heritability is studied by analyzing the correlations among family members. Twins are of particular interest: identical twins because they have the same genotype, and fraternal twins because they have similar environments. Identical twins reared apart provide an opportunity to isolate the effects of environment from heredity.

There is a series of heritability formulas that can be applied to correlations among family members. The formulas yield estimates of the relative contributions of heredity and environment. Cyril Burt (1958) and Burt and M. Howard (1956) provide some of the first estimates of the heritability of intelligence. From a sample of 826 children of varying relationships, they obtained an estimate of heritability of .93. This means that 93 percent of the variance in intelligence in that population could be explained genetically. It does not mean that the intelligence levels of individuals within that population were 93 percent a function of their genetic inheritance—although this is one way these results have been interpreted, albeit erroneously. When more sophisticated formulas were applied to these data, the estimates were revised downward to about .70 (Jinks & Fulker, 1970; Jinks & Eaves, 1974).

Until his death, Burt was considered the dean of British psychologists, but since then his work has become the center of controversy. He published articles that included identical coefficients for different samples, and used parameters that were estimated in ways that tended to increase the probability of finding the results he was seeking. In addition, some articles published in Burt's journal, the *British Journal of Statistical Psychology*, apparently were written by Burt himself and given fictitious authorship. Whether these events were the insignificant errors of an aging researcher, or of such magnitude to constitute fraud, necessitating the rejection of all of his work, has been debated by other researchers in the field. Because he had always been considered so eminent, and because he was one of the most prolific researchers on this subject, such severe criticisms of his work were a blow to the field. However, other than obtaining estimates that were somewhat higher than those found by other researchers, his results are generally in agreement with later studies. Even the rejection of all of his work would not substantially change our understanding of the heritability of intelligence.

Applying the heritability formulas developed by Fulker (1973) to the series of studies reporting the correlation in intelligence among members of the same family, which were reviewed by Jarvik and Erlenmayer (1967), Loehlin et al. (1975) concluded that the total genetic contribution to intelligence in Caucasian populations is .75 and that of environment .25. These estimates can be adjusted up or down, depending on the way that certain parameters are estimated, and on the treatment of the effects of the interactions between heredity and environment. Morton (1972) obtained heritability estimates of .67, and Arthur Jensen, in 1969, obtained values of .80. After revising his computational methods, Jensen came up with an estimate of .67. Christopher Jencks (1972) obtains somewhat lower values, around .45.

Criticisms of Heritability Studies

The major problems with all such studies is that they must be done "after the fact." This is because rules and laws regulating the use of human subjects prevent extensive controls for extraneous variables. We are therefore forced to examine subjects where and when they are available. This is of course as it should be, but it leads to studies characterized by flawed data samples. There are a number of additional problems associated with such studies.

Assessment of Intelligence Because many of the studies of this subject tend to be *ex post facto* in nature, intelligence is often assessed in ways that make the validity of the intelligence scores suspect. Sometimes it is only estimated, and at other times it is assessed by tests of varying reliability and/or validity. Occasionally only parts of intelligence tests are used. There tends to be a lack of concern about the particular method of assessing intelligence in these studies; the general attitude is that one measure of intelligence is probably as good as another. However, there is no evidence that heritability estimates should be the same across different types and aspects of intelligence.

Estimation of Parameters The formulas for estimating heritability tend to be complex and require numerous variables, some of which are not readily available. When this occurs they must be estimated in some way. There is a tendency for different researchers to make these estimates using different rationales, to obtain different parameters, and therefore to report estimates that may be inconsistent with other similar studies.

Interactions Another criticism of such studies concerns the difficulties in explaining the effects of interactions. Interactions are not easy to understand, and they are often confused with correlations. For instance, parents of high socioeconomic status are likely to have relatively high intelligence levels and therefore pass on the genotype for higher intellectual performance. At the same time, they may also provide a more stimulating environment. When the effects of these two are additive—that is, the child's intellectual level is the sum of the effects of genetics and environment—this is labeled a correlation, to differentiate it from statistical interactions. Statistical interactions occur when the child in such a situation does even better than would be expected, by the added effects of both environment and heredity. It is possible to have so many other types of interactions and correlations between specific individual characteristics of environment and genetic endowment that it is impossible to quantify heritability.

It is not easy to differentiate between correlations and interactions, but correlations apparently occur much more frequently. Plomin (1980) describes three types of correlations: passive, reactive, and active. *Passive correlations* are the type already described, where the intellectual level of the parents affects the intelligence of offsprings both by providing positive genes and by providing a stimulating environment. Children who inherit genes for high intelligence are likely to be double blessed by a stimulating environment. *Reactive correlations* occur when individuals in a child's environment interact differently as a result of geneotype. For instance, teachers might pay more attention to children that they perceive to be more attractive. *Active correlations* would occur when a person's behavior is affected by his or her genotype. A child from a deprived environment who has a positive intellectual genotype might seek out similar peers or spend a great deal of time reading.

Problems in Studies of Twins In most studies of twins, it is very difficult to differentiate between monozygotic (identical) and dizygotic (fraternal) twins. The assessment of the environment and determination of the degree that environments differ are also difficult to make. If monozygotic twins are placed in similar environments, the degree of heritability may be overestimated.

How Important Are Heritability Indexes?

First of all, it seems apparent that the proportion of variance in intelligence that can be explained by the genotype is substantial. It must be remembered, however, that heritability indexes are a function of variability across a population in three areas: intelligence, genetic properties, and environment. Changes in any one can affect the size of the heritability estimate. The aspect of the relationship that is most likely to vary is the environment, so the heritability of intelligence within a population is a function of how diverse the environment is. The more variable the environment, the less heritable intelligence will appear to be. In a given population, where there is little environmental variability, a heritability study might yield a very high heritability index. Of course, an individual's IQ might still be affected greatly by environments that are different from the majority population.

In interpreting the results of a heritability study, one must also be careful to ensure that the variability of the preceding three factors in the sample is the same as that found in the population. Because such studies typically include samples that were not assigned subjects randomly, the legitimacy of generalizations to other groups is not easy to establish.

The Inseparability of Heredity and Environment An example of the close relationship between heredity and environment occurs in the case of the genetic defect called phenylketonuria. This is a condition that can result in severe mental retardation. It is caused by a single recessive gene that, when neither parent contributes a dominant gene to offset it, prevents the production of the enzyme phenylaline hydroxylase. This substance is needed to convert phenylaline, a substance common in foods, to tyrosine. Although tyrosine is not harmful, excessive amounts of phenylaline lead to the buildup of substances that are destructive to the central nervous system and ultimately result in severe mental retardation. It is now possible to screen for this condition using a simple blood test and to prevent its occurrence by means of a special phenylaline-free diet.

Phenylketonuria is often used to illustrate the relationship between heredity and environment because it is caused by a single identifiable gene and because it provides a good example of the difficulty involved in attempts to separate heredity and environment. Consider the child with this genetic defect who has normal intelligence because of the intervention of medical science and the provision of the special diet. Is this child's intelligence a function of heredity or environment? Consider the child who suffers from phenylketonuria. Is he or she mentally retarded strictly as a result of genes inherited from parents or because their environment did not provide the phenalyline-free diet?

Although it is possible to estimate the relative contributions of heredity and environment across populations, this cannot be done for individuals. It is probably most accurate to say that all of our behavior is controlled by genes, and all of our behavior is controlled by the environment.

Conclusions About Heritability Studies

Existing studies of heritability can be criticized in many ways, but regardless of the study, they all conclude that genes explain a substantial amount of the intelligence test score variance in populations. Even though each study can be criticized for a combination of reasons, the same errors are not always repeated in every study.

It is reasonable to make an appeal to parsimony when a series of studies arrives at the same conclusion, but all are flawed in one way or another. We can either accept the hypothesis that intelligence is determined to a considerable degree by genetic factors, or we can substitute a different hypothesis and rationale to explain away each of a series of consistent findings. At some point it makes sense to accept the most general hypothesis as being more likely than a whole series of alternate hypotheses. It should be emphasized that although evidence is compelling, it is not conclusive. There is the possibility that new information may be revealed that will drastically downgrade the importance of genetics in intelligence. At the present time it is reasonable to believe that heredity makes a sizable contribution to the variance found in intelligence.

Differences in Cultural and Ethnic Performance on Mental Ability Tests

There is compelling evidence to support the position that a sizable proportion of the variance in intelligence test performance in Caucasian populations can be explained as being the result of heredity. However, this tells us nothing about the reasons for the differences in performance between Caucasians and other groups. Consider two fields of corn, each planted from the same set of seeds. In one field there is an abundance of nutrients and water, and in the other there is not. The variability in the height of the corn within each field might be almost entirely a function of heredity, but any difference between the two fields is clearly the result of environmental factors.

Heritability Indexes Among Non-Caucasian Populations

There are relatively few studies of the heritability of intelligence among non-Caucasian groups. In one of the few studies, Scarr-Salapatek (1971) concluded that inheritance explained less variance in standardized test performance in a black population than in a Caucasian population.

Studies of Blood Grouping

Because the blood-grouping structure of various ethnic groups differs, it is possible to correlate the degree of similarities in blood grouping with intelligence test scores. A high correlation between the similarities in blood groupings and the degree of intelligence would argue for a substantial genetic cause for the differences.

Loehlin et al. (1973), in a study of blacks, found no association between the prevalence of blood groupings inherited from Europeans and level of intelligence. Studies of racial mixture and level of intelligence have also failed to show more than a slight relationship with intelligence. These findings could be supportive of either an environmental or hereditarian view (Loehlin et al., 1975). These authors also report data that suggest that for blacks at the upper extremes of intelligence, 140 and above, there is a tendency to find less of an admixture of European ancestors. This is the opposite of what would be expected if differences in intelligence test performance were largely genetic.

Studies of Separate Abilities

Studies of differences in separate abilities across ethnic groups (Lesser, Feter, & Clark, 1961) do reveal some patterns. Jewish groups tend to do somewhat better on verbal tasks, as do black groups, whereas Oriental groups tend to do somewhat better on spatial and mathematical tasks. Although such differences have been used to support a genetic basis for overall differences, an environmental explanation is equally credible.

Conclusions

There are sizable mean differences in intellectual functioning among different ethnic groups. But when, within a group, variance is considered, between-group differences do not loom as large. Sex differences, which will be discussed in more detail in a following section, can also explain a considerable amount of variance.

Test bias is another factor that has been used as an explanation of differences among various ethnic and cultural groups. Depending on how it is viewed, it can play a large or small role in this phenomenon. (Test bias is discussed in this chapter and in even more detail in Chapter 8.)

The large amount of variance in intelligence that can be explained by heritability in Caucasian populations has made it tempting to conclude that the differences among cultural and ethnic groups might be explained by genetic factors. Such a conclusion is premature in the absence of evidence demonstrating a connection between the existence of such correlational characteristics in one population (in this case Caucasian) and the cause of differences between populations.

Sex Differences in Intelligence Test Performance

Discussions of the relative contribution of heredity and environment to intelligence test performance tend to stir emotions, mainly because of concern for the implications this might have for ethnic and cultural differences. Sex differences in intelligence test performance have been emphasized much less.

In the past, it has generally been assumed that there is no important difference between the sexes in intelligence. When differences occur, they are usually explained in terms of measurement error. In the construction of intelligence tests, items that discriminate between the sexes are usually either eliminated or balanced by other items that favor the opposite sex. The result is the creation of intelligence tests that yield equal test scores for males and females.

Studies of Sex Differences

The classic book on the subject of sex differences is *The Psychology of Sex Differences* by Eleanor Maccoby and Carol Jacklin (1974). The authors reviewed over two thousand articles and books, making a special effort to evaluate the methodological soundness of the research. In 1977 another book on this topic, written by Carol Tavris and Carole Offir, *The Longest War: Sex Differences in Perspective*, was published. This book builds on the work of Maccoby and Jacklin. Both books, coupled with enormous amounts of research done in this area, have resulted in a remarkable agreement among experts concerning the direction of sex differences in ability. There is not, however, any agreement concerning the cause of the differences. Females are superior to males in verbal ability from ten or eleven years on, and males are superior in quantitative skills and visual spatial ability from the onset of adolescence. Some explanations of these differences emphasize culture as the most important factor (Witterman, 1979), but the general consensus of those who have studied the issues most carefully is that these differences represent a real phenomenon (Tavris & Offir, 1977). Spatial ability has been the focus of greatest interest, both because this is the ability that shows the greatest differentiation between the sexes, and because differences in quantitative ability might be the result of spatial ability.

Spatial Ability as a Recessive Gene One early attempt to explain the cause of the differences as being other than an acquired characteristic, associated spatial ability with a single recessive gene carried in the *X* chromosome. Because males have only one *X* chromosome, the gene for good spatial ability could not be canceled by a dominant gene the way it could be for females, who have two *X* chromosomes. If the dominant and recessive genes exist in equal numbers, it would be expected that about half of all males would have good spatial ability while only about a fourth of all females would. In addition, males could be expected to more closely resemble their mothers, from whom they receive their *X* chromosome, whereas females would resemble their fathers more (only if the father contributed the recessive gene, which the father would manifest himself, would the daughter have the characteristic). The proportion of high spatially skilled males and females to be expected by this scenario has been manifested in a number of studies (Tavris & Offir, 1977). More recent studies have reported frequencies of good spatial abilities in males and females less supportive of this view. With the increased interest in the effects of brain laterality, this single-gene theory has found less support.

Brain Laterality The importance of the laterality of the brain has been known since the work of Broca and Wernicke in the nineteenth century. The nervous system is constructed in such a way that the left side of the body is connected to the right side of the brain and the right side of the body is connected to the left side of the brain. Verbal behavior and sequential processing of information are centered in the left brain, whereas simultaneous processing, and the perception of gestalts, take place primarily in the right brain. The halves are connected by the corpus callosum, which prevents us from becoming aware of the differentiation.

The simplest explanation for the differences in ability found between the sexes would be that females are dominant in their left brain and males are dominant in their right brain. However, this does not appear to be the case. Instead, it is generally agreed that males are more lateralized than females. This means that the performance by males on specific tasks is likely to be controlled by only one of the hemispheres, whereas females tend to use both. Apparently, restricting spatial tasks to the right brain is more efficient, but it is better to process verbal material across both hemispheres, as is done by females.

Up to this point, this discussion of laterality has been tentative, and it is clearly an oversimplification. The more that is learned about brain functioning, and in particular about the lateralization of the brain, the less clear the picture has become. Bryden (1982), in a review of the many studies of sex differences in the lateralization of the brain, points out that the studies are about equally divided between those that show greater lateralization for males and those that show no difference. He found only a few studies that showed a greater lateralization for females. However, whether or not a study finds greater lateralization for males is partially a function of the nature of the task used to assess laterality. Greater laterality in males is most likely to occur in studies that use nonmeaningful verbal material presented auditorily. Tasks requiring visual perception are less likely to show laterality for males. Nonverbal material (such as a melody) presented auditorily even tends to show greater laterality for females.

Researchers in this field now generally agree that ability differences between the sexes can best be explained in terms of differential brain structure. Earlier theories suggesting that it was the result of the slower development of males that led to greater lateralization have been rejected. Instead, the differences are attributed to physical differences in the brain that result from the effects of sex hormones at an early age.

Bias in Intelligence Testing

The validity of intelligence tests for assessing minorities is a major concern. We know that, as a group, blacks do less well on standardized mental ability tests than whites. Of course there is considerable overlap in scores across these two populations, with many blacks surpassing the mean for whites. On the average, across many tests, the difference is of a magnitude of about one standard deviation. These differences are of particular concern on general intelligence tests because there is a tendency for their authors to explain performance on the tests in terms of functional intelligence. This is done despite the fact that there is little evidence to show that intelligence tests are actually measuring functional intelligence.

The only construct for which intelligence test scores have been shown to be valid is academic aptitude. Of course validity is not absolute, and all that we can legitimately say is that intelligence tests are to some degree valid predictors of academic performance. Whether the amount of validity characterizing the tests is sufficient is a subjective decision to be made by those evaluating the test. The fact that blacks have lower scores on such tests does not establish that such tests are statistically biased against blacks. To prove this, it would be necessary to demonstrate that the predictive validity of the test is different for blacks than for whites. This would mean that the actual academic performance of the individuals tested could not be predicted in the same way across different ethnic groups, and that blacks consistently perform better academically than could be expected based on the prediction of the aptitude test. Existing studies fail to show differences in predictive validity—in fact, if anything, academic aptitude tests can be shown to be somewhat biased in favor of blacks. This means that there is a slight tendency for blacks not to perform as well on the criterion measure as might be anticipated by the predictor. This is most likely a statistical artifact resulting from a regression to the mean. Cronbach et al. (1972) provide a methodology for correcting for this sort of error.

Factor Analysis

The factor structure of ability tests for minority and nonminority groups has also been compared, and most evidence fails to show any difference among cultural and ethnic groups. For instance, Daniel Reschly (1978), in a study of the WISC-R, compared blacks, Chicanos, and native Americans and found no differences in factor structure across the groups. Therefore it is reasonable to conclude that the tests measure the same constructs when used with different ethnic groups.

Item Analysis

Inspecting a test, item by item, to detect bias has also been tried. Although there are many experts and lay persons who believe that they can determine if an item is biased by examining it, this is actually quite difficult. A more legitimate method of determining whether items are biased is by rank-ordering items in terms of difficulty, separately for each cultural ethnic group. Even though the group means may differ, we would expect the rank order of item difficulties to be the same. When the rank order is not the same because items are either easier or harder for one group than the other, conclusions about whether such items are biased rests on firmer ground. However, differences in relative item difficulty across different groups does not in itself prove bias. We would only be safe in assuming that an item was biased if we could assume that the two groups were similar with respect to the underlying ability being measured. The results of studies that have done this have generally shown that items that appear to be biased are not, and some items that look to be completely fair are in fact biased (Jensen, 1980). More sophisticated methods for accomplishing this sort of bias analysis are described in Chapter 8, page 166, in the section on latent traits.

Aptitude and Achievement

The focus of our concern should be on the lower performance of minority groups on achievement tests and general school performance, rather than on the aptitude tests that predict that performance. If the academic aptitude tests (intelligence tests) did not predict these differences, they would not be valid.

Although there is a substantial relationship between academic performance, as measured by grades, and scores on achievement tests, we must be careful not to assume that poor academic performance is caused by low intelligence. Poor achievement in school is also likely to cause poor performance on intelligence tests.

The connection between low socioeconomic status and poor performance in school is well established, and blacks are more likely to come from a low socioeconomic background than are nonminorities. There are many other factors, some of which are related to socioeconomic class and others that involve the cultural significance of being a minority that have been suggested as causes of poor performance in school. Among these are poor nutrition, discrimination, broken homes, overcrowding, poor school facilities, and lack of rewards for those who do succeed academically. For whatever reason, the fact that substantial segments of our society are not succeeding in school as well as they should, in order to increase the probability of success in society upon graduation, should be the major focus of concern.

The academic aptitude tests that anticipate that a child will encounter or is encountering problems in school must be judged according to criteria that go beyond concern about the inconvenience that such revelations may cause. The potential for misuse certainly exists in terms of labeling, self-fulfilling prophecies, and the damage to self-esteem. However, the question of their continued use should be answered by a determination of whether they have advantages that compensate for their disadvantages and whether the alternatives to their use would be more fair.

Culture-Fair Tests

One early attempt to deal with the problem of cultural bias was the development of the so called culture-fair test. The goal was to develop an intelligence test that was equally fair for all cultural groups. Although of major interest at one time, such attempts have generally been abandoned. The reason for the loss of interest is the fact that the idea of a culture-fair test is illogical, and the attempts to develop such tests were not successful. As has already been emphasized, the major aspect of an intelligence test that is useful and valid is the part that deals with academic aptitude, which is clearly related to culture. The fact that differences in ethnic background, culture, language, family structure, and socioeconomic level can result in lowered scores, on what is essentially a test of academic aptitude, is not evidence of a flaw in the instrument if these are factors that cause academic performance to be depressed. An instrument that was independent of these factors would be a poor predictor of academic performance.

Most so-called culture-fair intelligence tests have focused on nonverbal skills because these are believed to be more independent of culture. They are not only less adequate predictors of academic performance, but blacks tend to do somewhat better on verbal than nonverbal tests. This makes the selection of nonverbal tasks for inclusion on a culture-fair intelligence test intended for use with black students unfair.

SUMMARY

1. Under the heading of mental ability tests, it is reasonable to include intelligence tests, academic aptitude tests, and many other specific aptitude tests.
2. The term *intelligence* was not widely used until this century; since its introduction it has been extremely controversial.
3. Much of the controversy surrounding intelligence stems from disagreements concerning how it should be defined.
4. One useful approach to defining intelligence is to think of it in terms of two aspects: academic aptitude and functional intelligence.
5. We have no direct methods of assessing functional intelligence; as a result, standardized tests—both individual and group—measure mainly academic aptitude.

6. There are a number of fundamental issues surrounding the study of intelligence. Included are such issues as whether it is unitary or multifaceted, distinctions between fluid and crystallized intelligence, and differences in hemispherical functioning of the brain.
7. Perhaps the most important single controversy in the realm of intelligence assessment concerns the relative contributions of heredity and environment.
8. Although there is considerable evidence concerning the relative contribution of heredity to variance in intelligence across populations (geneticists would generally accept a proportion between 50 to 70 percent), the effect of these factors on the intelligence of an individual is unclear.
9. Although there are sizable differences in intelligence test performance among ethnic groups, there is a lack of clear evidence concerning the cause of these differences.
10. There are also sex differences in intelligence, with females having some advantage in verbal ability, while males do better on spatial ability and quantitative tasks.
11. Test bias can be categorized as either vernacular or statistical. Test specialists have generally concluded that although intelligence tests may appear biased (vernacular bias), they are not biased from a technical-statistical point of view.

SUGGESTED READINGS

BRYDEN, M. P. (1982). *Laterality: Functional asymmetry in the intact brain*. New York: Academic. [This is a technical, but complete and up-to-date, treatment of the significance of brain laterality to mental ability.]

GUILFORD, J. P. (1967). *The nature of human intelligence*. New York: McGraw-Hill. [The bulk of this book is devoted to Guilford's multifaceted theory of intelligence; the first three chapters, which cover the historical background of intelligence testing, the ways intelligence is studied, and a description of theories of intelligence, are excellent.]

JENSEN, A. R. (1979). *Bias in mental testing*. New York: Wiley. [This book represents the culmination of Jensen's study of individual differences in mental ability. It is scholarly and contains excellent descriptions of the different types of instruments used to assess mental ability. Technical methods of assessing bias are also included. Ninety percent of the material is of a very high scholarly level. Those who take exception to Jensen's theses may find themselves disagreeing with Jensen about the other 10 percent.]

LOEHLIN, J. C., LINDZEY, G., & SPUHLER, J. N. (1975). *Race differences in intelligence*. San Francisco: Freeman. [This is generally considered the authoritative source of information on the topic; most references to this subject use this book as their major source. Interestingly, it is quoted by those on both sides of the controversy.]

MACCOBY, E. E., & JACKLIN, C. N. (1974). *The psychology of sex differences*. Stanford CA: Stanford U.P. [Although it is somewhat dated now, this is still considered an important source of information about sex differences, including differences in mental ability.]

14

Individual Intelligence Tests

OVERVIEW

The first successful mental ability tests were individually administered, an assessment technique that continues to be used on a widespread basis. There are three groups of commonly administered individual intelligence tests, (1) the Stanford-Binet, (2) the series of tests developed by David Wechsler, and (3) the new individual intelligence test created by Alan and Nadeen Kaufman.

In this chapter the major individual intelligence tests are described, along with the setting in which they are likely to be employed. Accompanying this is a limited discussion of test interpretation. Adult intelligence tests typically are used either as one aspect of a clinical diagnosis or for vocational counseling; the scales for children are generally administered in connection with educational diagnosis, usually with the purpose of making decisions concerning special education placement. Because this is a procedure that has been severely criticized, the advantages, disadvantages, and controversies surrounding the practice are discussed.

OBJECTIVES

In this chapter you will become familiar with the major individual intelligence tests; their history, structure, and social significance. Specifically, you will learn the following:

- The historical development of individual intelligence tests.
- The structure of the three major groups of individual intelligence tests, including the Stanford-Binet, the Wechsler tests, and the Kaufman Assessment Battery for Children.
- The interpretation of these three tests.
- The reasons for the introduction of the SOMPA and why its use is not recommended.
- The appropriate uses for individual intelligence tests in special education placement.

Introduction

The first intelligence tests were administered individually. They consist of open-ended questions and performance tasks that involve the judgement and skill of the examiner. These tests must be administered on a one-to-one basis; several hours are required for administration, plus additional time for scoring and report writing. Because of the time required and because most states restrict the use of these tests to licensed psychologists and others legally permitted to function in this role through certification, they are expensive. They do have important advantages, however. Because all the questions are presented orally, these tests can be administered to young children not as yet socialized to testing. The process of administering the test enables the examiner to observe such behaviors as attention and effort. Through an interpretation of patterns of correct and incorrect answers and an examination of the actual responses, it is possible to obtain both clinical insight and an understanding of an individual's cognitive functioning. As a result, the examiner learns a great deal more about an individual than just test scores.

This can be contrasted with group tests, which are objectively scored, can be administered in large numbers, and do not require the extensive examiner training associated with individual intelligence tests. The information obtained from such tests is restricted to the scores themselves. They do provide reliable and valid estimates of intelligence, as long as the examinee is socialized to function in the testing situation and is capable of any reading that may be required. When these conditions are not met, the result may be a score that severely underestimates intelligence. Under these circumstances administering an individual intelligence test seems more appropriate.

From 1916 until 1939 there was only one major individual intelligence test, the Stanford-Binet. In 1939, the Wechsler-Bellevue intelligence test for adults was published; David Wechsler followed this test with a series of individual intelligence tests for other populations. In 1983 a third individual intelligence test was published, the Kaufman Assessment Battery for Children (K-ABC).

The Stanford-Binet Tests

Alfred Binet The individual most responsible for the way we measure mental abilities today is Alfred Binet. Born into a wealthy upper-class French family, his early inclination was to become a doctor like his father, but as the result of an unfortunate encounter with a cadaver being studied by his father, he chose instead the career of law (Matarazzo, 1976). In 1878, at the age of twenty-one, he earned his law degree. He never actually studied law, having instead switched to the study of psychology. His first interest was hypnotism, particularly the effect of magnets on the entranced subject. He was convinced that magnets could affect thought and cause illusions. He was so unsophisticated at this point that he did not understand that discussing the proposed experiments in front of the subject strayed far from accepted laboratory practice. Other investigators severely criticized his research methods, causing Binet no small amount of embarassment and humiliation

(Matarazzo, 1976). He then turned to child psychology, earned his doctorate, and like Piaget began studying child development by observing his own two daughters. He also began to compare the performance of children and adults on psychophysical indices such as reaction time, tapping, speed, and eye-hand coordination. When he found few meaningful differences, he began to wonder if there were other higher-level measurements that would show a difference.

As a project for the Society for the Psychological Study of Children, in which Binet was very active, and later at the request of a special commission set up by the Ministry of Public Education, Binet began to develop methods for discriminating between normal and mentally retarded children. This was intended to provide improved methods for screening children for possible placement in special education classes. It was already being done by means of medical and school achievement tests. Binet, along with the rest of the commission, believed that this practice should continue. But they also were interested in the kind of psychological tests that could measure higher-level cognitive process, believing that such instruments would increase the accuracy of these decisions. To this end, together with Theodore Simon, he developed the 1905 scale, which is considered the first real intelligence test. It consisted of thirty tests and was standardized on fifty normal and twenty-six institutionalized retarded children. It contained items such as the following:

1. A determination of whether the subject could recognize the difference between a square of chocolate and a square of wood.
2. Repeating three spoken digits.
3. Comparing two weights.
4. Telling how two common objects are different.
5. Defining abstract terms.

This 1905 scale was a preliminary experimental tool that provided only an approximation of the subject's mental functioning. Because the items were in order of increasing difficulty, a determination of how many items were completed provided an estimate of an individual's level of intellectual functioning.

With the 1908 revision, the number of items was increased from thirty to fifty-eight. They were grouped at age levels, which permitted the computation of mental ages. This gave the test the capability of estimating the intellectual functioning of all children, rather than just differentiating between normal and subnormal children.

His 1911 revision provided general improvements in the scale through more careful selection of items and a larger norm sample. The mental-age method of reporting scores was maintained because Binet believed that any finer gradations were unwarranted. He probably would have been dismayed by Terman's later adoption of the IQ.

With the introduction of these tests, Binet made major contributions to the nascent field of measurement. Although he was not necessarily the first to use all of the innovations that his test featured, he was the first to pull all of the parts together into a single instrument. First of all, and perhaps of greatest importance, Binet emphasized higher-level cognitive processing, instead of the sensory and anthropmetric measures that were so popular at the time. Second, he viewed a child's performance as a composite of a group of tests. Up until this point, test developers tended to examine the results of each item or test separately. With a composite score Binet was able to greatly simplify the decision-making procedures that were the ultimate purpose of the instrument and move in the direction of viewing intelligence as a unified construct. In addition, he pioneered the use of criterion groups to establish the validity of his items.

Binet's attitudes toward testing were also enlightened. He emphasized the scientific aspects of mental assessment, along with the importance of rapport. He urged the examiner not to be influenced by the information that he might already have about the subject. He also rejected the monarchic, single-score theory of intelligence in favor of the idea that intelligence is made up of many aspects. Paradoxically, his tests provided only a single mental-age score. Binet may be the single most important figure in the development of psychological and educational tests, and it is unfortunate that he died before he could see all of his ideas come to fruition.

Lewis Terman and the 1918 Stanford-Binet Terman obtained his masters degree from Indiana University, where his thesis was written on the subject of leadership, with emphasis on the traits that led to the adoption of that role. He was awarded a Ph.D. by Clark University in 1906. At the time Clark University enrolled only graduate students and was the nation's most important center for training psychologists. Terman was particularly interested in studying under G. Stanley Hall, one of the founders of American psychology.

Hall had obtained the nation's first Ph.D in psychology and is considered the founder of the child psychology movement in this country. He also started several of what were to become important psychological journals and was instrumental in the establishment of the American Psychological Association (APA), of which he was the president twice, an honor shared only with William James.

Terman's dissertation was titled, "Genius and Stupidity: A Study of Some of the Intellectual Processes of Seven 'Bright' and Seven 'Stupid' Boys." The seven boys at either extreme of the distribution were selected from a pool of five hundred by principals and teachers who knew the students. This process resulted in strongly contrasted groups. He compared these groups using a series of tests similar to those used by Binet. Included were such topics as mathematics, language mastery, interpretation of fables, memory, and motor ability. The bright boys were superior on mental tests, but there was less difference in inventiveness. On personality variables the subjects were highly individual (Seagoe, 1975).

After graduating from Clark University, Terman moved to California, where he began work as the principal of the San Bernardino high school. After a year he was appointed to the faculty of the Los Angeles Normal School. In 1910 he was appointed to the faculty of Stanford University, where he remained for the rest of his career.

Between his graduation from Clark University and his appointment at Stanford, Terman devoted his energy to interests other than mental testing. However, as a result of the publication of Binet's tests and the urging of his colleagues, Terman renewed his interest in mental testing. A number of psychometrists had translated the 1908 Binet scale into English, including Goddard, Huey, Whipple, Wallin, and Kuhlman, but none as systematically as Terman.

Although Terman greatly admired Binet and viewed his instrument as a major breakthrough, there were many weaknesses in the scale that he wanted to correct. He felt that chance factors played too great a part in the scoring, and that there were other related procedural problems. He also objected to the arbitrary cutoff scores for feeblemindedness and suggested an improved method of establishing the age levels of a test (Seagoe, 1975).

Like Binet, Terman believed that intelligence was a complex process, and that an intelligence test should emphasize abstract thinking. Unlike Binet, he believed intelligence was a unitary trait.

To the items from the tests developed by Binet, Terman added some that he borrowed from his dissertation and others where appropriate. His final instrument had six tests at each age level, with each test made up of one or more items. He used a sample of one thousand children and four hundred adults for the standardization of the test. The testing procedures involved the establishment of a basal age, with additional months added for each test passed. He then adopted the method of computing IQ scores first introduced by William Stern (1912), which was based on the ratio between mental age and chronological age. Later the IQ became the symbol for intelligence and the focus of attacks on the mental testing movement.

The test was titled the *Stanford Revision of the Binet* and later the *Stanford-Binet Intelligence scale*. Terman used this title rather than one that included his own name because he wanted to give full credit to those Stanford graduate students who had put in so much time on the development of the instrument. He also felt that he owed a debt to the pioneering work of Alfred Binet (Seagoe, 1975).

Terman believed that the 1916 Stanford-Binet was far from perfect, and that it would only be the first in a series of similar tests created by other psychologists, with each refinement an improvement. He was surprised when his test quickly gained widespread approval. It soon became the most widely used and generally accepted instrument of its kind, as well as the standard against which all subsequent tests of intelligence would be compared.

In 1937 the scale was revised, and two separate forms were developed (L and M). A norming sample of 3,184 was used for this version. In 1960 the scale was again revised, by combining the best items from forms L and M.

The criteria used to determine which items were to be included from the two scales involved both a consideration of item difficulty at different ages and the magnitude of the correlation coefficient computed between individual items and the total score. Emphasis on item correlations leads to a test with high internal consistency but restricts the interpretation of the test in terms of separate item types. The 1960 revision also included a reassignment of items to different age levels, based on the performance of the subjects on the 1937 scale.

Prior to the 1960 scale, IQ scores for the Stanford-Binet were computed by using the ratio between mental age and chronological age:

$$IQ = \frac{MA}{CA} \times 100$$

Such an approach is based on the assumption that intelligence increases at a constant rate. This assumption, somewhat questionable during a child's younger years, begins to make no sense at all as a child approaches adolescence. Modifications of the test must be made with great care because new items must have the same difficulty as those they replace. Any change in the difficulty of test items will affect variability, and without the use of standard scores, equal variability across the different age ranges on the test must be maintained by manipulating item difficulty. Instead of having the selection of better items and the improvement of the assessment of intelligence as the focus of test development, the test author must be concerned with obtaining uniform variability across all ages.

Many of these problems are eliminated with the introduction of deviation IQ scores. An individual's score is compared only to other individuals of the same age, and the variability of the test is maintained across all ages, regardless of item difficulties.

The use of standard scores to compute IQs was a major improvement in the 1960 scale. However, the standardization process and the method of computing the deviation IQs in the 1960 scale have been criticized because they were not based on the performance of subjects on the 1960 scale but had instead been extrapolated from the performance of subjects on the 1937 scale. In 1972 the test was restandardized, using improved procedures and the norms were derived from subjects who took the revised form.

The Stanford-Binet is based on a division of the life span into time periods, most of which are measured by six tasks. From year two to five, the periods are six months. From five to fifteen, the increments are yearly. Adults are divided into average adult and superior adult I, II, III. A basal age (the point where the subject gets all items correct) and a ceiling (the point where the subject misses all items) are established. An estimation of mental age is obtained by adding all tasks mastered, or assumed mastered. The construction of the test is such that different types of items are used at different ages. This means that qualitatively different types of intelligence can be measured depending on age. For instance, the early items administered prior to seven years are mostly nonverbal performance items, whereas the part of the test administered to adults includes mostly verbal items. Such discrepancies did not bother Terman because he had a strong belief that intelligence was unitary. He believed that all of those items, regardless of type, measured the same construct of intelligence.

Interpreting the Stanford-Binet

The Stanford-Binet yields a single score that is naturally the starting point for any interpretation of the test. The score provides information on the overall intellectual functioning of the subject being tested. A second focus can be on scatter or on the degree the subject's scores spread across age levels. The farther apart the basal and ceiling, the greater the scatter. A third focus of interpretation is on the degree to which the test is believed to reflect the intellectual functioning of the subject.

There seems to be a strong need on the part of the users of these tests to be able to categorize the items of the tests into subscales, to ease the chore of interpretation. Because Terman believed in the unitary nature of intelligence and because items from the two forms of the 1937 test were selected on the basis of their correlation with the total score, the Stanford-Binet seems impervious to factor analysis and to any empirical basis for categorizing items. There are many ways of conducting a factor analysis, but regardless of the methods employed, the Stanford-Binet yields only one important factor.

Some writers have attempted to delineate functional groupings (Lutey, 1977; Sattler, 1974; Valett, 1965), which are based on a given writer's opinions concerning what he or she believes to be the best classification. Not surprisingly, the three classification systems are not in agreement concerning the category in which each item should be placed. Three factors tend to make such a process difficult: (1) the Binet manual provides little documentation concerning what the test developers believe an item is measuring; (2) some items measure more than one ability, making it difficult to ascertain the single category in which they should be placed; and (3) the titles of the test are sometimes misleading because they might suggest one classification when the nature of the test implies a different classification.

The Wechsler Tests

As chief psychologist at Bellevue Psychiatric Hospital, working mainly with adults, David Wechsler found that the Stanford-Binet was not nearly as useful with this population as it was with children. Many of the items on the test were too childlike to be appropriately used with adults, and this sometimes interfered with rapport. In addition, the number of items actually involved in the computation of intelligence was smaller than desirable for adults. For brighter adults it was not always possible to reach a ceiling. He wanted to develop a test that not only could be used appropriately with adults, but also would have other features that he felt were desirable and that would be improvements over the Stanford-Binet. The test he developed, the Wechsler-Bellevue, provides not only an overall IQ score, which he called the Full-Scale Score, but Verbal and Performance scores and series of other subscale scores. On the Verbal Scale the reponses are made orally, whereas on the Performance section of the test the subject responds nonverbally, by gestures or motor responses, to tasks.

Global Intelligence

The selection of such a structure reflects Wechsler's position concerning the issue of whether intelligence is a unitary or multifaceted trait. The creation of a test that yields subscales might argue for a multifaceted view of intelligence, but instead of selecting subscales with small intercorrelations, he chose subscales on the basis of their correlation with the total score. If one genuinely believes that intelligence is made up of separate factors, he or she would create a test on which subscales would each measure something unique and the subscale scores would not intercorrelate.

Wechsler believed that intelligence was global. This is a position that occupies the middle ground between those who view intelligence as a single trait and those who believe it is multifaceted. According to Wechsler, intelligence is made up of separate aspects that, grouped together, measure the same global intelligence. According to this theory it makes sense that the subscales should intercorrelate. Providing subscales also made the test more attractive to psychologists because the inclusion of many subscales made it easier for them to write reports. This is the main reason why the Wechsler tests have become the predominant individual intelligence test used today.

Deviation IQs

Another major advantage of the Wechsler-Bellevue test, over the then existing version of the Stanford-Binet, was the use of deviation scores instead of mental-age ratios to compute IQs. The use of deviation scores gave the Wechsler tests an early advantage over the Stanford-Binet, which did not use this method of computing IQ scores until 1960.

Tests Developed by Wechsler

In 1955 the Wechsler-Bellevue was divided into two separate tests: the Wechsler Intelligence Scale for Children (WISC) and the Wechsler Adult Intelligence Scale (WAIS). In the development of the WISC, Wechsler was guilty of the same error that he had earlier criticized Binet and Terman for making. Just as the Stanford-Binet contained items too childlike for adults, he now included many items on the WISC that were too adult. In the early 1970s another test was introduced, the Wechsler Pre-School and Primary Scale of Intelligence (WPPSI) for children from four to six and a half years of age. In 1974 the WISC was revised, and the new test was titled the Wechsler Intelligence Scale for Children-Revised (WISC-R). The WISC-R featured a much improved norming sample, out-of-date items were modified, and those items that were too adult were eliminated, along with any that were shown not to contribute to subscale reliability. In 1981 the WAIS was revised; the new test is called the Wechsler Adult Intelligence Scale-Revised (WAIS-R).

Subscales on the WISC-R

There are five subscales and one alternate to be used when a subscale is spoiled, for both the Verbal and Performance sections of the WISC-R. The subscales on the tests are standardized to have a mean scaled score of 10 and a standard deviation of 3. The total of all subscale scores is computed, and by means of tables, the examiner obtains the Verbal, Performance, and Full-Scale scores. The subscales on the WISC-R follow:

Verbal Scale

1. Information—The child is asked questions about his or her environment. The content includes what is learned in school as well as at home. Example: When is Memorial Day? What is a carburetor?
2. Similarities—Here the child is asked to tell how two things are alike. The intention is to determine how well the child sees relationships and understands abstractions. Example: How are a needle and a thimble alike?
3. Arithmetic—The child is asked to solve computation problems presented orally in the form of a sentence. Not only is the child's ability to perform mental computations assessed, but he or she must be able to remember the numbers long enough to perform the computations and use simple logic. Example: If a store charges 25 cents for three pencils, how much would nine pencils cost?
4. Vocabulary—The child is asked to define a series of worlds. Example: What does *hesitate* mean?
5. Comprehension—The child is asked what he or she would do in a given situation, or why something happens. This task requires the child to have a real-world understanding of the environment. Example: Why is it wrong to set off a fire alarm when there is no fire?
6. Digit Span (alternate)—The child is asked to repeat a series of digits. Each trial includes an additional digit. After one set of trials, which includes repeating digits in the same order that they were presented, the child is asked to respond to another series of digits by repeating them in the reverse order of their presentation. This task measures short-term auditory memory and also has been used as a measure of anxiety.

Performance Subscales

1. Picture Completion—The child is shown a series of pictures, each with some part missing, and is asked to point to the missing part. For instance, the child might be shown a dog with a missing leg. The child must correctly recognize the leg as the missing part. Although the child is allowed to respond verbally, it is not required.
2. Picture Arrangement—The child is asked to place a series of pictures in order so that they tell a story. The child must first figure out what is going on in the story and then use logic to determine the correct sequence.
3. Block Design—The child is required to manipulate blocks, which have sides that are all red, all white, or half red and white, in such a way that they reproduce designs presented on cards.
4. Object Assembly—The child is given pieces of cardboard which, when properly aligned, form an object. The task is similar to constructing a jigsaw puzzle.
5. Coding—The child is given a code in which various geometric shapes are linked to numbers. The child must then fill in the appropriate shapes below a set of numbers. The score on this task is determined by how many correct shape-number matches are completed in two minutes.
6. Mazes (alternate)—The child is given a series of mazes and must find the way from the center to the outside without crossing a solid line or going up blind alleys.

Substituting Mazes for Coding

Alan Kaufman (1979) recommends that Mazes be substituted for Coding in the computation of IQs, and Wechsler (1974) permits this substitution. The recommendation was made because the Mazes task fits better with the other Performance tasks. Coding was selected to be used to compute IQs instead of Mazes because it is easier to administer and score, and because females do better than males on Coding. Its inclusion balances other tasks on which males do better.

Comparing the WISC-R and WAIS-R

On the WAIS-R the Verbal score is computed using six subscales because Digit Span is included in the computation of the verbal score and is not used as an alternate. Mazes are not included on the WAIS-R, so there is no alternate subscale available for the Performance scales either. In addition, the name of *Coding* is changed to *Digit Symbol* on the WAIS-R. Otherwise the items on the WAIS-R are similar to those used on the WISC-R, except for their level of difficulty.

Comparing the WISC-R and WPPSI

On the WPPSI the Verbal section differs from the WISC-R only by having Sentences replace Digit Span as an alternate. Sentences requires the recall of a series of words in the form of a sentence rather than a series of numbers. On the Performance section of the WPPSI, Picture Completion, Block Design, and Mazes are retained, but Picture Arrangement, Object Assembly, and Coding have been replaced by Animal House and Geometric Design. There is no alternate subscale provided. Animal House requires the child to associate colored pegs with animals in a Coding type of task, whereas Geometric Design requires the construction of Geometric Shapes from printed models, using pencil and paper.

Interpreting the Wechsler Tests

Unlike the Stanford-Binet, the Wechsler tests provide different types of scores. Although the difficulties in interpreting the Stanford-Binet seems to surround a dearth of scores, the overinterpretation of scores seems to be a major problem with the Wechsler tests. Attempts to provide empirical analyses of the WISC and WAIS through factor analyses have not been particularly successful because each new analyses seemed to yield different results. The factors isolated seemed to be more a function of the type of factor analysis selected and the rotation used than any underlying structure. The factor-analytic studies of the WISC-R have been much more successful. Kaufman's book, *Intelligent Testing with the WISC-R* (1979), which includes his interpretation of existing factor-analytic research on the WISC-R, provides very useful information on the interpretation of this instrument. He found that there were three factors on the test that were maintained across ten different factor-analytic studies characterized by differences in age, sex, race, IQ, and socioeconomic levels. The two major factors are verbal ability (Verbal Scale) and perceptual organization (Performance Scale). The third factor is usually referred to as freedom from distractability, although this may not be the best possible title.

Because the two main factors are congruent with the Verbal and Performance scales, an important step in interpretation is a comparison of scores on these two scales. A distinction must be made between diagnostic and educational importance. Although it takes large differences to justify the conclusion that the occurrence is so rare as to take on diagnostic importance, smaller differences may have important educational meaning. For instance, we might learn that a child performs better when not required to respond verbally. This information could be used to adapt the child's education program, but we should not conclude that the child has a specific disability in the area of verbal learning.

The third factor is more elusive. Kaufman calls it freedom from distractability, but it has also been associated with test anxiety, state anxiety, poor sequencing ability, a lack of skill in handling symbolic content, and numbers. The three subscales that make up this third factor are Arithmetic, Digit Span, and Coding. Before attaching meaning to this factor, it is necessary that all three subscales be consistently above or below the individual's mean for the section in which the subscale belongs, and that one of the three deviate by at least three scaled score units.

Since the introduction of the Wechsler tests, there has been interest in interpreting differences among subscale scores. This procedure must be approached with care because the existence of measurement error in the scores can result in small differences that are not statistically significant. The differences must be sufficiently large to be meaningful. The problem is in ascertaining how large these differences should be. A rule of thumb that seems reasonable and is advocated by Kaufman is to view as important any deviation of at least three scaled score units from the mean of the section in which the subscale is located.

Consider a child who received the following subscale scores on the Verbal section of the WISC-R.

Information	7
Similarities	9
Arithmetic	12
Vocabulary	9
Comprehension	8

The mean of the subscales is 9; therefore, it would be correct to say that this child scored above the mean on Arithmetic because, with a score of 12, he or she is 3 above the mean. It would not, however, be correct to say that the child was below average in Information because the score is only 2 points below the mean of 9.

Determining the appropriate magnitude of differences is not the only problem that one must face in examining subscale scores. There is a lamentable tendency among examiners to isolate deviant subscale scores and then make an interpretation based on what that scale presumably measures. This can result in faulty diagnoses because each subscale typically measures more than one thing, and there is no way for the examiner to know exactly what specific characteristics a subscale is measuring for a particular individual. Kaufman suggests that information provided by one deviant subscale be viewed as a hypothesis, and that the examiner seek confirmation or disconfirmation in other subscales or behaviors before reaching conclusions.

A *profile* is a pattern of scores in which some subscales are characteristically high and others low. Profiles are interpreted through their association with specific syndromes, problems, or disabilities. Scatter refers to the overall difference between the highest and lowest scores, regardless of what they are. There is little evidence to support the association of scatter with any particular syndrome or etiology. In fact, a spread of nine to ten points between the highest and lowest subscales on the WISC-R is typical.

The use of profile analyses has met with more success than scatter analysis. The profiles of mentally retarded and learning- and reading-disabled children show some consistency. The mentally retarded child is more likely to do better on Picture Completion, Object Assembly, and Block Design than he or she does on Information, Arithmetic, and Vocabulary. The learning- or reading-disabled child will typically do better on Picture Completion, Object Assembly, and Block Design, while doing poorly on Information, Arithmetic, Digit Span, and Coding (Kaufman, 1979).

Comparisons Between the Stanford-Binet and Wechsler

With the introduction of deviation scores to compute IQs on the Stanford-Binet, it and the WISC-R became almost equivalent for subjects between the ages of six and fifteen years; however, the WAIS-R is clearly better for adults. The WPPSI cannot be used with very young children (norms for the Stanford-Binet go as low as two years, whereas the WPPSI is used only for children as young as four years.) Young children suspected of mental retardation are also better tested with the Stanford-Binet.

As mentioned earlier, the Wechsler tests have become the tests of choice largely because they provide subscale scores. These are of great convenience to the psychologist faced with the task of writing a psychological report. The typical correlation between the two tests is .80.

Brighter students get higher scores on the Stanford-Binet than on the Wechsler, whereas duller students do better on the Wechsler. Older students get higher scores on the Wechsler, whereas younger students do better on the Stanford-Binet (Sattler, 1974).

Although the Stanford-Binet and Wechsler tests provide the best estimates of intellectual functioning, and overall are the best psychological instruments available, the score itself is not what makes these tests valuable. The tests are administered on an individual basis, with the entire session usually lasting over an hour. In this session the skilled examiner learns more than test scores about the subject. Depending on the skill of the person administering the test, the intellectual and emotional characteristics of the subject can be revealed.

The Kaufman Assessment Battery for Children (K-ABC)

A third individual intelligence test, published in 1982, can be expected to present a strong challenge to the dominance of the WISC-R. The test was developed by Alan and Nadeen Kaufman (1982) and is called the Kaufman Assessment Battery for Children (K-ABC). It is normed for use with children from the age of two and a half to twelve and a half, which makes it useful for about the same population as the WPPSI, WISC-R, and Stanford-Binet.

The test has a number of attractive features. The norming of the test was based on the 1980 census and includes handicapped children in about the same proportion as exists in the U.S. population. The psychometric properties of the test—reliability and validity—are very good and compare favorably with those of the WISC-R. In addition, even before the test was published, over forty reliability and validity studies were conducted on it. This is unusual, because such research is normally conducted only after a test is published.

The instrument consists of sixteen subtests; some subtests are administered to all the children tested, whereas others are administered only to a limited number of ages. The maximum number of tests administered at any age is thirteen. The instrument provides five scales: Sequential Processing, Simultaneous Processing, Mental Processing Composite, Achievement, and Non-Verbal.

The Sequential Processing Scale

The Sequential Processing Scale includes three subtests: Hand Movements, Number Recall, and Word Order. Each of these tasks requires a sequential response to stimuli.

The Simultaneous Processing Scale

The simultaneous processing scale includes seven subtests: Magic Window, Face Recognition, Gestalt Closure, Triangles, Matrix Analogies, Spatial Memory, and Photo Series. These subtests involve the perception of many stimuli at once, rather than sequential perception. There are more Simultaneous Processing Scale subtests than Sequential Processing Scale subtests because there are not as many possible tests of sequential processing and because simultaneous processing is a broader concept and thus must be measured in more ways. In addition, some Simultaneous Processing Subtests can only be given to children in a limited age range, so to cover all ages, additional subtests in this area were needed.

The Mental Processing Composite Scale

The mental processing composite scale consists of a combination of the Sequential and Simultaneous Processing Scales. The scales are weighted so that they count equally to correct for the fact that there are more Simultaneous Processing subtests. The Mental Processing Composite is considered *the* measure of intelligence on this instrument.

The Achievement Scale

The achievement scale consists of six subtests: Expressive Vocabulary, Faces and Places, Arithmetic, Riddles, Reading and Decoding, and Reading and Understanding. In contrast to the Mental Processing Scale, which focuses on novel situations, the Achievement Scale emphasizes skills and knowledge acquired in the environment—either in school, at home, or elsewhere. Unlike Wechsler and Terman, the Kaufmans have chosen not to include acquired ability as an aspect of intelligence. It is used to supplement the Mental Processing Composite and provide a measure of crystallized intelligence to compare with the fluid intelligence measured by the Mental Processing Composite.

The Nonverbal Scale

The nonverbal scale consists of a selected number of subtests from the Sequential and Simultaneous Processing Scales that can be administered without verbal instructions, either by example or by means of pantomine, and to which the subject can respond with gestures or by performing tasks that require no verbal response. This scale is considered comparable to the Mental Processing Scale and is included for use with subjects with communication problems or for those who do not speak English.

The Theoretical Basis for the K-ABC

The psychologist, encountering a client with a below-average level of intelligence, generally wants to go beyond a global description of intelligence in the psychological report and to be able to point to specific strengths and weaknesses. There is really no way to do this with the Stanford-Binet, and it is not easily done with the WISC-R. Wechsler grouped items according to their content and was not particularly interested in processes. Kaufman has made important contributions to the interpretation of the WISC-R, so it is not surprising that the K-ABC would be constructed in such a way that it would facilitate this sort of analysis.

In writing about the Stanford-Binet and Wechsler tests, Kaufman (1975) has criticized their structure and selection of items as not reflecting current theory about intelligence. He thinks that there is too much emphasis on content at the expense of processes. In particular, he has advocated that an intelligence test should reflect what is now known about the functioning of the brain. For these reasons the K-ABC places considerable emphasis on distinguishing between left-brain sequential processing and right-brain simultaneous processing. This is believed to have important implications for educational diagnosis, particularly for children with learning disabilities, who the Kaufmans believe are stronger in simultaneous than sequential processing. In addition, this dichotomy provides information for adapting instructions to a child's learning style. Most school instruction favors left-brained sequential processing. If the results of administering the K-ABC to a child suggests a right-brain preference, a teacher could focus on activities that match the child's preferred mode of functioning.

Throughout the technical manual the authors emphasize control of socioeconomic status, but this characteristic is estimated only by means of parental educational level. The problem with using parental education level to estimate socioeconomic levels is that the two affect intelligence test performances in different ways.

The Kaufman opposes the use of the term IQ because of the emotions that this term stirs, confusion concerning its meaning, and the way it has been misused. Although he applauds D. McCarthy for not including an *IQ* score with the McCarthy Scale of Children's Ability, he criticizes her for continuing to provide a standard score with a mean of 100 and a standard deviation of 16. The K-ABC does not employ an IQ score but instead uses a *Standard Score* with a mean of 100 and a standard deviation of 15. The Kaufmans are now faced with the irony that in some states the K-ABC cannot be used to certify children for special education placement because some state laws specify the use of an IQ score. Even though this test provides scores that seem comparable to the WISC-R or Stanford-Binet IQ scores, because they are not specifically called IQs, they are not acceptable to these states.

Nondiscriminatory Testing

Another important goal of the K-ABC test is to provide nondiscriminatory testing. After briefly reviewing the literature on the intellectual assessment of blacks, the Kaufmans (1983, p. 14) state that "despite frequent empirical findings of little racial bias in intelligence tests (e.g., Sandoval, 1979), a more humanistic approach to the controversy leads to one inescapable conclusion: more sensitive and thoughtful methods of intellectual assessment are required to meet the needs of minority group children." This is a curious statement because the Kaufmans are simultaneously arguing for different methods of assessing minority children while supporting the validity of existing tests.

In creating a test that is believed to be more sensitive and thoughtful, they have emphasized only fluid intelligence and have not included the crystallized ability assessed by the Achievement Scale as a part of the intelligence score. This is done despite the fact that the predictive validity of the Achievement Scale is better than the Mental Processing Composite, according to their own data. This is done because the items in the Mental Processing Composite are more novel and thus are less dependent on cultural experiences. The Kaufmans seem to have fallen into the trap of trying to measure intelligence independently of school performance. By taking this approach they lose the strongest claim such tests have for validity and the most useful purpose for their administration: the prediction of academic performance.

Although the technical manual emphasizes the dichotomy between sequential and simultaneous processing, the test seems mainly to emphasize memory. Of the ten subtests in the Mental Processing Composite, five are measures of short-term memory. By comparison, ony three of the ten subtests are measures of abstract thinking. This is in contrast with the WISC-R and Stanford-Binet, which emphasize abstract thinking and higher-level thought processing, rather than short-term memory and recognition. The theoretical approach of the K-ABC, in this respect, is consistent with Arthur Jensen's (1980) theory of intelligence. Jensen has proposed two types of intelligence: Level I, which includes memory and paired associate learning, and Level II, which emphasizes higher-level and abstract thinking. Jensen suggests that blacks are better at Level-I tasks, whereas Caucasians are better at Level-II tasks. The Kaufmans' selection of items seems to suggest that they have adopted Jensen's theory of intelligence and have used it to develop an intelligence test that diminishes differences between the performance of black and white children on this test.

The authors of the K-ABC report data that indicate that the difference between black and white children, in intellectual functioning, is much less on the K-ABC than on the WISC-R. The Kaufmans would like to think that the similarities in intellectual functioning are the result of sophisticated techniques of eliminating biased items. On the other hand, the similar performance of black and white students might reflect a vindication of Jensen's theories of the structures of intelligence.

In addition, the comparability of norm samples must be considered. These results were obtained using norm samples in which the educational level of blacks was much higher than that found in the 1980 U.S. census (see Table 3.7 of the *Kaufman Assessment Battery For Children Interpretive Manual*). Before it can be demonstrated that there is indeed little difference in the intellectual performance of blacks and whites on the K-ABC, it will be necessary to select a sample that more correctly matches that found in the U.S. census.

The K-ABC also provides sociocultural norms that allow for a comparison of a child with other children of the same race and level of parental education. Norms are presently available for only white children and black children. These norms allow, for instance, a black child with parents who lack a high school diploma to be compared with other black children of the same age and parental level of education.

This approach is similar to the Estimated Learning Potential (ELP) provided by the System of Multicultural and Pluralistic Assessment (Mercer, 1979), to be discussed in a following section. While Jan Mercer states that the ELP can be used as one criterion for identifying the mentally retarded and gifted (Mercer, 1979), the Kaufmans disavow this use stating that (p. 167), "We cannot advocate the use of these supplementary norms for diagnostic or placement decision" (1982). However, because they are provided, there is a good possibility that they will be misused in exactly the way that the authors disavow.

Conclusions About the K-ABC

The Kaufmans have created the first major new individual intelligence test since the Wechsler-Bellevue. The determination of whether this test represents an important advance over the other two tests is as yet unresolved. The issue will not be decided until the test is used by practitioners and research data on the test accumulate.

The predecessors of the Kaufmans (Binet, Terman, and Wechsler) focused on the accumulation of items that they believed assessed intelligence. They were motivated by pragmatism and were not overly concerned about theory. The Kaufmans have criticized existing individual intelligence tests for this reason and have attempted to incorporate existing theories of cognitive psychology into their test. Ultimately, this instrument must be evaluated in terms of the degree to which it has succeeded in doing this.

The System of Multicultural Pluralistic Assessment (SOMPA)

The System of Multicultural Pluralistic Assessment (SOMPA) is not really a separate test of intelligence because it includes performance on the WISC-R. It does, however, represent a break from traditional methods of assessment. It was developed as a response to concern about the fact that minorities, on the average, obtain lower scores on tests of intelligence than do nonminorities. It also reflects a related concern about school systems labeling so many minority children as mentally retarded. The implementation of the SOMPA in a school district would eliminate this problem because it is so constructed that instead of the traditional estimates of 2 percent (MacMillan, 1977; Robinson & Robinson, 1976), it can be expected to identify less than .5 percent of the school population as mildly mentally retarded (Reschly, 1981).

The SOMPA is a battery of separate measures intended to provide information on a child's level of functioning in different areas. It requires a considerable amount of time for each assessment—as much as five hours according to Thomas Oakland (1979). In addition to including such traditional measures as the WISC-R and Bender Visual-Motor Gestalt, it requires the acquisition of a considerable amount of information from each child's parents.

The SOMPA is made up of three models: the Medical Model, the Social System Model, and the Pluralistic Model.

The Medical Model

The Medical Model includes such tasks as fine motor sequencing, physical dexterity, performance on the Bender Visual-Motor Gestalt test, the relationship between weight and height, and visual and auditory acuity, as well as the health history of the child. These data are provided in order to eliminate the possibility that the child's poor school performance has an organic cause. If such problems are detected, they can be treated before, or along with, any educational deficits.

The Social System Model

The Social System Model has two parts: the Adaptive Behavior Inventory for Children (ABIC) and the WISC-R scores. Because the WISC-R has already been described, it will not be discussed in any more detail at this point.

The ABIC consists of a series of multiple-choice questions that are answered by the parents and that provide an estimate of a child's adaptive behavior in a nonschool setting. Parents are asked about their child's functioning in such areas as the family, community, and among peers. A total score is also computed. Scores on different sections of the ABIC can be converted into standard scores and percentiles that permit comparisons with the norm group. The main purpose of the ABIC is to determine whether a child who appears mentally retarded, based only on the WISC-R, is mentally retarded when out-of-school functioning is considered.

Although the ABIC has generally been reviewed favorably (Oakland, 1979), this instrument does have disadvantages. It relies exclusively on the parent or guardian as the source of information, which can lead to unverified results and unreliable conclusions. It contains some middle-class items that cause children from this background to obtain higher scores than others, and the use of a norm sample selected only from a California population may make generalization to other parts of the country inappropriate. Finally, there is no way to determine what expectations the child's community has for the child. The group on which the instrument was normed may have one set of expectations, and the child's community may have another. There are really no adaptations made for children from economically deprived environments, for instance. Accounting for these differences would seem to be a fundamental requirement of an adaptive behavior scale. It is difficult to see how one can determine which behaviors are adaptive without knowing what is expected in the community.

The most important question about the ABIC concerns its role in decisions concerning which children should be placed in special classes and which should not. Because the assessment of adaptive behavior is mandated by PL-94-142, some such instrument must be used; as Oakland (1983) has pointed out, however, most clinicians lack training in how to use the information the ABIC provides. At issue is the relevance of information about a child's ability to function in his or her community to the task of determining the optimum academic setting. Because there is little relationship between scores on the ABIC and academic performance (Sattler, 1982; Oakland, 1980; Yonge, 1982) it is unclear just how information about a child's capacity to function in his or her community relates to the issue of school or class placement. Its inclusion as a criterion for eligibility is one of the major reasons that the incidence of mild retardation declines so rapidly with the implementation of SOMPA assessment procedures. Although the purpose of its inclusion was to counter the purported bias of the WISC-R against minority groups, it tends to also make many students, who are not minorities, ineligible for special class placement (Reschly, 1981).

The Pluralistic Model

The Pluralistic Model is the most controversial aspect of the SOMPA. It is divided into two sections: the Sociocultural Scales provide information in four areas: family size, family structure, socioeconomic status, and urban acculturation. Information from these questions is then used in a regression equation that transforms a child's WISC-R score into an Estimated Learning Potential (ELP) score. There are different regression equations for blacks, whites, and Hispanic children. The effect of this process is to determine a child's level of intellectual functioning through a comparison with children of similar backgrounds. Sattler (1982) demonstrates how a black child with a full-scale score of 69 on the WISC-R who came from a large family, poor family structure, low socioeconomic status, and limited urban acculturation can receive a full-scale ELP of 108. The intention is to estimate what a child's IQ would have been had the disadvantages not occurred. However, there is no evidence that this is indeed what happens. The effect is to add a constant to the score of disadvantaged children. Because ELPs are computed with different norm groups, there is no way to compare the scores of children from different backgrounds. The child whose ELP score was elevated from a WISC-R score of 69 to 108 is simply not the same intellectually as the child with a WISC-R score of 108.

George Yonge (1982) points out that what is being done is the equivalent of saying that a third-grader who is at the 50th percentile in math is the same as a 10th-grader at the 50th percentile. The capacity of the ELP to predict academic performance is much less than the WISC-R's. For the ELP the correlations are in .4s, whereas for the WISC-R they are in the .6s (Oakland, 1980). In addition, the use of ELPs discriminates against white children who are disadvantaged. This is because the regression equations used for this group do not elevate low IQs nearly as much as those used for black and Hispanic disadvantaged children.

There is one further irony. When estimating academic potential with the SOMPA, the authors correct for the child's sociocultural background, despite the fact that children are expected to compete in school against a single set of academic criteria. However, in evaluating adaptive behavior that can be expected to vary greatly according to sociocultural background, and where such consideration would be legitimate, a single scale is used.

Conclusions About the SOMPA

The development of the SOMPA has one major goal: to rectify the disproportionate number of minority children being labeled mentally retarded and placed in special education classes. The implementation of the SOMPA can eliminate this problem, but not only does it remove large numbers of minority children from special education classes, it does the same for nonminority children. The use of the ABIC and ELP leads to large discrepancies among scores because academic achievement tends to be similar to WISC-R performance, which falls below the ELP and ABIC score. The result is that the disadvantaged children who are no longer eligible for classes for the educably mentally retarded meet the requirements for placement in classes for the learning disabled. This, in fact, is what has happened in some school districts where the SOMPA has been tried. What is gained are slightly smaller classes and a label (learning disabled) that is less offensive than mentally retarded. The instructional methods are about the same for the two types of classes, but it is somewhat easier to mainstream LD than EMH students.

The Use of Individual Intelligence Tests to Determine Special Education Placement

Although individual intelligence tests are used in research and as one aspect of an individual's clinical assessment, their broadest application in educational settings is as part of the process for determining whether a child should be placed in a special education setting. Once it is established that a child would benefit from an educational setting different from the normal classroom, a decision concerning the particular type of special education also must be made.

At one time, children were placed in special education classes on the basis of teacher recommendations alone. It was considered a major reform when federal and state funding for special education classes became tied to the requirement that an assessment of individual intelligence become part of the placement process.

Children are not screened using individual intelligence tests. Such a procedure would be far too expensive, even if it could be justified on any other grounds. PL 94-142 requires that the intelligence test be only one part of the assessment process. Therefore, children are not labeled mentally retarded and put into self-contained classes because of the WISC-R or any other single test. Children are recommended for special education consideration by teachers, and the administration of an intelligence test is only one part of a lengthy and complex assessment procedure. No one advocates that intelligence test scores be the sole criteria for special education placement. The role of the intelligence test is to ensure that children are placed in the appropriate educational setting. The use of these tests is more likely to prevent children from being placed in special classes than it is to cause children to be assigned to them.

Disproportionality

At the present time, there is some sentiment in support of a ban on the use of intelligence tests. This opposition is particularly strong among civil rights groups that believe that their use has led to a disproportionally large number of black students in classes for the mentally handicapped. There are several court cases that are relevant to the question of whether mental ability tests should be used as a criterion for determining placement in special education classes. The ruling in *Diana et al.* vs. *State Board of Education of California* (1970) criticized the use of English language IQ tests for placing bilingual children in special classes and recommended that justification be provided for any instance where the proportion of an ethnic group's enrollment in special classes exceeds the proportion of that group in the population as a whole.

The most important legal action so far is probably *Larry P. et al.* vs. *Wilson Riles, Superintendent of Public Instruction for the State of California*, which has resulted in a cessation of the use of intelligence tests as a criterion for making decisions about the placement of black students in special education classes in California. The court's main objection to the use of intelligence tests as a basis for placing children in EMH classes centered on the belief that their use had resulted in disproportionately large numbers of nonwhite students in those classes. The objection was based on the belief that intelligence tests measure innate ability and that innate ability is evenly distributed across ethnic groups. When special education classes contain a disproportionate number of a minority group, this is used as evidence that the intelligence test used for placement is biased.

Innate ability is a construct that no one has been able to isolate and validly measure. The question of whether this construct is evenly distributed across cultural and ethnic groups remains not only unanswered, but probably unanswerable. Academic performance is not evenly distributed across cultural and ethnic groups but is substantially related to socioeconomic status. It should surprise no one that academic aptitude tests reflect this reality.

Conclusions About Special Education Placement

The problem is that we are able to identify large numbers of students who cannot benefit from the normal classroom and are being traumatized by the experience of total failure. We also know that there are funds available to help children who are assigned a special education label, but there is little money for children who are not.

The child identified as having a severe educational handicap must either be given a special education label or be denied services. Advocacy groups representing minorities have taken the position that identifying members of an ethnic group in this way constitutes a slur against that ethnic group. The practice of labeling is now being called pernicious and the result of a conspiracy by the forces of the upper classes to suppress the lower classes.

It is unfortunate that those who criticize existing procedures are more concerned about the large number of children labeled educationally deficient than the fact that our schools have failed to provide effective educational programs for those children.

As federal and state funding for special classes diminishes, a point will soon be reached when the elimination of classes from a budget will become increasingly attractive. When those classes are gone, there will be few services available for the children who are failing to benefit from regular programs.

The decision to place a child in a special class is a weighty one. If the classes are only ineffectual dumping grounds for unwanted students, then no student should be placed in them. If, however, they are legitimate educational settings for students who are behind their peers academically, and they provide the opportunity for these students to lead useful lives, then failing to place a child in such a class who belongs there is as serious as putting a child in a class in which he or she does not belong.

Finally, if we decide not to use general ability tests for special education placement, we are left with subjective decisions made by various school personnel. The danger of bias seems much greater when trusting personal judgment. The inappropriate placement of students in special classes was far worse prior to the general adoption of individual intelligence as a major part of the process of special education placement.

SUMMARY

1. Alfred Binet, together with Theodore Simon, developed the first individual intelligence test in Paris in 1905.
2. The Binet test was revised and expanded by Louis Terman, who published the Stanford-Binet in 1916.
3. David Wechsler introduced a series of individual intelligence tests that relegated the Stanford-Binet to alternate use.
4. The most recently introduced individual intelligence test is the K-ABC. It differs from the other major tests by placing an emphasis on differentiating simultaneous from sequential cognitive processing.
5. The SOMPA was introduced as a response to concern about the disproportionate numbers of minority children who are placed in special education classes.

SUGGESTED READINGS

KAUFMAN, A. S. (1980). *Intelligent testing with the WISC-R*. New York: Free Press. [Unlike most books on the subject of psychological test interpretation, this one does not depend solely on the author's clinical experience. It is, instead, research based and provides the clearest, most complete description of the interpretation of the WISC-R available.]

LUTEY, C. (1977). *Individual intelligence testing: A sourcebook and manual*. Greeley, CO: Lutey. [This textbook started out as a manual for use in the classes that Carol Lutey was teaching in individual intelligence testing. The manual was so well received that she has made it available for commercial use. It is, as one might expect, very practical and provides a great deal of how-to suggestions. Her philosophy of test interpretation is somewhat different from that of Sattler or Kaufman, in that she advocates a highly precise mathematical approach to test interpretation.]

MATARAZZO, J. D. (1976). *Weschler's measurement and appraisal of adult intelligence*. Baltimore: Williams & Wilkins. [The focus of this book is on adult intelligence, but it also includes a very thorough discussion of the history of the development of individual intelligence.]

SATTLER, J. M. (1982). *Assessment of children's intelligence and special abilities*. Boston: Allyn. [This is the most often used textbook for training individuals in the use of individual psychological instruments and is an excellent source of information on the topic.]

15

Group Mental Ability Tests

OVERVIEW

Following the successful introduction of individual intelligence tests at the beginning of this century, group intelligence tests were developed to provide a more efficient method of assessing an individual's level of intellectual functioning. Group mental ability is a general heading for instruments that measure the same construct, although they may be given different names. At one time these tests were widely and uncritically used, but during the last twenty years their use has been questioned. For this reason they are not used as often as they once were. When they are used it is usually for a specific purpose and more care is taken in interpreting them.

Included in this chapter are descriptions of several of the major group intelligence tests, accompanied by information about when they should be used and how their results should be interpreted. Also included in this chapter is a description of the major scholastic aptitude tests and a discussion of the issues and controversies that surround their use. The chapter concludes with a discussion of multiple aptitude tests.

OBJECTIVES

From this chapter you will learn about the different types of group intelligence tests: scholastic aptitude tests, multiple aptitude tests, and job-related tests. Specifically, you will learn the following:

- The historical development of group intelligence tests.
- The characteristics of the Cognitive Abilities Test and the Test of Cognitive Skills.
- The characteristics of the different scholastic aptitude tests.
- The controversies surrounding scholastic aptitude tests.
- The use of group mental ability tests to screen job applicants and assess specific aptitudes.

Introduction

Individual intelligence tests such as those described in the previous chapter are most useful as clinical psychological instruments because they can tell us a great deal about the cognitive functioning of an individual. If we are just interested in an estimate of overall intellectual functioning, there are group tests of mental ability that can be administered to many individuals at once, inexpensively and efficiently, and that yield results similar to those obtained using individual intelligence tests. These group tests seem to work best with individuals of average and above-average intelligence. Those who cannot read, have communication problems, or have other disabilities are not easily or validly evaluated using group methods and can be assessed better with individual tests.

There are three types of group ability tests: group intelligence tests, scholastic aptitude tests, and multiple-aptitude tests.

Group Intelligence Tests

The Army Alpha and Beta

The United States entered World War I on April 16, 1917. The president of the APA at that time was Robert Yerkes. Yerkes called together the leading psychologists of the day to determine how their organization could best contribute to the war effort. It was decided that the newly developing field of mental testing offered the best opportunity for them to be of assistance. Later they were formally given this charge by the Department of War.

Assembled at the Vineland New Jersey training school was the cream of the crop of the then burgeoning field of psychology. In addition to Yerkes, the committee included such luminaries as Terman, Boring, and Walter Bingham among others. The committee decided that the focus of their work should be on assessing the mental ability of recruits for the purpose of determining how the armed forces could best use their talents. They also decided to not use individual tests because the number of recruits to be tested was so vast that the testing sessions would have to be brief, which would impair the reliability of their results. In addition, differences among a large number of examiners would further degrade the precision of the test. At this point Terman shared with the committee the work that Arthur Otis was doing in this area, and so Otis was invited to participate as a member of the committee.

Otis had been hired as a graduate assistant to perform the laborious mathematical computation associated with the development of the Stanford-Binet. Later, in connection with Otis's dissertation, Terman encouraged his development of a paper-and-pencil analogue to the Stanford-Binet that could be given on a large scale cheaply and efficiently and be scored in such a way as to maintain the highest possible scoring reliability. Otis suggested that the recall items that dominated the Stanford-Binet be replaced by recognition items in the form of multiple-choice questions (Robertson, 1972).

Otis's approach was adopted by the committee. They eventually developed the *Army Alpha* for literates and the *Army Beta* for illiterates; the test was administered to over 1,700,000 recruits. The results were used to make determinations that ranged from which men were to be officers and which noncommissioned officers, all the way down to who would be rejected for service. Although the actual usefulness of the test for the army is in some dispute (Samuelson, 1977; Gould, 1981) it certainly had a major impact on future testing. At the end of the war there was a great proliferation of similar tests used in the civilian sector.

Otis played an important role in the development of those tests and published the Otis Group Intelligence Scale in 1918. In 1921 he published the Otis Self-Administering Tests of Mental Ability. Finally, in 1967, the Otis-Lennon Mental Ability Test was published. At the same time that Otis was developing his tests, others were publishing similar ones. Such tests began to be used on a regular basis, mainly for the purpose of grouping. Serious opposition to the use of these tests did not occur until the 1960s, when opposition to group testing focused on the discrepant performances of minorities and nonminorities.

When desegregation became more widespread, the use of these tests for grouping was believed to be causing resegregation, and educators and civil rights advocates began to question their use. This opposition was manifested in a series of court cases, the most prominent of which was *Hobson v. Hansen* (1967), in which Circuit Court Judge Skelly Wright ruled that the District of Columbia could no longer track students. Tracking is the once widespread practice of administering group intelligence tests to students in early grades and then assigning them either to an academic or nonacademic track. If a child did well on the test, he or she was assigned to such courses as college math, advanced English, science, and foreign languages; the student who did poorly found him- or herself enrolled in vocational and shop courses. Tracking tends to be permanent because when students do not enroll in introductory academic courses in the lower grades, they lack the prerequisites for the more advanced courses in the higher grades.

Because grouping on the basis of mental ability has been interpreted by the courts to be illegal, the use of these tests has declined. They are no longer administered on a widespread basis except in private schools and for the purpose of screening students for admission to gifted programs.

Test publishers have responded to criticism of these tests by avoiding the use of such terms as *intelligence*, *mental ability*, and *IQ*. They have substituted more neutral terms that focus on the capacity of the tests to assess academic ability. The Lorge-Thorndike became the Cognitive Abilities Test (CAT); the Otis-Lennon Mental Ability Test became the Otis-Lennon School Ability Test; and the Short Form Test of Mental Maturity became the Short Form Test of Academic Ability, and later the Test of Cognitive Skills. However, the content of the tests did not change along with the title. Changing the name of what had previously been called an intelligence test to something suggesting academic ability assessment was reasonable because that is, in fact, what the tests measure. Their validity is determined by their capacity to make good predictions about academic performance.

Some test authors also have disavowed the use of the term *IQ*. For instance the CAT uses *Standard Age Scores*, whereas the Test of Cognitive Skills (TCS) has a *Cognitive Skills Index*. These scales have means of 100 and standard deviations of 15 or 16 and therefore look like—and are treated as though they are—IQ scores. There are groups in education and psychology that find the use of IQ scores anathema, and others who would not purchase a test that did not include them. The compromise solution is to include IQ scores and then call them by another name.

Two group intelligence tests have been selected as examples of this type of instrument and will be described briefly. The two tests are the CAT, published by Houghton Mifflin, and the TCS, published by McGraw-Hill.

The Cognitive Abilities Test (CAT)

This test includes a Primary Battery for children in first and second grade and a Multilevel Edition for children in grades 3 through 12. The Primary Battery is a nonreading test, divided into two sections labeled Level 1 and Level 2. Level 1 is for kindergarten and first-grade students of below-average ability. Because of the need for early intervention, the test was constructed so that it can discriminate best among children in the bottom three fourths of their class. For children in the upper quarter of the first grade, there are few items difficult enough to provide good discriminations. Level 2 is intended for higher-functioning first-graders and second-graders and does a better job than Level 1 in discriminating among members of this group.

The Multilevel Edition is divided into three sections: Verbal, Quantitative, and Nonverbal. The test is called multilevel because within each section the items are ranked from easy to difficult and divided into eight levels. This allows for one level for each grade from grades 3 to 8 and two levels divided among the four remaining grades. Each student takes the level that is appropriate for his or her ability, which is not necessarily the level corresponding to grade in school. Brighter children should take levels above their grade and less bright students levels below their grade. This is done in order to ensure that the maximum discriminations occur at a child's ability level and should result in more reliable test scores. This is not difficult to accomplish administratively because the testing material for all levels is available in a single test booklet.

The *Verbal Battery* includes Vocabulary, Sentence Completion, Verbal Classification, and Verbal Analogies. The *Quantitative Battery* includes Quantitative Relations, Number Series, and Equation Building. The *Nonverbal Battery* includes Figure Analogies, Figure Classification, and Figure Synthesis.

The Verbal and Quantitative Batteries emphasize the skills needed in school and consist of measures of current functioning in these domains. The inclusion of the Nonverbal Battery provides a measure of ability that at least gives the appearance of being independent of cultural background. This may be more apparent than real because there is no evidence that nonverbal items are really more fair to individuals from different cultural and ethnic groups. At the same time, this battery is not as accurate in predicting school performance as the other batteries, so it is not entirely clear what its purpose is. Reliabilities, as computed using measures of internal consistency, range from .89 to .90 for the Primary Battery, .91 to .94 for the Verbal Battery, .87 to .91 for the Quantitative Battery, and .90 to .93 for the Nonverbal Battery.

The test is well established, has a good reputation, and is given favorable reviews in the Mental Measurement Yearbooks. It was developed by three of the premier measurement experts in the country: Robert Thorndike, Elizabeth Hagen, and Irving Lorge. The manuals provided are thorough and well constructed. The test's most attractive feature are the norming procedures, which allow a child to be tested on any one of several levels. This makes it possible always to provide an appropriate level of difficulty for a child.

There are two criticisms of the test: (1) the instructions may be somewhat difficult for children to understand, and (2) the answer sheets provided are poor. Alternative answer sheets can be ordered.

The Test of Cognitive Skills (TCS)

The Test of Cognitive Skills (TCS), published by McGraw-Hill, evolved from what was first the Short Form Test of Mental Maturity and later the Short Form Test of Academic Ability. The test is intended as a measure of school aptitude and focuses on abstract thinking and, in particular, the skills of education. There are five test levels for the TCS:

Level 1	Grades 2–3
Level 2	Grades 3–5
Level 3	Grades 5–7
Level 4	Grades 7–9
Level 5	Grades 9–12

For each test level there are four subtests: Analogies, Sequences, Memory, and Verbal Reasoning.

Analogies requires the student to recognize the relationship between two pictures, picture *A* and picture *B*. In order to demonstrate that the relationship is understood, the student must examine a third picture (*C*) and then select a fourth picture (*D*) from a series of pictures, such that *C* and *D* are related in the same way as *A* and *B*. *Sequences* requires the student to identify which figure, number, or letter comes next in a sequence. *Memory* assesses the student's ability to recall previously presented material. *Verbal Reasoning* involves several different types of tasks: finding the necessary part of a word (for example, that a car must have wheels and a motor, but it could still be a car without windshield wipers), determining which word comes next in a sentence, and solving logic problems.

The test was developed to be administered along with the Comprehensive Test of Basic Skills (CTBS). Because the CTBS is so widely used, the TCS is also frequently administered. The justification for the administration of the TCS along with the CTBS is that it permits the computation of Anticipated Achievement Scale Scores (AASS). These are transformed scores derived from multiple-regression estimates that use performance on the TCS to predict CTBS scores. They provide an estimate (the Anticipated Achievement Scale Score), of how well a student should do on the subscales of the CTBS. This permits comparisons between actual and estimated performance that presumably allow for estimates of whether the child is an under- or overachiever.

Although this may seem logical to those unfamiliar with testing, it makes no sense in light of what is known about the way that mental abilities are structured. The idea that aptitude and achievement tests are measuring qualitatively different constructs is a misconception that supposedly had been corrected many years ago (Anastasi, 1982). Aptitude and achievement tests differ mainly in terms of how we use them and how they are validated. There is some difference in content, but there is more overlap. Discrepancies reflect little more than differences in the capacity of a child to perform tasks requiring different degrees of abstract thinking and measurement error.

School system personnel who should know better are attracted to the use of AASS scores because they help alleviate public relation problems associated with the administration of achievement tests. When a school system receives the results of standardized achievement testing, newspapers immediately want to publish them and parents want to see how their child's school compares with other schools in the system. In such a process there are winners and there are losers. Principals of schools that do poorly tend to yell "foul" because they perceive that, as a result of forces over which they have no control, such as their particular mix of students, their school is being made to look bad. By reporting results in terms of the relationship between AASS and actual scores, a school has two chances to look good. It can shine either in terms of the actual score on the CTBS or in terms of its position relative to the AASSs. In schools where students are performing at a below-average level on the CTBS, most discrepancies will involve achievement scores that are higher than the AASS because it is more likely that such students will do better on concrete than on abstract tasks.

The TCS seems to be a legitimate group intelligence test, although it is more dependent on short term memory than other comparable tests. It is particularly attractive to school systems that already administer the CTBS because it can be easily administered. The use of the AASS cannot be justified on psychometric grounds and serves mainly as a clever and effective marketing ploy and public relations tool.

College Aptitude Tests

Tests used as a criteria for admission to academic programs from undergraduate to graduate and professional schools are similar in content to group intelligence tests. Their format and norming also are essentially the same. Because group intelligence tests have been shown to be an effective predictor of academic performance, it is logical that they would serve as a model for college aptitude tests. The main difference between group tests of intelligence and college aptitude tests is difficulty. College aptitude tests are constructed to be more difficult because they are used with a select group of students—those being considered for admission to colleges, universities, or graduate schools.

The two tests that are most often used for admission to undergraduate schools are the SAT and the American College Testing Program (ACT).

The Scholastic Aptitude Test (SAT)

At the turn of the century, a student who wanted to apply to more than one university or college might be required to take a separate exam for each school, a procedure that made applying to several schools difficult; it also forced each school to develop its own testing program. The College Entrance Examination Board (CEEB) was established in order to provide standardized procedures for testing students for college admittance. The CEEB is a nonprofit organization now made up of over two thousand member schools. The first tests used were essay tests, but in 1926 an objective test titled the Scholastic Aptitude Test (SAT) was introduced. The test is now administered by the Educational Testing Service (ETS) under a contract with the CEEB. Separate editions of the test are developed each year, and test booklets are varied so that all students do not take the various sections of the test at the same time. Different forms of the test are designed and equated so that they have the same meaning, regardless of which is taken. The test is administered at specified testing dates under close supervision and with great concern for security.

The SAT consists of 150 multiple-choice questions divided into verbal and mathematical sections designated SAT-V and SAT-M. Scores range from 200 to 800. The standard deviation for the test is 100, and the mean for the original standardization was 500.

The verbal section emphasizes reading comprehension; the mathematical section assesses the student's ability to solve mathematical problems through reasoning, rather than by recalling knowledge of high school mathematics (Karmel & Karmel, 1978).

The standard error of measurement for both sections of the test is 30 points. Internal consistency is estimated at .90 for the SAT-V and .88 for the SAT-M.

The American College Testing Program (ACT)

The ACT was developed as a test that could be used not only as a criteria for college admission, but as an aid in achieving the best match possible between colleges and prospective students. The authors of the ACT tried to assess the sort of skills that a high school student needed in order to be successful in college. Those good intentions are mitigating by the fact that the publishers must make certain that they include no material that is specific to individual curricula or they will find themselves unfairly discriminating against students from public schools whose course of studies differed from the content of the test.

All items on the test are multiple choice; a student receives five scores: English Usage, Mathematical Usage, Social Studies Reading, Natural Sciences Reading, and Composite Score. Raw scores on the subtests are transformed to standard scores that range from 1 to 36, with a mean of 16 for all high school seniors and 19 for college-bound seniors. The standard deviation is set at 5, and the test's measurement error is 1.

The validity of the ACT, like the SAT, is usually estimated by means of correlations or multiple correlations between scores on the aptitude tests and GPA in college. The results of a large number of studies for both tests yield a wide range of coefficients ranging between .30 and .70, with scores around .40 probably being average. Most experts in this area (Karmel & Karmel, 1978; Anastasi, 1976) consider the ACT to be inferior to the SAT in terms of some psychometric qualities (reliability and standard error), but there is general agreement that the two are about equal in terms of predictive validity. In studies directly comparing their predictive validity, almost identical values were obtained (Pugh, 1965). The correlation between the two tests was found to be .86. It is generally believed that the two tests measure the same types of skills found on other group intelligence tests; in fact, such instruments seem to be equally valid for predicting GPA. The sizable intercorrelations among subtests on the ACT render their use for placement suspect.

The Graduate Record Exam (GRE)

The Graduate Record Exam (GRE) is published by ETS and is used as an admissions criteria for graduate and professional schools. It provides Verbal and Quantitative scores, along with twenty advanced achievement tests from which students can choose, depending on the requirements of the school to which they are applying. Like the SAT, its scores range from 200 to 800. In 1952 the original norm group had a mean of 500 and a standard deviation of 100.

The content of the GRE is similar to the SAT, but it is more difficult. A smaller norm sample was used than for the SAT, and although its reliability is similar to the SAT's, its validity is less impressive. Across thirty studies, the median correlation between the GRE score and GPA in graduate school was .33, whereas the predictive validity of previous GPA was .31. When the two are combined, a value of .45 is obtained (ETS, 1980). It is not unusual to find studies that report little or no relationship between the GRE and graduate school GPA. This can be partially explained by the fact that there is often a minimum amount of variability in a graduate school GPA because of grade inflation. Also, schools that accept only students with high GREs restrict the range of that variable as well.

The Millers Analogies Test (MAT)

The Millers Analogies Test (MAT) is published by the Psychological Corporation and was first used in 1926. It is an exclusively verbal test consisting of one hundred analogy problems. Students are given fifty minutes to answer as many of them as they can. Items range in difficulty from easy to extremely hard. The test's biggest strength is its difficulty, which enables it to make good discrimination among students of very high ability. Standard scores are not available, and only raw scores are reported. Reliability is adequate and validity is comparable with the GRE—which means that it is not particularly impressive. The MAT is used primarily as an admission requirement for graduate schools, but it has also been used as a screening instrument and an aptitude test for personnel decisions in business and industry.

Controversies Surrounding Tests of College Aptitude

As was the case with individual and group intelligence tests, tests of college aptitude have aroused considerable controversy. There have been calls for their elimination as a criterion for college admission as part of a general disapproval of standardized testing (Hoffman, 1962), as well for their replacement by achievement tests (Jencks & Crouse, 1982). Most of the criticism and discussion of such tests has focused on the SAT, but criticism of the SAT applies equally to the ACT and other scholastic aptitude tests. The four most important issues surrounding scholastic aptitude testing follow: the decline in test scores, the effect of coaching, the validity of the test, and the social cost-benefit of the test's use.

The Decline in SAT Scores

When the SAT was originally standardized, it had a mean of 500 and a standard deviation of 100. The standard deviation has stayed about the same, but now relatively few students obtain scores as high as 500—only about 20 percent of white students and 2 percent of black students (Stanley, 1971). The national averages in 1980–81 were 424 for the SAT-V and 466 for the SAT-M. In 1982 the averages were 426 and 467, which was the first time in nineteen years that the scores had not declined. The declines over the previous years have been a source of national concern. Despite the fact that this test is not an achievement test and is not constructed in such a way as to make it an effective overall tool for academic evaluation, it is the closest thing we have to a nationally administered standardized test of academic achievement.

Although the cause of the decline is not known, there are some hypotheses that have been eliminated, and it is possible to speculate about others that may be responsible for at least some of the decline. First of all, there is no evidence that the declines resulted from changes in test content, in composition of the groups taking the tests, or because of changes in the scaling methods used on the test (Harnischfeger & Wiley, 1976).

The decline is not restricted to the SAT but is paralleled in most other standardized tests. The verbal scores of females, which once exceeded males, have now declined to the point that they are nearly equal to those of males. One of the most troubling aspects of the decline is that it is most noticeable at the upper ends of the distribution.

Some possible explanations involve events inside and outside of school that occurred concomitantly with the decline. One must be very careful about such speculations because the mere fact that two events occur at the same time does not mean that one caused the other.

There have been a number of events that have occurred at the same time as the test score decline in terms of the schools. For instance, during this period there has been an increased absentee rate and indications that students are taking fewer academic courses (Harnischfeger & Wiley, 1976).

The most prominent nonschool activity that has been suggested as having a negative effect on SAT scores is television. Increased television viewing might also explain the fact that the achievement test performance of children in the early grades has increased at the same time that the performance of children in the upper grades had declined. Perhaps the stimulation of television, both verbal and visual, along with educational programs such as Sesame Street, benefit children in the early grades. At the same time, the existence of television may prevent older students from participating in beneficial educational activities. There are other factors that have occurred along with the test-score declines, such as increases in the number of working mothers and single-parent families, as well as the number of illegitimate children. Robert Zajonc (1976) has even suggested, by means of some clever statistical manipulations, that the decline can be explained in terms of the number and spacing of children, with students who have siblings close to them in age being at a disadvantage.

The most important nonschool cause of the decline is not really quantifiable but involves a general trend away from a belief in the importance of reading and other academic pursuits. We are reaching the point where reading, as a means of obtaining information, is declining in importance.

The Effect of Coaching on SAT Performance

Opponents of the SAT have tried to show that coaching, training, and other academic preparation can result in students raising their test scores. At one time this might have been viewed as an attack on the very foundation of the test: its capacity to measure innate ability. However, because the hierarchy at ETS and CEEB no longer cling to this view and are quite willing to admit that the test is a measure of acquired skills—albeit acquired over long years of schooling—establishing that the test is susceptible to teaching no longer has the sting it once did.

A much more important concern is the income level of a student's family. To the extent that it is possible for middle-class students to enroll in expensive training programs, enhance their skills, obtain higher scores, and thereby increase their chance to be admitted to selective schools, the more such tests will favor higher socioeconomic status (SES) students. Of course upper SES students already enjoy a tremendous advantage by virtue of just being able to afford the tuition at exclusive colleges and universities.

One impediment to arriving at an answer to the question of whether such training programs are effective stems from the variability among programs. Test preparation can range from short-duration instruction in test taking and testwiseness to practice on sample tests, all the way to intensive programs with the goal of improving underlying verbal and mathematical ability.

Interpreting the results of research is difficult because the usual way to determine if programs are effective is to compare test performance before and after instruction. Students do not usually take the test for a second time or enroll in programs to increase their score unless they have done poorly (or anticipate that they will do poorly). Improvement over two administrations tends to appear larger because of the imperfect reliability of the test, which causes the scores to regress toward the mean on the second administration.

The experience of having taken the test once seems to have a positive effect, as does practicing with one of the commercially prepared workbooks. These are helpful because they familiarize the student with the test instructions and the different types of items that appear on it. They are also much less expensive than commercial programs.

The general consensus among those who have studied the issue is that a short-term course will not improve the scores more than about 10 points, whereas intensive training over an extended period of time may be more helpful. Most efforts to improve performance have focused on vocabulary, but memorizing vocabulary is difficult and not likely to be successful. The best advice to someone who wants to improve his or her scores is to read a great deal, particularly difficult books with sophisticated vocabulary.

Performance on the quantitative section of the test seems to be more easily improved than the verbal section. This section of the test is structured to assess math reasoning more than to assess specific operations. The more knowledgeable about mathematics a student becomes, the quicker he or she can work, and the higher the score obtained. Even though it is possible to obtain average scores relying on logical thinking alone, high scores on the quantitative section of the test are likely to be attained only by students with a strong math background. A review of basic mathematical concepts and experience with practice problems can have a positive effect on performance on this section.

Validity

The validity of an aptitude test is generally assessed by means of establishing the relationship between the test score and a criterion measure. In this case freshman college achievement (FCA) in the form of GPA. Such an approach has the advantage of simplicity; it would seem that nothing could be easier than establishing the relationship through correlation and then resolving the issue once and for all. However, as has been illustrated throughout this textbook, there is nothing simple and straightforward about the interpretation of correlations.

There are a large number of studies of the predictive validity of the SAT that tend to yield a wide range of results. There are studies that show virtually no relationship, and others that show correlations as high as .70 (Jensen, 1981). ETS (1980) reports that the median validity coefficient for 827 studies was .37 for the verbal section and .32 for the math section. When the two are combined, a multiple correlation of .41 is obtained. The correlation with the high school record (HSR) was .52; when the SAT and HSR are combined, a value of .58 is obtained. These are the figures to which both those who believe the test is valid and those who criticize its validity agree. The only exception to this acceptance is that Allan Nairn (1980), a critic of the SAT, in a study of the SAT commissioned by Ralph Nader, erroneously averaged the verbal and mathematical sections to obtain a combined prediction of .345. This is wrong. A combination of the two should predict better than either by itself. If this were not the case, it would make sense to use only the SAT-V and ignore the SAT-M.

These validity coefficient are conservative because they are medians of a large number of studies conducted over a long period of time. Recent trends are for the SAT to increase in validity while HSR becomes a poorer predictor. The predictive validity for HSR is declining because of grade inflation in high school, which restricts the range of the GPAs (Bejar & Blew, 1981). Because the pool of available high school seniors is declining and schools are being forced to become less selective (Bracey, 1980), the range of SAT scores is increasing—which will also cause the validity coefficient for the SAT to increase.

Although there is agreement about the magnitude of the validity coefficient, it is the interpretation of its values that has led to controversy. Nairn (1980), together with Ralph Nader, and with the support of Warner Slack and Douglas Porter (1980), has severely criticized the SAT in general; in particular he has taken issue with the position that the coefficients presented should be interpreted as supportive of the view that the SAT is valid.

Nairn interprets the validity coefficient in two ways. First, he squares the correlation between SAT and FCA (incorrectly using the value of .345, rather than .41), which yields an index of determination of .12. Although this is not generally considered a legitimate method of interpreting the validity coefficient (ETS, 1980; Cronbach & Gleser, 1965), it is at least credible if it were used as a means of explaining variance in HSR by the SAT. Instead, Nairn asserts that the obtained value represents the percentage of times that the SAT would predict FCA better than by chance. There is no known support in any manual or textbook for this interpretation. This is not only an egregious use of statistics, but it makes no sense intuitively. The worst possible test, one with no reliability whatsoever, would predict better than chance, half of the time.

Nairn also uses a statistic called the index of forecasting efficiency. This is another statistical method of transforming a correlation that causes the validity coefficient to look smaller and that, according to the statistical and testing literature, is used incorrectly by Nairn. These values are then interpreted by using percentages that make the increase in knowledge obtained by the SAT look trivial. Rex Jackson (1980) and ETS (1980) interpreted the data differently and obtained percentages that are very supportive of the test's validity.

It seems futile to take on ETS and its allies in the testing and statistics field, on their home court, using the weapons of sophisticated correlational statistics. R. A. Weitzman (1982) provides an elegant example of how statistics can be used to defend the validity of the SAT. He begins with the same basic values that all parties seemed to have accepted (the correlation between SAT and FCA set at .41, between HSR and FCA at .52, and a combination of the two being .58). He begins by demonstrating, statistically, a point that Slack and Porter (1980) had arrived at intuitively. Weitzman shows that admissions officers in colleges and universities place more weight on the SAT than HSR, despite the fact that the HSR is a more valid predictor. He shows that the correlation between admission to college and SAT is .49, whereas it is only .33 for HSR. He then feeds these data into other regression formulas that correct for the restriction in range resulting from the higher weighting of the SAT; he comes up with a corrected validity for the SAT of .64, .60 for HSR, and .76 for a combination of the two.

The basic agreed on coefficients have been interpreted in ways that stretch from the position that 88 percent of the time you are better off flipping a coin rather than using the SATs, to a corrected validity coefficient of .76. Although this does not illustrate very much that is profound about the validity of the test, it does show the futility of ever resolving the issue statistically.

Cost/Benefit of College Aptitude Tests

The widespread use of college aptitude tests was once heralded as a force for social change because they allowed decisions concerning who would be favored by admittance to selective schools to be based solely on ability. Those with ability could rise on the social ladder regardless of family background, while those at the top who lacked ability would find it difficult to maintain their position. Testing, therefore, could be viewed as a potent force for social mobility. Unfortunately, this seemed to work only along socioeconomic lines and not in terms of cultural and ethnic background. For blacks it tends to be regressive because it provides a concrete basis for denials of admissions to desired schools and is thus more difficult to reverse.

As with other mental ability tests, black students do not, on the average, perform as well as white students on the SAT. In 1980–81, of 75,000 blacks who took the test, only 70 scored higher than 700 on the Verbal section; 156 scored higher than that value on the Quantitative section. In that year, for white students the average scores were 442 and 483 for the Verbal and Quantitative sections, respectively; for blacks the averages were 332 and 362 (Connell, 1982).

Although blacks are attending undergraduate and graduate schools in much greater numbers than in the past, they are still woefully underrepresented. One compromise is not to require minority candidates to meet requirements in terms of test scores. For instance, some graduate schools waive the requirement for graduate exam test scores in the case of black applicants. This approach leads to admission policies that are biased in favor of upper-middle-class blacks because instead of tested ability, background and interviewing skills become paramount. This procedure also creates the situation where students are placed in a highly competitive academic climate lacking the same chance of success as those with whom they are competing. Such a situation is damaging to the involved students' self-esteem and is probably a net loss to the minority group involved. A better solution, albeit one that it of doubtful legality, is the use of quotas. The same criteria can be used for all students, but the best students of every group are admitted according to predetermined proportions.

Are the Tests Really Used?

According to the popular press, the importance of performance on scholastic aptitude tests has never been higher. Changes in national averages are headline news, and controversies about coaching and questions about validity have received extensive coverage. Despite the publicity, the importance of performance on such tests is actually declining. As a result of the diminishing pool of high school graduates intending to enter higher education, universities and colleges are being forced to become less selective. Their only alternative is to face drastically reduced enrollments and suffer the severe economic penalities that such a change would necessitate. The change in admissions policies gets little publicity because there is not much to be gained from informing school alumnae and boards of trustees that standards are being lowered.

This brings us to the strongest criticism of the use of scholastic aptitude tests: they often are not really used (Bracey, 1980). A panel of educators formed by the National Academy of Sciences has suggested that, except for highly selective schools, scholastic aptitude tests are an unnecessary expense and inconvenience.

It certainly seems unfair to require all students to pay a fee approaching $20 to take a test that is not really necessary. High school seniors should not be expected to bear the cost of sparing alumnae the dreary news that high standards cannot be maintained. Gerald Bracey (1980), reports that some schools have requested that students retake the test, even though they have already been accepted, in order to raise the average score of incoming freshmen. Some schools with open admissions policies require students to take the tests, even though all students with high school diplomas are accepted.

There is also some movement in the opposite direction. Some schools that previously maintained an open admissions policy are now requiring that students meet minimum levels of performance on the tests. This presents some problems because the tests are constructed to make the best discriminations at the upper ends of the scale. They are likely to be much less reliable for making decisions at the low end.

Screening Job Applicants

Mental abilities tests are used both in civil service exams and for screening job applicants. They are used not because they are particularly effective, but because something is needed and there are no better alternatives. Success on most jobs depends on a variety of skills that are independent of academic aptitude.

The test developer for an industry or branch of the civil service who sits down to build an instrument that can discriminate between those who are likely to be successful and those who are likely to fail at a given job has few alternatives. Because we lack good criteria for determining who will be successful and who will not, an empirical approach to item selection is ruled out. What has usually happened is that, in the process of development, the tests have evolved into an assessment of the same skills measured on other group mental ability tests. Because validity is difficult to establish and reliability is relatively easily obtained, the focus shifts to this criteria. The items that lead to the greatest internal consistency are those that measure verbal ability, such as vocabulary, analogies, reading comprehension, and general word-use skills. Through the process of selecting and rejecting items, regardless of how they started out, such tests pick up more and more verbal content because those items contribute to high reliability.

Such tests are usually made to at least look as though they are measuring what they are supposed to measure. It is unacceptable to have entry into the police force be based on performance on a test of verbal ability. Vocabulary tests are constructed to include words such as *jurisprudence*, *habeas corpus*, *interrogation*, and the like; this makes them look like a test for policemen, which makes them more acceptable. These kinds of requirements sometimes are imposed by the courts.

Civil service and other job-related tests should be required to have at least a modicum of predictive-related validity. If it can be shown that the job requires a high level of verbal intelligence, a test measuring that construct could be justified; otherwise, it is unfair to use such a test.

This position is supported by such federal regulations as the *Uniform Guidelines on Employee Selection Procedure*, adopted by the Equal Employment Opportunity Commission, the Office of Personnel Management, and the departments of Justice and Labor. These rules were developed as a response to the Civil Rights Act of 1964 and the litigation that followed with the support of civil rights groups. The rules require that the tests be valid, as defined by the *Standards for Educational and Psychological Tests* (1985), published by the American Psychological Association.

Even if a test is valid, according to these standards it still must be shown that the testing program does not have an adverse effect on any minority group. The burden of proof that the test is fair rests with the employer, and he or she is also required to keep records to demonstrate that the effects of the screening procedures are nondiscriminatory.

Multiple-Aptitude Tests

As discussed in Chapter 13, one of the most prominent issues surrounding intelligence testing concerns the question of whether intelligence is unidimensional or multidimensional—that is to say, whether the term *intelligence* refers only to a set of separate abilities or to a single entity called intelligence. The authors of most intelligence tests have constructed instruments that yield a single score, which indicates support for a unitary view of intelligence. In many cases, despite the inconsistency of the practice, they go on to report subscores along with the unitary intelligence score. There have been some instruments developed that are based on multifactor definitions of intelligence. Most of those tests are not well known or often used. Those that are include a series of instruments that have for their focus the provision of information that is intended to be used to assist individuals making career and educational decisions. Unlike group intelligence tests, the use of which has declined, multiple-aptitude tests are being administered on a widespread basis in secondary schools. Engen, Lamb, and Prediger (1982) report that, in a survey of standardized test use in 597 junior high schools, 93 percent of the schools made some use of career guidance tests, and most of that use involved the administration of multiple-aptitude tests.

For those involved in career and/or educational counseling, a test capable of specifying the college major or job for which a person is best suited seems like a wonderful tool for facilitating the process. The construction and use of such tests are based on the following assumptions: (1) that human mental ability is defined by a series of relatively independent separate abilities, (2) that different career choices and college majors require separate abilities or combinations of abilities for success, and (3) that it is possible to match individual profiles of abilities to the requirements of careers and majors. The legitimacy of such tests depends on the degree to which these assumptions can be met.

The three most often-used multiple-aptitude tests are the Differential Aptitude Test (DAT), the General Aptitude Test Battery (GATB), and the Armed Services Vocational Aptitude Battery (ASVAB).

The Differential Aptitude Test (DAT)

The Differential Aptitude Test (DAT) first appeared in 1947 and was authored by George K. Bennett, Harold G. Seashore, and Alexander G. Wesman. It is used primarily with high school students, and it is intended to assist them in making decisions concerning their choice of a college major. The scales on the test were selected because they seemed to reflect useful categories to meet the practical needs of counseling. They were not selected using factor analysis and tend to be factorially complex, which means that each scale may measure more than one factor. The scales on the test areas follow:

1. Verbal Reasoning *(VR)*—Completion of verbal analogies.
2. Numerical Abilities *(NA)*—Mathematical computations.
3. Abstract Reasoning *(AR)*—Pattern recognition in geometric shapes.
4. Space Relations *(SR)*—Mental rotation of geometric shapes.
5. Mechanical Reasoning *(MR)*—Answering questions that require mechanical knowledge.
6. Clerical Speed and Accuracy *(CSA)*—Copying patterns onto answer sheets.
7. Spelling *(Sp)*—Discrimination between correctly and incorrectly spelled words.
8. Language Usage *(LU)*—Identification of poor grammar.

The *VR* and *AR* scales assess the same broad intellectual abilities that are generally included on mental ability and intelligence tests. *NA*, *Sp*, and *LU* represent school-related achievement tests. *SR*, *CSA*, and *MR* include tasks that appear job related and are intended to be useful in vocational counseling. Except for *CSA*, which assess how quickly the student works and is therefore labeled a speeded task, the DAT is a power test.

Scores are reported using stanines and percentiles on well-constructed reporting forms that utilize normalized percentile charts to correct for unequal differences between percentiles. Percentile bands are provided to aid in distinguishing between those differences that are significant and those that are more likely to have occurred by chance. Procedures of test construction and norming are carefully described in the technical manual, giving the impression of technical expertise. The test is characterized by good reliability, with coefficients on the individual scales in the .90s.

With a test intended to measure individual abilities, it is important that the intercorrelations among scales be as small as possible. This is unfortunately a difficult goal to achieve, and it was not reached in the case of the DAT. Many correlations between scales are in the .50s and .60s. This is most likely the result of the general ability that underlies the different scales and the decision not to construct the test using factor analysis.

The DAT has been shown to be a reasonably good predictor of school performance as measured by both concurrent high school grades and college GPA. A combination of *VR* and *NA* provides the best prediction. The DAT is therefore able to do what other scholastic aptitude tests do—predict GPA—and it does it in much the same way, by assessing verbal and quantitative abilities. Evidence to show that there are unique profiles associated with specific college majors is lacking. To demonstrate the advantages of DAT scores over SAT and ACT scores, one should be able to advise high school students legitimately that they would be more successful in one major than another—for instance, in English rather than in engineering. There is no evidence that such advice can legitimately be rendered, for which there are two probable causes: (1) the individual scales measure general, rather than unique, abilities; and (2) the criterion of grades is dependent on so many complex factors that specific abilities and skills play only a small part.

A DAT Career Planning Program is available that utilizes additional information about interest obtained from the student taking the test. A computer printout containing recommendations about approximate college majors and careers is then provided. Although the program appears carefully constructed and is based on the best existing expertise, there is a lack of substantiation for the interpretations provided. If it cannot be shown that student profiles can be matched with career and college majors, there is no magic within a computer that can make the recommendations valid. There is a risk that the computer and its printout will confer a degree of legitimacy and certitude to interpretations that should be made only with considerable reservation.

The General Aptitude Test Battery (GATB)

The GATB was introduced in 1947 by the United States Employment Service (USES) to be used in career counseling in its state employment offices. It has also been made available to nonprofit organizations, including high schools and colleges. It consists of twelve subtests that are used to measure nine factors. The subtests follow:

1. Name Comparisons—The examinee must indicate if two names are the same.
2. Computation—Speed of answering simple computations.
3. Three-Dimensional Space—Correctly matching a three dimensional figure with a two dimensional figure.
4. Vocabulary—Identification of synonyms and antonyms.
5. Tool Matching—Selection of a specific tool from tools that appear similar.
6. Arithmetic Reasoning—Solving arithmetic word problems.
7. Form Matching—Selection of a stimulus from among several similar stimuli.
8. Mark Making—Speed of making a pattern on an answer sheet with a pencil.
9. Place—Moving pegs from one hole to another.
10. Turn—Speed of manipulation of pegs (turning them over).

11. Assemble—Speed of placing washers on rivets.
12. Disassemble—Speed of removing washers from rivets.

The ability factors and the tests on which they are based follow:

1. General Mental Ability—Vocabulary, arithmetic, and reasoning.
2. Verbal Aptitude—Vocabulary.
3. Numerical Ability—Computation, arithmetic, and reasoning.
4. Spatial Aptitude—Three-dimensional space.
5. Form Perception—Tool matching and form matching.
6. Clerical Perception—Name Comparison.
7. Motor Coordination—Mark making.
8. Manual Dexterity—Place and turn.
9. Finger Dexterity—Assemble and disassemble

Scores for the nine ability factors were determined by converting the raw scores to standard scores with a mean of 100 and a standard deviation of 20, using norms based on a 1940 sample of four thousand subjects selected to be representative of workers at that time. An analysis of each occupation was made to determine which factors were critical for it. These are called Special Aptitude Test Batteries, or SATBs. This analysis was based on such considerations as their importance to the job, correlation with a criterion variable, high means, and low variability. Once the factors associated with an occupation were identified, minimum scores for each factor were set for each occupation. This use of minimum acceptable scores is called the multiple cutoff method of determining profiles. Cutoffs for factor scores for groups of occupations, called Occupational Ability Patterns (OAPs), were also determined.

The reliability of the GATB using equivalent form and test-retest is in the acceptable .80 to .90 range. There is a massive amount of data available on the validity of the GATB, which primarily consists of correlations of SATBs with measures of job success or performance in training. The correlations tend to be in the .30s and .40s, the samples are small, and there is a lack of cross-validation. The biggest limitation is the ex post facto nature of the analysis. Under these circumstances it is not clear to what degree aptitude could have developed once a person was on the job. It is also unclear to what degree individuals select a job because of certain aptitudes they have, despite the fact that those aptitudes are unnecessary for success in the job. Even with the limitations of these studies, their volume is impressive.

There are some criticisms of the GATB. First of all, the use of multiple cutoff scores is difficult to defend. A person is not deemed to have an aptitude for a specific occupation if his or her scores on even one factor are below the cutoff. This is so even if the individual has extremely high scores in the other relevant factors. Multiple regression techniques could be used, and they would permit such compensation. When the test was developed such sophisticated techniques were not available, but with the availability of computers today there is no reason to stick with such an outmoded approach.

The test is also too dependent on the speed of the examinee, which may not be appropriate as a predictor for occupations where this trait is less important. It also makes the test inappropriate for individuals with handicapping conditions that affect their response speed but that may not interfere with their ability to perform on the job. This would be true of older examinees because response speed tends to decline as a function of age.

The Armed Services Vocational Aptitude Battery (ASVAB)

Since World War I the armed forces have been administering group ability tests for the purpose of obtaining the most appropriate assignment of recruits. In 1958 the Air Force made an abbreviated version of their aptitude test available for use in high schools; shortly afterward the Army and Navy did the same thing with their aptitude tests. This was done for several reasons: first, to assist students in making decisions about military careers; second, as a service to students who wanted to understand their own abilities so that they could make better decisions about careers; and last, but not least, as a recruiting tool. The provision of this service gave recruiters entry into the school system and access to high school students that they might want to recruit. The awkwardness of having different recruiters trying to have their test administered in the same school resulted in the Office of the Assistant Secretary of Defense for Manpower requiring the creation of a single test that could be used primarily for placement of recruits in the different branches of the military services and secondarily as a service to high schools for purposes of career counseling (Cronbach, 1979). The test that was developed was titled the Armed Services Vocational Aptitude Battery (ASVAB). There have been a series of versions and forms since its introduction, the most recent of which is ASVAB 14, which was first administered in July 1984.

The ASVAB is administered by military service representatives and scored using their facilities. The results are returned to the school counselor, without charge. The results also are sent to recruiters for each of the military branches in the area, who use the information to contact students for purposes of recruitment. Counselors can specify a broad range of limitations to this recruiting: they can specify the time period that they would like to have pass before the results are passed on to recruiters; and they can specify that no telephone contacts be made or that no recruiters contact the students. Because most school counselors are limited in the resources that they have available for administering vocational tests, this free service is very attractive. As a result, the ASVAB has become the most often administered standardized test used in secondary school today. Engen, Lamb, and Prediger (1982) reported that 93 percent of junior high and senior high schools surveyed used career guidance tests; of those, 66 percent were administering the ASVAB, 34 percent reported using the DAT, 24 percent the GATB, 20 percent the Kuder Occupational Inventory Scale, and 19 percent the Strong-Campbell Interest Inventory.

The appropriateness of using these test services as a means for recruiters to gain entry into the school has been questioned, as have the test's poor psychometric qualities. In 1976, Lee J. Cronbach, a highly respected testing specialist, was asked to review the test for the *Eighth Mental Measurements Yearbook*. Although it is not unusual for a reviewer to criticize a test that he or she has been asked to review, Cronbach's displeasure with the test was extreme. He was convinced that the test was so flawed that its use should be halted immediately. He sent letters and copies of his review to members of Congress and other organizations, with this goal in mind. The version of the test being used at the time was ASVAB 76. The response to the criticism, of Cronbach and others was to revise the test with a version called ASVAB 77 Form 5. Although this version was an improvement, Cronbach (1979) remained critical. He felt that the general reliability was too low, that the reliability of the differences between subscales was not satisfactory, and the validity of the test for military occupations could not necessarily be generalized to civilian occupations. Furthermore, the manuals that accompanied the test for use by counselors made recommendations that were neither supported by research nor logic.

A new version, the ASVAB 14, first used in July 1984, is made up of ten subtests, eight which are power tests and two which are speeded:

1. General Science—Knowledge of basic science facts.
2. Arithmetic Reasoning—Ability to solve arithmetic word problems.
3. Word Knowledge—Ability to define words.
4. Paragraph Comprehension—Ability to answer questions about short paragraphs.
5. Numerical Operations—Speed in answering simple arithmetic operations.
6. Coding Speed—Speed with which numbers can be associated with words from a given code.
7. Auto and Shop Information—Knowledge of tools and shop techniques and practices.
8. Mathematics Knowledge—Knowledge of high school level mathematical principles.
9. Mechanical Comprehension—Ability to solve mechanical problems.
10. Electronics Information—Knowledge of electrical, radio, and electronics information.

Scores on the subtests are not used for counseling; instead, the focus is on composites made up of combinations of subtests. There are three academic composites and four occupational composites:

Academic Composites

1. Academic Ability—Word Knowledge, Paragraph Comprehension, and Arithmetic Reasoning.
2. Verbal—Word Knowledge, Paragraph Comprehension, and General Science.
3. Math—Mathematics Knowledge and Arithmetic Reasoning.

Occupational Composites

1. Mechanical and Crafts—Arithmetic Reasoning, Mechanical Comprehension, Auto and Shop Information, and Electronics Information.
2. Business and Clerical—Word Knowledge, Paragraph Comprehension, Mathematics Knowledge, and Coding Speed.
3. Electronics and Electrical—Arithmetic Reasoning, Mathematics Knowledge, Electronics Information, and General Sciences.

4. Health, Social, and Technology—Word Knowledge, Paragraph Comprehension, Arithmetic Reasoning, and Mechanical Comprehension.

Numerical operations is used only in military career guidance.

For ASVAB 14, information on the reliability of the subtests is not yet available. Instead, reliability for the composites is reported, and they are in the .90s. Reliabilities such as these are not necessarily desirable. It would be better if the reliabilities of the subtests were in the .90s. Reliability for the composite should be much lower and not be reported. If each subtest is measuring a unique ability, the subtests would not be correlated; consequently, the reliability of a combination of subtests would not be very high. The cause of the homogeneity within the composites stems from the similar content of the subtests. School-related ability, knowledge, and information are the main focus of the subtests. Unlike the GATB, which is also intended to assess job-related skills, the ASVAB does not assess spatial ability or include manipulative performance tasks. The DAT, which is primarily intended to assist students in making decisions about a college major, includes the assessment of a broader range or abilities than does the ASVAB.

The composite scores also are highly intercorrelated. This occurs both because the same subtests are used in different composites and because the subtests appear to be measuring similar constructs. An examination of Table 15.1 reveals the magnitude of the intercorrelations—in many cases just slightly below their reliabilities. The smallest is 78, between the Verbal and Math composites. The DAT has been criticized for intercorrelations in the .50s and .60s, but the ASVAB is far worse, with intercorrelations mostly in the .80s and .90s. This is unacceptable in a test intended to assess separate abilities. The most obvious conclusion is that this is a test that tries to look like it is measuring separate abilities by reporting subtest and composite scores, but is in fact measuring only general ability. The main result of such a high intercorrelations is that most who take the test will have a flat profile—all of the scores will be about the same—which defeats the purpose of differential aptitude testing.

Validity of the Test for Nonmilitary Use The case for the validity of the ASVAB is based largely on studies that show correlations between composites and criteria associated with job success in the military or grades in a military school. Individuals with high scores on the Business and Clerical composite are likely to be successful in a business or clerical-related position in the armed services, whereas a low score is more likely associated with a lack of success. Of course, a high score on the Mechanical and Crafts composite will also predict success in business or clerical

TABLE 15.1 Intercorrelations of Composites of the ASVAB for Males in Grades 11–12

Composites	AA	Verbal	Math	MC	BC	EE
Verbal	.93					
Math	.92	.78				
Mechanical and crafts	.87	.83	.80			
Business and clerical	.91	.88	.89	.78		
Electronics and electrical	.94	.90	.93	.92	.89	
Health, social, and technology	.97	.91	.89	.94	.89	.96

occupations, as will any of the other composites because they are so highly correlated. The most important use for a multiple-aptitude test is not to provide information about general ability—which is already available from other sources—but to provide information about which of several career choices should be made. In most cases students will do about the same on the different composites. Therefore, they are not given useful information to help them in making decisions about the particular job for which they are best suited.

The case for the validity of the ASVAB for civilian occupations is based on the assertion that for military occupations there is generally an equivalent civilian occupation. Unfortunately, there are large numbers of civilian occupations for which there is no equivalent military speciality. Evidence that military and civilian occupations with the same titles require the same abilities for success is not presented. In all likelihood there are occupations that are the same and others that are different.

Further evidence for the validity of the ASVAB is based on the idea of *validity generalization*, in which the validity of one test is generalized to another. Using this approach the validity of the GATB is somehow generalized to the ASVAB. Not only is the validity of the GATB less than sparkling, but the content of the two tests is far from identical.

Conclusions About the ASVAB ASVAB 14 does include several improvements over previous versions of the test. The reliability of the composites is certainly high but, as pointed out earlier, it is probably too high. The manuals have toned down their claims for the test and are more conservative in their recommendations.

The biggest problem with the test is that it is not capable of serving the purpose for which it is intended. The test is so dominated by a general ability factor that it provides little differential information. By being so closely tied to military career choices, most of the professions are excluded and the student is left with mainly technical and skilled occupations.

In summary, even though the test booklet, test administration, test scoring, and reporting of results are provided for free, this may not be a bargain. The scores provided may not make any real contribution beyond the information provided by the SAT and ACT.

Conclusions About the Use of Multiple-Aptitude Tests

The goal of developing an assessment tool that can provide information to individuals concerning the career for which they are best suited is certainly worthy. The attractiveness of such an instrument to vocational counselors is obvious. However, success in the construction of such tests is not easily achieved. Human abilities are not easily differentiated, and it is difficult to isolate the specific abilities required for different careers.

The task of determining the most appropriate college major differs from the task of selecting occupations. The prediction of college majors has the advantage of a relatively good criterion of success in GPA, but there does not seem to be a sufficiently large difference among the abilities required for success in different college majors. They all seem dependent on verbal ability. For the selection of occupation there do appear to be differences in required abilities, but there is seldom a satisfactory criterion of success. We are usually left with nothing but supervisor ratings to measure job success.

The authors of multiple-aptitude tests have failed to show that they can isolate a reliable profile of abilities in individuals and match it to the requirements of college majors and/or occupations. It is difficult to show that these instruments are more effective than measures of general ability. Information about general ability is less useful because a high score merely suggests that the individual could succeed at all careers and a low score suggests that he or she could succeed at few.

Conclusions

The case for the continued use of individual intelligence tests as one part of a psychological assessment to determine whether to place a child in special classes seems strong. The elimination of such instruments would ultimately work to the disadvantage of those children most needing help. The case for the use of aptitude tests for admissions to colleges, universities, and graduate schools is somewhat equivocal, but it can be made, based on the assumption that this is the best method we presently have. The use of mental ability tests for occupational screening is weak, and their use is hard to justify on other than utilitarian grounds.

The question of whether mental ability tests should continue to be used can be answered on a case-by-case basis, as has been done in preceding sections of this book. They can be viewed as a useful, if somewhat dangerous, tool whose value, under certain circumstances, is great enough to justify their continued use, despite their potential for abuse.

Philosophical positions concerning mental abilities testing can be categorized into three groups: (1) those espousing a meritocracy, for which the tests are viewed positively because of their beneficial affect on social mobility; (2) classic elitist views that oppose the tests because they pose a threat to the status quo and a rigid class system; and (3) egalitarian positions that oppose the tests because they emphasize differences that are believed to harm the disadvantaged. The pose of egalitarianism also provides a good cover for classic elitism.

The bulk of the last three chapters has provided a defense of mental testing, and it is an area much in need of being defended. The defense of mental ability testing depends on its value in sustaining the meritocracy in which we now find ourselves. Unfortunately, the benefits of our meritocracy have not, for the most part, accrued to minorities. Instead, our society is experiencing a process of reordering; power is shifting into the hands of those who control information to the technocrats and their "staff," who have gotten where they are based on demonstrated ability, rather than on any other factor. This is all right if you possess characteristics that are valued and are a beneficiary of that system. If you do not and are not, and there is no way that your deficiencies can be remedied, you will feel trapped, with no chance for success. It is unlikely that your sympathies will favor the meritocratic view of society.

The history of the development of intelligence tests also should give the advocate of these tests reason to pause. Some of the founders of the mental abilities testing movement, for instance, Sir Francis Galton and Karl Pearson, opposed the immigration of Jews into England on the basis of genetic inferiority. Goddard viewed immigrants as a class as being inferior. The view of the early developers of intelligence tests was that intelligence was immutable, permanent, and determined largely by genetics. There is no great leap from eugenics to genocide. It was recently revealed that in Virginia in the 1920s a sterilization program was implemented for those considered mentally defective. If members of minority groups remain skeptical of the intelligence tests movement, here is evidence that they are justified. Others can argue that mental tests are valuable and useful tools, like screwdrivers, and no one should complain if screwdrivers drive nails poorly. However, although we also might agree that dynamite is useful and effective for removing an unwanted tree stump from our backyard, we might not want to advocate that it be sold at the corner hardware store.

SUMMARY

1. Group testing of intelligence got its start with the Army Alpha and Army Beta tests, which were used to screen inductees into the armed services during World War I.
2. Care should be taken to ensure that test publishers and consumers alike do not attach too much importance to the distinction between aptitude and achievement.
3. Academic aptitude tests such as the SAT and the ACT are similar to group tests of intelligence.
4. The decline in scholastic aptitude test scores cannot be attributed to any single cause; it is most likely the result of multiple factors.
5. Existing evidence suggests that coaching can increase scholastic test scores only by relatively small amounts.
6. Evidence concerning the validity of scholastic aptitude tests is mixed. There is evidence to support the view that they are highly valid, invalid, or somewhere in between.
7. Test developers have not met with much success in predicting occupational success when they stray from the prediction of academically related skills.
8. There are three major multiple-aptitude tests. The DAT is a power test primarily used to help high school students select appropriate college majors. The GATB is used as an aid in vocational guidance for nonprofessional occupations. It is primarily a speeded test. The ASVAB is mainly intended to guide the assignment of recruits within the armed services, but it is now being used extensively with high school students. It is made available free of charge by armed forces recruiters.

SUGGESTED READINGS

ANASTASI, A. (1982). *Psychological testing*. New York: Macmillan. [This book is an excellent source of information on group intelligence and multiple-aptitude tests.]

CRONBACH, L. J. (1979). The armed services vocational aptitude battery—a test battery in transition. *The Personnel and Guidance Journal, 57,* 232–237. [In this article Cronbach presents an extremely critical discussion of this particular aptitude test.]

NAIRN, A., & ASSOCIATES. (1980). *The reign of ETS: The corporation that makes up minds*. Washington, D.C.: Ralph Nader. [This book presents the arguments against the use of standardized tests, in particular the SAT.]

SHERTZER, B., & LINDEN, J. D. (1979). *Fundamentals of individual appraisal*. Boston:

Houghton. [This is a good source for brief descriptions of group ability tests.]
THORNDIKE, R. L., & HAGEN, E. P. (1977). *Measurement and evaluation in psychology and education, (4th ed.).* New York: Wiley. [Chapter 11 in this book contains a particularly good discussion of the subject of assessing the validity of multiple-aptitude tests.]
TURNBULL, W. W. (1980). *Test use and validity*. Princeton, NJ: ETS. [This is a spirited defense of the use of scholastic aptitude tests. It presents the specific rebuttals of Nairn and the Ralph Nader organization's criticisms of the SAT.]

16

Personality Assessment

OVERVIEW

This chapter covers the methods of assessing human traits that were not included in previous chapters. All traits not classified as measures of ability are considered measures of personality. No attempt has been made to include all possible methods of assessing personality because there are far too many. The most representative are discussed, along with a description of the theoretical and methodological approaches with which they are associated. The chapter is divided into four sections based on different ways of learning about an individual's personality. These include learning about personality by asking the examinee directly (self-reports), asking others (rating scales), observing behaviors (systematic observations), and interpreting an examinee's response to ambiguous stimuli (projective methods). Of these approaches, the most often used is the self-report, which receives the greatest emphasis here.

OBJECTIVES

From this chapter you will learn about personality measures from simple self-report instruments to projective instruments. Specifically, you will learn the following:

- The four ways of assessing personality.
- The three methods of selecting items for objectively scored self-report adjustment scales.
- The different types of interest inventories and how they are developed.
- The best ways to assess attitudes.
- How to learn about personality through intermediaries.
- How direct observations can provide information about personality.
- How projective tests are used to provide information about personality.

Introduction

The assessment of human abilities can be roughly divided into two parts: mental abilities and personality. The assessment of mental abilities, including educational, achievement, intelligence, and various aptitude tests, has appeared in previous chapters in this book. This chapter is devoted entirely to personality assessment. Personality is a broad topic and encompasses a wide range of human characteristics, such as character, temperament, adjustment, interests, and attitudes.

The assessment of mental abilities, although embroiled in controversy, contains methods and instruments that can make a strong claim for respectability. They can be compared favorably to any assessment of human characteristics, including those used in the medical profession. Unfortunately, this is not the case with personality assessment. The methods used tend to be subjective, imprecise, and lacking in validity and reliability.

There are two diametrically opposing theoretical positions, *nomothetic* and *idiographic* (Allport, 1961), that are relevant to the assessment of personality. The nomothetic view is characterized by the belief that personality functions in a rational and predictable manner and that traits exist that are common to all people. It follows from this view that theories and laws can be propounded that are relevant to personality. If one accepts the nomothetic view, it is possible to formulate general rules of personality behavior based on observations. This permits the prediction and explanation of future behaviors and the creation of assessment instruments that yield numerical values.

The idiographic view of personality emphasizes the unique character of personality and asserts that everyone is different—not only different along each of a set of established dimensions (traits and characteristics), but different in the actual structure of the domain. This makes it difficult to devise a systematic theory of personality. According to this view, general categories of personality are precluded. If this view of personality is adopted, then the systematic assessment of personality has no basis because personality is unpredictable.

In this chapter a nomothetic perspective is taken, and it is assumed that it is possible to formulate models of personality that are valid across individuals, permitting us to make predictions about human behavior. Without this assumption, there would be no need to include this chapter. In fact, there seems to be a trend in measurement textbooks, particularly in those that focus on education, to deemphasize the assessment of personality. However, a discussion of measurement that excluded personality would be incomplete.

At one time, personality assessments of all kinds were common in public schools, but with the exception of the widespread use of interest inventories, personality testing in the schools has become increasingly rare. This has occurred because of the stiffer requirements for parental permission that must be satisfied before any testing is permitted. Federal laws related to the education of the handicapped have also tended to restrict the use of personality testing in the schools. For instance, PL 94-142, which is the federal legislation mandating the availability of special education, can be interpreted to require a school that identifies a child as having a personality problem to provide school services adapted to the child's needs. This is an expense that schools prefer to avoid.

There are four major ways of assessing the personality of an individual: (1) by asking the examinee directly (self-reports); (2) by asking others (rating scales); (3) by observing behavior (systematic observation); and (4) by interpreting an examinee's response to ambiguous stimuli (projective methods).

Learning About Personality From An Individual's Self-Report

Learning about a person by analyzing his or her responses to questions has been a commonly used method for assessing, quantifying, and/or explaining personality. Assessments of this type can range from informal interviews all the way to highly structured objective measures of personality. Such approaches are based on the assumption that the information obtained provides an accurate description of an individual. However, the description will be accurate only to the extent that the individual is willing and able to reveal him- or herself.

There are many reasons why individuals might not want to answer questions about themselves honestly. Often they are being assessed because a decision is going to be made about them. It is to be expected that people would hesitate to reveal something that would make them look bad and cause decisions to be made against what they perceive to be their best interests.

In a therapeutic setting, where the presumption can be made that the individual is seeking help and should be willing to be self-revelatory, the person being assessed may be unable to provide accurate information even if he or she wants to. This becomes increasingly true, the deeper the personality is being probed. Insightfulness and the ability to explicate one's deepest feeling are rare traits. The essence of many theories of personality has this conflict between inner-most feelings and what a person consciously reveals as a focus. They emphasize the difficulty in obtaining access to these inner feelings.

Interviews

The interview can be thought of as a purposeful conversation. It is intended to provide information on a quasi-informal basis and is adaptable and flexible. This is usually an advantage, but such procedures can be so unstandardized that they are meaningless. The approach remains one of the most often used types of assessment, simply because it fulfills a need for human involvement in decision-making. There are a number of disadvantages to this approach. Its unstructured nature can result in circumstances where there is little similarity among separate interviews of individuals that are intended to be assessing the same thing. The quality of an interview is determined by the skill of the interviewer. There are many who consider themselves to be good, or at least competent, interviewers, but it is an uncommon skill.

The process is also subject to considerable bias. This can be as fundamental as overt racial and sexual bias, or as subtle as the interactions between the characteristics of the interviewee and the likes and dislikes of the individual conducting the interview. For instance, the interviewer may dislike assertive women or men with blond hair.

When the purpose of the interview is to provide information that is to be used as the basis for important decisions, such as selection for a job or admission to a university, we not only need to be concerned about the degree of truthfulness of the response, but of the possibility of outright faking. Most people, when placed in this setting, are likely to speak and behave in whatever way they believe will result in decisions favorable to themselves. Expressed attitudes and interests may be determined almost entirely by what they think is expected. Under these circumstances, the subject of the interview is likely to concentrate on providing whatever responses they perceive are dictated by the situation.

Unlike mental ability tests, where we are seeking an assessment of an individual's maximum performance, personality tests are intended for the purpose of assessing typical performance. Herein lies the major disadvantage of the interview as an assessment tool. The person being interviewed for a job or possible acceptance by a college or university is likely to be in a state of maximum performance, which means that the personality assessment is likely to provide a misleading perception of the subject's typical level of functioning.

The reliability of the interview tends to vary depending on the degree of standardization of the content of the interview and the degree that interviewers are trained to obtain a common set of data. Moving in the direction of greater standardization of the interview process has the advantage of increasing the similarity of the data collected. This approach is seldom used because it restricts the flexibility of the process. It can also prevent the interviewer from tailoring the process to the unique characteristics of the person being interviewed.

Questionnaires

The use of interviews continues on a widespread basis because of the human need to make decisions about people after having personal contact with them. As a tool for collecting information, it can be inefficient because of the large amount of time that it requires. A more efficient means of collecting information is the questionnaire. It can be administered to large numbers of individuals at once and be structured in such a way that it facilitates the retrieval of information.

One of the most important goals in the development of a questionnaire is ensuring that its construction has a rational basis. Although this abjuration may seem obvious, an examination of questionnaires in use will indicate the lack of thought with which many of those instruments were developed. Instructions need to be clear and concise. When a question is poorly written, the reliability of responses can drop to an unacceptable level. Given the conditions that prevail when most questionnaires are completed, there is usually no opportunity to clarify any confusions. Similarly, the reading level of those filling out the forms must be taken into account because this can place limits on the accuracy of the obtained information.

The biggest problem with the structure of questionnaires is that decisions about what is to be included are too often based on the "kitchen sink approach," where anything and everything is included. Any time a decision is required concerning whether something should be included, it is placed in the questionnaire, on the theory that it is better to have too much information than not enough. Any time it is believed possible that any information might be useful in the future, it is included on the off chance that its usefulness might eventually be established. The result is a loss for all concerned. The person filling out the questionnaire is required to spend an excessive amount of time and experience unneccessary agony to provide all of this information. There is a greater probability that the responses will be provided in a cursory fashion when the instrument is too long. The cost of the questionnaires, as well as their storage increases, and useful information may be submerged under a sea of irrelevancies.

Instead of using this approach, the questionnaire should be developed after decisions have been made concerning what information is needed. The questionnaire should then request only that information. In this way, the resulting questionnaire will be less burdensome to the person completing it, more efficient, and less expensive.

The structure of the questionnaire will depend on whether the results are to be stored in computer memory. Whether this is to be done immediately or is likely to occur at a later point, the questionnaire needs to be developed in such a way that the process is facilitated. As much as possible, responses should be coded numerically to facilitate their storage. Open-ended questions should be avoided whenever possible. Unless these responses can be placed into categories and assigned numbers, they cannot be easily stored in a computer.

When a large number of individuals are to be administered a questionnaire, it is desirable to create forms that can be machine scored. The process of transferring data from the questionnaire to memory storage is the most expensive and difficult part of the analysis process. Using machine-scorable answer sheets can greatly facilitate this process. It is advisable to include a computer consultant in the planning stages of this data collection process. There are methods of questionnaire design that can greatly facilitate the transfer of information to computer storage.

Objectively Scored Self-Report Instruments

Interviews and questionnaires, even when standardized, are dependent on open-ended questions. As a result of subjective interpretations, they do not usually have good psychometric characteristics. The success of the Army Alpha and the Army Beta mental ability tests, and the commercial versions that followed, led psychologists to consider the possibility that personality could be measured in the same objective fashion. Using a format that restricts the examinee to a limited number of responses, these approaches can almost completely eliminate the error resulting from subjective scoring. The adoption of these techniques has led to the development of a large number of objective personality instruments. Their development proceeded in three main directions: adjustment scales, interest scales, and attitude scales.

Adjustment Scales

There are three main approaches to developing adjustment scales: through logical-theoretical analysis, empirical criterion keying, and factor analysis.

Logical-Theoretical Analysis The simplest way to create an instrument is to select items either in terms of what seems to fit logically with the construct under consideration, based on clinical and/or professional experience, or according to a theoretical rationale.

The Woodsworth Personal Data Sheet. One of the earliest attempts to standardize personality assessment using a logical-theoretical approach was the Woodsworth Personal Data Sheet (Woodsworth, 1920) developed during World War I and intended to identify soldiers likely to break down in combat. The need for this test arose from the impracticality of interviewing all recruits. It contained 116 questions that were to be answered yes or no. It included such questions as, "Do you often have nightmares?" and "Did you ever try to commit suicide?" It yielded a single score intended to assess a recruit's degree of maladjustment.

The Mooney Problem Checklist. The Mooney Problem Checklist (Mooney & Gordon, 1950) is an example of a currently administered test illustrating the use of the logical-theoretical approach to selecting items. The test is intended to be used for facilitating counseling interviews, locating students with problems, conducting group guidance, increasing the understanding of the normal student, and as a basis for research. Items for the instrument were obtained from problems that reoccurred in clinical case histories and from statements of problems submitted by four thousand high school students. There are four forms: Junior High (J), High School (H), College (C), and Adult (A).

The examinees check those problems that they believe apply to them. Although it is possible to obtain a score by counting the number of items endorsed, no norms are provided, and it is better to interpret the test clinically on the basis of the counselor's or psychologist's experience. The authors emphasize that this instrument does not measure the intensity of an individual's problems. Objective scoring is not recommended because high scores could be the result of an individual having many problems or a greater-than-usual willingness to admit problems. A low score could either indicate that a person had few problems or that he or she was unwilling or unable to admit to them. Under these circumstances, scores from the test are difficult to interpret.

The Edwards Personal Preference Scale (EPPS). The Edwards Personal Preference Scale (EPPS) is an example of a personality assessment instrument for which items were selected based on theory and on the judgment of the test author. The theory was that of Henry Murray (1938), who articulated a series of human needs that he believed determined personality. Each statement on the EPPS was selected according to its fit with one of fifteen needs described by Murray's theory.

Examples of these needs are achievement, affiliation, and nurturance. The instrument contains 210 items, with each item made up of two statement, each from a different needs scale. The subject chooses the one statement in each pair that is most characteristic of him- or herself.

Allen Edwards, the author of this scale, was very concerned about the fact that on self-report personality tests there is a tendency for the examinee to make only responses that he or she perceives to be socially acceptable. Edwards believed that instruments intended to measure adjustment were inadvertently likely to become measures of an examinee's ability to differentiate between responses that are socially acceptable and those that are unacceptable, rather than a measure of what is intended. To avoid this tendency, the items on the EPPS are arranged in such a way that the paired statements are of equal social desirability.

Because of the forced-choice format used, the structure of the test is ipsative. This means that the scale scores are interdependent. Consequently, a subject's score is most meaningful in terms of within-subject differences, rather than in terms of how the examinee compares with others in a norm group. The test has been normed using about fifteen hundred college students, but the interpretation of the scores using either the percentiles or *T*-scores provided is not very meaningful. A student's high score on a particular need can either be the result of the possession of the trait or because other traits are relatively unimportant.

Anne Anastasi (1982) states that the validity of this test is in doubt because most validity studies have yielded equivocal or contradictory results. This is partially because the ipsative nature of the test does not permit easy evaluation using ordinary methods of validation. Because the magnitude of the subscales is dependent on the relative size of the other subscales, correlations among the subscales tend to be negative, and correlations with outside criteria tend to be near zero.

Empirical Criterion Keying Assessment instruments that must depend on the clinical judgment of their authors, even when objectively scored, maintain a considerable amount of subjectivity. In addition, these tests tend to be vulnerable to faking and can be influenced by the ulterior motives of the examinee.

Empirical criterion keying provides a method for addressing these problems. Items are selected based on how well they discriminate between two criterion groups. For instance, items endorsed by individuals who have been identified as depressed, but not endorsed by nondepressed normal individuals, can be used to make up a depression scale. When the test is administered, individuals who endorse those items are given a higher score on the depression scale. This approach gives the impression of validity and may alleviate, to some degree, a subject's tendency to provide only socially acceptable responses. This works to the extent that items are subtle and do not have an obvious connection with the trait. By endorsing a seemingly innocuous statement, an individual may reveal the existence of a characteristic that he or she might prefer to hide.

The Minnesota Multiphasic Personality Inventory (MMPI). The most widely used personality test is the Minnesota Multiphasic Personality Inventory (MMPI), which employs an empirical criterion keying approach. The MMPI was developed by S. R. Hathaway and J. C. McKinley and was first published in 1943 by the

Psychological Corporation. It was designed to aid in making psychiatric diagnoses. The original intention was to use it to differentiate among specific types of mental illness and not as a general measure of adjustment. Its use has now expanded enormously from this modest beginning.

The MMPI can be administered either individually, using a card-sorting technique, or on a group basis with machine-scorable answer sheets. Items are classified under twenty-six headings. The headings include general health habits, occupational interests, obsessive and compulsive states, and phobias. There are ten clinical scales:

1. Hypochondriasis (*Hs*)—Abnormal concern about health.
2. Depression (*D*)—Lack of hope, poor morale, and dissatisfaction with self.
3. Hysteria (*Hy*)—Complaints about specific physical symptoms.
4. Psychopathic Deviate (*Pd*)—Lack of emotional responses and disregard of social mores.
5. Masculinity-Femininity (*Mf*)—Tendency toward masculine or feminine interests.
6. Paranoia (*Pa*)—Suspicions of persecution.
7. Psychasthenia (*Pt*)—Obsessive-compulsive behavior.
8. Schizophrenia (*Sc*)—Bizarre and unusual thought patterns and divergence from reality.
9. Hypomania (*Ma*)—Overproductivity in thoughts and action.
10. Social Introversion–Extroversion (*Si*)—Withdrawal from social contact.

In addition, there are three validity scores:

1. *The Lie Score* (*L*) consists of items that place the subject in an unrealistically positive light. Persons who respond to too many of these items are believed to be "faking good."
2. *The Validity Score* (*F*) includes items so negative that they are rarely endorsed. High scores on this scale indicate either scoring errors, a subject who is responding in a random fashion or trying to make him- or herself look bad.
3. *The Correction Score* (*K*) is based on the response of individuals who, while having normal profiles, are judged to have clinical syndromes.

The norm sample was made up of clinically diagnosed psychiatric patients categorized into one of eight classifications and a control group that consisted of visitors to Minnesota hospitals. The clinical scales were derived by comparing the specific clinical group, consisting of about fifty subjects, with the normal, or control, group. Items for each scale were selected because they differentiated between the clinical and normal groups. The mean and standard deviation for the norm group on these items was then obtained and used as the basis for the computation of *T*-scores with a mean of 50 and a standard deviation of 10. The masculinity-femininity scale was obtained by determining which items differentiated between males and females in the normal population. The Social Introversion–Extroversion scale was developed by comparing two groups of college students—one group characterized by high scores on a test of introversion-extroversion, and the other by low scores.

Modern use of the MMPI does not emphasize the original scales. They are avoided because they represent outdated clinical categories, are based on inadequate norm groups, are intercorrelated, and are unreliable. Their use with normal populations is awkward because of their emphasis on pathology. There is an additional problem that results from changes in what is considered acceptable behavior that have occured between the 1940s when the test was developed and the present. Because of those differences, it is not unusual to obtain scores of 70 or higher in the normal population. For instance, the personality characteristics of present-day college students turn out to be similar to those labeled as psychopatic in the original norming population.

Although factor analysis might suggest better subscales, the original classifications have not been abandoned because of the extensive research, tradition, and clinical experience associated with the scales. Instead, the interpretation of the original scales has been replaced by the use of profiles. Rather than interpret scales individually, the pattern of all of the scales is examined. Although the original scales are still the basis for the profiles, numbers are used instead of the original scale names. This not only eliminates the obsolete terminology, but also facilitates the coding of profiles. Books called atlases are available that match clinical syndromes with profiles, and vice versa. Once a clinician knows a profile, he or she can look up the diagnosis. Given a diagnosis, the profile with which it is associated can be identified. The information from such atlases also can be stored in computer memory, and the computer can be programmed so that it quickly generates a complete diagnosis from the machine-scorable answer sheets. At first this was only possible on large computers and the answer sheets had to be sent away for this scoring. Disks are now becoming available that can be used with personal computers to obtain the same types of diagnoses that were at one time available only from mainframe computers. Personal computers can analyze results and generate interpretations, but data entry can be laborious. When the analysis is done at a large computer center, machine scorers are available that interpret the answer sheets and then feed the data directly into the computer.

The computer-analysis approach is limited by the difficulties associated with considering the effect of the myriad of factors that have been shown to affect the way a subject responds on this instrument. Sex, race, age, SES, intelligence, and cultural background all can affect the scores on the MMPI. Presumably, the good clinician can take these factors into account better than a computer program, although there is no reason to think that the factors could not eventually be added to the analysis program.

Like any self-report approach to assessing personality, the MMPI is subject to deliberate as well as unintentional distortions by the person taking the test. In most cases this means that the individual is trying to place him- or herself in an unrealistically positive light. Occasionally, individuals might wish to make themselves look bad.

Theoretically, the empirical criterion-keying approach used with the MMPI can correct for these tendencies. Tendencies toward responding in ways that are socially desirable presumably occurred at the same level in the norm groups as in present-day populations taking the inventory. Of greater importance is the fact that the set of items that differentiates between the various syndromes and the normal group is presumed to contain subtle items. For instance, individuals identified in the original norm sample as being paranoid may be more likely to endorse a statement that indicates that they like the color red. A paranoid examinee who wanted to hide this characteristic would have no way of knowing that he or she should avoid endorsing such a statement because there is no obvious connection between a like for this color and a tendency toward paranoia. This does not work as well as the authors intended because most syndromes are defined by rather obvious items.

The *L*, *F*, and *K* scales are intended to detect the subject who is not making a sincere attempt to respond honestly. Unfortunately, these scales represent a somewhat unsophisticated attempt to accomplish this. Whereas the *F* scale may detect the individual who responds haphazardly, or the individual who is trying to appear mentally ill, the *L* scale serves mainly to intimidate the naive examinee who is told that the test has a "lie score" that can detect dishonest responses.

The *K*-scale is somewhat more sophisticated and includes items endorsed by individuals who, despite being mentally disturbed, have normal profiles. This scale is intended to be sensitive to the same sort of tendencies detected by the *L* and *F* scales. Elevated *L* scale scores can be expected to be accompanied by elevated *K* scale scores. Normal subjects who are overly candid and willing to engage in self-criticism and to identify symptoms, even when they are minimal, may obtain low scores on the *K* scale. Low *K*-scale scores are also associated with elevated *F* scales. The *K* scale can be used to correct mathematically an examinee's score either by increasing the scores of those whose maladjustment is masked by a normal profile or by lowering the scores of the individual who is being too open. These transformations seem to have a radical effect on the meaning of the scale scores, greatly altering correlations with criterion variables. Although some studies have supported the view that this approach results in better diagnoses, other research has not been so supportive (Cronbach, 1970).

An example of a computer-generated profile is provided in Figure 16.1. This is from a sample Minnesota Personnel Interpretive Report, which is a trademark owned by the University Press of the University of Minnesota.

Factor-Analytic Approaches The two methods of developing objectively scored personality tests already discussed have statistical characteristics that are often less than desirable. The scales on these instruments are sometimes different from those that would be obtained through factor analysis, which suggests a lack of construct-related validity. Futhermore, the scales often have low internal consistency and tend to be intercorrelated to an unacceptable degree.

The use of factor analysis is intended to eliminate these problems. Unfortunately, the nature of factor analysis is such that it fails to provide a wholly satisfactory solution to the problem of selecting scales.

There are two major problems with using factor analysis for developing scales on a personality test. First, the items on such scales tend to intercorrelate to such a small degree that factor analysis tends to be unstable. Second, there are only two factors that are likely to emerge from such an analysis: introversion–extraversion and degree of adjustment. This latter factor could also be interpreted as either a manifestation of social desirability or the willingness of a person to say negative things about him- or herself (Cronbach, 1970). Edwards (1957) provided dramatic evidence for this, although its existence had long been suspected. He had 152 subjects rate the social desirability of 140 items from the MMPI and found a .86

Figure 16.1
MMPI profile.

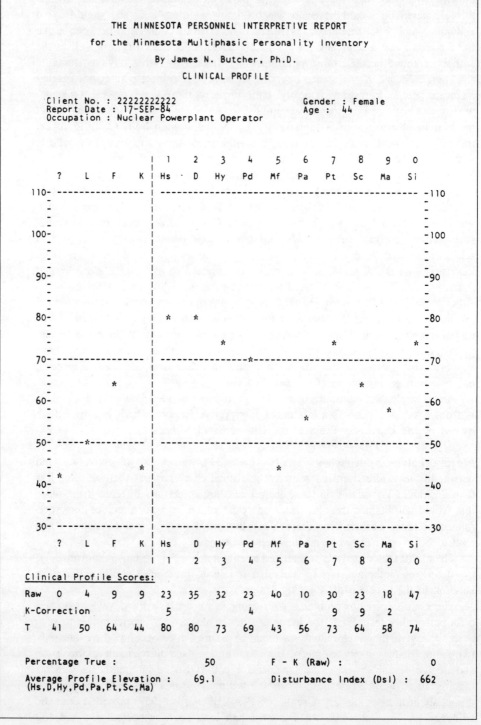

THE MINNESOTA PERSONNEL INTERPRETIVE REPORT

for the Minnesota Multiphasic Personality Inventory

By James N. Butcher, Ph.D.

CLINICAL PROFILE

Client No. : 22222222222
Report Date : 17-SEP-84
Occupation : Nuclear Powerplant Operator

Gender : Female
Age : 44

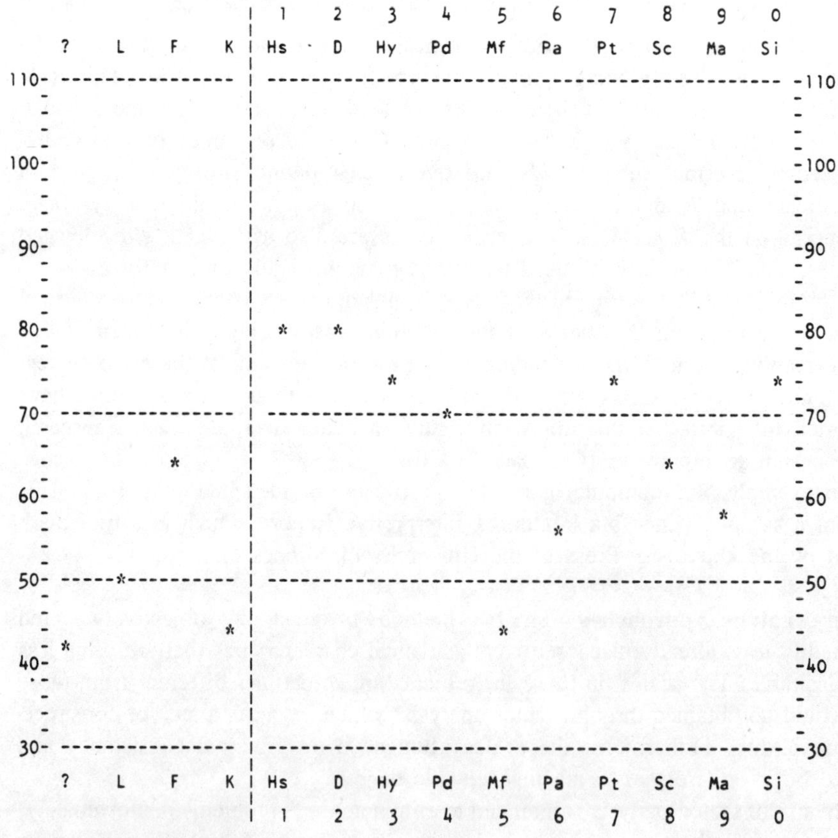

<u>Clinical Profile Scores:</u>

	?	L	F	K	Hs	D	Hy	Pd	Mf	Pa	Pt	Sc	Ma	Si
Raw	0	4	9	9	23	35	32	23	40	10	30	23	18	47
K-Correction					5			4			9	9	2	
T	41	50	64	44	80	80	73	69	43	56	73	64	58	74

Percentage True : 50

F - K (Raw) : 0

Average Profile Elevation : 69.1
(Hs,D,Hy,Pd,Pa,Pt,Sc,Ma)

Disturbance Index (DsI) : 662

correlation between the social desirability of items and the probability that a subject would state that the item described him- or herself.

The variability in social desirability or willingness to say negative things about oneself is of interest in understanding personality dynamics but tends to distort the results of most self-report instruments. The authors of personality tests usually want to have more than these two factors on their tests, and it requires a considerable amount of statistical manipulation to accomplish this goal. The result, too often, is an instrument with a factor structure that is not a great improvement over those developed using a logical-theoretical or an empirical criterion keying approach.

The Sixteen Personality Factor Questionnaire (16 PF). The Sixteen Personality Factor Questionnaire (16 PF) was developed for use with individuals sixteen years old or older. It is objectively scored and intended for use in research and as a means of providing a clinical description of personality.

In developing the instrument, Raymond B. Cattell began with a list of all the adjectives that could be used to describe human behavior and then reduced that list to 4,504 traits. This list was then pared down to 171 traits that accounted for the meaning of the traits in the original list. Factor analysis was used to reduce these further, to 36 of what were called surface traits. From them, a final group of 16 traits with the greatest variance were selected (Cattell, 1970).

The 16 factors are labeled with the symbols *A, B, C, E, F, G, H, I, L, M, N, O,* Q_1, Q_2, Q_3, Q_4. Note that *D, J,* and *K* are not included. These are scales that were considered for inclusion and have been used in other versions of the test but are not included in the final instrument. These symbols and their associated bipolar traits are as follows:

A	Cool, critical, and aloof	vs.	Warm hearted, outgoing
B	Low intelligence	vs.	High intelligence
C	Emotionally unstable	vs.	Emotionally stable
D	Submissive	vs.	Dominant
F	Silent and introspective	vs.	Talkative and cheerful
G	Frivolous	vs.	Persevering and responsible
H	Shy and restrained	vs.	Adventuresome, friendly, and impulsive
I	Tough minded and unsentimental	vs.	Tender minded and sensitive
L	Trusting and conciliatory	vs.	Suspicious and jealous
M	Conventional	vs.	Imaginative and absent minded
N	Unpretentious and forthright	vs.	Shrewd and worldly
O	Self-assured and placid	vs.	Insecure and anxious
Q_1	Conservative	vs.	Liberal
Q_2	Dependent on group	vs.	Self-Sufficient
Q_3	Unconventional and unconcerned about social rules	vs.	Controlled and socially precise
Q_4	Relaxed and tranquil	vs.	Tense and frustrated

There are also additional second-order factors derived from a factor analysis of these 16 primary factors.

Computer analysis of test results can be obtained from The Institute for Personality and Ability Testing (P.O. Box 188, Champaign, IL 61820). It provides not only the scores for the different scales, but a narrative interpretation of what the scores mean. There are a number of different reports available: the 16 PF Narrative Score Report, the Marriage Counseling Report, the Personal Career Development Profile, the 16 PF Clinical Report, the Human Resource Development Report, and the Law Enforcement Assessment and Development Report. The cover page from the 16 PF Narrative Score Report is provided in Figure 16.2. (The remainder of the report can be found in the Appendix).

Because personality is integrated, it is not easy to describe it in terms of independent factors. To the developers of a factor-analytically derived test, this is a concern because, to the extent that items are correlated, they are measuring the same thing. The manual for the 16 PF (1977) states that

> These sixteen dimensions, or scales, are independent. All items on the test contribute to the score on one and only one factor so no dependencies are introduced at the level of scale construction. Moreover, the experimentally obtained correlations among the sixteen scales are generally quite small, so that each scale provides some new piece of information about the person being tested.

In the *Handbook for the 16 PF* (Cattell, Eber, & Tatsuoka, 1970) the intercorrelations among the scales are presented. They are far from being "quite small". The correlations range from the negligible to the substantial. For instance, the correlation between *O* (self-assured vs. insecure and anxious) and Q_4 (relaxed and tranquil vs. tense and frustrated) is .75 for males and .67 for females. For males, out of a possible 120 correlations, there are 29 above .30. If there were no correlations among the scales, it would not be possible to obtain the second-order factors.

There is a bewildering array of test forms—*A, B, C, D, E*, and *F*. *A* and *B* are equivalent forms and are intended for individuals who are at least at the seventh-grade reading level, but they are also appropriate for college-level students. *C* and *D* are written at the fifth-grade level and are intended for the "man in the street," whereas *E* and *F* are written at the third-grade level and are intended for the subliterate. As long as the reading-level requirement is met, any individual can take any of the forms. Because the reliability of individual forms can be expected to be low, it is recommended that, where possible, examinees be given all six forms. With only one form, a trait is measured only by a few items and this is the cause of the low reliability. With all six forms, there are an acceptable 32 to 38 items per trait.

Most writers (Cronbach, 1970; Shertzer & Linden, 1979; Anastasi, 1982) are critical of the 16 PF, citing its questionable factor structure, low reliability, and correlation among scales. They urge that the test be used as a research instrument rather than a clinical instrument. This criticism may be too harsh. Despite its limitations it is probably as good as any of the other objective measures of personality adjustment. Besides, none of those instruments can really stand alone as a means of either diagnosing personality disturbances or describing the normal personality. They must be used by a trained clinician who is able to corroborate or reject the hypotheses suggested by the test results.

The Guilford-Zimmerman Temperament Survey (GZTS). The Guilford-Zimmerman Temperament Survey (GZTS) instrument was developed by J. P. Guilford

Figure 16.2 16 PF profile.

THE INSTITUTE FOR PERSONALITY AND ABILITY TESTING
P. O. BOX 188 CHAMPAIGN, ILLINOIS 61820

THIS COMPUTER INTERPRETATION OF THE 16 PF IS INTENDED ONLY FOR PROPERLY QUALIFIED PROFESSIONALS AND SHOULD BE TREATED AS A CONFIDENTIAL REPORT.

4/20/1984

NAME-JOHN SAMPLE AGE-29
ID NUMBER- SEX-M

* * * * * * * * * V A L I D I T Y S C A L E S * * * * * * * * * *

THERE IS REASON TO SUSPECT SOME DISTORTION IN HIS TEST RESPONSES.
THIS IS SOMETHING THAT SHOULD BE EXPLORED FURTHER.
FAKING GOOD/MD (STEN) SCORE IS VERY LOW (2.0).
FAKING BAD (STEN) SCORE IS HIGH (8.0).

* *

16 PF
PERSONALITY PROFILE

SCORES R	U	C		LOW MEANING	1 2 3 4 5 6 7 8 9 10	HIGH MEANING	%
8	4	4	A	COOL, RESERVED	<---	WARM, EASYGOING	23
10	8	8	B	CONCRETE THINKING	----->	ABSTRACT THINKING	89
10	2	3	C	EASILY UPSET	<-----	CALM, STABLE	11
22	10	10	E	NOT ASSERTIVE	--------->	DOMINANT	99
21	9	9	F	SOBER, SERIOUS	------->	HAPPY-GO-LUCKY	96
11	4	4	G	EXPEDIENT	<---	CONSCIENTIOUS	23
19	7	7	H	SHY, TIMID	--->	VENTURESOME	77
9	6	6	I	TOUGH-MINDED	->	TENDER-MINDED	60
11	8	8	L	TRUSTING	----->	SUSPICIOUS	89
16	7	7	M	PRACTICAL	--->	IMAGINATIVE	77
4	2	2	N	FORTHRIGHT	<-------	SHREWD	4
15	8	7	O	SELF-ASSURED	--->	APPREHENSIVE	77
15	9	9	Q1	CONSERVATIVE	------->	EXPERIMENTING	96
14	8	8	Q2	GROUP-ORIENTED	----->	SELF-SUFFICIENT	89
12	5	5	Q3	UNDISCIPLINED	<-	SELF-DISCIPLINED	40
14	7	6	Q4	RELAXED	->	TENSE, DRIVEN	60

NOTE: "R" DESIGNATES RAW SCORES, "U" DESIGNATES (UNCORRECTED) STEN SCORES, AND "C" DESIGNATES STEN SCORES CORRECTED FOR DISTORTION (IF APPROPRIATE). THE INTERPRETATION WILL PROCEED ON THE BASIS OF CORRECTED SCORES.

PERSONAL COUNSELING OBSERVATIONS

ADEQUACY OF ADJUSTMENT IS ABOVE AVERAGE (6.5).
ACTING-OUT BEHAVIOR TENDENCIES ARE HIGH (7.9).
EFFECTIVENESS OF BEHAVIOR CONTROLS IS LOW (3.3).

INTERVENTION CONSIDERATIONS

THE INFLUENCE OF A CONTROLLED ENVIRONMENT MAY HELP. SUGGESTIONS INCLUDE-
A GRADED SERIES OF SUCCESS EXPERIENCES TO IMPROVE SELF-CONFIDENCE

using a somewhat different factor-analytic approach than was used by Cattell in the development of the 16 PF. The GZTS consists of three hundred items of which the examinee can endorse as many or as few as he or she wishes. The ten scales on the test follow:

1. General activity (*G*).
2. Restraint (*R*).
3. Ascendance (*A*).
4. Sociability (*S*).
5. Emotional stability (*E*).
6. Objectivity (*O*).
7. Friendliness (*F*).
8. Thoughtfulness (*T*).
9. Personal relations (*P*).
10. Masculinity (*M*).

Reliabilities range from .75 for Objectivity to .87 for Sociability (Thorndike & Hagen, 1977). Some intercorrelations between scales are unacceptably high.

Ethical Considerations Associated with Objective Scored Adjustment Inventories Objective personality scales were originally developed for the purpose of providing a systematic alternative to existing subjective methods, but they also share characteristics that have caused ethical problems. Their objectivity, the fact that they can be given to large groups, and the availability of machine scoring and computer analysis has led to a great deal of abuse.

These personality tests are intended for use by clinicians trained in their use. Although considerable attention has been given to these instruments, the reader should not conclude that these discussions are sufficient to qualify them to administer and interpret the tests. However, the ability of the reader to understand reports based on the results of these instruments, should be enhanced.

These instruments are not and should not be used in school settings except by trained psychologists when their use is justified and all appropriate permissions and informed consent have been secured. Their use as a screening instrument or as a criterion for admission to colleges and universities is clearly inappropriate. In the hands of a skilled clinician, they can play a useful role in diagnosis and therapy, but they also have a great potential for misuse.

Interest Inventories

One of the most important decisions that a person makes in a lifetime is the choice of a career. Unfortunately, this decision is often made on the basis of faulty data and lacks a rational basis. When this occurs, particularly in the case of careers requiring extensive education and/or training, the result can be discontent and unhappiness. One cause of this irrational decision making is that students are influenced by the urging of parents, friends, and relatives and are swayed by misconceptions they pick up from the media. For instance, a student might believe that he or she wants to be a psychologist, without any real idea of what such a career entails. When a student starts studying for that career he or she may become discouraged because it is not what was expected. Students are also likely to be restricted in the sorts of careers that they consider. There may be many jobs for which they might be suited, but they end up considering only a small proportion of them.

Interest inventories have the potential for providing useful information to individuals, as well as to the counselors and psychologists who are trying to help them make career choices. Of course, obtaining employment in a chosen field requires more than an interest and the proper personality profile. One must have the prerequisite aptitudes to train for the occupation as well as to succeed in it. It also helps if there are actually jobs available in the chosen field.

Interest inventories provide information about each individual's personality and interest, as well as about how he or she compares either to those already in the occupation or to clusters of occupations. It is assumed that careers differ in terms of the personality characteristics and interests that those in the careers must have in order to be happy and successful. Furthermore, it is assumed that individuals differ in terms of those characteristics. The purpose of interest inventories is to match the individual's characteristics to the career.

The process of achieving this match is far from simple. There are few standardized tests that are as complex as interest inventories. The development of interest inventories requires an enormous amount of time and technical expertise. Two general approaches are taken. Interests can be described either in terms of specific jobs or groups of jobs. At one time, each interest inventory selected one of these approaches. Now, the two major interest inventories, the Strong-Campbell Interest Inventory and the Kuder scales provide information about the characteristics of people in specific occupations as well as clusters of occupations.

The Strong-Campbell Interest Inventory One of the pioneers in the field of interest assessment was E. K. Strong who published the Strong Vocational Interest Blank (SVIB) in 1927. The emphasis of that test was on professions and occupations that required a college degree. The 399 items included in the instrument focused on likes or dislikes for specific occupations and activities. The examinee responded to each item with an *L* for like, an *I* for indifferent, or a *D* for dislike. The test was scaled using an empirical criterion-keyed approach similar to that used in the development of the MMPI.

Individuals were identified who had worked in a specific occupation for three years and were judged to be satisfied and reasonably successful. Each of these criterion groups contained about three hundred subjects. The norm groups were then compared with a general reference sample composed of all other occupational groups. Items that differentiated between a specific occupational group and the general reference group were used to make up each occupational scale.

A separate form was developed for use with women, but it was less successful than the scale for men. It included only traditional occupations, and women in this limited range of jobs did not tend to endorse items differently based on their jobs. As a result there was a lack of variance among jobs, which resulted in the instrument doing a poor job of discriminating.

In 1974 a newer and more sophisticated instrument was developed to take the place of the SVIB, titled the Strong-Campbell Interest Inventory (SCII). It has a single form for males and females. The instrument consists of 325 items grouped into seven categories. The first five categories are occupations, school subjects, activities, amusements, and day-to-day contact with various types of people. Each statement is scored with an *L, D*, or *I*, as was done with the SVIB. The sixth category consists of pairs of activities. The examinees respond by indicating the one they prefer. The seventh section contains a series of descriptive statements to which the subjects respond either yes or no, depending on whether they agree with the statement.

The scoring of the test is complex and requires computer analysis. The responses must be made on machine-scorable answer sheets. Machine scoring costs about $4 per analysis, with lower rates for volume scoring. The four types of scales on the SCII, developed using different procedures of scale development, are (1) Special Scales, (2) General Occupational Themes, (3) Basic Interest Scales, and (4) Occupational Scales.

Special scales. The Academic Comfort Scale (ACS) was developed by identifyng items that differentiate between college students with good grades and those with poor grades. The scale is not a measure of academic ability but is a measure of the degree of comfort in and/or liking for an academic setting.

The Introversion-Extroversion Scale (IE) was designed to correlate with the Social Introversion Scale of the MMPI. The scale appears to measure a subject's preference for working with people versus working alone.

General occupational themes. The six general occupational theme scales are based on John Holland's theory of vocational development. Holland is a leading theoretician in the field of occupational interest. He postulates that individuals develop a combination of six personality types, which make up the general occupational themes:

1. Realistic.
2. Investigative.
3. Artistic.
4. Social.
5. Enterprising.
6. Conventional.

Patterns of these personality types can be matched with different occupational environments.

The six general occupational theme scales were developed logically by choosing twenty items that correspond to the definition of each of Holland's six areas. A high score on a general Occupational Theme reflects the subject's liking for a number of items in that general occupational area.

Basic interest scales. The 23 Basic Interest Scales were developed by clustering groups of highly correlated items. The groups of items were examined and the scale was named according to item content. This resulted in scales with labels such as Agriculture, Law/Politics, and Teaching. The Basic Interest Scales are grouped on the profile form according to the Holland personality type with which they fit.

Occupational scales. The Occupational Scales were developed using empirical criterion keying in the same manner as the SVIB. There is a single form of the instrument for males and females, but the occupational scales are normed separately.

One of the goals of the authors of this instrument is to have norms available for both males and females for each occupation. In order to reach this goal, it is necessary to obtain samples of successful workers who match the established criteria for success and happiness in the job. This is often difficult because, despite the advances that have been made in breaking down traditional occupation barriers, there are still occupations where the workers are either almost exclusively male or female. In the 1981 version of the test, there is a total of 162 separately normed occupational groups representing 85 occupations. Of these, 77 are matched pairs and only 8 are not matched—4 for males and 4 for females. The 4 occupations for females that are not matched are dental assistant, dental hygienist, home economics teacher, and secretary. For males the unmatched occupations are agribusiness manager, investment fund manager, and skilled crafts and vocational agriculture teacher. These are occupations for which they could not obtain a sufficient sample of the appropriate sex. The test authors went to great length to find appropriate samples, but despite considerable effort, they were unsuccessful.

Examinees obtain a standard score with a mean of 50 and a standard deviation of 10 on each scale, indicating how similar, their individual interests are to those in each occupation. A score of 45 or more is considered similar, whereas 24 or less is considered dissimilar. Similarity is defined in terms of the degree to which an individual's scores match the likes and dislikes of the individuals in the occupations. This is done for those items that differentiate an occupational group from the responses of the entire sample, which includes all occupations.

The Occupational Scales, like the Basic Interest Scales, are categorized according to the six Holland Occupational Themes. The coding of the different scale types according to Holland's theory of occupational choices allows subjects to see consistencies across the scale types and aids in profile interpretation.

Report forms. As a result of the complexity of the instrument, the SCII must be scored using a computer. An example of the type of report provided by Consulting Psychologists Press, Inc. can be seen in Figure 16.3. An example of their interpretive report can be found in the Appendix.

Interpretation. Occasionally there will be inconsistencies between the Basic Interest Scales and the Occupational Scales. One reason for this is the fact that the Basic Interest Scales were derived only from likes, whereas the Occupational Scales were based on likes and dislikes. An individual might have a high score on the Mathematics Scale but a low score on the Mathematician Scale because he or she likes those things that place people in the Mathematics category but does not dislike the same things that mathematicians dislike. Another factor that might lead to inconsistencies between the two scales is that the Occupational Scales are based on a wider range of items, any that distinguish the criterion group from the entire sample. The Basic Interest Scales are based on only those items that are directly related to the scale. Furthermore, the Basic Interest Scales tend to be homogeneous, whereas the Occupational Scales tend to be heterogeneous. This is a function of the scaling process used in their respective development.

Figure 16.3 SCII profile.

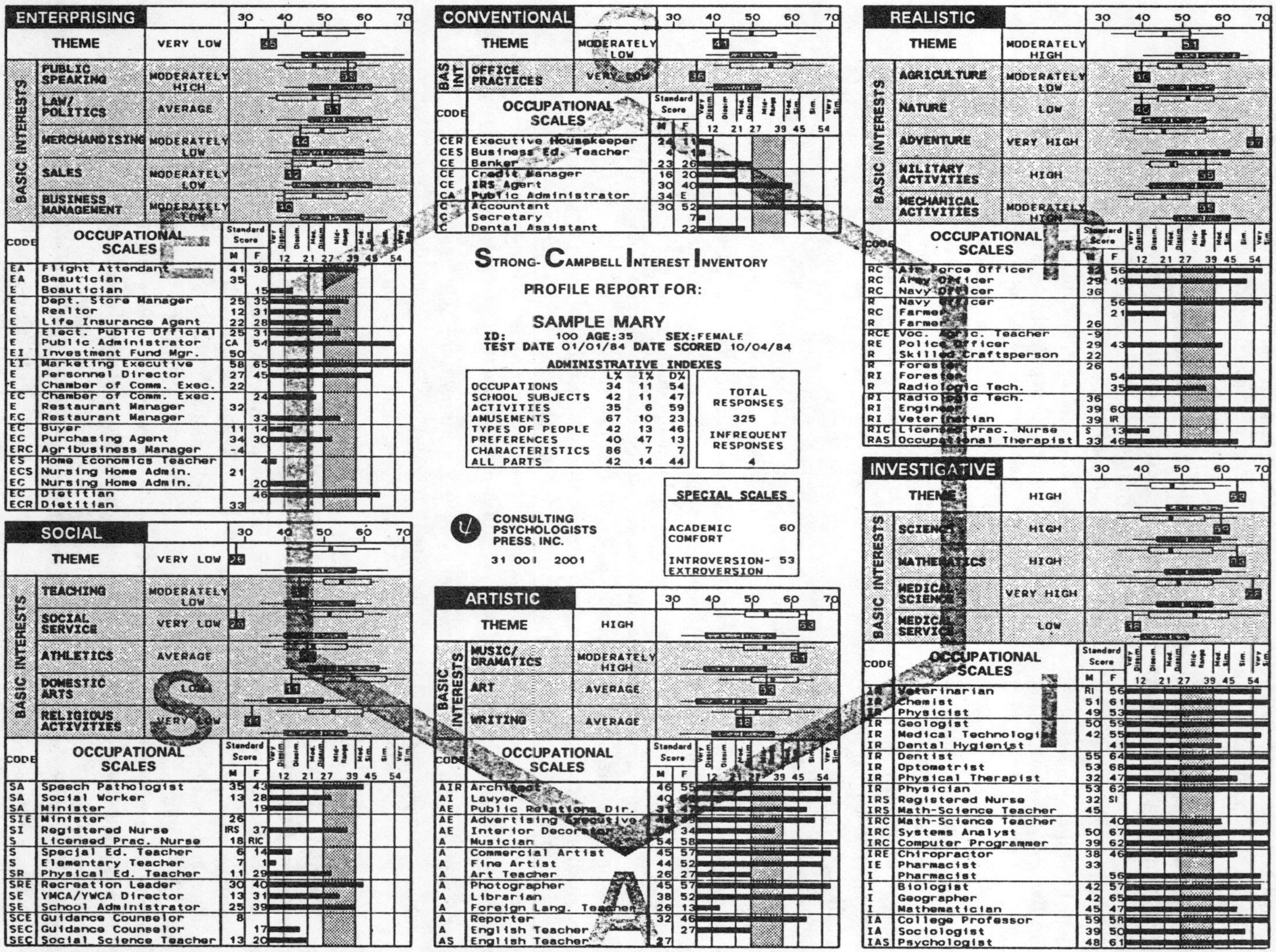

The Kuder Inventories The first Kuder inventory, the Kuder Vocational Preference Record, provided a useful alternative to the SVIB because its focus was quite different. The SVIB focused on occupations, and the Kuder reported general occupational categories, or interest scales: Outdoor, Mechanical, Scientific, Computational, Persuasive, Artistic, Literary, Musical, Social Service, and Clerical, plus a Verification Score. The instrument consists of 168 triads of activities; the examinee selects the most preferred and least preferred. In this manner the instrument controls for acquiescense—the tendency of an individual always to agree—and other response sets. This structure causes an instrument to be ipsative. It is difficult to make normative comparisons with an ipsative instrument because the magnitude of any scale is not independent from other scales. A high score can represent interest in an area or a relative lack of interest in other occupations.

The Kuder inventories were developed for use with high school students and young adults. The scales were developed through a combination of content analysis and the use of intercorrelations. This was done with the goal of obtaining scales that were relatively independent.

At one time it was of some advantage to administer both the Kuder Vocational Preference Record and the SVIB because each provided different types of information about interests. However, the SVIB has been revised into the SCII, which provides extensive information on occupational categories.

The Kuder Occupational Interest Survey (KOIS), Form DD, was developed in 1970; it provides information on specific occupations, as does the SCII. Administering both the SCII and KOIS is redundant and even confusing.

The KOIS uses 100 triads in the same format as the earlier Kuder test and includes a total of 114 occupational scales and 48 college major scales. An examinee's score on a given scale is determined by the computation of the correlation between his or her responses and the responses of the criterion groups.

The Career Assessment Inventory (CAI) The Career Assessment Inventory (CAI) instrument is intended for use with non-college-bound, nonprofessionals. It utilizes the same general approach as the SCII, with six Occupational Themes, 22 Basic Interest Scales, and 89 Occupational Scales. The test is comparable to the SCII in its interpretation, but the problems of differential responses by males and females are somewhat more acute because of the occupations being assessed. Jobs that do not require a college degree are more identified with one sex than jobs that do. A great deal of effort has been devoted to correcting for these differences, and the instrument is appropriate for use with both males and females.

The Self-Directed Search (SDS) The Self-Directed Search (SDS) also was developed by Holland. It takes a different approach to assisting individuals in understanding the nature of their interests and developing an awareness of the occupations in which they might be interested. The individual administers the instrument to him- or herself and then tabulates the results. The individual is then guided through the booklet by means of a series of questions about occupational daydreams, preferences for occupations, competencies, preferences for activities, and estimates of abilities. Each subsection has items relating to Holland's six occupational themes. At the end of the booklet, the examinees summarize their scores and determine the occupational themes that best describe their interests. They can then use *The Occupations Finder* in which are listed 456 jobs coded by three or sometimes two letters representing the Holland themes. It also lists the *Dictionary of Occupational Titles* code, which provides a source of information about each occupation and the level of education it requires.

The Reliability and Validity of Interest Scales The use of interest inventories is predicated on the assumption that a person's interests remain stable. If they do not, then knowledge of present-day interests is of no value in predicting future job satisfaction. Similarly, it must be assumed that the interest structure of jobs remains stable. There is evidence to support both views (Campbell, 1968; McArthur, 1968). Robert Thorndike and Elizabeth Hagen (1977) also cite evidence for the predictive validity of these instruments. The tests are susceptible to faking, but when used appropriately the examinee should have no reason not to give honest answers. Using these instruments as a device to screen prospective employees is not an appropriate use and will likely lead to responses that are not entirely honest, as well as to distorted interpretations.

Sex Bias in Interest Inventories Because they emphasize the status quo in existing occupations, interest inventories are inherently conservative. Historically they have reflected sex differences in employment and placed most of their emphasis on males and male occupations. In the late 1960s and 1970s, concern about sex equity and women's rights began to increase. This led to a careful examination of existing interest inventories, which had been developed with males as their focus and for which women were a secondary consideration. These instruments were criticized for their use of sexist language and their perpetuation of sex and occupation stereotypes. Separate norms for men and women were used, and traditional male and female occupational roles were emphasized. Insensitivity to the needs and feelings of women in interest-inventory construction probably reached its nadir when the 1969 SVIB appeared with a blue cover for the male version and a pink one for the female version.

Concern about sex bias in interest inventories led to the National Institute of Education (NIE) forming a panel to investigate the subject that included experts in career guidance, education, and measurement. The result was a set of guidelines titled *NIE Guidelines for Assessment of Sex Bias and Sex-Fairness in Career Interest Inventories*. These were not legal requirements, but they were intended to provide guidance to the authors and publishers of interest inventories. The guidelines include directions for how the instruments should be constructed, the types of technical information that should be provided, and the ways the instruments should be used. With respect to the structure of the instruments, the guidelines state that the same interest-inventory forms should be available and appropriate for both males and females; that information about all occupations should be reported for both sexes; that the item pool should be made up of items appropriate for both males and females; and that all wording and occupational terms should be nonsexist.

The satisfaction of these requirements is a relatively straightforward but expensive process; any interest inventory that was to remain competitive in the marketplace had to be modified to meet these requirements. Meeting guidelines, however, does not ensure an unbiased instrument. One crucial aspect of interest-inventory construction that was left unresolved in the guidelines involved the question of whether such instruments should include combined or separate norms for the two sexes. On the surface at least, interest inventories based on combined norms would seem to be the least sex biased. But because of the considerable differences between the interests of males and females, combined scales are likely to result in males consistently obtaining high scores on traditional male occupations and low scores on traditional female occupations, while females do just the opposite. The result of this approach would be an interest inventory that is clearly biased, and its use could be expected to cause even greater sex stereotyping.

One alternative is to eliminate those items to which males and females respond differently. This unfortunately results in the loss of items that are useful in understanding occupational preferences and can lead to a subsequent loss of validity. Campbell and Hansen (1981), in a study intended to provide information for use in the revision of the SCII, report the results of comparisons among four approaches to interest-inventory construction:

Method 1—Separate norms; biased items retained.
Method 2—Separate norms; biased items removed.
Method 3—Combined norms; biased items retained.
Method 4—Combined norms; biased items removed.

They found that for six occupations studied, method 1 was always the most valid approach for either males or females, and that for most occupations where method 1 was more valid for one sex, method 3 was more valid for members of the opposite sex. In no cases was method 2 or 4 (biased items removed) more valid. The elimination of sex-biased items appears to detract too much from the capacity of an interest inventory to assess interest in specific occupations accurately. Therefore, separate scales were determined to be more valid and reliable than combined scales. Other studies (Hansen, 1976; Webber & Harmon, 1978) came to much the same conclusion. As a result, the decision was made that the SCII would continue to use separate norms, and that sex differentiating items would not be removed. The authors of the KOIS came to much the same conclusion; as a result, it uses separate norms for males and females. Both the SCII and KOIS report scores based on both norms, although it is not altogether clear how these two norms should be used or how they should be interpreted when they are not in agreement. The manuals for these two instruments are not very helpful in this respect. The latest version of the Career Assessment Inventory has switched to combined norms that include males and females. It seems reasonable to conclude that eventually all interest inventories will be constructed in this fashion.

Concern about sex bias in interest inventories goes beyond the structure, language, and appearance of these tests and is closely tied to the philosophy of career counseling: specifically, the degree to which a counselor wants to take an activist role in urging men and women to enter nontraditional occupations. The traditional view that the purpose of interest inventories is to match an individual with an occupation in which he or she is most interested, has shifted to the view that these instruments should provide the individual being counseled with a broad range of occupations for which he or she might be suited.

Measuring Attitudes

Unlike the self-report assessments described up to this point, measures of attitudes usually focus on a single construct rather than on a set of scales. Like other self-report measures, they are limited by what the individual knows about his or her attitudes and is willing to communicate. Most people have similar perceptions of the social desirability of the items measuring personality traits, so there is a tendency for everyone to respond to items on such instruments in a similar fashion. Because there is considerable variability in the social desirability of attitudes, scores on attitude measures are not as affected by this factor. When we are seeking the overall attitude level of a group and do not need to know about the attitudes of individuals, it is possible to keep responses anonymous. This increases the probability that responses will represent a more genuine reflection of attitudes.

Verbalized attitudes may not be the same as actual behaviors, or underlying feeling, but they are still important because they tend to influence behavior. For example, parents who withdraw their children from public schools and place them in private schools, at the time that their children's schools are desegregated, often express support for school desegregation (Cunningham & Husk, 1980). They attribute the withdrawal of their children from public schools to factors other than opposition to school desegregation. Their attitudes and behaviors seem to be dissonant, but this articulation of an accommodating view toward these social changes may be the result of a desire to make what they perceive to be an acceptable response. Such responses still represent a more positive attitude than that of the parent who expresses adamant opposition to school desegregation. In this case attitudes may indicate willingness to modify behavior.

The biggest problem with attitude-assessment instruments is the ease with which they can be constructed. This ease is misleading. Just because items can be collected quickly and an instrument put together easily does not mean that the instrument will measure the constructs it is intended to measure in a reliable fashion. Unless attitude scales are created in a systematic fashion, utilizing what is known about good instrument construction, the results may be meaningless. The following section includes suggestions for ensuring that the scores obtained actually reflect the attitudes they are supposed to measure.

Summative Ratings Attitude scales are usually constructed by gathering statements that are related to an attitude. The examinee responds to the statements with a numerical indication of the strength of his or her feeling toward a statement. Those responses can then be summed to obtain an estimate of the attitude. The most often-used approach for accomplishing this is to have the respondent indicate the degree to which he or she agrees or disagrees with statements. This is called a summative rating, or Likert scale, after Reneis Likert who first introduced the use of this technique. The following key illustrates the options provided to the subject:

6—Strongly agree.
5—Mildly agree.
4—Somewhat agree.

3—Somewhat disagree.
2—Mildly disgree.
1—Strongly disagree.

If you want to measure attitude toward school desegregation, you might include statements such as the following:

1. I am in favor of school desegregation.
2. Students benefit from attending school with students from different cultures.
3. School desegregation causes school achievement to decline.
4. I would not allow my child to attend school with children of different races.
5. It is morally wrong to separate children in school by race.

The respondents than place a number adjacent to each statement, indicating their degree of agreement with the statements. Some items are stated positively and some negatively. This is intended to correct for the tendency of respondents to agree always. During the process of summing across items to attain the assessment of the attitude, the scoring of negatively stated items is reversed. In order to increase variability, the statements are also written in such a way that they represent different degrees of commitment to school desegregation.

Graphic scales. Although the preceding procedure takes up little space (and many items can be placed on a single page), graphic scales seem to be more appealing to respondents. This approach is implemented by following each statement with an agree–disagree dimension laid out in such a way that the respondent can make a mark along the dimension to indicate the degree of agreement:

Strongly Disagree	1	2	3	4	5	6	Strongly Agree

Number of steps. The number of steps in the scale is also of importance. The more steps, the greater the reliability of the scale. This increase is noticeable up to seven steps, but the increase in reliability declines as twenty steps are reached. Items with more than seven steps are seldom used because the increase in reliability resulting from the additional steps is slight. It is easier to increase reliability by adding more items.

Types of anchors. Even though the agree-disagree anchors are particularly flexible, there is no reason why other anchors could not be used when they fit the meaning of the statements. For instance, factors such as effective-ineffective, important-unimportant, or like me–not like me have been successfully employed for this purpose.

An odd or an even number of steps. Another issue in the construction of attitude-rating scales involves the decision about whether to include an odd or even number of steps. Most respondents seem to prefer an odd number, so that they have an appropriate response when they feel neutral. With an even number of steps, they might feel as though they are being forced to make a distinction where none exists. On the other hand, the neutral position can be an easy way out for the person unwilling to devote an appropriate amount of time to the task of responding to all items. They may simply endorse the middle step. There is some evidence that, when forced to make a commitment other than the neutral one, respondents can still make a reliable decision (Nunnally, 1967).

One drawback to using an even number of steps, and denying the subject the opportunity to make a neutral response, is that this procedure can result in an increase in the amount of missing data. The respondent may simply refuse to respond if he or she cannot make a neutral response.

Single-item scales. Although single-item assessments of attitudes are not unusual, they provide a poor method of assessment. The use of one item prevents the assessment of internal consistency, and, if the one item is misunderstood, the results become invalid. The single item used also may be written in a way that biases the results. Consider the following two statements.

1. Parents should be forced to bus their children long distance for the purpose of integrating schools.
2. The courts should use any reasonable means for implementing school desegregation.

Even though both statements are related to the use of busing as a means of implementing school desegregation, used as single items they would be likely to yield quite different results. This is often a problem in the opinion polls so often published in newspapers and magazines. This bias could occur to some degree with any attitude scale, but with many items there is a greater likelihood that the positive and negative items will cancel each other.

Another problem with the single-statement attitude-rating scale is that it can end up being constructed so that there is no variability among the respondents. If the single statement being used to evaluate school desegregation is worded in such a way that everyone responds in the same way, then it will do a poor job of discriminating among the various attitudes held by the respondents. If a single-item scale is to be used, it is recommended that it include at least ten steps (Nunnally, 1967).

Improving the Summative Rating Scale The first step in developing a good summative rating scale is the selection of good statements. The goal is to select a broad range of statements that are representative of all possible items in the domain of observables. These can be generated by the test author, found in magazines and newpaper articles, or obtained from individuals asked to write on the subject (Edwards, 1957). It is important to avoid statements of facts to which all respondents may respond in the same way regardless of their attitude. For instance, the statement, "The use of busing to implement school desegregation is controversial," would be a sentiment with which most respondents would agree to approximately the same degree. Edwards (1957) provides a useful list of suggestions for selecting statements to be included in an attitude-rating scale.

1. Avoid statements that refer to the past rather than to the present.
2. Avoid statements that are factual or capable of being interpreted as factual.
3. Avoid statements that may be interpreted in more than one way.
4. Avoid statements that are irrelevant to the psychological object under consideration.

5. Avoid statements that are likely to be endorsed by almost everyone or by almost no one.
6. Select statements that are believed to cover the entire range of the affective scale of interest.
7. Keep the language of the statements simple, clear, and direct.
8. Statements should be short, rarely exceeding twenty words.
9. Each statement should contain only one complete thought.
10. Statement-containing universals such as *all*, *always*, *none*, and *never* often introduce ambiguity and should be avoided.
11. Words such as *only*, *just*, *merely*, and others of a similar nature, should be used with care and moderation in writing statements.
12. Whenever possible, statements should be written in simple sentences rather than compound or complex sentences.
13. Avoid the use of words that may not be understood by those who are to be given the completed scale.
14. Avoid the use of double negatives (p. 14).

Once you have collected the best set of statements that you can, using the preceding suggestions, they should be administered to a pilot group. Then the same sorts of item-analysis procedures that were used with ability tests can be employed. For this process to be practical, it should be done with the aid of a computer. Instructions for accomplishing this are found in Chapter 4, page 92. The item analysis will indicate which items are good and which are poor. By deleting, replacing, or revising bad items, the reliability of the test can be greatly improved.

Other Methods of Deriving Scales Up to this point, only one method of deriving scales has been discussed, the summative rating scale. This is the easiest method of scaling; other approaches are encountered much less often.

The method of paired comparisons. One alternative to the use of summative ratings utilizes a series of statements with which values are associated according to how strongly they reflect an attitude. Knowing which items are endorsed by an individual provides a measure of their attitude.

Such an approach requires that we scale the statements before we scale people. The simplest method of doing this is to have judges rank-order the statements. Because it has been found that judges tend to be imprecise in their ranking, alternative methods have been devised for scaling statements. The method of paired comparisons is one approach. It requires the construction of an instrument that includes all of the possible pairs of statements given to a group of judges.

The judges then choose, for each pair, the statement that represents the more favorable position in relation to the attitude. The statements are then ranked in terms of how many times they are chosen over other attitudes, and a weighting value is assigned to each item using that information. The set of statements can then be administered to respondents who endorse the best descriptor statements. A quantitative estimate of attitude is computed by finding the median value of the items endorsed.

The number of possible pairs can be determined by the following formula:

$$\text{Number of pairs} = n\,(n - 1)\,/\,2 \qquad \textbf{[16.1]}$$

where n equals the number of statements. If there were 10 statements, the number of pairs would equal 45 [10 (10 − 1) / 2 = 45). As can be seen, you would not need many statements before this approach became unworkable.

The method of equal appearing intervals (Thurstone method). The preceding method of weighting statements according to the degree to which they reflect an attitude is workable only if there are a relatively few statements to be rated. With a large number of statements, the Thurstone method, or method of equal appearing intervals, is more practical. With this approach, judges are given a set of cards with the letters *A* through *K* on them. These cards are then laid out on a table with the instruction that *K* represents favorable responses and *A* unfavorable responses, while *F* is neutral. The statements are arranged by the judges according to their favorableness. The placement on the scale is then converted to weightings, and the attitude of an individual is determined in the same way as was done with paired comparisons.

Q-sorts are similar to equal appearing intervals, but instead of allowing judges to arrange the statements in any order, they are required to place them on the scale in such a way that they are normally distributed.

Semantic differential. The semantic differential is an approach to assessing attitudes that is quite different from those discussed up to this point. It was developed by C. E. Osgood (1962) as an approach to quantifying attitudes based on word meanings. Instead of collecting a set of statements to define an attitude, the investigator starts with the subject he or she wants to assess. A set of concepts is selected that is intended to define the psychological space of the subject. The concepts are selected based on their capacity to elicit a range of responses. Associated with each concept is a set of bipolar adjective pairs, such as good–bad, wise–foolish, valuable–worthless, fair–unfair, and so forth. The same set of adjective pairs is listed under each concept. Example 16.1 illustrates what the format for one concept would look like.

EXAMPLE 16.1. School Desegregation

GOOD	:____	:____	:____	:____	:____	:____	:____	BAD
	1	2	3	4	5	6	7	
FOOLISH	:____	:____	:____	:____	:____	:____	:____	WISE
	1	2	3	4	5	6	7	
VALUABLE	:____	:____	:____	:____	:____	:____	:____	WORTHLESS
	1	2	3	4	5	6	7	
UNFAIR	:____	:____	:____	:____	:____	:____	:____	FAIR
	1	2	3	4	5	6	7	

Osgood used a set of fifty adjective pairs; most semantic-differential instruments are made up of either the entire list or a subset of it. The adjective pairs used by Osgood do not exhaust the possibility of pairs, and depending on what is being studied, additional or different pairs could be used. The pairs are reversed either randomly or systematically to ensure that the subject think about each response, rather than just go down the page marking the same point on the scale for each adjective pair.

After many factor-analytic studies of semantic-differential scales, Osgood concluded that there are three major factors. The first, and the one with the most consistently high loadings is *evaluation*; the other two are *potency* and *activity*. The adjective pairs in each factor are not always the same, and occasionally there are other factors; over many extremely diverse factor-analytic studies, however, these three factors consistently appear.

An important advantage of the semantic differential is the ease with which such scales are assembled. Because a standard set of adjective pairs can be used, the test constructor need only assemble the concepts. There is no requirement for pilot testing before use, although such a procedure can be useful. This approach is also economical because a great deal of information can be collected on a few pages, and respondents can make a large number of responses in a short amount of time.

The one disadvantage of this approach is the complexity of the interpretation of the results. It requires knowledge of factor analysis and the interpretation of a large amount of data. This is in contrast to the summative-rating approach, where a single score assessing an attitude is obtained.

Learning About Personality Through the Perceptions of Others

The major disadvantage of the methods of assessing personality based on asking a person about him- or herself is that we have no way of being sure that the responses to our questions will be honest. Even if respondents want to do this, they might not be able to.

The second method of assessing personality involves finding out about a person by asking others. This approach appears to provide some advantages over the previous methods because the observer can be expected to be more objective and more willing to give honest interpretations than the individual whose personality is being assessed. At the same time, the observer is likely to be limited in his or her ability to make accurate judgments, both by a lack of insight and opportunity to observe.

Letters of Recommendation

Letters of recommendation are often used for making decisions about whether an individual should be admitted to a college, university, graduate program, professional school, or some form of employment. Letters of recommendation are often routinely requested under these circumstances.

Unfortunately this is not a particularly useful method of finding out about others. Letters are usually solicited by the subject of the letters, and, therefore, there is every reason to think that the writer will be more loyal to the person about whom he or she is writing than to the individual for whom the letter is intended.

Now that individuals have increased rights to examine materials that contain information about them, there is a greater hesitancy on the part of the writers of letters of recommendation to make negative statements. They are afraid that the subject of the letter will learn its content. Not only are they reluctant to displease the subject of the letters, but they have the additional fear of lawsuits. There also is a reluctance on the part of most people to say negative things about others, which increases when they must put such thoughts on paper. It is much easier and more pleasant to accentuate the positive.

As a result of these factors, letters of recommendation tend to be uniformly positive and, therefore, are characterized by little variability. When these factors are added to the biases and response styles of the letter writer, which are unknown, letters of recommendation become quite difficult to interpret. Only the rare negative letter, the letter that is studiedly neutral, or the letter that continues for page after page, extolling the virtues of the individual discussed, are likely to influence our judgments.

Rating Scales

Everyone has the opportunity to be rated or to fill out rating forms on someone else. They are the most popular method of evaluating others. Rating can either be retrospective or current, but they always require interpretive skills on the part of the person doing the rating.

The construction of rating scales follows the same format as is used for self-report measures of personality. In the place of statements, the rater is usually given a list of personality traits that must be evaluated and assigned a value in the same fashion as the summative scales discussed previously.

Rating scales are seldom used to understand the underlying personality of others; this can be done better with a self-report approach. They are instead used to evaluate an individual's surface qualities to facilitate decision making. A typical use is in the evaluation of job performance, where a supervisor rates employees for purposes of making personal decisions.

These instruments resemble tests of ability because they are used to make decisions about job performance. At the same time they are similar to personality tests in terms of the ways they are constructed and the types of things they measure. Rating scales are not selected as a means of evaluation because of proven effectiveness. They are used because there are no real alternatives. The inefficiency of this method generally results from either the rater's unwillingness or inability to accurately assess the person being rated.

The Unwillingness to Do a Good Job of Rating The rater may be faced with a situation in which the rating form is so long and there are so many persons to be rated, that the task is just not worth the effort. Or, the person doing the rating may identify with those being rated, and therefore try to make them look good. Morale in many jobs requires that those in superior positions take care of those who work for them. The results of the rating in some cases becomes a matter of public record. The person being rated sees the results, and this causes raters to be reluctant to give low evaluations.

The Inability to Do a Good Job of Rating Even if the rater is willing to do a good job, there are certain factors that might prevent it. There may be little or no opportunity for the subject to be observed, or the trait may be covert or unrevealed in the atmosphere in which the observation is taking place. Inconsistencies in the standard of reference used by different raters may also cause the ratings to be inaccurate.

The Limitations of Rating Scales The result of the preceding two factors is that most raters err on the side of generosity. Jum C. Nunnally (1967) has found that ratings tend to be dominated by a single factor that he labels leniency, or the willingness to say positive things about others. This causes rating to be affected by the traits of the raters, which supress the reliability and validity of the evaluation. There is also a tendency for a rater who has a positive perception of one aspect of an individual's personality to let that feeling influence the rating of other traits. The result is called the halo effect.

Improving Rating Scales Ratings can be improved by making them easier to complete and brief enough for their completion to be a realistic goal. Sometimes a forced-choice approach is used to eliminate the tendency to make only positive responses. The rater must either rank individuals in terms of their characteristics, or evaluate them by choosing between choices of descriptions that are equally desirable. This means that the rater may be forced to choose between *punctual* and *competent* as descriptions of the individual being rated. There is often resistance to such an approach because it makes rating difficult. It also takes control away from the rater; the rater may not know whether his or her response will result in a high or low evaluation.

Careful training of the raters is also important and can prevent some of the problems encountered with rating scales. The ratings of several observers can also be pooled, which leads to fairer, more reliable ratings. This is expensive, however.

Direct Observations

Systematic Observations

The use of systematic observations differs somewhat from the types of assessment studied up to this point. The use of ratings focuses on the use of observable behavior to assess personality, but the person doing the observing is expected to make interpretations. With systematic observations the behaviors are observed, and recorded, and the personality is explained in terms of what an individual actually does. The goal is to obtain the most objective recordings of behavior, and every attempt is made to *prevent* the observer from doing any interpretation.

This approach to assessing human behavior is particularly favored by behaviorists, who are skeptical of the process of transforming behaviors into distances on a continuum and then forming constructs. They assert that because we cannot accurately evaluate what a person is thinking, we should assess only actual behavior. Because behavior-modification approaches to therapy focus on changing specific behaviors, it is necessary to have techniques to measure behavior objectively so it can be determined whether the behavior has changed.

Conducting Observation of Behavior Before we can begin observing behavior we must first define the behavior to be observed. This must be done in such a way that ambiguity is avoided. The behavior to be observed must be unitary and discrete. The goal is to define it so well that after reading its definition anyone could recognize it when it occurs.

After the behavior is defined, observation can begin. Observations are based on three considerations: (1) frequency, which is the number of times a specific behavior occurs within a given time period; (2) duration, the length of time a behavior continues at each occurrence; and (3) conditions, the circumstances and/or setting that exists at the time the behavior occurs. After watching and recording what may seem to be haphazard or random behavior, it is usually possible to see some pattern emerging. It is necessary at this point to be aware of the antecedents and consequences of the observed behavior. When the behavior occurs several times and each time is of some duration, the recording of both frequency and duration is useful. If the behavior has a fairly fixed duration, frequency by itself may be an adequate measure. Some behaviors occur infrequently. Duration, not frequency, may then be the desired measure.

It is important to be aware of the effect that the observation itself is having. The person may become uncomfortable, begin "performing," or perhaps just stop exhibiting whatever behavior you are observing. This phenomenon is referred to as a reactive effect to observation.

Using Graphs If behavior observation occurs over time, the data obtained may be graphed. By charting the collected data, the observer may note any trends or variations in the target behavior. If an intervention strategy is to be employed, this observing and charting can continue throughout the treatment condition. These observations can then be compared with those made in the preintervention phase to note if the behavior was altered in the desired direction.

Understanding Personality Through an Examinee's Interpretation of Ambiguous Stimuli

The psychologist or counselor who has a need to assess personality in something more than a purely subjective sense faces a dilemma. The main instruments available that can make any claim to avoiding subjectivity are the self-reporting objective personality tests. As has been discussed, these instruments have some important drawbacks. Primary among those is the fact that they require the subject to provide information about him- or herself in the form of a self-report. Under many circumstances the client has good reasons not to respond honestly and may be intentionally trying to provide erroneous information. This is most likely to occur when objective tests are used outside of the normal therapeutic setting. In the therapeutic setting the examiner can develop a relationship likely to result in a client being willing to disclose information that might otherwise be suppressed.

There also are situations where the client may want to reveal information about his or her personality but is unable to do so. After all, it is generally considered evidence of progress when a person suffering from some form of emotional maladjustment reaches a point where he or she can admit having a problem. This implies that many people with such problems are unable to reveal the characteristics of their own personality. This is the circumstance where projective tests are most useful. They provide techniques for learning about personality despite the unwillingness or inability of a client to disclose information about his or her personality. The development of techniques of projective personality testing can be traced back at least as far as Carl Jung's use of word association as a means of getting patients to reveal their personality.

The psychoanalytic view of personality emphasizes the point that, rather than being fully integrated, a personality is divided into a conscious and an unconscious. Norman Sundberg (1977) calls these primary and secondary process of thinking. The secondary process is the conscious everyday mode of thinking and communicating. It is generally rational and logical, whereas the primary, or subconscious, is controlled by more primitive forces and drives.

There is now increasing evidence that physiological brain structure explanations exist for this phenomenom. The explanations are based both on hemispherical differences in the brain and the relationship between the cerebral cortex and the limbic system. Dreams, which are an illustration of subconscious brain functioning, appear to serve important purposes in information processing for humans as well as other mammals.

According to theories of the unconscious, we are capable of acting in ways that are inconsistent with our conscious needs in order to satisfy subconscious desires. An insecure man might create an air of great manliness; someone who really hates his or her mother might treat her with greatest solicitude; an individual unsure of his or her own sexuality might campaign with great fervor against homosexuality.

This is a view diametrically opposed to that espoused by the behaviorists, who believe that the best measure of personality is obtained from observing what a person does. The essence of projective testing is the idea that personality is never revealed directly.

Projective tests, or techniques, provide an opportunity for an individual to reveal his or her characteristics, traits, feelings, attitudes, and behavior patterns through a response to relatively unstructured material. To stimulate the subject to respond in his or her own way, the material presented is usually ambiguous, vague, or incomplete. The instructions are brief and general so that the imagination and the expression of feelings can be given free play. In addition, the procedure may be disguised by presenting the task as a test of imagination or storytelling ability, or it may be introduced without any explanation of its purpose. One of the major advantages of the method is that the subject is not likely to fake his or her responses because they do not require factual information or answers to specific questions; he or she has no way of knowing how the responses will be interpreted by the clinician interpreting the test. The materials are usually interesting, which makes them useful for establishing rapport.

The Rorschach Test

The Rorschach test is named after its creator, Hermann Rorschach (1884–1922), a Swiss psychiatrist. Although he died shortly after introducing the test, its potential was seen by five American psychologists who developed systems for its interpretation: Bruno Klopfer, S. J. Beck, Marquerite Hertz, Zygmunt Piatrowski and David Rapaport. John Exner extended the theory and techniques of scoring to the point where it became the dominanat projective technique. Its use has declined somewhat, but it remains a routine technique for personality testing in many settings. The test is administered by presenting ten cards of bilaterally symmetrical inkblots. During the development of the test, a number of different types of inkblots were used, but the current test is composed of those that elicited the widest variety of responses. Five of the cards are monochrome, two are black and red, and three use other color shades. The inkblots are generally ambiguous, like cloud formations, and the usefulness of the test stems from the idea that people react emotionally to such ambiguous stimuli. It is hoped that the tested subject will read or project his or her own feelings and interpretations into the inkblots, thus revealing deep personality characteristics to the skilled examiner.

After presenting each of the ten cards, the subject is asked what he or she sees or what the inkblot is reminiscent of, or even perhaps a more formal, "what might this be?" The responses are recorded. Then the subject is asked to go over the cards again and point out where what was reported was seen and why he or she called it what he or she did.

There have been disagreements concerning whether quantitative efforts at scoring are better than loosely structured interpretations, which are highly subjective. Obviously the examiner's knowledge of personality dynamics is the real key to the instrument's validity. Examiners who read their own theory into test results, or in some cases, project personal problems onto the results have been criticized.

When a quantitative approach is used, three criteria determine scores:

1. Location Scores
   - Was the whole inkblot interpreted?
   - Were unusual details emphasized?
2. Determinant Scores
   - Was form more important than color?
   - Was the object moving?
   - Did the response fit the inkblot's objective form?
3. Content Score
   - Did the examinee make popular responses?
   - Were animals, humans, or objects emphasized?

The interpretation of the scores is a process that involves extensive training, but some general considerations can serve as examples of how the data are used.

1. Responses involving humans in motion indicate creativity and imagination.
2. Responses that are overly original or unusual indicate a schizophrenic tendency.
3. Preoccupation with color shows problems controlling emotions.
4. Rejecting both color and human movement signifies a rigid personality.
5. Preoccupation with the details of the inkblots indicates a compulsive behavior type.

Attempts to establish the reliability and validity of this instrument have met with limited success. Interjudge reliability tends to be low, and attempts to validate the test against outside criteria have not been successful. Stability over time using the same examiner is more satisfactory. The justification for its use is derived from the testimonies of clinicians who believe it to be valuable and who have had success with it as a clinical tool.

The most important criticism of the instrument, in addition to low reliability and validity, concerns the excessive commitment of time required before a clinician is deemed skilled in its use. Six or more credit hours plus more time in practicums and internships are usually required, and it is questionable whether the benefits of the instrument justify the time spent learning to administer it.

When an alternate form is desired with the same general characteristics as the Rorschach, the Holtsman Inkblot Technique can be used. It includes ninety inkblots in pairs, and computer scoring is available.

The Thematic Apperception Test (TAT)

The Thematic Apperception Test (TAT) is a projective assessment technique used by clinical psychologists who are specially trained in its use. It is used to gain insight into a subject's personality through fantasies and motives. The author of the TAT was Henry A. Murray, a psychologist particularly interested in needs structures. It was first published by The Harvard University Press in 1943.

The test consists of thirty ambiguous cards that depict scenes ranging from individuals in conversation to bizarre dreamlike images. Each was chosen to evoke an emotional response. For instance, a man may be shown in conversation with an older woman. In their response to such a picture, men are likely to reveal their feelings about their mother. A young girl may be shown arguing with an older man, and this could elicit feelings for a father or fatherlike figure. There is also one blank card.

The subject is asked to make up a story about each picture and is asked the following questions:

1. What led up to what is happening in the story?
2. What is happening in the story?
3. How does the person (or persons) feel in the story?
4. What is the final outcome of the story?

Interpretation emphasizes consistency in dominant themes. It is felt that these represent the inner thoughts and feelings of the subject.

The test is administered in two fifty-minute sessions, one day apart. Ten cards are used per session, with a maximum of five minutes per card. It is suggested for use with individuals aged four and over. There are four separate sets of cards chosen from among the thirty for different combinations of the subject's sex and age.

Themes emphasized in the instrument's interpretation are perception of authority, reaction to a difficult task, originality, belief in the importance of luck, magical intervention, happiness versus unhappiness, and feeling about parents. There is some relationship between the stories generated and actual behavior, but this relationship is not always direct. Aggressive stories may be associated with aggressive behavior, but aggresive stories combined with stories containing plots in which agression is justified may indicate that this inclination is being repressed. Sometimes the adult responses to the TAT are more closely related to adolescent behavior than the TAT stories of adolescents.

The Assessment of Personality Through the Interpretation of Drawings

The Figure Drawing Test is a projective personality test that utilizes interpretations of drawings of the human figure. It is based on the assumption that these figures and the way they are executed reveal the examiner's personality, including self-image and attitudes toward other people. This approach works best with children and can be used with illiterates and those who do not know the language. Administration is easy, and the task is ambiguous enough to make it difficult to fake.

Having been given a pencil and a piece of paper, the examinee is asked to draw a person. If the examinee asks questions or objects to the task, he or she is told that artistic ability is unimportant and to draw whatever he or she wishes, except that it should be a complete figure and not just a head. Abstract stereotyped cartoons or stick figures are not acceptable.

After the first figure is drawn, the examinee is asked to draw a person of the opposite sex on the reverse side of the paper. Verbalizations, sequence of drawing, bodily gestures, and other behavior are noted, as well as manner (confident, cautious, impulsive), need for more directions, and anything else that indicates how the individual copes with the task.

There is no single approach to interpreting the drawings. Some psychologists use graphological analysis, and others apply psychoanalytical concepts such as self-image and ego ideal. Most examiners use an approach based on individual clinical experience. It is helpful to examine the drawings as a whole, in order to note the attitudes and tone they convey, and then look for cues in specific aspects of each figure. It is always assumed, unless otherwise indicated, that the subject is drawing him- or herself.

SUMMARY

1. Personality tests include the forms of assessment that do not fall under the rubric of mental ability testing.
2. Theoretical views of personality can be classified as either nomothetic or idiographic.

3. There are four major ways of assessing personality: (1) by asking the examinee directly (self-report), (2) by asking others (rating scales and letters of recommendation), (3) by observing behavior (systematic observations), and (4) by means of interpreting an examinee's response to ambiguous stimuli (projective tests).
4. Directly questioning the examinee is the most common approach to assessing personality and includes interviews, questionnaires, and objectively scored personality tests.
5. Objectively scored personality-assessment instruments can be categorized according to their use: adjustment scales, interest inventories, and attitude scales.
6. The three main approaches to selecting items for an adjustment scale are logical-theoretical, empirical criterion keying, and factor analysis.
7. The Edwards Personal Preference Scale (EPPS) is an example of an adjustment scale based on the logical-theoretical approach.
8. The most often-used adjustment scale, the MMPI, was developed using empirical criterion keying.
9. The items for the 16 PF and the Guilford-Zimmerman Temperament Survey were selected by means of factor analysis.
10. The most often-used interest inventory is the SCII, which provides information about an individual's overall areas of interest (General Occupational Themes), more specific areas of interest (Basic Interest Scales), and the specific occupation with which he or she has most in common (Occupational Scales).
11. One of the most important issues surrounding interest inventories concerns the issue of sex bias. Such instruments are inherently conservative because they reflect existing job satisfaction. There has been pressure to have these instruments restructured in such a way that they encourage males and females to enter nontraditional occupations.
12. Attitudes are usually assessed by means of a summative rating scale (sometimes called the Likert scale), which consists of a series of items with which the subject indicates his or her degree of agreement or disagreement.
13. Information about personality obtained through the perceptions of others is obtained by means of letters of recommendation and rating scales.
14. Direct observations involve the understanding of personality through careful and systematic observations.
15. Projective tests provide a means of learning about an individual's personality that promises to avoid an examinee's conscious or unconscious attempts to supress such information.

SUGGESTED READINGS

ANASTASI, A. (1982). *Psychological testing*. New York: Macmillan. [This textbook contains excellent chapters on personality, particularly Chapter 17, which covers self-report inventories, and Chapter 18, which is on interest inventories.]

SHERTZER, B., & LINDEN, J. D. (1979). *Fundamentals of individual appraisal: Assessment techniques for counselors*. Boston: Houghton. [This book is a good source for brief descriptions of the various types of personality instruments.]

SUNDBERG, N. D. (1977). *Assessment of persons*. Englewood Cliffs, N.J.: Prentice-Hall. [This textbook contains useful information about personality assessment, particularly the use of projective techniques.]

17

Selecting Tests, Reporting Results, and the Future of Measurement

OVERVIEW

The purpose of this chapter is to pull together some of the themes that have been introduced throughout this book. Like most aspects of our culture, the measurement field is an institution that is undergoing rapid change. In this chapter the ways that tests are used and the decisions that must be made in the process of their selection are described. Also included is a description of the available sources for obtaining information about tests and suggestions about presenting their results. Finally, some thoughts about the ways that measurement and evaluation can be expected to change in the future are presented.

OBJECTIVES

From this chapter you will learn about how tests are selected and how their results are conveyed, and you will gain some insights about the future of testing. Specifically, you will learn the following:

- The levels at which selection takes place.
- The various purposes of testing.
- How to find out about tests and assessment instruments.
- The best ways of reporting the results of tests and conveying this information to others.
- The changes in measurement and evaluation that can be expected in the future.

Introduction

The importance of testing in our society tends to run in cycles that range from public acceptance to general hostility. The swings in these attitudes do not always cut completely across society, but we seem to be in a state where test use is either increasing or declining. The demise of testing is either being proclaimed or its pervasiveness decried.

During the late 1960s and early 1970s, there was considerable opposition to testing and testing-related activities. The National Education Association (NEA) was calling for a moratorium on all standardized testing in public schools at the same time that an association of black psychologists was demanding a ban on mental ability testing. The causes of this opposition were diverse but seemed to center on egalitarian sentiments fueled by opposition to the Vietnam War and the expansion of the civil rights and feminist movements. There was the belief that as a society we should avoid establishing hierarchies in which only those at the top reap the rewards. It was further asserted that individual differences and testing programs that promoted their existence should be deemphasized, and that our society should provide more benefits for those who were most in need. In the 1980s egalitarianism has declined and seems to have been replaced by the goal of establishing a meritocracy that has testing as one of its major components.

At the present time there is a great deal of concern about the poor quality of our educational systems. One response to this concern is the use of standardized achievement tests to improve student performance. A current manifestation of this view is the threat of diploma denial based on performance on minimum competency tests.

Selecting an Assessment Instrument

A large number of issues and problems accompanies this growing interest in tests and test use. In order to make good decisions in this area we must first of all consider the level at which testing decisions are to be made and who is to make the decision. Second, there must be a determination of the purposes of testing and the methods of obtaining information about tests.

The Level of Selection

The first big issue in test selection concerns the level at which the selection takes place and who does the selecting. There is a tendency for the level of test selection to be related to the cost of the testing program. In general the greater the financial outlay, the higher the level of the decision. Test-selection decisions can be divided into four levels: teacher, school, school district, and state.

Teacher-Level Decisions Teachers have relatively few opportunities to select tests other than the ones they create. This is mainly because they are not given funds for such purposes. Occasionally they may be in the position to obtain achievement tests in specific subject matter areas, or diagnostic tests may be made available to them. Generally they must select from a set of tests that have been chosen by someone at a higher level.

School-Level Decisions In high schools, counselors are responsible for most of the decisions about test selection. These decisions generally involve the selection of interest inventories and/or aptitude tests. There are only certain types of tests that the counselor can choose. The use of personality tests in schools is declining because the permission of parents must be secured before such instruments can be administered. Parents also have the right to see the reports from any tests given to their children. This is the result of the 1974 Family Educational Rights and Privacy Act, often referred to as the Buckley Amendment. This regulation eliminates the practice of administering personality tests and placing the results in a student's file without his or her parents knowing such information exists. There is also a reluctance to become too involved in the mental health of students because P.L. 94-142 requires that public schools provide an adapted educational program for any student who has been identified as needing such as program. The administration of personality tests can lead to more students being labeled emotionally disturbed and eligible for adapted educational programs. To avoid the expense of providing such programs, schools try to avoid the identification of these problems.

District-Level Decisions Most decisions regarding the choice of standardized tests are made at the local school-district level. These are difficult decisions because there are many factors involved, and it is easy to underestimate the difficulty of the choice. The technical characteristics of the test must be evaluated, which requires someone with background and skill in this discipline. The most fundamental decision concerns whether to use an existing test or develop a new one, but the costs and practical aspects of the test-administration process must also be understood and considered. Finally, teachers, counselors, administrators, and parents need to feel that they are a part of the decision-making process. Committees are often used because they can be set up in such a way that they include representatives of the different interested constituencies and the expertise needed for a good decision. The committee then makes recommendations to the individual, who ultimately must make the decision.

State-Level Decisions States are increasingly becoming involved in decisions about the administration of standardized achievement tests. The selection of a single test for an entire state permits comparisons among school districts that can be useful for purposes of evaluation. It also centralizes the test-purchasing procedures. As a result of the financial commitments involved, this can have important political significance. States also make decisions regarding the instruments to be used for placing children in special education classes. They make these decisions in conjunction with the setting of standards to determine who is eligible for such classes and who is not. This needs to be centralized at the state level because much of the funding for special education programs comes from the state. States want to control who is identified as a special education student so that they can control how much money each district receives.

No single test can serve all purposes. Generally, each instrument does only one thing well, but nothing prevents a test publisher from making claims to the contrary. Most standardized tests are promoted as being able to do far more than there is evidence to show that they can do.

Before a test is selected, it is necessary to specify the goals it is supposed to achieve. There are four main purposes for administering standardized measures of achievement: the diagnosis of learning problems, the determination of what a student has learned, the assessment of minimum competency, and evaluation. It is possible to use the same test to accomplish several of these purposes or to have one tests that purports to be useful for all of the purposes, but this will usually mean that none of the purposes are accomplished with maximum efficiency.

Diagnosis Diagnostic tests must be constructed quite differently from tests intended for overall evaluation. They are most reliable, and have the smallest standard error of measurement, at the low end of their scale, which is where students who are having problems are likely to be located. This is in contrast to most tests, which endeavor to be most reliable in the middle of the distribution where the majority of students are found. Diagnostic tests also must have reliable subscale scores so that a student's strengths and weaknesses can be isolated. It is not enough to point out the items that he or she gets wrong. A single item or even several items are not enough to measure a specific ability reliably. Furthermore, diagnostic tests should not be routinely administered to all students. It is a waste of time for average and above-average students to take a test intended to isolate the specific weaknesses of low-performing students.

Determining Specifically What a Student Has Learned Criterion-referenced tests are structured to provide information about what a student has learned. Unfortunately, this is more likely to be what educators think they want to know than what they really want to know. When you consider a set of objectives, a sufficient number of items to assess each objective, and the large number of students being tested, the amount of data generated by criterion-referenced tests is overwhelming. Such information may have some value to teachers and parents in terms of understanding what a student has learned, but it is of no real use to anyone else. Once this is realized, performance on individual subscales is ignored and tallies of the total number of items correct are obtained. Once this is done, the integrity of the criterion-referenced approach is compromised, and the information derived will be greatly inferior to what would have been obtained with norm-referenced tests.

An important, but often unrecognized, difference between norm- and criterion-referenced tests is that the criterion-referenced test can only sample a restricted range of material. In order to have a sufficient number of items to assess each objective, only a limited number of objectives can be reliably assessed. With a norm-referenced test, on which a much more limited number of summary scores is reported, a broader range of abilities can be assessed. True, it is not possible to specify the level of achievement in a large number of areas, but it is the overall score that usually is of most interest anyway.

Minimum Competency As was emphasized in Chapter 11, minimum competency is a movement of great importance in education today. Virtually every state has already implemented such programs, is in the process of doing so, or is studying its possible implementation. Unfortunately the approaches to accomplishing this goal have not always been consistent with what is known about the best ways of assessing student performance.

The ideal approach would be to make a determination of the areas in which a student's minimum competency is to be assessed and then locate the best instrument for accomplishing this goal. This is seldom done. More often a criterion-referenced format is selected. This is too bad because there are more reasons for not using this approach than for using it. With a criterion-referenced test one obtains a separate score for each objective. This is usually more information than anyone wants. What is needed is a summary score intended to determine if the student has reached a level that permits the conclusion that he or she is competent. As a result, the criterion-referenced aspect of the test is often ignored, and decisions about competence are based on the percent of items correctly answered. Furthermore, items chosen for a criterion-referenced test are selected because they differentiate those students that are competent from those who are not. This is okay if you want to examine each item separately, but if you are summing across items, greater variability in difficulty is needed. Generally, this requires items that are more difficult than those that would be selected using a criterion-referenced approach. It can be expected that minimum competency tests contructed using a criterion-referenced approach will be of considerably lower reliability than those constructed using a norm-referenced format.

With all of the disadvantages, you might be wondering why such an approach would ever be selected. There are three possible reasons. First of all, although criterion-referenced testing methods have been around since the late 1960s, they are still perceived as a recent innovation, so there is the belief that because it is newer, it is better. Second, the emphasis on objectives creates the impression that such a test is more constructive, in that it focuses on student strengths and weaknesses and therefore may have a greater value in modifying educational practices. When only summary scores are used, this aspect of the test is lost. Third, there is the naive belief that the only fair way a test can be constructed to assess competency is to make each item capable of assessing mastery. Such an approach lends an air of legitimacy to such assessment and makes it easier to establish the content, curriculum, and instructional validity of a test. This makes the job of selling the test to the public easier. Paradoxically, this method of constructing minimum competence tests, which appears to be the most legitimate, is in fact a poor way of constructing such a test.

Another important decision encountered in the process of selecting a minimum competency test concerns the question of whether to use an available test or construct a new one. For economic and test-quality reasons, existing tests should always be used when they are available and appropriate. The cost of developing good tests is staggering; it makes no sense for individual school districts or states to create their own tests when this is not necessary.

The decision to develop a local test is often rooted in a concern for content related validity: the need to ensure that the test assesses the objectives designated as appropriate for the school system. Standardized achievement tests are capable of assessing only a limited number of objectives. They must only include objectives that are common to all states and school districts if they are to be marketable on a nationwide basis. No school district would want to use a test that assessed objectives that were not included in their curriculum because this would not be fair to the students taking the test. This is a particular problem for subject-matter areas with which specific content is associated, like science and history. It is less of a problem for reading and math because school districts nationwide require students to achieve about the same objectives in these two areas. Because most school districts that are implementing minimum competency testing start out with the assessment of these two areas, one would expect school districts and states to utilize existing commercially available tests. This is not what happens and, instead, they generally construct their own tests. One reason they do this is that it is easier to convince the public and the courts that the test is legitimate when it can be shown that the test was based directly on the instructional objectives of the school district.

School districts probably should be constructing their own tests to assess such areas as science and social studies. It is very difficult to find appropriate existing instruments in these areas because school districts and states differ so much in their specific objectives and in the grade level at which that content is introduced to students.

Another reason locally constructed tests are preferred concerns the problem of setting cutoff scores to determine who passes and who does not. This is a big problem in criterion-referenced and minimum competency testing that seems to resist technical solutions. There is no satisfactory method of setting cutoff scores, although many have been tried. The setting of cutoff scores can easily become a political problem because a high failure rate reflects badly on the school system that is doing the testing. There is a strong temptation to set cutoff scores in ways that make the system looks good. Cutoff scores are usually set in terms of some percentage of items passed. The number of students passing the test then becomes a function of the difficulty of the test. Because the difficulty of a test is in the hands of the test's constructors, there is no real accountability concerning what a score means. If a standardized test is used, anyone with access to the test's manual can translate the cutoff score into grade equivalents. Although it might reflect well on a school district to be able to say that 90 percent of its students got more than 70 percent of the items on a test correct, it would not be nearly as impressive to say that minimum competency means performing at a fifth-grade level. A minimum competency test should not be used for purposes of evaluating a state or school district, but it is difficult to prevent this from happening.

Evaluation Because standardized test scores usually are available and because they appear to be objective, there is a temptation to use them for purposes of evaluation. Certainly it is useful to include test data as a part of an evaluation of a school or school district. However, it takes a great deal of skill and sophistication to interpret the scores correctly. The test data available are not usually a fair measure of a system's effectiveness because the testing process is controlled by those being evaluated. This is a big enough problem when standardized tests are administered, but when a system creates its own tests, sets their own criteria for passing, and uses the results as evidence of how good of a job it is doing, the question of credibility arises. For test results to be legitimate, the test should be administered by an outside agency that also defines the level of performance necessary for satisfactory performance.

Finding Out About Tests and Assessment Instruments

Before a new drug can be marketed it must undergo years of rigorous testing. The process is very expensive and there are periodical complaints that useful drugs, successfully used in other countries, are not yet available in the United States. On the other hand, there have been some truly dangerous drugs kept out of this country that were used with devastating effects elsewhere. Thalidomide, which caused terrible birth defects when administered to pregnant women, is one example. Although it was used extensively in Europe, it was never licensed for use in this country. This process of licensing drugs is intended to protect the public not only from dangerous drugs, but also from those that are ineffective. Drug companies are also restrained from making claims about their products that are not supported by evidence.

Even though standardized tests may not have the same potential for harm that drugs have, their unrestricted use can lead to abuses. No official and systematic review of tests exists. There are no real limitations on test publishers concerning either the tests they sell or the claims that they make about these instruments. The only accountability is their occasional evaluation in journals and other publications that review tests. The only constraint is the marketplace, where the rule seems to be *caveat emptor*, "let the buyer beware."

The worst abuses are not the result of poorly thought-out, unreliable, and invalid tests developed by publishers or authored by individuals who do not know what they are doing. The worst abuses occur with what starts out as good tests, developed using the best expertise but then marketed using unsubstantiated claims or including unjustified scores and interpretations.

There is little hope for a change in these circumstances in the near future, and no new federal agency to oversee standardized tests is being advocated. Perhaps all that can be done is to urge the users of tests to read the claims of test publishers with a critical eye.

A new potential abuse comes from the use of computer-generated interpretations of test scores. As tests become more complex, more of them can only be scored using a computer. This includes tests in many areas such as standardized achievement tests, personality tests, and interest inventories. If a test must be scored by a machine scorer and its results are already stored within the computer, then it is a simple step, assuming the availability of appropriate programming, to have an interpretive report generated. Examples of such reports can be found in the Appendix. It is very difficult for a user to evaluate the validity of such reports. One is forced to accept the integrity of the company producing the software that generates them.

Those who read the reports may not even know they are reading a computer-generated report. The format of some reports is such that they are clearly and easily identified as being computer generated, but others appear to be written by a counselor or psychologist. It can be expected that the use of such reports will proliferate because diagnoses by trained personnel are expensive and difficult to obtain, whereas computer-generated reports are relatively inexpensive. Unless they are valid, they are no bargain and have the potential for great harm, especially because they seem to eliminate the need for a trained individual to interpret their results.

Because there is no centralized source of information about tests, it is not easy to find out about them. This is not too big of a problem for the most well-known tests, but it is for those that are even slightly less well known. It is particularly difficult to obtain the sort of critical evaluations in which someone is willing to say "Yes, this is a good test for these purposes" or "No, this test should not be used." In finding out about tests, there are three types of information that potential users need to know, including finding out what tests are available, their characteristics, and evaluative information about them.

Finding Standardized Tests

In the case of standardized achievement and mental ability tests, the major available tests are well known, and when a new test is introduced the publishers go to great lengths to make sure that everyone in the field is made aware of its introduction. Major new entries into the field are greeted with considerable fanfare. Tests assessing constructs that are more specialized may be less well known, and there are so many that no one person can be familiar with all of them. This is true of tests used to assess specific aspects of cognitive functioning, but it is even more clearly the case with personality tests used to assess specific aspects of personality.

In the case of large-scale achievement, mental ability, group personality, and interest inventories, the standards for content validity, reliability, and norm sampling are so high that developing a new test is prohibitively expensive. For this reason there are relatively few new tests that enter the market in these areas. In settings where tests are used without extensive norms, there is a proliferation of new tests being developed every day. The individual who seeks information about these instruments has a difficult task.

There are three main ways of learning about what tests are available. First of all, one can become familiar with the literature and follow up references to tests. Second, catalogs can be obtained from publishers that list all of the tests available. Publishers are more than happy to send these catalogs to individuals interested in purchasing tests and test materials. A third way of becoming aware of available tests is through published compilations of available tests: for instance, *Tests in Print* (Buros, 1974), which supplement his *Mental Measurement Yearbooks*, and endeavors to compile all commercially available tests in the English language. Of course, with a 1974 publication date, it does not include recently published tests. A more recent publication is *Tests* (Sweetland & Keyser, 1983) which is described by its authors as "a comprehensive reference for assessments in psychology, education, and business." These two books list tests with a brief description of their characteristics but do not include critical reviews or evaluations. There are other sources that list available tests for such specialized areas as reading, math, and special education.

Finding Out About the Characteristics of Tests

Some information about a test's characteristics can be obtained from the sort of compilations already mentioned. Measurement textbooks can also provide information about specific tests. You will find only a small proportion of available tests described in these publications; however, if you are interested in a well-known and often-used instrument, this may be a quick source of information. To really get a grasp of what a test is like, you need to examine a copy of the test and its manuals. The plural is used because with large-scale tests there is often more than one manual. Some publishers provide administration manuals, interpretive manuals, and technical manuals. The details of such topics as reliability and validity are likely to be included only in the technical manual. Most publishers will provide specimen tests along with the manual or manuals to those professionals who it is felt should have access to the test. There is a need to maintain the security of the test so that copies do not become available to the general public. Psychological tests, including individual intelligence and personality tests, are made available only to those who are qualified to use them. The publishers of college and graduate school aptitude tests also are restrictive in disseminating their tests and will release only sample items, never the tests themselves.

It is only through an examination of the actual instrument and a thorough reading of the accompanying manuals that you will be able to understand whether a particular test should be selected. It must be kept in mind, however, that one purpose of preparing test manuals and making them available is to convince individuals like you, who are considering the use of a test, that this is the one you should select. You cannot expect to find anything critical in a test manual, and any weakness of the test will be carefully hidden.

The experienced and knowledgeable test user will be able to read between the lines of the manuals and make an evaluation of a test based both on what it says and what it doesn't say. Often what a manual leaves out is as significant as the claims that are made. Those who lack the prerequisite knowledge to make such judgments should refer to sources of critical reviews of tests.

Finding Critical Reviews of Tests

The most important source of reviews about tests are the Buros *Mental Measurement Yearbooks* published by the Buros Institute of Mental Measurements. There is a total of eight yearbooks now available; the *Eighth Mental Measurement Yearbook*, published in 1978, is the most recent. Each yearbook emphasizes those tests that have been published since the previous yearbook, so it may be necessary to consult earlier volumes for information about older tests. For some tests, only minimal descriptive information is provided, but for most, one or more critical reviews of the test are included. This provides the reader with the best single source of evaluative information about tests. The reviews are well written and objective, and the reviewers are not hesitant to criticize and point out weaknesses in tests when they find this warranted. Another source of critical evaluations is professional journals. Two good sources are the *Journal of Educational Measurement* and *Measurement and Evaluation in Guidance*. Other professional journals in psychology, counseling, and education may contain test reviews either as a regular feature or as the subject of articles in the journal.

When none of these sources turns up information about a test in which you are interested, it is possible to find references to tests in *Education Index* and *Psychological Abstracts*. If an examination of the abstract suggests that articles might be of use, then you can go to this original source for information. Additional sources of information can be found in the services provided by the Educational Resources Information Center (ERIC). These include the *Current Index to Journals in the Education* (CIJE) and *Resources in Education* (RIE). This information is available through computer network systems that permit access over telephone lines by means of a computer terminal or microcomputer with a modem. It is important that test reviews be examined because it is easy to get only a one-sided view of a test. Talking to others who already use the test is not necessarily helpful because they may not be knowledgeable or they may already have too much invested in the test to be critical.

Evaluating Tests and Assessment Instruments

The first step in making a decision about which test to use is to make sure that you have a clear understanding of exactly what purpose or purposes you want the test to serve. Publishers may make a claim to the contrary, but as a general rule, each test can serve only one purpose, and it is unlikely that a single test will be effective in meeting several diverse needs. The next step involves obtaining relevant information about the test. This will generally include the test itself, the manuals that accompany it, and critical evaluations made by experts in the field. Once this information is obtained, it is possible to initiate an evaluation of the test instrument.

Test Objectives

The first step in evaluating a test is to determine whether its purposes are the same as yours. You must examine how the publisher or test authors believe that the test should be used, understanding that they may make claims concerning the flexibility of their tests that are not supported by evidence. This is an area where critical reviews will be helpful.

In the case of a standardized achievement test, the set of specific learning objectives that the test assesses will be included in the manual. Each potential user must compare this list with the objectives of their particular school or district. The test will usually cover a more restricted number of objectives than desired because of the need to make the test appropriate for the widest range of users. In addition, the limitations of the objective-testing format restricts the types of information about student performance that can be gathered.

Norm Sampling

The test manuals should include a description of the procedures that were used in setting up the norm sample. The quality of the norming procedure is not simply a function of the size of the sample, although for large-scale tests it is not unusual for norm samples to be in the hundreds of thousands. The representativeness of the sample is even more important. If the test is reporting results that purport to compare an individual fifth-grader's score with that of all other fifth-graders, it is important that the norms represent the performance of all fifth-graders. This will only happen if the procedures used in selecting the norm sample are such that they reflect the population as a whole. This means that when the sample is selected, the test developers must take into account such factors as the type of school and school size; whether is is located in an urban, suburban, or rural setting; socio-economic status; parental education, and so on. Each of these factors must be represented in the norm sample in the same proportions that exist in the population (all fifth-graders in the United States). It also means that the process for deciding who would be included in one of these categories is based on a process of random selection. This does not usually happen because the selection of a norm sample is determined by the school districts that are willing to participate in the norming process. The schools most likely to be willing to participate are those already using an earlier version of the test being normed or another test from the same publisher. The use of such a nonrandom selection process can sometimes adversely affect the representativeness of the norm sample.

In constructing a norm sample, the goal is to make the sample as similar as possible to the population about which generalizations are being made. The major problem with a sample that is not representative is that derived scores based on norms will misrepresent the abilities of those who take the test. The score may over- or underestimate an individual's ability. If the norm sample contains a disproportionate number of above-average students, ability will be underestimated. A child who obtains a score that places him or her at the 50th percentile when compared to the norm group for this particular test would actually be above average and would have a higher percentile if a norm sample that more accurately reflected the population were used. A norm sample with a disproportionate number of below-average students would similarly have the effect of inflating the magnitude of percentiles.

It is important to remember that the main impact of incorrectly constructing a norm sample is that the resulting derived scores will be biased estimators of ability. However, the relative standing of those taking the test will not be affected, nor will the predictive validity of the test be impaired. For instance, the inclusion of handicapped children as part of the norm sample is only significant if they are included in significant numbers and their scores are deviant enough to affect the mean score at different grade levels. Otherwise the score obtained by a handicapped child would be the same whether the norm sample with which they are compared included handicapped children or not.

Types of Derived Scores Provided

When using standardized tests that are scored by a computer, the availability of derived scores is not a problem because it is simple for the scoring program to include algorithms for computing any desired types of scores. All the user needs to do is select the type of derived score desired. Other tests not developed for such large-scale use may not provide as many options in the way of derived scores. If the technical manual provides detailed summary statistics, it may be possible for you to compute your own standard scores. Some test manuals provide only a few types of derived scores and include an insufficient amount of information to permit you to compute your own scores.

Reliability and Standard Error of Measurement

Reliability constitutes one of the most important types of information that should be included in test manuals or other sources of test descriptions. As a rule you will find that test publishers provide large amounts of data on reliability because such data are easy to generate. The quantity of this data is not as important as its quality. First of all, the reliability of data should be in the form of internal consistency. This might be labeled as KR20, KR21, or coefficient alpha reliability. Split-half reliability provides an estimate of internal consistency, not quite as good as those already mentioned but still acceptable. Alternate-forms reliability can also be useful, but because of the expense of generating separate versions of a test it is seldom included. Test-retest reliability is appropriate only for speeded tests or when the stability of the construct being measured is of particular importance. It is acceptable to include this type of reliability along with internal consistency, but it can substitute for internal consistency only in the case of speeded tests.

When subscale scores are included, reliability coefficients should be reported separately for each subscale. It is inappropriate to report the reliability of combined subscales. It is assumed that each subscale is assessing something unique. If not, why bother to include such scores? If the reliabilty of a combination of subscales is very high, they must be intercorrelated.

The reliability of a scale is partially dependent on the number of items, and publishers who want to include many subscales are faced with the problem of subscales with few items, which are likely to have poor reliability. Because subscales are seldom independent, it is tempting to combine them in some way for purposes of determining reliability.

It is difficult to specify an acceptable level of reliability, although it is easier to specify good than poor reliability. Reliability coefficients in the .90s are clearly indicative of high reliability. But coefficients lower than this are not necessarily an indication of poor reliability. Certain subject matter lends itself to high reliability. For instance, tests of verbal intelligence can be expected to have high reliability, often in the .90s. Personality tests, on the other hand, have a much lower reliability.

The standard error of measurement cannot be used to compare tests because its magnitude is dependent on the scale of the test being analyzed. Some users like to have the SEM available because they can use it to compute confidence intervals, as explained in Chapter 5.

Tests developed through the use of latent-trait or item-response theory, because of the sophistication of the data analysis procedures employed, can report SEMs for each scaled score, instead of reporting a single overall SEM, as is done with the most tests. This sort of data is available with the CTBS, and it is very useful in pointing out how misleading a single reliability coefficient or SEM can be. An examination of reliabilities converted from SEMs across different scaled scores shows that, with scores around the mean, the reliability of the test is very high, usually in the mid-.90s. At one standard deviation above or below, the reliabilities generally drops to the mid-.80s. As scores deviate further from the mean, the reliabilities become smaller—almost zero as you approach two standard deviations from the mean. The lesson should be clear. Scores that deviate very far from the mean are unreliable.

Validity

In contrast with reliability, the test user can expect only meager information regarding validity in the typical text manual. Many publishers choose to ignore this characteristic because it is so difficult to establish. The type of evidence for validity provided in the past was usually restricted to one form, determined by the type of text. However, it is better thought of as being unitary, with each method used as evidence for validity.

Achievement tests should always include information about content-related validity, which generally consists of a description of how the test was developed, including the procedures used for selecting objectives and generating items. The test authors usually start with a lengthy list of objectives obtained from a large number of school districts. This list is then reduced to a workable number, with the emphasis on those that all school districts have in common. The objectives are then used as the basis for selecting test items.

Contingency tables are a related feature that shows how items are matched to objectives. They provide the user with an idea of the number of items at each level associated with an objective. The level of an item indicates how abstract it is. The level can range from simple recall of information to the application of principles.

Information about content-related validity, although useful, really does not tell us much about validity. It does not tell us the degree to which inferences made based on scores are legitimate. Generally speaking, this is the only type of validity evidence one can expect to obtain from a test manual for a standardized achievement test. This is true despite the fact that the addition of other types of evidence would provide a more convincing case for validity.

Individual intelligence tests should at least include information on criterion-related validity. However, the manuals for the Wechsler tests and the Stanford-Binet hardly mention validity of any kind. The new Kaufman Assessment Battery for Children (K-ABC) does include some data on concurrent criterion-related validity, primarily correlations between it and the WISC-R and Stanford-Binet. The manuals for individual intelligence tests really should include evidence for predictive criterion-related validity because these tests are so often used to predict student performance in school. Even though you will seldom find such evidence in manuals, it is readily available from other sources.

Group mental ability tests also should provide evidence of predictive criterion-related validity. Some manuals do, but most don't. Predictive-related validity data are widely available for scholastic aptitude tests, such as the SAT and ACT.

With the exception of interest inventories, the manuals for personality tests typically include little or no direct evidence of validity of any kind. The most appropriate evidence for validity for most personality tests is construct-related validity, but it is seldom included in the manuals for these instruments.

Regardless of the type of test, few manuals provide adequate evidence for validity. This is because test manuals are primarily a form of promotional material; they are seldom a reliable source of information about assessment instruments. This is because publishers are unlikely to include any material that does not strongly support the adoption of their tests.

All test manuals really should provide evidence of construct-related validity supplemented, in the case of achievement tests, by content-related validity. In the case of mental ability tests, it should be supplemented by predicitve criterion-related validity. Unfortunately, construct validity is seen almost exclusively in measurement textbooks and is actually applied only in the occasional journal article.

The Practical Aspects of Instrument Evaluation

Once an instrument has been evaluated in terms of the preceding criteria, it is still necessary to consider some additional characteristics that, although not critical, can have an important influence on the usefuleness of a particular instrument. The first consideration is cost effectiveness. This requires a balance between what is absolutely essential and what it would be nice to have, considered in the light of what can be afforded. Testing is a process that can require a considerable outlay of funds. This expense stems from a number of factors: test booklets; answer sheets, where required; and the expense of producing printed results for school-system records and for the individual and/or his or her parents. How much these cost is a function of the length and technical sophistication of the test. Conducting a high-quality item analysis and obtaining a large norm sample are expensive, and these costs must be passed on to the user. Publishers that cut corners in these areas can be expected to produce tests that are less expensive, but users must understand what they are not getting. If one does not want to make comparisons with a national sample, then elaborate norm samples may not be necessary. The purchase and use of a test that is deficient in its technical charactersistics may lead to a testing program that is not really cost effective because the results obtained may be so deficient in reliability and validity that they are not useful.

In addition to the expense of test development, the cost of a test is a function of test length and the type of test booklet used. Some tests use a single multilevel test booklet that can be administered across all grades, with students in each grade using only a portion of the book. Other tests have different booklets for each level. If answers are recorded in the test booklet, a new booklet will need to be purchased for each child for each administration of the test. It is less expensive to use separate answer sheets to record answers because that allows the test booklets to be reused. This technique cannot be used effectively with younger children, because they lack the test-taking skills and motor and cognitive coordination to identify an answer on one page and then transfer their response to another sheet.

The scoring system used and the availability of machine scoring are other important considerations. Hand scoring large numbers of answer sheets is not a very productive way to spend time. For any more than a few tests, machine scoring is much more efficient. Therefore, the availability of machine scoring is an important factor to be considered when adopting a test.

From the standpoint of costs, it also is important to know if a test can only be scored by machine and interpreted by a computer. This is an increasing trend in standardized tests because their complicated scoring systems do not permit hand scoring. It also increases costs, providing another source of income for the test's publisher. Not only do you need to know whether a test can or must be machine scored, you also need to know which of several versions of this service are available. The most common method is to provide scoring at a central location, which requires that tests be sent by mail. With these types of services, you need a quick turnaround. For large school districts that administer a single test to many students, it may be more cost effective to lease the scoring program from the publisher and do the scoring locally. Another option being made available for some tests, particularly personality tests, involves the use of local machine scorers attached to a micro-computer with a modem. These transfer the results by phone line to a central location where the instruments are interpreted. The results are then returned almost immediately to the microcomputer, from which they can be printed.

Test results obtained through the medium of a computer introduce the possibility of computer-generated interpretations and reports. The user needs to know about the availability of such services and about their quality. It is easy to be impressed by a single example of a computer-generated interpretation, but you may find yourself less impressed by succeeding reports if they lack originality.

Tests differ in terms of the complexity of their administration and the completeness of the directions that are included in the manuals that accompany them. If the directions are particularly complex, they might best be included in a separate manual. The directions should be clear and full and should specify the correct conditions for testing. The precise directions to be used by the examiner should be provided word for word, preferably in boldface type. The specification of allowable materials, timing, and permissible responses to inquiries from the examinees also should be included along with sample problems that show the examinee exactly what he or she is to do. To be avoided is the circumstance where an examinee performs poorly and it is then unclear whether his or her performance was the result of a lack of ability to complete the required tasks or an inability to comprehend the instructions. This problem is less of a concern with individually administered tests because the examiner can observe the examinee's performance and determine if he or she understands the instructions. With group tests the individuals who do not understand what they are supposed to do can easily go undetected.

In selecting a test one should also consider the appearance of the test itself. Of importance is the quality of the paper on which the test is printed, the size of the print, the attractiveness of the test layout, the reading level of the test, and the clarity of pictures and illustrations. Items and illustrations should not be split between two pages. In short, nothing in the appearance of the test should increase its difficulty.

It must be remembered that all of the characteristics mentioned here carry a price tag. It is less costly to create a poor test than a good one. The individual charged with the responsibility for selecting a test must seek value, but it is unlikely that one can get more or better test results than are paid for. On the other hand, it is important to avoid paying for expensive characteristics or services for which you have no need.

Reporting Results

It doesn't make sense to commit resources to assessment programs if the results are not conveyed to those who need to use them. There is sometimes a reticence about revealing test results, even among colleagues. This stems from the belief that test results, although useful to a small coterie of experts, can be harmful if they are disseminated too widely. It is believed that those who lack the appropriate expertise and experience to interpret the results may use them incorrectly. There is also the realization that in our society knowledge is often equated with power. Those who know more tend to be perceived as being more important. Counselors and school psychologists are sometimes tempted to withhold test results from teachers for the stated reason that there is a risk that they will misuse the information, when the real reason lies somewhere in the power relationships among school personnel. Teachers are sometimes guilty of the same types of patronizing behavior toward parents.

Although not everyone is equal in his or her ability to understand and use the results of tests, almost all test data can be presented in a manner comprehensible to any audience. This requires that the person who is presenting the information be knowledgeable; he or she may require, under some circumstances, that experts be brought in as consultants to explain test results, either from within or from outside of the system.

Conveying Test Results to Colleagues

The assumption must be made that colleagues are indeed professional and should share all available data that are relevant to the population with which they work. This sharing of information does require some limits. It should be shared on a need-to-know basis. Test results should not be disseminated to those who do not have a direct use for them.

Those with whom the information is being shared may also need individual or group in-service instruction on the appropriate techniques for interpreting scores, as well as on the ethical considerations associated with test use. If the data are misused, administrative interventions may be required; however, test results should not be denied because of this possibility.

The types of scores reported to colleagues and other professionals should be high-level, standard scores such as *T*-scores or scaled scores. Grade equivalents, and percentiles because they are not of an interval scale, can be very misleading when used for the purpose of making comparisons. Stanines are intentionally made imprecise, so they are a poor choice for communicating results among professionals.

Communicating with Parents

In communicating with parents, the foremost concern is that the information provided facilitate understanding. Those who do the communicating must anticipate the level of presentation at which they are likely to be understood. This requires that the person doing the communicating understand what the results mean. Nothing is more disconcerting than to have parents ask questions for which you have no answer or to be caught in an obvious contradiction. Consultants and other experts need to be available when particularly complex results must be communicated. Care must be taken in the case of the explanation of the reults of psychological tests. Their administration presumes highly trained examiners, but too often the explanation of their results is left to those who lack formal training in interpretation. Ideally, a school psychologist should be available to assist in interpreting such tests.

Grade equivalents, percentiles, and stanines are the traditional means of communicating test results to parents. It has generally been assumed that more complicated standard scores are too difficult for parents to understand. But parents have no apparent difficulty in understanding the meaning of IQ scores (at least at a superficial level) or SAT and ACT scores, all of which are standard scores. The biggest problem with reporting results using standard scores involves helping teachers feel more comfortable with them. There is no reason why this could not be accomplished in training sessions for teachers and other interested professionals.

Communicating Test Results to the Community

Naturally most test results are only shared among those who have a need to know. This generally includes other involved professionals, the examinee, and the parents, when the examinee is a minor. The public has no need or reason to know about individual test results. However, in the area of standardized achievement tests, as well as for some group mental ability tests, the public has a great interest in test results that can be used as indicators of school effectiveness or as an evaluation tool. Newspaper reporters demand such information because it makes a good story. The community is very interested in how the school system does as a whole on such tests and in how individual schools compare. Real estate salespersons use this information to influence the house purchases of buyers with children who wish to locate in an area with good schools.

There are a number of problems with publishing test scores in newspapers. First of all, such test scores are not valid indicators of the quality of schools because performance on standardized tests is mainly a function of the underlying ability of students. Changing the characteristics of a school, or the quality of the education provided, has a relatively small effect on test-score performance. Test performance seems to be much more closely associated with family background and socio-economic and minority status. A school with children from upper-middle-class homes and few minorities will have relatively high scores, even if the quality of education provided by the school is poor. The school whose student population consists of less-advantaged children and a higher proportion of minority children will have lower scores, no matter how skilled the teachers and principals and regardless of the quality of the educational program provided. If test scores are used as the only criterion of school performance, the public will have misconceptions about the quality of the education provided in different schools. In other words, test results may give us good information about the level at which students are performing but tell us little about the quality of education they receive. There is another problem. Standardized achievement tests are constructed to provide accurate information about student performance to the schools and through them to parents. This works as long as the school system, principals, and teachers want the test results to be reliable. If the results are used to evaluate schools, principals and teachers will want their students to perform as well as possible on the tests. Because they control the administration of the tests and are aware of test content, and because the tests are revised only every five to ten years, the validity of the results for evaluation purposes is suspect. It is just not reasonable to assume that any individual will be able to suppress the temptation to do things that will ultimately make them look good. For standardized achievement tests to be a legitimate basis for school evaluation, they must be administered by a disinterested neutral organization. The test content will have to be changed each year, and care in test security will have to be a major administrative consideration. In addition, a standard policy concerning who takes and does not take the test will have to be set. There is a great temptation to exclude those students who can be expected to perform poorly on the test.

Even if we disapprove of the policy, tests are being administered and newspapers are demanding the results so that they can publish them. If these data are to be released, it is important that a high level of expertise and knowledge surround the process. Newspaper reporters can be expected to know little about testing and will therefore accept what they are told by the school system. The use of *change scores*, which reflect the difference between tested aptitude and achievement (called AASS scores when used with the CTBS and explained in Chapter 12), should be discouraged. This practice is inconsistent with modern measurement theory. Those scores are also characterized by such low reliability that they are almost meaningless. Results are best reported in the form of *T*-scores. Initially they may be more diifficult to understand than grade equivalents or percentiles, but with increased exposure they will become comprehensible and as acceptable as any other score.

The Future of Measurement and Evaluation in Education

There is a temptation to describe a world of measurement and evaluation for the future that is very much different from the one that presently exists. Of course it is possible that it will be quite different, but using the past as a predictor, there will not be enormous changes because the field is conservative and changes come slowly. There have been several changes over the past twenty years that can be expected to have a lasting effect on future assessment practices. They were introduced with great promise, and it has been anticipated that they would greatly alter the way assessments are conducted. The four most important follow:

1. Criterion-referenced testing.
2. MCT.
3. The use of computers in measurement.
4. The application of latent-trait theory.

Criterion-Referenced Testing

There was a time when criterion-referenced testing was expected to dominate the future of educational testing. During the 1970s it was hard to find critics willing to question that inevitability. The technology promised to solve many of the problems that were plaguing testing; in particular it appeared to provide a method of testing that was nonthreatening and thus likely to calm some of the fears of those who viewed testing as evil. Unfortunately, criterion-referenced testing is associated with such technical problems as how to compute reliability, establish validity, and rationally determine cutoff scores. In addition, to report student performance on a diversity of different objectives is a massive bookkeeping chore. As the difficulty associated with solving these problems became more apparent, the enthusiasm of testing specialists began to wane. At the same time that interest among testing specialists began to decline, the techniques began to be used on an increasingly more widespread basis under conditions where the technical limitations could be conveniently ignored. Criterion-referenced testing is being used by local and state school systems on a widespread basis to construct educational tests. It seems to have an intuitive appeal to the public, even if the resulting tests are often of low quality. Tests are sometimes constructed using criterion-referenced methodology, but the scores reported are not criterion-referenced because only the total score is reported. Despite the dubious effectiveness of this method and its declining popularity among testing specialists, it can be expected that this approach to constructing tests will continue to be used in the future. However, this is an approach that has already passed its apex.

MCT

The MCT movement is one of the most important developments in the field of testing today. Every state has either already developed, is in the process of developing, or is actively considering some form of MCT. Most of the legal roadblocks that at first were threatening to impede such programs have been eliminated, but their technological problems remain. No one really knows how best to conduct minimum competency testing, and there are almost as many versions as there are states and school districts. The measurement problems associated with this form of assessment have not limited the spread of the movement because it is primarily political rather than educational or measurement oriented. It is a response to the widespread belief that our school systems are not performing their job adequately. This is a highly visible, yet relatively inexpensive, way for state legislatures to create the impression that they are on top of the problem and are working hard to improve education.

It is difficult to construct an MCT test that actually does what it is supposed to do: to distinguish between those who are competent or incompetent (or whatever synonyms are used by a state). Those who develop and administer the tests have a vested interest in not having too many students fail, and there is a tendency to structure tests in such a way that only a small percentage of students are actually denied diplomas. After all, such assessment programs are only one part of broader educational reforms, and a high failure rate would reflect badly on other programs. As a result, such programs can be expected to go through a cycle. They begin with a large amount of initial fanfare and high expectations about what such a program can do for an educational system and are followed by implementation and the realization that almost all students are passing. The result that can be expected is a gradual decline in interest in such programs when it is realized that the quality of education has not been markedly improved.

Computers in Measurement

Computer measurement is a development that may end up having the biggest impact on the way that testing and evaluations are conducted in the future. Of course predictions about computers are very risky. Articles written about the future of education twenty years ago hardly mentioned computers. Even *Future Shock* written by Alvin Tofler in 1971 makes little mention of computers in general and says nothing about personal computers. The tendency now is to react to the underestimation of the importance of computers in the past by overdramatizing their future impact. With respect to education in general, it is probably wise to recall the early predictions about programmed instruction and instructional television, which were expected to dominate education in the 1980s. Testing is a little different in that there are certain tasks associated with it that can be done much more easily and economically with a computer. The most important applications are test scoring and interpretation. Large-scale standardized tests are being constructed so that they can only be scored by a computer. Because a test interpretation is so labor intensive, the general trend is to have computers also do the interpretation. Other applications, such as having teachers' test records stored in computer memory and using computers in test construction are a little farther down the road. The problem is that such use requires high-level and clever programming expertise that can only be purchased at high cost. It is not clear that the results can justify the outlay of expenses. In the area of individual testing, there may be a trend toward more testing using the computer to record responses directly. Again, this approach saves a great deal of time and permits the use of less highly trained examiners.

Latent-Trait Theory

Latent-trait theory is another recent and important development in the field of testing. Its impact has mainly been on the users of standardized achievement and aptitude tests. It provides a more sophisticated and effective method of developing and interpreting such tests. Although there are other possible applications throughout testing, it is not at all clear that latent-trait theory will ever be used on a widespread basis. It may simply be too complex and difficult for most in the field to understand. When you realize how poorly much simpler theoretical aspects of measurement are applied, pessimism about the application of this far more sophisticated technique seems warranted.

Conclusions About the Future of Testing

One clear trend in the field of measurement is that computers will play an increasingly more important role in testing and evaluation. Although to predict a future in which all or even most testing is done using this medium, or to expect that pencil and paper tests will cease to be used, is unjustified.

Predictions about the future of standardized testing must be guarded because we are, after all, talking about a field where the majority of decisions are made by the consumer, who is not necessarily well informed. What those in the field of testing feel is best for the testing field is subordinate to what the test buying public wants. If there is a demand, there will be a publishing company willing to meet that demand. Concerns about the fact that certain tests or approaches to testing are neither useful nor justified by what is known about measurement may fall on deaf ears. It might be true that a small fuel-efficient, easy-to-operate automobile, constructed to be safe in a crash, is the only type of vehicle that should be marketed. However, it is clear that the public wants a choice of different cars. They demand them and are willing to pay for them, and there are manufacturers more than happy to accede to their fantasies. The same holds true for testing. Whatever sort of test someone wants and can pay for, particularly if he or she can pay for them in volume, will be created, marketed, promoted, and sold.

SUMMARY

1. Our society seems to be entering a stage where testing, and particularly standardized testing, is increasing in importance.

2. The increased importance of testing has forced educators to make many decisions related to testing. Decisions must be made concerning the level at which the choice about a test should be made and who should make that decision. The purposes of the test, which test is to be selected, and how the results are to be disseminated must also be determined.

3. There is no centralized objective source of information about tests, so users should be skeptical about the claims made by test publishers.
4. Information about what tests are available can be obtained from publisher's catalogs, references in journals and books, and reference books that list available tests.
5. Some information about the characteristics of a test can be obtained from the sources named in 4. Additional information can be obtained from measurement textbooks and from an examination of actual tests and the manuals that accompany them.
6. Critical reviews of tests can be obtained either from journals related to the type of test that is of interest or from the mental measurement yearbooks.
7. Tests need to be evaluated in terms of the objectives they assess, their norm sampling, the types of derived scores they provide, their reliability, their validity, the quality of their manuals, the instructions provided, their appearance, and their cost.
8. Results of tests should be disseminated as widely as is appropriate. Although individual results should not be shared with those who have no real need to know, results should not be hidden from those who need them out of an exaggerated fear that the results will be misused.
9. The future of testing can be examined along the lines of criterion-referenced testing, minimum competency testing, latent-trait theory, and the application of computer technology.

SUGGESTED READINGS

GRONLUND, N. E. (1985). *Measurement and evaluation in teaching*. New York: Macmillan. [This textbook includes excellent articles on obtaining information about tests and the most effective methods of disseminating information about results to parents and the community.]

HISCOX, M. D. (1984). A planning guide for microcomputers in educational measurement. *Educational Measurement Issues and Practice, 3*(2), 28–34. [This provides an excellent discussion of the future of computers in the testing field. The author cautions about overselling the significance of computers in the future of testing.]

THORNDIKE, R. L., & HAGEN, E. (1977). *Measurement and evaluation in psychology and education*. New York: Wiley. [This book contains a useful chapter on obtaining information about tests.]

APPENDIX Statistical Tables and Sample Reports

Included in this appendix are two tables and two sample reports. Table A.1 provides the percentage of cases between the mean and proportions of the standard deviation. Table A.2 provides the magnitude of the correlation needed for significance at the .05 level for sample size ranging from one to five hundred. Following the tables are two sample computer generated counseling or psychological reports. The first report is based on the 16 PF and the second report on the Strong-Campbell Interest Inventory.

TABLE A.1 Percentage of Cases That Can Be Found Between the Mean and a Given Proportion of a Standard Deviation (*z*-score)

Proportion of Standard Deviation (*z*)	Proportion of Cases Between $\overline{X}$ and *z*	Proportion of Standard Deviation (*z*)	Proportion of Cases Between $\overline{X}$ and *z*	Proportion of Standard Deviation (*z*)	Proportion of Cases Between $\overline{X}$ and *z*
0.00	.0000	0.40	.1554	0.80	.2881
0.01	.0040	0.41	.1591	0.81	.2910
0.02	.0080	0.42	.1628	0.82	.2939
0.03	.0120	0.43	.1664	0.83	.2967
0.04	.0160	0.44	.1700	0.84	.2995
0.05	.0199	0.45	.1736	0.85	.3023
0.06	.0239	0.46	.1772	0.86	.3051
0.07	.0279	0.47	.1808	0.87	.3078
0.08	.0319	0.48	.1844	0.88	.3106
0.09	.0359	0.49	.1879	0.89	.3133
0.10	.0398	0.50	.1915	0.90	.3159
0.11	.0438	0.51	.1950	0.91	.3186
0.12	.0478	0.52	.1985	0.92	.3212
0.13	.0517	0.53	.2019	0.93	.3238
0.14	.0557	0.54	.2054	0.94	.3264
0.15	.0596	0.55	.2088	0.95	.3289
0.16	.0636	0.56	.2123	0.96	.3315
0.17	.0675	0.57	.2157	0.97	.3340
0.18	.0714	0.58	.2190	0.98	.3365
0.19	.0753	0.59	.2224	0.99	.3389
0.20	.0793	0.60	.2257	1.00	.3413
0.21	.0832	0.61	.2291	1.01	.3438
0.22	.0871	0.62	.2324	1.02	.3461
0.23	.0910	0.63	.2357	1.03	.3485
0.24	.0948	0.64	.2389	1.04	.3508
0.25	.0987	0.65	.2422	1.05	.3531
0.26	.1026	0.66	.2454	1.06	.3554
0.27	.1064	0.67	.2486	1.07	.3577
0.28	.1103	0.68	.2517	1.08	.3599
0.29	.1141	0.69	.2549	1.09	.3621
0.30	.1179	0.70	.2580	1.10	.3643
0.31	.1217	0.71	.2611	1.11	.3665
0.32	.1255	0.72	.2642	1.12	.3686
0.33	.1293	0.73	.2673	1.13	.3708
0.34	.1331	0.74	.2704	1.14	.3729
0.35	.1368	0.75	.2734	1.15	.3749
0.36	.1406	0.76	.2764	1.16	.3770
0.37	.1443	0.77	.2794	1.17	.3790
0.38	.1480	0.78	.2823	1.18	.3810
0.39	.1517	0.79	.2852	1.19	.3830

TABLE A.1 (continued)

Proportion of Standard Deviation (z)	Proportion of Cases Between $\bar{X}$ and z	Proportion of Standard Deviation (z)	Proportion of Cases Between $\bar{X}$ and z	Proportion of Standard Deviation (z)	Proportion of Cases Between $\bar{X}$ and z
1.20	.3849	1.60	.4452	2.00	.4772
1.21	.3869	1.61	.4463	2.01	.4778
1.22	.3888	1.62	.4474	2.02	.4783
1.23	.3907	1.63	.4484	2.03	.4788
1.24	.3925	1.64	.4495	2.04	.4793
1.25	.3944	1.65	.4505	2.05	.4798
1.26	.3962	1.66	.4515	2.06	.4803
1.27	.3980	1.67	.4525	2.07	.4808
1.28	.3997	1.68	.4535	2.08	.4812
1.29	.4015	1.69	.4545	2.09	.4817
1.30	.4032	1.70	.4554	2.10	.4821
1.31	.4049	1.71	.4564	2.11	.4826
1.32	.4066	1.72	.4573	2.12	.4830
1.33	.4082	1.73	.4582	2.13	.4834
1.34	.4099	1.74	.4591	2.14	.4838
1.35	.4115	1.75	.4599	2.15	.4842
1.36	.4131	1.76	.4608	2.16	.4846
1.37	.4147	1.77	.4616	2.17	.4850
1.38	.4162	1.78	.4625	2.18	.4854
1.39	.4177	1.79	.4633	2.19	.4857
1.40	.4192	1.80	.4641	2.20	.4861
1.41	.4207	1.81	.4649	2.21	.4864
1.42	.4222	1.82	.4656	2.22	.4868
1.43	.4236	1.83	.4664	2.23	.4871
1.44	.4251	1.84	.4671	2.24	.4875
1.45	.4265	1.85	.4678	2.25	.4878
1.46	.4279	1.86	.4686	2.26	.4881
1.47	.4292	1.87	.4693	2.27	.4884
1.48	.4306	1.88	.4699	2.28	.4887
1.49	.4319	1.89	.4706	2.29	.4890
1.50	.4332	1.90	.4713	2.30	.4893
1.51	.4345	1.91	.4719	2.31	.4896
1.52	.4357	1.92	.4726	2.32	.4898
1.53	.4370	1.93	.4732	2.33	.4901
1.54	.4382	1.94	.4738	2.34	.4904
1.55	.4394	1.95	.4744	2.35	.4906
1.56	.4406	1.96	.4750	2.36	.4909
1.57	.4418	1.97	.4756	2.37	.4911
1.58	.4429	1.98	.4761	2.38	.4913
1.59	.4441	1.99	.4767	2.39	.4916

TABLE A.1 ***(continued)***

Proportion of Standard Deviation (z)	Proportion of Cases Between $\overline{X}$ and z	Proportion of Standard Deviation (z)	Proportion of Cases Between $\overline{X}$ and z	Proportion of Standard Deviation (z)	Proportion of Cases Between $\overline{X}$ and z
2.40	.4918	2.75	.4970	3.10	.4990
2.41	.4920	2.76	.4971	3.11	.4991
2.42	.4922	2.77	.4972	3.12	.4991
2.43	.4925	2.78	.4973	3.13	.4991
2.44	.4927	2.79	.4974	3.14	.4992
2.45	.4929	2.80	.4974	3.15	.4992
2.46	.4931	2.81	.4975	3.16	.4992
2.47	.4932	2.82	.4976	3.17	.4992
2.48	.4934	2.83	.4977	3.18	.4993
2.49	.4936	2.84	.4977	3.19	.4993
2.50	.4938	2.85	.4978	3.20	.4993
2.51	.4940	2.86	.4979	3.21	.4993
2.52	.4941	2.87	.4979	3.22	.4994
2.53	.4943	2.88	.4980	3.23	.4994
2.54	.4945	2.89	.4981	3.24	.4994
2.55	.4946	2.90	.4981	3.25	.4994
2.56	.4948	2.91	.4982	3.30	.4995
2.57	.4949	2.92	.4982	3.35	.4996
2.58	.4951	2.93	.4983	3.40	.4997
2.59	.4952	2.94	.4984	3.45	.4997
2.60	.4953	2.95	.4984	3.50	.4998
2.61	.4955	2.96	.4985	3.60	.4998
2.62	.4956	2.97	.4985	3.70	.4999
2.63	.4957	2.98	.4986	3.80	.4999
2.64	.4959	2.99	.4986	3.90	.49995
2.65	.4960	3.00	.4987	4.00	.49997
2.66	.4961	3.01	.4987		
2.67	.4962	3.02	.4987		
2.68	.4963	3.03	.4988		
2.69	.4964	3.04	.4988		
2.70	.4965	3.05	.4989		
2.71	.4966	3.06	.4989		
2.72	.4967	3.07	.4989		
2.73	.4968	3.08	.4990		
2.74	.4969	3.09	.4990		

TABLE A.2 Magnitude of Correlation Necessary to Obtain Significance at the .05 Level (only 5 times in 100 would such a correlation occur by chance)

df = *N* − 2	One-tailed	Two-tailed	*df* = *N* − 2	One-tailed	Two-tailed
1	.988	.997	26	.317	.374
2	.900	.950	27	.311	.366
3	.805	.878	28	.306	.361
4	.729	.811	29	.301	.354
5	.669	.754	30	.296	.349
6	.622	.707	40	.257	.304
7	.582	.666	50	.231	.273
8	.549	.632	60	.211	.250
9	.521	.602	70	.196	.232
10	.497	.576	80	.183	.217
11	.476	.553	90	.172	.205
12	.458	.532	100	.164	.194
13	.441	.514	200	.116	.137
14	.426	.497	500	.074	.087
15	.412	.482			
16	.400	.468			
17	.389	.455			
18	.378	.444			
19	.369	.433			
20	.360	.423			
21	.352	.413			
22	.344	.403			
23	.337	.396			
24	.330	.388			
25	.323	.381			

Sample computer-generated report for the 16 PF.

THE INSTITUTE FOR PERSONALITY AND ABILITY TESTING
P. O. BOX 188 CHAMPAIGN, ILLINOIS 61820

THIS COMPUTER INTERPRETATION OF THE 16 PF IS INTENDED ONLY FOR PROPERLY QUALIFIED PROFESSIONALS AND SHOULD BE TREATED AS A CONFIDENTIAL REPORT.

4/20/1984

NAME-JOHN SAMPLE
ID NUMBER-

AGE-29
SEX-M

* * * * * * * * * V A L I D I T Y S C A L E S * * * * * * * * * *

THERE IS REASON TO SUSPECT SOME DISTORTION IN HIS TEST RESPONSES. THIS IS SOMETHING THAT SHOULD BE EXPLORED FURTHER.
FAKING GOOD/MD (STEN) SCORE IS VERY LOW (2.0).
FAKING BAD (STEN) SCORE IS HIGH (8.0).

* *

16 PF
PERSONALITY PROFILE

SCORES R	U	C		LOW MEANING	1 2 3 4 5 6 7 8 9 10	HIGH MEANING	%
8	4	4	A	COOL, RESERVED	<---	WARM, EASYGOING	23
10	8	8	B	CONCRETE THINKING	----->	ABSTRACT THINKING	89
10	2	3	C	EASILY UPSET	<-----	CALM, STABLE	11
22	10	10	E	NOT ASSERTIVE	--------->	DOMINANT	99
21	9	9	F	SOBER, SERIOUS	------->	HAPPY-GO-LUCKY	96
11	4	4	G	EXPEDIENT	<---	CONSCIENTIOUS	23
19	7	7	H	SHY, TIMID	--->	VENTURESOME	77
9	6	6	I	TOUGH-MINDED	->	TENDER-MINDED	60
11	8	8	L	TRUSTING	----->	SUSPICIOUS	89
16	7	7	M	PRACTICAL	--->	IMAGINATIVE	77
4	2	2	N	FORTHRIGHT	<-------	SHREWD	4
15	8	7	O	SELF-ASSURED	--->	APPREHENSIVE	77
15	9	9	Q1	CONSERVATIVE	------->	EXPERIMENTING	96
14	8	8	Q2	GROUP-ORIENTED	----->	SELF-SUFFICIENT	89
12	5	5	Q3	UNDISCIPLINED	<-	SELF-DISCIPLINED	40
14	7	6	Q4	RELAXED	->	TENSE, DRIVEN	60

NOTE: "R" DESIGNATES RAW SCORES, "U" DESIGNATES (UNCORRECTED) STEN SCORES, AND "C" DESIGNATES STEN SCORES CORRECTED FOR DISTORTION (IF APPROPRIATE). THE INTERPRETATION WILL PROCEED ON THE BASIS OF CORRECTED SCORES.

PERSONAL COUNSELING OBSERVATIONS

ADEQUACY OF ADJUSTMENT IS ABOVE AVERAGE (6.5).
ACTING-OUT BEHAVIOR TENDENCIES ARE HIGH (7.9).
EFFECTIVENESS OF BEHAVIOR CONTROLS IS LOW (3.3).

INTERVENTION CONSIDERATIONS

THE INFLUENCE OF A CONTROLLED ENVIRONMENT MAY HELP. SUGGESTIONS INCLUDE-
A GRADED SERIES OF SUCCESS EXPERIENCES TO IMPROVE SELF-CONFIDENCE

Sample report for the 16 PF (*continued*).

JOHN SAMPLE PAGE-2 4/20/1984

PRIMARY PERSONALITY CHARACTERISTICS OF SIGNIFICANCE

CAPACITY FOR ABSTRACT SKILLS IS HIGH.
INVOLVEMENT IN PROBLEMS MAY EVOKE SOME EMOTIONAL UPSET AND INSTABILITY.
IN INTERPERSONAL RELATIONSHIPS HE LEADS, DOMINATES, OR IS STUBBORN.
HIS STYLE OF EXPRESSION IS OFTEN LIVELY, OPTIMISTIC, AND ENTHUSIASTIC.
HE TENDS TO PROJECT INNER TENSION BY BLAMING OTHERS, AND BECOMES JEALOUS OR SUSPICIOUS EASILY.
IN HIS DEALINGS WITH OTHERS, HE IS EMOTIONALLY NATURAL AND UNPRETENTIOUS, THOUGH SOMEWHAT NAIVE.
HE IS EXPERIMENTING, HAS AN INQUIRING MIND, LIKES NEW IDEAS, AND TENDS TO DISPARAGE TRADITIONAL SOLUTIONS TO PROBLEMS.
BEING SELF-SUFFICIENT, HE PREFERS TACKLING THINGS RESOURCEFULLY, ALONE.

BROAD INFLUENCE PATTERNS

HIS PERSONALITY ORIENTATION IS EXTRAVERTED. THAT IS, HIS ATTENTION IS DIRECTED OUT INTO THE ENVIRONMENT. THIS TENDENCY IS ABOVE AVERAGE (7.5).
AT THE PRESENT TIME, HE SEES HIMSELF AS SOMEWHAT MORE ANXIOUS THAN MOST PEOPLE. HIS ANXIETY SCORE IS ABOVE AVERAGE (6.6).
TASKS AND PROBLEMS ARE APPROACHED WITH EMPHASIS UPON RATIONALITY AND GETTING THINGS DONE. LESS ATTENTION IS PAID TO EMOTIONAL RELATIONSHIPS. THIS TENDENCY IS HIGH (8.1).
HIS LIFE STYLE IS INDEPENDENT AND SELF-DIRECTED LEADING TO ACTIVE ATTEMPTS TO ACHIEVE CONTROL OF THE ENVIRONMENT. IN THIS RESPECT, HE IS EXTREMELY HIGH (10.0).

VOCATIONAL OBSERVATIONS

AT CLIENT'S OWN LEVEL OF ABILITIES, POTENTIAL FOR CREATIVE FUNCTIONING IS VERY HIGH (9.0).
POTENTIAL FOR BENEFIT FROM FORMAL ACADEMIC TRAINING, AT CLIENT'S OWN LEVEL OF ABILITIES, IS HIGH (7.6).
IN A GROUP OF PEERS, POTENTIAL FOR LEADERSHIP IS AVERAGE (5.6).
CONDITIONS OF INTERPERSONAL CONTACT OR ISOLATION ARE IRRELEVANT, BUT EXTREMES SHOULD BE AVOIDED.
NEED FOR WORK THAT TOLERATES SOME UNDEPENDABILITY AND INCONSISTENT HABITS IS VERY HIGH (9.0).
POTENTIAL FOR GROWTH TO MEET INCREASING JOB DEMANDS IS BELOW AVERAGE (4.1).
THE EXTENT TO WHICH THE CLIENT IS ACCIDENT PRONE IS HIGH (8.3).

OCCUPATIONAL FITNESS PROJECTIONS

IN THIS SEGMENT OF THE REPORT HIS 16 PF RESULTS ARE COMPARED WITH VARIOUS OCCUPATIONAL PROFILES. ALL PROJECTIONS SHOULD BE CONSIDERED WITH RESPECT TO OTHER INFORMATION ABOUT HIM, PARTICULARLY HIS INTERESTS AND ABILITIES.

1. ARTISTIC PROFESSIONS

ARTIST	ABOVE AVERAGE (7.1).
MUSICIAN	EXTREMELY HIGH (10.0).
WRITER	VERY HIGH (8.9).

Sample report for the 16 PF (*continued*).

JOHN SAMPLE PAGE-3 4/20/1984

2. COMMUNITY AND SOCIAL SERVICE

EMPLOYMENT COUNSELOR	AVERAGE (5.7).
FIREFIGHTER	BELOW AVERAGE (3.8).
NURSE	AVERAGE (4.9).
PHYSICIAN	HIGH (8.1).
POLICE OFFICER	BELOW AVERAGE (3.8).
PRIEST (R.C.)	LOW (3.3).
SERVICE STATION DEALER	VERY LOW (2.4).
SOCIAL WORKER	BELOW AVERAGE (3.6).

3. SCIENTIFIC PROFESSIONS

BIOLOGIST	ABOVE AVERAGE (6.9).
CHEMIST	ABOVE AVERAGE (6.8).
ENGINEER	BELOW AVERAGE (4.3).
GEOLOGIST	HIGH (7.9).
PHYSICIST	AVERAGE (6.3).
PSYCHOLOGIST	HIGH (7.7).

4. TECHNICAL PERSONNEL

ACCOUNTANT	ABOVE AVERAGE (7.5).
AIRLINE FLIGHT ATTENDANT	ABOVE AVERAGE (7.0).
AIRLINE PILOT	VERY HIGH (8.7).
COMPUTER PROGRAMMER	VERY HIGH (8.7).
EDITORIAL WORKER	AVERAGE (6.0).
ELECTRICIAN	EXTREMELY LOW (1.4).
MECHANIC	BELOW AVERAGE (3.7).
PSYCHIATRIC TECHNICIAN	AVERAGE (5.1).
TIME/MOTION STUDY ANALYST	AVERAGE (6.4).

5. INDUSTRIAL/CLERICAL PERSONNEL

JANITOR	LOW (2.9).
KITCHEN WORKER	EXTREMELY LOW (1.2).
MACHINE OPERATOR	LOW (2.9).
SECRETARY-CLERK	AVERAGE (5.0).
TRUCK DRIVER	VERY LOW (1.6).

6. SALES PERSONNEL

REAL ESTATE AGENT	ABOVE AVERAGE (7.2).
RETAIL COUNTER CLERK	HIGH (8.1).

7. ADMINISTRATIVE AND SUPERVISORY PERSONNEL

BANK MANAGER	HIGH (7.6).
BUSINESS EXECUTIVE	VERY HIGH (9.1).
CREDIT UNION MANAGER	AVERAGE (5.1).
MIDDLE LEVEL MANAGER	AVERAGE (4.8).
PERSONNEL MANAGER	HIGH (8.4).
PRODUCTION MANAGER	EXTREMELY HIGH (10.0).
PLANT FOREMAN	AVERAGE (4.6).
SALES SUPERVISOR	AVERAGE (5.8).
STORE MANAGER	LOW (2.8).

Sample report for the 16 PF (*continued*).

JOHN SAMPLE PAGE-4 4/20/1984

8. ACADEMIC PROFESSIONS

TEACHER-ELEMENTARY LEVEL	AVERAGE (5.6).
TEACHER-JUNIOR HIGH LEVEL	VERY HIGH (8.6).
TEACHER-SENIOR HIGH LEVEL	VERY HIGH (9.1).
UNIVERSITY PROFESSOR	AVERAGE (6.0).
SCHOOL COUNSELOR	ABOVE AVERAGE (6.6).
SCHOOL SUPERINTENDENT	AVERAGE (5.1).
UNIVERSITY ADMINISTRATOR	AVERAGE (6.1).

THIS PROFILE SHOWS THE 3233 PATTERN TYPE. FOR ADDITIONAL INTERPRETIVE INFORMATION REGARDING THIS PATTERN, SEE "INTERPRETING 16PF PROFILE PATTERNS" BY DR. SAMUEL KRUG. THIS PUBLICATION IS AVAILABLE THROUGH IPAT.

Sample computer-generated report for SCII.

CONSULTING PSYCHOLOGISTS PRESS

INTERPRETIVE REPORT FOR THE STRONG-CAMPBELL INTEREST INVENTORY

By Jo-Ida C. Hansen, Ph.D.

Name: SAMPLE MARY
ID #: 100
Sex: Female
Date: 10/04/84

You responded to all 325 SCII items.

The following interpretive comments are based on scores obtained from your pattern of responses. The SCII results are indicators of vocational interests, not aptitudes, and they should be used to help identify overall patterns of interests rather than to focus on one or two high scores. The SCII may aid you in exploring educational and occupational options, increase your knowledge of the relationship of occupations to the world of work, and help you identify avocational or leisure interests. As a tool for vocational exploration, the SCII will assist you in increasing your occupational options.

The following narrative will explain your highest General Occupational Themes, which are scales that measure six vocational types described by Dr. John L. Holland in his Theory of Careers (1973). Holland's theory states that people can be divided into six types -- Realistic, Investigative, Artistic, Social, Enterprising, and Conventional -- or some combination of the six types such as Realistic-Investigative or Artistic-Social. The narrative will also explain your Basic Interest Scale and Occupational Scale scores that are high and that are related to your General Occupational Themes.

Basic Interest Scales are sub-divisions of the General Occupational Themes and contain items that are highly consistent in content. They represent an important focus around which people group their own interests.

There are 162 Occupational Scales (male or female) representing 85 occupations. Your scores on each Occupational Scale show how similar your interests are to the interests of people in that occupation. Your SCII profile organizes the Occupational Scales by their relationship to the Holland Themes. The diagram below displays the six General Occupational Themes, your standard score on each, and how high or low your scores are compared to Women-In-General.

Sample report for SCII (*continued*).

INTERPRETIVE REPORT FOR THE STRONG-CAMPBELL INTEREST INVENTORY
Page 2

REALISTIC	INVESTIGATIVE
51	63
moderately high	high

CONVENTIONAL
41
moderately low

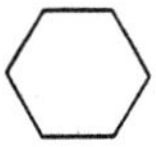

ARTISTIC
63
high

ENTERPRISING	SOCIAL
35	26
very low	very low

These six themes are arranged in a hexagon with the themes most similar to each other falling next to each other, and those most dissimilar falling directly across the hexagon from each other. Types adjacent to one another on the hexagon such as Realistic and Investigative, or Social and Enterprising, have more in common with one another than do types diametrically opposed to each other on the hexagon, such as Realistic and Social, or Investigative and Enterprising.

Your profile shows many high scores. Pay the most attention to the highest General Occupational Scale scores and the highest Basic Interest and Occupational Scale scores.

Your Highest General Occupational Theme:

You expressed preferences in Investigative areas, particularly mathematics, physical sciences, and medical and biological sciences. These areas include occupations in research; mathematics and measurement; sciences that study physical objects and chemical composition of substances; medicine; and sciences that deal with living beings and life processes.

Investigative types tend to view themselves as persistent, self-controlled, analytical, scholarly, and achievement-oriented.

You often prefer to work independently on ambiguous and theoretical tasks.

You probably like to work with numbers, symbols, words, and ideas. And, you may already have computational and numerical skills.

Occupationally, your interests are like the following Investigative type(s):

Veterinarian	Chemist
Physicist	Geologist
Medical Technologist	Dental Hygienist
Dentist	Optometrist
Physical Therapist	Physician
Math-science Teacher	Systems Analyst
Computer Programmer	Chiropractor
Pharmacist	Biologist
Geographer	Mathematician
College Professor	Sociologist

Sample report for SCII (*continued*).

INTERPRETIVE REPORT FOR THE STRONG-CAMPBELL INTEREST INVENTORY
Page 3

Psychologist

You probably enjoy spending your leisure time participating in complex activities that require learning many new facts, theories, and principles such as astronomy, computer science, sailing, or skiing. Your approach to both avocation and your vocation will be analytical.

Your Second Highest General Occupational Theme:

Your responses to the SCII indicate Artistic interests and appreciation of musical and dramatic activities. Examples of vocational choices of this type are actors/actresses, directors, and drama coaches; and musicians, possibly in performance, composition, or conducting.

Your aestheticism may be expressed through the creation of an original art work, or may take the form of appreciation (i.e. as observer rather than participant).

Artistic types may perceive themselves as independent, expressive, intuitive, and complex. They usually prefer to work alone and to participate in fields that require originality and imagination.

Your interests are most similar to Artistic workers in the following pursuits:

Architect	Lawyer
Public Relations Director	Advertising Executive
Musician	Commercial Artist
Fine Artist	Photographer
Librarian	Reporter

Your Third Highest General Occupational Theme:

You indicated Realistic interests encompassing military and mechanical activities. People with these interests often like to work with machines and tools in activities that involve mechanical and motor skills. They choose technical, skilled trade, or law enforcement occupations.

You also may like the structure and organization of the military, or situations that have a well-defined hierarchy of authority.

Realistic types regard themselves as practical, rugged, persistent, and robust; they like concrete problems, activities that require physical exertion, and outdoor work.

Your Realistic interests resemble those of people in the following occupation(s):

Air Force Officer	Army Officer
Navy Officer	Police Officer
Forester	Engineer
Occupational Therapist	

Sample report for SCII (*continued*).

INTERPRETIVE REPORT FOR THE STRONG-CAMPBELL INTEREST INVENTORY
Page 4

Your Lowest General Occupational Theme(s):

It is often helpful to compare your areas of high interest with your areas of lowest interest, to consider the types of occupations or avocations that you would not likely find as enjoyable or satisfying.

Your score on the C-Theme reveals that you do not have many interests in common with Conventional types. Conventional types may prefer well-ordered and systematic environments, perform structured tasks very effectively, and enjoy work that requires precision and attention to detail. You probably perceive Conventional people as orderly, practical and inflexible.

Basic Interest Areas With High Scores:

You have a response pattern that reflects a willingness to be involved in risky undertakings. This may be expressed as physical risk-taking such as mountain climbing or skydiving; as financial risk-taking, for example, working strictly on a commission basis; or perhaps as a readiness to make changes. People who have the wanderlust, or like to travel, also have risk-taking response patterns.

Your areas of interest are:

Military Activities, Mechanical Activities, Science, Mathematics, Medical Science, Music / Dramatics, Public Speaking

You may wish to think about your basic areas of interest to determine if the interests are related to vocational possibilities, or recreational and avocational activity.

Occupational Scales with High Scores:

You have interests <u>similar</u> to people in the following occupations:

Air Force Officer	Navy Officer
Forester	Engineer
Occupational Therapist	Veterinarian
Chemist	Physicist
Geologist	Medical Technologist
Dentist	Optometrist
Physical Therapist	Physician
Systems Analyst	Computer Programmer
Chiropractor	Pharmacist
Biologist	Geographer
Mathematician	Sociologist
Psychologist	Architect
Lawyer	Public Relations Director
Advertising Executive	Musician

INTERPRETIVE REPORT FOR THE STRONG-CAMPBELL INTEREST INVENTORY
Page 5

Commercial Artist	Fine Artist
Photographer	Librarian
Reporter	Public Administrator
Marketing Executive	Dietitian
Accountant (C.P.A.)	

You have interests moderately similar to people in the following occupations:

Police Officer	Dental Hygienist
Math-science Teacher	Speech Pathologist
Recreation Leader	Personnel Director
I.R.S. Agent	

You have interests that are very dissimilar to people in the following occupations:

Elementary Teacher	Home Economics Teacher
Executive Housekeeper	Business Education Teacher
Secretary	

Your score on the College Professor scale suggests that you may want to work in an academic environment, teaching adults and associating with colleagues who have intellectual interests.

Your score on the Army Officer scale denotes managerial interests, which means that you like to be in charge of other people, to have supervisory responsibility, to participate in competitive activities, and to resolve personnel problems. These are interests similar to people, no matter what their specialty, who assume supervisory or administrative positions.

Of course, Occupational Scale scores only evaluate how similar interests are to people already in the occupation. The scores give no indication of ability or probability of success. Therefore, consider your abilities as well as interests.

Non-Occupational Scales: Academic Comfort and Introversion-Extroversion

There are two non-occupational scales derived from your SCII responses that may give you additional insight into your interests and expectations:

The Academic Comfort Scale differentiates between people who enjoy being in an academic setting and those who do not. About two-thirds of all people who take the SCII score in the range of 32 to 60. High scores are associated with continuation to high academic degree programs. Your score on this scale was 60.

The Introversion-Extroversion Scale is associated with interests that require working with people as opposed to working alone. About two-thirds of all people who take the SCII score in the range of 38 to 62. High scores (60 and above) indicate introversion, and low scores (40 and below) extroversion. Your score on this scale was 53.

Sample report for SCII (*continued*).

INTERPRETIVE REPORT FOR THE STRONG-CAMPBELL INTEREST INVENTORY
Page 6

Additional Resources

You have just had the opportunity to examine your interests in general areas of occupational activities and to compare them with interests of people in specific jobs. You can find out more about your high-interest occupations by talking to your counselor, reading about and talking to people employed in those jobs, and volunteering in work environments that you enjoy.

Career planning is a lifelong process. It is helpful to collect information from a variety of sources to make informed choices about possible career paths. The following resources are recommended to learn more about occupations and about yourself; the list on the left contains books that are typically found in the library, and the list on the right contains books that may be purchased from the publisher or a local bookstore.

Library Resources

Dictionary of Occupational Titles
Occupational Outlook Handbook
Exploring Careers
the above books are published by
the U.S. Department of Labor)

Making Vocational Choices
by John L. Holland
Published by Prentice-Hall, Inc.

For Your Personal Library

What Color Is Your Parachute?
by Richard Bolles

Up Your Career
by Dean C. Dauw

Who's Hiring Who
by Richard Lathrop

The Career Game
by Charles Guy Moore

The publisher of this report, Consulting Psychologists Press, distributes the books listed "For Your Personal Library," and may be contacted at:
577 College Avenue, Palo Alto, CA 94306

BIBLIOGRAPHY

ALLEN, M. J., & YEN, W. M. (1979). *Introduction to measurement theory*. Monterey, CA: Brooks/Cole.

ALLPORT, G.W. (1961). *Pattern and growth in personality*. New York: Holt.

AMERICAN PSYCHOLOGICAL ASSOCIATION. (1985). *Standards for educational and psychological testing*. Washington, DC: Author.

ANASTASI, A. (1982). *Psychological testing*. New York: Macmillan.

ANDERSON, N. C., & FAUST, G. W. (1973). *Educational psychology: The science of instruction and learning*. New York: Dodd.

ANGOFF, W. H. (1971). Scales, norms, and equal scores. In N. L. Thorndike (Ed.), *Educational measurement* (pp. 508–600). Washington, DC: American Council on Education.

ARTER, J. A., & JENKINS, J. R. (1979). Differential diagnosis—prescriptive teaching: A critical appraisal. *Review of Educational Research, 49*, 517–555.

ASHBURY, R. R. (1938). An experiment in the essay-type question. *The Journal of Experimental Education, 7*, 1–3.

BAGLIN, R. F. (1981). Does "nationally" normed really mean nationally? *Journal of Educational Measurement, 18*(2), 97–107.

BARATZ, J. C. (1980). Policy implications of minimum competency testing. In R. M. Jaeger & C. K. Tittle (Eds.). *Minimum competency achievement testing: Motives, models, measures, and consequences*. Berkeley, CA: McCutchan.

BEJAR, I., & BLEW, E. O. (1981). Grade inflation and the validity of the scholastic aptitude test. *American Educational Research Journal, 18*(2), 143–156.

BENNETT, G. K., SEASHORE, H. G., & WESMAN, A. G. (1972). *Differential Aptitude Test*, New York: Psychological Corporation.

BERK, R. (Ed.). (1980). *Criterion referenced measurement: The state of the art*. Baltimore: Johns Hopkins.

——— (1980). A consumer guide to criterion referenced tests. *Journal of Educational Measurement, 17*(4), 323–349.

——— (1980). A consumer's guide to criterion-referenced test reliability. *Journal of Educational Measurement, 17*(4), 323–349.

BIEHLER, R. F., & SNOWMAN, J. (1982). *Psychology applied to teaching*. Boston: Houghton.

BIRNBAUM, A. (1968). Some latent trait models and their use in inferring an examinee's ability. In G. M. Lord & M. R. Novick (Eds.). *Statistical theories of mental test scores*. Reading, MA: Addison-Wesley.

BLOCK, J. H. (1971). *Mastery learning*. New York: Holt.

BLOOM, B. S. (1968). Learning for mastery, UCLA-CSEIP. *Evaluation Comment*, 1, (Whole No. 2).

BLOOM, E. (Ed.). (1956). *Taxonomy of educational objectives: Handbook 1, Cognitive domain*. New York: McKay.

BORING, E. G. (1923). Intelligence as the tests test it. *New Republic, 34*, 35–37.

BRACEY, G. W. (1980). The SAT, college admissions, and the concept of talent: Unexamined myths, unexplained perceptions, needed explorations. *Phi Delta Kappan, 34*, (3), 197–199.

BRELSFORD, W. M., & RELLES, D. A. (1981). *STATLIB: A statistical computing library*. Englewood Cliffs, NJ: Prentice-Hall.

BRYDEN, M. P. (1982). *Laterality: functional assymetry in the intact brain*. New York: Academic.

BURT, C. (1957). The distribution of intelligence. *British Journal of Psychology, 48*, 161–175.

——— (1958). The inheritance of mental ability. *American Psychologists, 13*, 1–15.

———, & HOWARD, M. (1956). The multifactorial theory of inheritance and its application to intelligence. *British Journal of Statistical Psychology, 9*, 95–131.

CAMPBELL, D. P. (1968). Stability of interests within an occupation over thirty years. In W. L. Barnette, Jr. (Ed.). *Readings in psychological tests and measurements* (rev. ed.). Homewood, IL: Dorsey.

———, & HANSEN, J. C. (1981). *Manual for the SVIB-SCII*. Stanford, CA: Stanford U.P.

CARROLL, J. B. (1963). A model of school learning. *Teachers College Record, 64*, 723–733.

CATTELL, R. B. (1971). *Abilities: Their structure, growth and action*. Boston: Houghton.

——— (1968). Some practical implications of the theory of fluid and crystallized general ability. In W. L. Barnette (Ed.). *Readings in psychological testing and measurement*. Homewood, IL: Dorsey.

——— (1965). *The scientific analysis of behavior*. Baltimore: Penguin.

———, EBER, H. W., & TATSUOKA, M. M. (1970). *Handbook of the Sixteen Personality Factor Questionnaire (16PF)*. Champaign, IL: Institute for Personality and Ability Testing.

CLEARY, T. A., HUMPHREY, L. G., KENDRICK, S. A., & WEISMAN, A. (1975). Educational uses of tests with disadvantaged students. *American Psychologist, 30*, (1), 15–41.

COFFMAN, W. E. (1971). Essays examinations. In R. L. Thorndike (Ed.). *Educational Measurement*. Washington, DC: American Council on Education.

COHEN, J. A. (1960). A coefficient of agreement for nominal scales. *Educational and Psychological Measurement, 20*, 37–46.

COLEMAN, J. E. (1966). *Equality of educational opportunity*. Washington, DC: U. S. Government Printing Office.

CONNOLLY, A. J., NACHTMAN, W., & PRITCHETT, E. M. (1976). *KeyMath Diagnostic Arithmetic Test*. Circle Pines, MN: American Guidance Services.

CRONBACH, L. J. (1951). Coefficient alpha and the internal structure of tests. *Psychometrika, 16*, 297–334.

——— (1984). *Essentials of psychological testing*. New York: Harper.

——— (1975). Five decades of public controversy over mental testing. *American Psychologist, 30*, 1–14.

———, GLESER, G. C., NANDA, H., & RAJARATNAM, N. (1972). *The dependability of behavioral measurements: Theory of generalizability for scores and profiles*. New York: Wiley.

——— (1979). The Armed Services Vocational Aptitude Battery—A test battery in transition. *The Personnel and Guidance Journal, 57*, 232–237.

CTB/McGraw-Hill. (1981). *CTBS: Comprehensive test of basic skills* (Forms U and V). Monterey, CA: Author.

CTB/McGraw-Hill. (1981). *CTBS: Comprehensive test of basic skills preliminary technical manual* (Forms U and V). Monterey, CA: Author.

CTB/McGraw-Hill. (1981). *CTBS: Comprehensive test of basic skills test coordinator's handbook Forms U and V*. Monterey, CA: Author.

CTB McGraw-Hill. (1981). *TCS: Test of Cognitive Skills*. Monterey, CA: Author.

CUBAN, L. (1980). Response to Dr. Baratz: "Policy implications of minimum competency testing." In R. M. Jaeger & C. K. Tittle (Eds.). *Minimum competency achievement testing: Motives, models, measures, and consequences*. Berkeley, CA: McCutchan.

CUNNINGHAM, G. K. (1981). Nonpublic school alternatives to busing: Attitudes and characteristics. *Urban Education, 16*(1), 3–12.

DARWIN, C. (1967). *On the origin of species by means of natural selection, or the preservation of favored races in the struggle for life*. London: J. Murray. (New York: Modern Library.)

Debra P. vs. *Turlington*, 644F. 2d 397, 404 (5th Cir. 1981).

Debra P. vs. *Turlington*, No. 78-892 Civ. T-C (M.D. Fla. July 12, 1979) at 2380.

Debra P. vs. *Turlington*, No. 78-892 (N.T. M.D. Florida, January 18, 1982) at 6.

Department of Education Office for Civil Rights. (1983). *Technical assistance and alternate practices related to the problem of the overrepresentation of blacks and other minority students in classes for the educable mentally retarded*. Washington, DC: U.S. Government Printing Office.

Diana vs. *California State Board of Education*. (1970). U. S. District Court for the Northern District of California (consent decree).

DUBOIS, P. H. (1970). *A history of psychological testing*. Boston: Allyn.

DUNN, L. M., & MARKWARDT, F. C. (1970). *Peabody Individual Achievement Test*. Circle Pines, MN: American Guidance Service.

EBEL, R. L. (1979). *Essentials of educational measurement* (3rd ed.). Englewood Cliffs, NJ: Prentice-Hall.

EDWARDS, A. L. (1957). *Techniques of attitude scale construction*. New York: Appleton.

——— (1953). The relationship between the judged desirability of a trait and the probability of it being endorsed. *Journal of Applied Psychology, 37*, 90–95.

——— (1957). The social desirability variable in personality assessment and research. New York: Dryden.

Educational Testing Service. (1980). *Test use and validity*. Princeton, NJ: Author.

ENGEN, H. B., LAMB, R.A., & PREDIGER, D. J. (1982). Are secondary schools still using standardized tests? *The Personnel and Guidance Journal, 60*, 287–290.

FALLS, J. D. Research in secondary education. *Kentucky School Journal, 6*, 42–46.

FISHER, T. H. (1978). Florida's approach to competency testing. *Phi Delta Kappan, 59*, (90), 599–602.

FRAZIER, J. G. (1917). *The golden bough*. London: Macmillan.

FULKER, D. W. (1973). A biometrical genetic approach to intelligence and schizophrenia. *Social Biology, 20*, 266–275.

GAGNÉ, R. M. (1977). *The conditions of learning*. New York: Holt.

GALTON, F. (1967). Classification of men according to their natural gifts. In Stephen Wiseman (Ed.). *Intelligence and ability*. Baltimore: Penguin.

GLASER, R., & KLAUS, D. J. (1962)). Proficiency measurement: Assessing human performance. In R. M. Gagné (Ed.). *Psychological principles in systems development*, New York: Holt, Reinhart and Winston.

GLASER, R. (1963). Instructional technology and the measurement of learning outcomes: Some questions. *American Psychologist, 18*, 519–521.

GLASS, G. V. (1978). Minimum competence and incompetence in Florida. *Phi Delta Kappan, 59*, 602–605.

——— (1978). Standards and criteria. *Journal of Educational Measurement, 15*, 237–261.

——— (1970). *Statistical methods in education and psychology*. Englewood Cliffs, NJ: Prentice-Hall.

GOULD, S. J. (1980). Jensen's last stand (Review of *Basic mental testing* by A.

Jensen). *The New York Review of Books, XXVII* (7), 38–44.

GRONLUND, N. E. (1982). *Constructing achievement tests*. Englewood Cliffs, NJ: Prentice-Hall.

——— (1985). *Measurement and evaluation in teaching*. New York: Macmillan.

——— (1985). *Stating educational objectives*, (3rd ed.). New York: Macmillan.

GUILFORD, J. P. (1967). *The nature of human intelligence*. New York: McGraw-Hill.

GUION, R. M. (1977). Content validity—the source of my discontent. *Applied Psychological Measurement, 1*, 1–10.

HAMBLETON, R. K. (1980). Latent ability scales: Interpretations and uses. In S. T. Mayo (Ed.). *New directions for testing and measurement interpreting: Interpreting test performance*. San Francisco: Jossey-Bass.

——— (1980). Test score validity and standard-setting methods. In Berk, R. A. (Ed.). *Criterion referenced measurement: The state of the art*. Baltimore: Johns Hopkins.

———, & NOVICK, M. R. (1973). Toward an integration of theory and method for criterion-referenced tests. *Journal of Educational Measurement, 10*, 159–170.

———, SWAMINATHAN, H., COOK, L. L., EIGNOR, D. R., & GIFFORD, J. A. (1978). Developments in latent theory: Models, technical issues, and applications. *Review of Educational Research, 48*, 467–510.

HANSEN, J. C. (1976). Exploring new directions for SCII occupational scale construction. *Journal of Vocational Behavior, 9*, 147–160.

HARNSICHFEGER, A., & WILEY, D. E. (1976). Achievement test scores drop. So what? *Educational Researcher, 5*(3), 5–12.

HATHAWAY, S. R., & MCKINLEY, J. C. (1943). *The Minnesota Multiplastic Personality Inventory*. New York: Psychological Corporation.

HILLS, J. R. (1981). *Measurement and evaluation in the classroom*. Columbus, OH: Merrill.

Hobson vs. *Hansen*. (1967). U. S. District Court for the District of Columbia, 269 F. Supp. 401.

HODGSON, G. (1974). Do schools make a difference? in H. F. Clarizio, R. C. Craig, & W. A. Mehrens. (Eds.). *Contemporary issues in educational psychology* (2nd ed.). Boston: Allyn.

HOFFMAN, B. (1962). *The tyranny of testing*. New York: Macmillan.

HOPKINS, C. D. (1978). *Classroom measurement and evaluation*. Itasca, IL: F. E. Peacock.

HORN, J. L. (1979). Intelligence—why it grows, why it declines. In L. Willerman & R. G. Turner. (Eds.). *Readings about individual and group differences*. San Francisco: Freeman.

HUYNH, H. (1976). On the reliability of decisions in domain-referenced testing. *Journal of Educational Measurement, 13*, 253–264.

Institute for Personality and Ability Testing. (1972)). *Manual for the 16PF*. Champaign, IL: Author.

JACKSON, R. (1980). The scholastic aptitude test: A response to Slack and Porter's "Critical appraisal." *Harvard Educational Review, 50*, 381–392.

JANIS, I. L., & MAHL, G. F. (1969). *Personality: Dynamics, development, and assessment*. New York: Harcourt.

JARVIK, L. F., & ERLENMEYER-KIMLING, L. (1967). Survey of familial correlations in measured intellectual functions. In J. Zubin & G. A. Jervis (Eds.). *Psychopathology of mental development*. New York: Grune.

JASTAK, J. F., & JASTAK, S. (1978). *Wide Range Achievement Test 1978 revision*. Wilmington, DE: Jastak Associates.

JAYNES, J. (1976). *The origin of consciousness in the breakdown of the bicameral mind*. Boston: Houghton.

JENCKS, C., & CROUSE, J. (1982). Should we relabel the SAT or replace it? *Phi Delta Kappan, 63*, 10, 659–663.

JENCKS, C. (1972). *Inequality: A reassess-*

ment of family and schooling in America. New York: Basic.

JENSEN, A. R. *Straight talk about mental tests*. New York: Free Press.

——— (1969). How much can we boost IQ and scholastic achievement? *Harvard Educational Review, 39*, 1–123.

——— (1980). *Bias in mental testing*. New York: Free Press.

JINKS, J. L., & EAVES, L. J. (1974). IQ and inequality: Review of Hernstein (1973) and Jencks (1972). *Nature, 248*, 287–289.

JINKS, J. L., & FULKER, D. W. (1970). Comparison of the biometrical, genetical, MAVA, and classical approaches to the analysis of human behavior. *Psychological Bulletin, 73*, 311–349.

JOHANSSON, C. B. (1978). *Manual supplement for Career Assessment Inventory*. Minneapolis, MN: Interpretive Scoring Systems.

KAISER, C. J. (1974). *Theoretical positions and baysian estimations of learning disability specialists*. Doctoral dissertation, University of Arizona.

KAMIN, L. J. (1975). Social and legal consequences of IQ tests as classification instruments. Some warnings from the past. *Journal of School Psychology, 13*, 317–323.

KANTER, H. M. (1985) *Computer applications of educational measurement concepts*. New York: Macmillan.

KARMEL, L. J., & KARMEL, M. O. (1978). *Measurement and evaluation in the schools* (2nd ed.). New York: Macmillan.

KAUFMAN, A. S. (1979). WISC-R research: Implications for interpretation. *School Psychology Digest, 8*(1), 5–27.

———, & KAUFMAN, N. L. (1983). *Kaufman Assessment Battery for Children interpretive manual*. Circle Pines, MN: American Guidance Service.

——— (1979). *Intelligent testing with the WISC-R*. New York: Wiley.

KERLINGER, F. N. (1973). *Foundations of behavioral research*. New York: Holt.

KRATOCHWILL, T., & DEMUTH, D. (1976). An examination of the predictive validity of the KeyMath Diagnostic Arithmetic Test and the Wide Range Achievement Test in exceptional children. *Psychology in the Schools, 13*, 404–406.

KUDER, F. (1976). *Occupational Interest Survey general manual*. Chicago: Science Research Associates.

———, & RICHARDSON, M. W. (1937). The theory of the estimation of test reliability. *Psychometrika, 2*, 151–160.

Larry P. vs. *Wilson Riles*. (1972). U.S. District Court for the Northern District of California, No. C-71-2270RFP.

LESSER, G. S., FIFER, G., & CLARK, D. H. (1965). Mental abilities of children from different social-class and cultural groups. *Monographs of the Society for Research in Child Development, 30* (4).

LEVY, J., & REID, M. (1976). Variations in writing posture and cerebral organization. *Science, 194*, 337–339.

LINN, R. L. (1984). Selection bias: multiple meanings. *Journal of Educational Measurement, 21*(1), 33–47.

LOEHLIN, J. C., LINDZEY, G., & SPUHLER, J. N. (1975). *Race differences in intelligence*. San Francisco: Freeman.

LORD, F. M. (1980). *Applications of item response theory to practical testing problems*. Hillsdale, NJ: Erlbaum.

———, & NOVICK, M. R. (1968). *Statistical theories of mental test scores*. Reading, MA: Addison-Wesley.

LUTEY, C. (1977). *Individual intelligence testing: A sourcebook and manual*. Greeley, CO: Lutey.

LYMAN, H. B. (1978). *Test scores and what they mean*. Englewood Cliffs, NJ: Prentice-Hall.

MACCOBY, E. E., & JACKLIN, C. N. (1974). *The psychology of sex differences*. Stanford, CA: Standord U. P.

MACLEAN, P. D. (1973). *A triune concept of brain and behavior*. Toronto: U. of Toronto Press.

MACMILLAN, D. (1977). *Mental retardation in school and society*. Boston: Little, Brown.

MADAUS, G. E. (1981). NIE clarification

hearing: The negative team's case. *Phi Delta Kappan, 63*, 92–94.

MAGER, N. F. (1962). *Preparing instructional objectives*. Palo Alto, CA: Fearon.

MARSHALL, J. C. (1967). Composition errors and essay examination grades reexamined. *American Educational Research Journal, 4*, 375–386.

MARSHALL, J. L., & HAERTEL, E. H. (1980). The mean split-half coefficient of agreement: A single administration of reliability for mastery tests. Unpublished manuscript, University of Wisconsin. From Subkovilak (1980).

MATARAZZO, J. D. (1976). *Wechsler measurement and appraisal of adult intelligence*. Baltimore; Williams & Wilkins.

MCARTHUR, C. (1968). Long-term validity of the strong interest test in two subcultures. In W. L. Barnette, Jr. (Ed.). *Readings in psychological tests and measurements* (rev. ed.). Homewood, IL: Dorsey.

MCCLUNG, M. S. (1979). Competency testing programs: Legal and educational issues. *Fordham Law Review, 47*, 652.

MCLOUGHLIN, J. A., & LEWIS, R. B. (1981). *Assessing special students*. Columbus, OH: Merrill.

MEHRENS, W. S., & LEHMAN, I. J. (1975). *Measurement and evaluation in education and psychology*. New York: Holt.

MERCER, J. R. (1979). *System of Multicultural Pluralistic Assessment (SOMPA): Technical manual*. New York: Psychological Corporation.

MESSICK, S. (1981). Evidence and ethics in the evaluation of tests. *Educational Researcher, 10*(9), 9–20.

MOONEY, R. L., & GORDON, L. V. (1950). *The Mooney Problem Check Lists' manual*. New York: Psychological Corporation.

MORTON, N. E. (1972). Human behavioral genetics. In L. Ehrman, G. S. Omenn, & E. Caspari (Eds.). *Genetics, environment and behavior*. New York: Academic.

MURRAY, H. A. (1938). *Explorations in personality*. New York: Oxford U. P.

NAIRN, A. (1980). *The reign of ETS: The corporation that makes up minds*. Washington, DC: Ralph Nader.

NEDELSKY, L. (1954). Absolute grading standards for objective tests. *Educational and Psychological Measurement, 14*, 3–19.

NIE, N.H., HULL, C. H., JENKINS, J. G., STEINBRENNER, K., & BENT, D. H. (1975). *Statistical package for the social sciences* (2nd ed.). New York: McGraw-Hill.

NITKO, A. J. (1983). *Educational tests and measurement: An introduction*. New York: Harcourt.

NUNNALLY, J. C. (1967). *Psychometric theory*. New York: McGraw-Hill.

——— (1978). *Psychometric theory* (2nd ed.). New York: McGraw-Hill.

OAKLAND, T. (1983). Joint use of adaptive behavior and IQ to predict achievement. *Journal of Consulting and Clinical Psychology, 51*(2), 298–301.

——— (1979). Research on the ABIC and ELP: A revisit to an old topic. *School Psychology Digest, 8*(3), 172–178.

———, & FEIGENBAUM, D. (1980). Comparisons of the psychometric characteristics of the adaptive behavior inventory for children for different subgroups of children. *Journal of School Psychology, 18*, 307–315.

OSGOOD, C. E. (1962). Studies on the generality of affective meaning systems. *American Psychologist, 17*, 10–28.

PEDHAZUR, E. J. (1982). *Multiple regression in behavioral research*. New York: Holt.

PIPHO, C. (1978). Minimum competency testing in 1978: A look at state standards. *Phi Delta Kappan, 59*, 585–589.

——— (1978). *Minimum competency update*. Denver: Education Commission of the States.

PLOMIN, R., DEFREIS, J. C., & MCCLEARN, G. (1980). *Behavioral genetics: A primer*. San Francisco: Freeman.

POPHAM, W. J., & HUSEK, T. R. (1969). Duplication of criterion-referenced measurement. *Journal of Educational Measurement, 6*, 1–9.

POPHAM, W. J. (1980). Domain specification strategies. In R. J. Beck (Ed.). *Criterion referenced measurement*. Baltimore: Johns Hopkins.

——— (1981). *Modern educational measurement*. Englewood Cliffs, NJ: Prentice-Hall.

PRICE, M. F., & ROGERS, B. R. (1981). Book review of the *KeyMath Diagnostic Arithmetic Test. Measurement and Evaluation in Guidance, 14*(2), 108–111.

PUGH, R. C. (1968). Tests for creative thinking—potential for the school testing program. *Indiana University Bulletin of the School of Education, 44*, 1–30.

RASCH, G. (1960). *Probablistic models for some intelligence and attainment tests*. Copenhagen: The Danish Institute for Educational Research.

RESCHLEY, D. J. (1981). Evaluation of the effects of SOMPA measures on classification of students as mildly mentally retarded. *American Journal of Mental Deficiency, 86*(1), 16–20.

——— (1978). WISC-R factor structures among Anglos, blacks, Chicanos, and Native American Papagos. *Journal of Consulting and Clinical Psychology, 46*, 417–422.

RESTAK, R. M. (1979). *The brain: The last frontier*. New York: Warner.

Riverside Publishing Company (1982). *Technical manual: Cognitive Abilities Test* (Form 3, Levels 1 & 2; and Levels A-H). Chicago: Author.

ROBERTSON, G. J. (1972). The development of the first Group Mental Ability Test. In G. H. Bracht & K. D. Hopkins (Eds.). *Perspectives in educational and psychological measurement*. Englewood Cliffs, NJ: Prentice-Hall.

ROBINSON, N., & ROBINSON, H. (1976). *The mentally retarded child* (2nd ed.). New York: McGraw-Hill.

ROSS, D. D. (1982). Competency based education: Understanding a political movement. *Educational Forum, 46*, 438–490.

SAS Institute, Inc. (1979). *SAS users guide* (1979 ed.). Raleigh, NC: Author.

SAMELSON, F. (1975)). On the science and politics of the IQ. *Social Research, 42*, 467–488.

SANDOVAL, J. (1979). The WISC-R and internal evidence of test bias with minority groups. *Journal of Consulting and Clinical Psychology, 47*, 919–927.

SATTLER, J. M. (1982). *Assessment of children's intelligence and special abilities* (2nd ed.). Boston: Allyn.

——— (1974). *Assessment of children's intelligence*. Philadelphia: Saunders.

SAX, G. (1980). *Principles of educational and psychological measurement and evaluation*. Belmont, CA: Wadsworth.

SCARR-SALAPATCK, S. (1971). Race, social class, and IQ. *Science, 174*, 1285–1295.

SCHWARTZ, M. D. (1983). *Using computers in clinical practice: Psychotherapy and mental health applications*. New York: Haworth.

SEAGOE, M. V. (1975). *Terman and the gifted*. Los Altos, CA: Kaufmann.

SENDERS, V. L. (1958). *Measurement and statistics*. New York: Oxford U.P.

SHEPHERD, L., & CAMILLI, G. (1984). Accounting for statistical artifacts in item bias research. *Journal of Educational Statistics, 9*(2), 93–128.

SHERTZER, B., & LINDEN, J. D. (1979). *Fundamentals of individual appraisal*. Boston: Houghton.

SIEGEL, S. (1956). *Nonparametric statistics for the behavioral sciences*. New York: McGraw-Hill.

SKINNER, B. F. (1954). The science of learning and the art of teaching. *Harvard Educational Review, 24*, 86–97.

SLACK, W. V., & PORTER, D. (1980). *The Scholastic Aptitude Test: A critical appraisal. Harvard Educational Review, 50*(2), 154–175.

SPEARMAN, C., & HOLZINGER, K. J. (1924). The sampling error in the theory of two factors. *British Journal of Psychology, 15*, 17–19.

SPENCER, H. (1895). *The principles of psychology* (3rd ed.). New York: Appleton.

STANLEY, J. C. (1971). Predicting college success of the educationally disadvantaged. *Science, 171*, 640–647.

SUBKOVIAK, M. J. (1976). Estimation reliability from a single administration of a mastery test. *Journal of Educational Measurement, 13*, 265–276.

——— (1980). Decision consistency approaches. In R. A. Berk (Ed.). *Criterion-referenced measurement: The state of the art*, Baltimore: Johns Hopkins.

SUNDBERG, N. D. (1977). *Assessment of persons*. Englewood Cliffs, NJ: Prentice-Hall.

SWAMINATHAN, H., HAMBLETON, R. K., & ALGINA, J. (1974). Reliability of criterion-referenced tests: A decision-theoretic formulation. *Journal of Educational Measurement, 11*, 263–268.

TAVRIS, C., & OFFIR, C. (1977). *The longest war: Sex differences in perspective*. New York: Harcourt.

TERMAN, L. M. (1916). *The measurement of intelligence*. Boston: Houghton.

———, & MERRILL, M. A. (1937). *Measuring intelligence*. Boston: Houghton.

———, & MERRILL, M. A. (1960). *Stanford-Binet Intelligence Scale*. Boston: Houghton.

THORNDIKE, R. L., & HAGEN, E. P. (1986). *Measurement and evaluation in psychology and education* (5th ed.). New York: Wiley.

THURSTONE, L. L., & THURSTONE, T. G. (1941). Factorial studies of intelligence. *Psychometric Monographs, 2*.

U.S. Department of Labor: Manpower Administration. (1970). *Manual for the USES General Aptitude Test Battery*. Washington, DC: U.S. Employment Service.

U.S. Military Entrance Processing Command (1984). *ASVAB Counselor's Manual*. Chicago: Author.

WECHSLER, D. (1981). *Manual for the Wechsler Adult Intelligence Scale-Revised*. New York: Psychological Corporation.

——— (1974). *Manual for the Wechsler Intelligence Scale for Children-Revised*. New York: Psychological Corporation.

——— (1967). *Manual for the Wechsler Preschool and Primary Scale of Intelligence*. New York: Psychological Corporation.

——— (1944). *Measurement of adult intelligence* (3rd ed.). Baltimore: Williams & Wilkins.

WEITZMAN, R. A. (1982). The prediction of college achievement by the scholastic aptitude test and the high school record. *Journal of Educational Measurement, 19*, 179–191.

WILLERMAN, L. (1979). *The psychology of individual and group differences*. San Francisco: Freeman.

WILSON, E. O. (1978). *On human nature*. Cambridge, MA: Harvard U.P.

——— (1975). *Sociobiology: The new synthesis*. Cambridge, MA: The Belknap Press of Harvard U.P.

WOLF, F. E. (1981. *Taking the quantum leap*. New York: Harper.

WOOD, R. L., WINGERSKY, M. S., & LORD, F. M. (1976). LOGIST—A computer program for estimating examinee ability and item characteristic curve parameters. *Research Memorandum 76-6*. Princeton, NJ: ETS.

WOODCOCK, R. W. (1973). *Woodcock Reading Mastery Tests*. Circle Pines, MN: American Guidance Service.

WOODSWORTH, R. S. (1920). *Personal data sheet*. Chicago: Stoelting.

WRIGHT, B. D., & STONE, M. H. (1979). *Best test design*. Chicago: MESA Press.

YALOW, E. S. (1983). Content validity at the crossroads. *Educational Researcher, 12*(8), 10–14, 21.

YEN, W. M. (1980). The extent, causes and importance of context effects on item parameters for two latent trait models. *Journal of Educational Measurement, 17*, 297–311.

——— (1981). Using simulation results to choose a latent trait model. *Applied*

Psychological Measurement, 5, 245–262.
——— (1982). Obtaining some degree of correspondence between unequatable scores. Paper presented at the annual meeting of the American Educational Research Association in New York City.
——— (1982). Use of three-parameter item response theory in the development of CTBS, Form U, and TCS. Paper presented at the annual meeting of the American Educational Research Association in New York City.

YONGE, G. D. (1982). Some concerns about the estimation of learning potential from the System of Multicultural Pluralistic Assessment. *Psychology in the Schools, 19*, 482–486.

ZAJONC, R. B. (1976). Family configuration and intelligence. *Science, 192*, 227–236.

NAME INDEX

E

F

G

H

J

K

L

M

N

O

P

Q

R

S

SUBJECT INDEX

B

C

J

K

L

M

N

O

P

Q

R

S

T

U

V

W